Lafcadio Hearn has seemed a marginal figure in literary history because the general orientation of Hearn scholarship has been biographical, concentrating on his life and personality rather than on his art and thought. Critics have tended to read in Hearn's writings his life experiences and translate his words into his life pattern. *An Ape of Gods* contends that if Hearn's outer life is a romantic voyage, his inner life is incomparably more romantic and stirring, and that his works comprise the remarkable record of a mental traveler.

Beong-cheon Yu considers Hearn's total achievement in the framework of art, criticism, and philosophy, focusing on specific areas which he believes important for a re-evaluation of Hearn's art and thought: first, his translations, stylistic experiments, romances, twice-told legends, and travel books; second, his contribution to American literary criticism during the 1880's, Japanese lectures, aesthetics of organic memory, and proposal for a world literature of humanity; third, his opinion of Japan, critique of the Western cults of individualism and passionalism, reconciliation of science and faith in terms of evolutionism and Buddhism, and final plea for integration of East and West on the basis of man as a whole being.

An
Ape
of
Gods

*"And your Western philosopher was really
teaching a Buddhist parable when he proclaimed
man but a higher kind of ape. For in this world
of illusion, man is truly still the ape, trying
to seize on water the shadow of the Moon."
—"Ape indeed," I made answer,—"but
an ape of gods,—even that divine Ape of
the Ramayana who may clutch the Sun!"*

Hearn, "Of Moon-Desire,"
Exotics and Retrospectives

Detroit, 1964, Wayne State University Press

An

Ape

of

Gods

The Art
and
Thought
of
Lafcadio
Hearn

by
Beongcheon
Yu
Wayne
State
University

Published simultaneously in Canada by Ambassador Books, Limited,
Toronto, Ontario, Canada

Library of Congress Catalog Card Number 64-10090

Two chapters in this book have been published as essays: "Lafcadio
Hearn's Aesthetics of Organic Memory," in the English Literary Society
of Japan publication, Studies in English Literature, XXXVIII, No. 1
(November 1961), 1–28; and "Lafcadio Hearn's Twice-Told Legends
Reconsidered," American Literature, XXXIV, No. 1 (March 1962),
56–71. They are reprinted through the courtesy of the publishers.

Grateful acknowledgment is made to the FORD FOUNDATION for finan-
cial assistance in the publication of this book.

to HYATT H. WAGGONER
this book is gratefully dedicated

Acknowledgments

In writing this book, I have been indebted to many persons. My gratitude is due to the distinguished scholars whose opinions on Lafcadio Hearn have helped me to view him in perspective, even though I often had to disagree with them.

I wish also to thank Professor Samuel F. Damon of Brown University, who first directed my interest to Hearn's art and thought; and my friends, Richard C. Bedford, Robert M. Farnsworth, Emerson R. Marks, and J. S. Wolkenfeld, who read the manuscript and offered me invaluable criticism at its several stages of revision. Harold A. Basilius, Director, Wayne State University Press, offered his scholarly interest and encouragement; Mrs. Barbara Woodward, editor, assisted me with care and insight in preparing the manuscript for the printer; and Miss Marilyn Fryzel kindly helped me to proofread.

Special mention must be made of the generosity of the Wayne State University Graduate Research Committee for two grants-in-aid, and of the English Department Planning and Policy Committee for the grant of time, which facilitated immensely my research and my final revision.

B. Y.

Preface

In *Father and I,* Kazuo Koizumi talks of a prediction made to his late father, Lafcadio Hearn, by a Takagi:

". . . under a big rock is hidden a great treasure. Surely, some time it will appear on earth and draw the attention of the people, but that stone is in the way." Then father said, "If I die, that stone will move, but I should like to see the treasure before I die." Takagi replied, "Don't be in haste—don't be in haste"; but father said that he could not wait.

The prediction remains to be fulfilled. Some have even doubted the existence of the treasure under the big rock, whereas others have only idolized the rock with no intent of removing it. Here is the origin of the Hearn myth, as E. C. Stedman foresaw years ago: "Hearn will in time be as much of a romantic personality and tradition as Poe is now." By now various epithets have been painted on the rock: a sensual Romantic, a wandering dreamer, a rootless cosmopolite, a self-styled exile, a frightened escapist, a heartless lover, a shameless friend, an ignoble traitor, and so on. When F. L. Pattee called him "that strangest of literary comets shot into our literary system," he was voicing a common estimate of Hearn's position in modern literature.

For such a twist of fate, it is true, Hearn is doubly responsible: First, there is his life, a series of flights across both hemispheres, which alienated him physically farther and farther from the world into which he had been born; and then there is the peculiarly anomalous nature of his achievement, which resists the literary historian's neat classification. But beyond this, it is we who are largely responsible for the common image of Hearn as an isolated marginal figure, because few of us have seriously questioned its accuracy. Almost all the Hearn studies undertaken in the past fifty years have not only accepted this image as their point of departure but also unanimously reaffirmed its truthfulness. For this reason the majority of Hearn studies, whether biographical or critical, seem to tend toward one or the other of two extremes, that is, Dr. Gould's oracular denouncement and Yone Noguchi's impassioned defense, neither of which helped to restore the genuine stature of Hearn. As a result, we have an image of Hearn not whole but split into fragments. This may be what made Oscar Lewis epitomize Hearn as "the most loved and the most hated figure in recent literary history."

Glancing at Hearn studies as a whole, one may easily see there the results of misdirected biographical interest: first, most of the studies are frankly biographical and concentrate on his life rather than his art and thought; second, those few critical or interpretative works are overly eager to read his life experience into his writings and to translate his words into his life pattern; and third, since even the critical works are concerned with some particular facet rather than an overall synthesis of his achievement, their method tends to entail distortions of the subject. This is especially true when the critic bases his arguments on biographical studies reflecting not so much judicious objectivity as partisan spirit.

The one-sidedness in Hearn scholarship may be due in part to the fact that, despite its enormous bulk, some difficulties have nonetheless remained to hinder our better access to the subject. We have still no definitive biographies of Hearn, the difficulty being that any good account of his life must encompass thoroughly and evenly four periods, European, American, West Indian, and Japanese. Nor do we have a complete collection of his writings, especially his newspaper articles, lectures, notebooks, and other miscellanies, a fact which disappoints those interested primarily in his art and thought. Besides, there are two more difficulties: first, the unavailability to Western scholars of the Japanese scholarship in the field; second, the kind of literary and cultural provincialism to which we are often prone. If one be aware of both the present state of Hearn scholarship and these difficulties, he should all the more appreciate the recent efforts by Vera McWilliams, Marcel Robert, Fumio Hozumi, O. W. Frost, Elizabeth Stevenson, and others toward providing Hearn scholarship with balance and objectivity.

Questioning the traditional notion of Lafcadio Hearn in our literary history, the present study attempts to reconsider him in the light of his literary and cultural milieu; in other words, to determine how intimately Hearn participated in the collective experience of his own generation. Although it makes use of the established facts of his life, it is not intended to be a biographical account. It is basically a critical examination of Hearn's achievement in its entirety. After all, there is no good reason why one has to wait until that "big rock" is cleared away. Would it not be better to delve into the "great treasure"? True, Hearn's life, now crystallized into almost a myth, is a highly romantic voyage; but it is my contention that his inner voyage is incomparably more romantic and more stirring. His was a mind such as Wordsworth described, "a mind forever voyaging through strange seas of thought, alone." His writings, taken all together, comprise a remarkable record of this mental traveler.

I have tried to avail myself of all Hearn materials within my reach, draw together those manifestations of his mind, and reconstruct his sphere of thought. I have discarded the form of critical biography and have instead considered his achievement in the three major phases: art, criticism, and philosophy. Within this general framework my method of approach is basically topical. Each of the fourteen chapters focuses on one particular facet of Hearn's achievement, examines possible relationships, consistency, and maturity, and assesses whatever significance it may claim. Each chapter is thus topically independent, yet progresses toward a final synthesis. Furthermore, his art is related, by way of his developing theories, to criticism, and they both grow into his philosophy. In a word, the entire plan is designed to acquaint the reader with the major aspects so that he may be able to perceive afresh one complete image of Hearn.

In view of the difficulties that have faced previous Hearn critics it would be best if I clarify my fundamental method at the start. My aim is to present the work of Hearn as a meaningful totality. Biographical material is of no special interest to me except insofar as it helps us to see Hearn's achievement. Second, I take it as my task not to defend Hearn, not to convert others to his point of view, but merely to elucidate his position and evaluate it in terms of his time and our own. It is indeed when relating Hearn to our own time that the most obstinate difficulties will enter. Hearn's ideas not only run counter to accepted ways of thinking today; many of them would also be unusual, not to say unpopular, at any time.

Each part of my study, corresponding to the three important sub-divisions of Hearn's work, brings up special problems of its own. When considering his creative work, for instance, we are faced with the problem of classification. His work just will not fit the clear academic distinctions among poetry, fiction, essay, and travel literature. If we are to take it seriously at all we will have to consider it as a unique kind of work; whatever outward form it may take, it is really what we might call the literature of philosophical voyage. His aesthetics of organic memory, with its emphasis on the collective unconscious, leads us even further away from what is commonly accepted today. Although Hearn is close to the aesthetic tradition of Poe and Baudelaire, and also to the ideas of Jung, still his attitude is esoteric and of a kind now generally ignored. Nevertheless, it is vital to any reasonable understanding of him. Most controversial are the ideas of Hearn which I discuss in Part III—his hopes for integration between the East and the West. I have no doubt that Hearn will provoke strong disagreement at the least, not only in suggesting integration but more especially in the kind of integration he suggests; however, controversy should not deter those of us who are interested in his work. In fact, it imposes on us an obligation to give him a fair hearing.

I have attempted to correct deep-rooted misconceptions about him long shared by many Hearn scholars, critics, enemies, friends, and even lovers, and to search for the "something permanent" which Edmund Gosse found in the fame of Lafcadio Hearn. I hope that the reader will consider my rather elaborate method of approach as justifiable and even necessary in view of the peculiar aspects of Hearn's achievement and the general state of Hearn scholarship, and that I have remained faithful to my expressed intention.

Contents

III *Philosophy*

1 Art

I

"Only the First Step"

Translation as an Art

There is good reason why our study of Hearn's art begins with 1882, the year which saw the publication of *One of Cleopatra's Nights,* first of his books to be printed. True, we do find the first sign of his awakening literary conscience in his early years in New Orleans, and even in his Cincinnati period (1869–77), especially in his Bohemian revolt against journalism. One might even say that his art grew out of his subsequent struggle to "get rid of newspaper life"; yet, these years are important largely as an embryonic stage of his literary career.

Early in 1882, when *One of Cleopatra's Nights* came out, perhaps Hearn alone knew the significance of the moment. To others it might have meant simply that this collection of six Gautier tales was his first publication in book form, but the fact that he willingly bore half the publishing expenses indicates that to him at least it meant a great deal more. After all, it was the book for which he had "tried for six years to obtain a publisher." [1] He must have looked back at the long way he had come since the difficult years in Cincinnati when he decided to devote all his scanty time to the translation of some French masters, especially the long nights when he was translating Gautier's tale, "One of Cleopatra's Nights," "under merely a poor jet of gas, with his one useful eye close to book and manuscript." [2] Probably he started this task to maintain the dignity of art against journalistic drudgery, but when it was all over he found that it had turned out to be a search for an artistic medium. His feelings are made clear in a letter to H. E. Krehbiel, his friend in Cincinnati, written about this time:

> What you say about the disinclination to work for years upon a theme for pure love's sake, without hope of reward, touches me,—because I have felt that despair so long and so often. And yet I believe that all the world's art-work—all that which is eternal—was thus wrought. And I also believe that no work made perfect for the pure love of art, can perish, save by strange and rare accident. Despite the rage of religion and of time, we know Sappho found no rival, no equal. Rivers changed their courses and dried up,—seas became deserts, since some Egyptian romanticist wrote the story of Latin-Khamois. Do you suppose he ever received $oo for it?
>
> Yet the hardest of all sacrifices for the artist is this sacrifice to art,— this trampling of self under foot! It is the supreme test for admittance into the ranks of the eternal priests. It is the bitter and fruitless sacrifice which the artist's soul is bound to make,—as in certain antique cities maidens were compelled to give their virginity to a god of stone! But without the sacrifice can we hope for the grace of heaven?
>
> What is the reward? The consciousness of inspiration only! I think art gives a new faith. I think—all jesting aside—that could I create something I felt to be sublime, I should feel also that the Unknowable had selected me for a mouthpiece, for a medium of utterance, in the holy cycling of its eternal purpose; and I should know the pride of the prophet that had seen God face to face. [3]

It seems significant that this formal declaration of his artistic ambition, so to speak, coincided with the publication of *One of Cleopatra's Nights,* and that Hearn launched into his literary career by way of translation. Translation indeed was to have a decisive bearing on his entire career.

From the start Hearn entertained a genuine conviction about translation as a legitimate form of art; accordingly, he approached it with characteristic sincerity. As a veteran practitioner he not only strove to live up to the highest standards of that art but also demanded the same from his fellow translators. Since his own debut in the New Orleans newspaper world with his translation of Gautier's "The Mummy's Foot" (*Item,* June 16, 1878), he wrote about the art of translation as much as he translated. His interest is evident in many of his articles, especially those dealing with some recent American translations of Gautier, Flaubert, and Zola. [4] In these Hearn considered two important aspects of the question, the translator's artistic conscience and his necessary qualifications. "Translating and Mutilating" (*Item,* January 30,

1880), the first of the series, was occasioned by John Stirling's version of Zola's *Nana*. (It matters little whether Hearn knew that "John Stirling" was actually the pen name of Mary Neal Sherwood.) In spite of his personal objection to Zola's scientific determinism, Hearn demanded a full translation of the original with no expurgation, and insisted that one should criticize the result only from an artistic standpoint. It was his belief that "a purified version of Zola is not Zola. Zola is nothing if not impure." In another article, *"Captain Fracasse"* (*Item*, April 11, 1880), he continued to call for artistic integrity on the part of the translator. This time he summed up the whole issue more succinctly, saying that "only an artist could have translated this work properly."

About a year later, Hearn resumed his attack on the prolific Stirling's translations, and more bluntly questioned his artistic qualifications. Apparently Hearn grew intolerant of Stirling's rapid production. In a third article, *"Madame Bovary"* (*Item*, January 28, 1881), Hearn denounced the translator as a humbug, and demanded that he be suppressed. Such translation, he pointed out, was only "a disgrace to American literature," and "a shame to the Publishing house which issued it." In fact, he insisted that it was not a translation at all. In a fourth article, "Some American Translations" (*Item*, January 30, 1881), printed two days later, Hearn remarked that New Orleans, the once French city, ought to expose Stirling's "contemptible" translations as nothing but literary frauds. The last of this series, "How Stirling Translates Zola" (*Item*, January 31, 1881), was Hearn's *coup de grâce*. After making a detailed comparison of the French and English texts of Zola's *Madeleine Férat*, he let his patience give way to cool contempt: "With a knowledge of English inferior to that of a dime novelist, and a knowledge of French equal to that of a ten-year old school boy, it is hardly likely that Stirling could introduce Emile Zola to American readers." [5]

To explain all this as merely professional jealousy on Hearn's part would miss the point. It seems more reasonable that his severity is due to both his self-confidence as a translator and his zeal for artistic perfection. Since translation is distinctly art, a translator must be an artist first of all. But the point should not be misunderstood; Hearn held that to do justice to the original a translator must be qualified doubly, both linguistically and artistically. All this he set forth in his usual manner in his editorial "For the Sum of $25":

> When an attempt is made to make anything like a fair estimate of the labour needed to effect a faithful and meritorious translation of the great masters of the French language, we cannot imagine it possible to translate

more than five or six pages a day (long primer, leaded, 16mo). For it is by no means sufficient to reproduce the general meaning of the sentence: —it is equally necessary to obtain a just equivalent for each word, in regard to force, colour, and form;—and to preserve, so far as possible, the original construction of the phrase, the peculiarity of the rhetoric, the music of the style. And there is a music in every master style,—a measured flow of words in every sentence;—there are alliterations and rhythms; there are onomatopoeias; there are tints, sonorities, luminosities, resonances. Each word in a phrase is a study in itself, and a study in its relation to other words in the phrase; and the phrase in its relation to the sentence and the sentence in its relation to the paragraph, and the paragraph in its relation to other paragraphs. Then besides precise shades of meaning must be studied, harmonies of tones and their relation to other tones, and their general interrelation with the music of the entire idea. A most laborious, cautious, ingenious, delicate and supple work;—a work demanding perhaps even a greater knowledge of one's own language than of the French tongue,—a work to be aided, not by French dictionaries, but by English dictionaries of synonyms and derivations and antonyms and technicalities and idioms and rhymes. A work requiring intense application, wearisome research and varied linguistic powers. A work of giants, indeed;—easily flowing as its results may seem to careless eyes thereafter;—eyes unable to analyze the secret of the art that pleases them. There is no more difficult and scholarly task than to translate perfectly a masterpiece from one tongue to another. Wherefore the proverbs— French, Spanish and Italian:—*traduir c'est trahir; traductor, traidor,* and *tradultor traiditore,* synonymizing "translator" and "traitor." Faithless indeed must be the translator who imagines that he can produce in one week or one month a fair translation of some work which cost its author years of literary labour.

And this very new school of French literature,—the school of Daudet, Goncourt, Zola and Flaubert,—so ruthlessly treated by persons who produce these bogus translations, is that which of all others demands the most careful labour. The sense, forms, force, sonority, colour of every word must be studied; the shape of every phrase chiselled out; the beauty of every naked sentence polished like statuary marble. Men have killed themselves at this terrible literary labour, so utterly ignored by American translators. One of the brothers Goncourt perished from the nervous exhaustion entailed by intense application. And it is such works as this, the labour of years,—work produced in nervous tortures, prostrating fatigues, brain agonies unspeakable,—a work of blood and tears,—a work in whose every line quivers the vitality of the creator,—that some vulgar scribbler sits down to translate at a bar-room table under a contract to complete the task in one week for the sum of $25.[6]

Hearn is undoubtedly right in enumerating all the factors involved in translation, in demanding that the effort of the translator who deals with a masterpiece should parallel the author's own efforts, and finally in defining what a perfect translation ought to effect beyond linguistic and ideational transference. For this, few of us would hesitate to give him credit. Although the task set down here sounds formidable, perhaps too formidable to be fulfilled by him or by any other, Hearn set out to emulate the ideal translator, whatever his and our estimate of the actual result. Toward the end of his New Orleans period (1877–87) he still continued to ridicule French translations then appearing in the *States* and the *Picayune,* both the *Times-Democrat's* rivals in the city. When the *States* issued a challenge for a competition between their translator and Hearn of the *Times-Democrat,* the editor of the latter, rejecting such "a purely local contest," countered with a national contest. The episode indicates Hearn's solid stature as translator at this time.

Scanning Hearn's remarks on the art of translation, we may wonder how he would have reacted had he known that much the same opinion had been voiced by Henry James only a few years before. Reviewing two recent American translations of Gautier's travel books, James said: "Omission in translation is rarely absolutely justifiable." He went on to describe a good translator as one who gives "care, and taste, and imagination" to the original.[7] It would be interesting to conjecture what James would have said of Hearn's translations, since care, taste, and imagination are the very qualities that make his translation creative art.

For an example of Hearn's translation as creative art one may well take his first extended work, *One of Cleopatra's Nights,* a choice that is justifiable for more than one reason. As his introduction to this Gautier translation suggests, Hearn is acutely aware of the significance of his attempt. In its concluding passage he states explicitly that the artist alone can judge Gautier's creations, and that what he is really trying to recapture is "the loveliness of the antique world," "physical beauty and artistic truth," and "the charm of youthful dreams and young passion in its blossoming." He hopes that "the first English version of these graceful fantasies" may not be found wholly unworthy of the original. Moreover, Hearn students customarily cite this work as an example of his fidelity to the original. One reviewer went still further, declaring that "he [Hearn] also improved upon it and many a scholar who knows both French and English has confessed under the rose that Gautier is outdone."[8] Gautier was the very artist whom James believed untranslatable, his fantasies being "four-fifths verbal to one-fifth intellectual." As James put it, Gautier is "precisely one of the writers who are everything in their own tongue, and nothing, almost nothing, out of it." [9] Although it is certain that Hearn would have opposed James vehemently, James is quite right in pointing out that to translate Gautier into English calls for rare skill.

In the same introduction Hearn, noting Gautier's graphic power in particular, observes that his art is that of "painting carried to the highest perfection in literature." The following passage is typical of what Hearn designated as Gautier's "occasional abuse of violent coloring":

> While Cleopatra sleeps, let us ascend upon deck and enjoy the glorious sunset view. A broad band of violet color, warmed deeply with ruddy tints toward the west, occupies all the lower portion of the sky; encountering the zone of azure above, the violet shade melts into a clear lilac, and fades off through half-rosy tints into the blue beyond; afar, where the sun, red as a buckler fallen from the furnace of Vulcan, casts his burning reflection, the deeper shades turn to pale citron hues, and glow with turquoise tints. The water, rippling under an oblique beam of light, shines with the dull gleam of the quicksilvered side of a mirror, or like a damascened blade. The sinuosities of the bank, the reeds, and all objects along the shore are brought out in sharp black relief against the bright glow.[10]

Hearn's fidelity to the French original is undeniable. Yet, upon closer examination we cannot fail to notice what has been added to Gautier's verbal painting. The translator's addition of two slight locatives "above" and "beyond" gives the canvas three-dimensional perspective. Although substitution of "the deeper shades" for "la nuance" may be unnecessary, it is evidence of his effort to approximate the otherwise untranslatable French. In rendering "produit des teints pareilles à celles des turquoises" into simply "glow with turquoise tints," he makes good use of dynamic force, a virtue inherent in English. But his noun-adjectives, "the glorious sunset view" for "l'admirable spectacle du soleil couchant," sound a bit forced, though Hearn is concerned with balance. This may be more easily overlooked than his excessive fondness for such words as "color," "tints," and "hues." Despite these minor additions, the piece on the whole exemplifies what Hearn called literalism.

The term "literalism" is misleading, since Hearn thereby means a great deal more than linguistic literalism. There is a revealing episode in his correspondence with Jerome A. Hart, of San Francisco, one of his early admirers. Reviewing Hearn's Gautier collection for the *Argonaut,* Hart wrote: "Mr. Hearn has few equals in this country as regards translation, and the stories lose nothing of their artistic unity in his hands." "But his hobby is literalism," he complained, and compared the original of the famous epitaph in "Clarimonde" with Hearn's translation: "Ici-gît Clarimonde/Qui fut de son vivant/La plus belle du monde" (Here lies Clarimonde,/Who was famed in her lifetime/As the fairest of women). After referring to Hearn's footnote that "the broken beauty of the lines is unavoidably lost in the translation," Hart advanced his own version: "Here lieth Clarimonde,/Who was, what time she lived,/The loveliest in the land." Therewith he concluded: "The fleeting archaic flavour of the original is not entirely lost here, and the lines are broken, yet metrical." In reply to this suggestion Hearn wrote: "Your translation of the epitaph seems to me superb as far as the first two lines go; but I can hardly agree with you as to the last." He does not believe that "La plus belle du monde" can be perfectly rendered by Hart's "The loveliest in the land," because of "the circumscribed idea it involves." As Hearn sees it, the French original, though simple, is "an expression of paramount force." What it attempts to convey is "the idea of beauty without an equal, not in any one country, but in the whole world." After complimenting Hart's second line as a masterpiece of faithfulness, he adds, ". . . and, as you justly remark, my hobby is literalism." [11]

As such, Hearn's literalism should not be taken too literally. As our first example shows, the more he labors to effect the complex nuance of the original, not only its general meaning but also its peculiar architectonics, he goes beyond literalism, often verging on paraphrase. Another example comes from Flaubert's philosophical pageant, *The Temptation of St. Anthony*, which Hearn undertook to translate in Cincinnati along with "One of Cleopatra's Nights," but which was not published during his lifetime. It is also a work in which James had earlier discovered little but a series of pictorial observations.[12] To illustrate his point James chose one of the most graphic passages, describing an eerie appearance of the Queen of Sheba. James believed that Flaubert must be "especially satisfied" with the passage, "both as a piece of description and a piece of dramatization," and then ventured his own translation:

Her dress, in golden brocade, divided regularly by furbelows of pearls, of jet, and of sapphire, compresses her waist into a narrow bodice, ornamented with applied pieces in color representing the twelve signs of the zodiac. She wears high skates, of which one is black and spangled with silver stars, with the crescent of the moon, while the other is white, and covered with little drops in gold, with the sun in the middle.
Her wide sleeves, covered with emeralds and with feathers of birds,

expose the nakedness of her little round arm, ornamented at the wrist by a bracelet of ebony; and her hands, laden with rings, terminate in nails so pointed that the ends of her fingers look almost like needles.

A flat gold chain, passing under her chin, ascends beside her cheeks, rolls in a spiral around her hair, which is powdered with blue powder, then, falling, grazes her shoulder and comes and fastens itself on her bosom in a scorpion in diamonds which thrusts out its tongue between her breasts. Two great blood [sic] pearls drag down her ears. The edges of her eyelids are painted black. She has on her left cheek-bone a natural brown mole, and she breathes, opening her mouth, as if her bodice hurt her.

She shakes as she walks, a green parasol surrounded with gilt bells, and twelve little woolly-headed negroes carry the long train of her dress, held at the end by a monkey, who occasionally lifts it up. She says: *"Ah, bel ermite! bel ermite! mon coeur défaille!"*

Why a pointless description such as this is distasteful to James is plain enough. He questions caustically: "What is M. Flaubert's historical evidence for the mole on the Queen of Sheba's cheek and the blue powder in her hair?" On the other hand, this is the kind of scene which Hearn could hardly resist, and he translates it thus:

Her robe of gold brocade, regularly divided by furbelows of pearls, of jet, and of sapphires, sheaths her figure closely with its tight-fitting bodice, set off by coloured designs representing the twelve signs of the Zodiac. She wears very high pattens—one of which is black, and sprinkled with silver stars, with a moon crescent; the other, which is white, is sprinkled with a spray of gold, with a golden sun in the middle.

Her wide sleeves, decorated with emeralds and bird-plumes, leave exposed her little round bare arms, clasped at the wrist by ebony bracelets; and her hands, loaded with precious rings, are terminated by nails so sharply pointed that the ends of her fingers seem almost like needles.

A chain of dead gold, passing under her chin, is caught up on either side of her face, and spirally coiled about her coiffure, whence, redescending, it grazes her shoulders and is attached upon her bosom to a diamond scorpion, which protrudes a jewelled tongue between her breasts. Two immense blond pearls depend heavily from her ears. The borders of her eyelids are painted black. There is a natural brown spot upon her left cheek; and she opens her mouth in breathing, as if her corset inconvenienced her.

She shakes, as she approaches, a green parasol with an ivory handle, and silver-gilt bells attached to its rim; twelve little wooly-haired negro-boys support the long train of her robe, whereof an ape holds the extremity, which it raises up from time to time. She exclaims:

"Ah! handsome hermit! handsome hermit!—my heart swoons!" [13]

Both versions can be compared in many ways. Where Hearn gains, James loses; and vice versa. The fundamental difference lies in the approach to translation. Hearn approximates French; James approximates English.

Whatever his intention, Hearn's renderings, such as "sheaths her figure closely with its tight-fitting bodice" (for James's "compresses her waist into a narrow bodice"), "Two immense blond pearls depend heavily from her ears" (for "Two great blood [sic] pearls drag down her ears"), "and she opens her mouth in breathing, as if her corset inconvenienced her" (for "and she breathes, opening her mouth, as if her bodice hurt her"), etc., are all heavy-handed when compared with James's, which are simple, natural, and straightforward.

Since it is his policy to retain the flavor inherent in the French original, Hearn never would exchange "very high pattens" for "high skates," "her coiffure" for "her hair," or even "her robe of gold brocade" for "her dress, in golden brocade." To this sort of literalism few would object, but why he should have "redescending" or "a natural brown spot," instead of James's simple "falling" or "a natural brown mole," we cannot but wonder.

Hearn still has the love for noun-adjectives that we saw in his Gautier piece, and at times he uses them successfully. His "ebony bracelets" and "diamond scorpion" sound better than James's "a bracelet of ebony" and "a scorpion in diamonds." But Hearn's gallicism in "a moon crescent" is almost as uncomfortable as James's literalism in "the crescent of the moon" (for "un croissant de lune").

Now what is peculiar about Hearn's translation, compared with James's? It is that Hearn is not wholly satisfied with literalism, and goes on to amplify or paraphrase the original when he believes it not only justifiable but even indispensable. Notice the additions, such as "a *golden* sun," "*precious* rings," "*sharply* pointed," and "*jewelled* tongue," none of which is found in the French original, "un soleil," "bagues," "pointus," and "la langue." Whether these should be considered an improvement on the original is hard to decide. Emphasis is another device Hearn often resorts to. Perhaps the best example is his "exclaims" for James's "says," which is literally closer to the French word *"dit."*

All in all, Hearn attempts to catch the rhythm of French as much as James attempts to catch the rhythm of English. If there is one thing for which we have to criticize Hearn, it is not for falling short of the original but for being too faithful to it, almost to the point of sounding artificial. Now we may wonder which of these English versions Flaubert would prefer.

The freedom Hearn takes in translation, of the kind our second example illustrates, is not the result of linguistic slovenliness or technical incompetency. It seems instead to be the result of a zealous artistic conscientiousness. Undoubtedly, he believed that genuine translation is possible only by going beyond a literal rendering. One must translate not only the colors, forms, and sounds, but also the sensations, emotions, and thoughts which are found in the original. Translation in this sense is something quite different from a linguistic equivalent of the original; it should be a recreation of the original, a process which naturally involves interpretation, too. Yet the result ought to be one with the original. Since it recreates the original in body and soul, translation demands a fundamentally aesthetic approach. This is Hearn's concept of translation, and it accounts for both the merits and the weaknesses we notice in all his translations.

Bearing this in mind, let us look at one more example. It is "Les Bienfaits de la lune," one of Baudelaire's prose poems, a great favorite with Hearn for a very personal reason. Under the title of "The Moon's Blessings" his translation appeared in the Sunday issue of the *Times-Democrat,* March 12, 1882:

> The Moon, who is herself the embodiment of caprice, looked through the window while thou wert slumbering in the cradle, and said to herself:—"this child pleaseth me." And softly she descended her stairway of clouds, and noiselessly passed through the window-panes. Then did she extend herself upon thee, with all the supple tenderness of a mother, and deposed her colors upon thy face. Therefore have thine eyes ever remained green, and thy cheeks extraordinarily pale. And it was through contemplating that strange visitor that thine eyes became so weirdly large; and so tenderly did she press thy throat that thou hast ever retained within thy heart a vast desire to weep.
>
> Meantime, in the expansion of her joy, the Moon filled all the chamber like a phosphoric atmosphere, like a luminous poison; and all that living light thought and spake:—"Thou shalt eternally feel the influence of my kiss. Thou shalt be beautiful after my fashion. Thou shalt love all that I love and all that loves me:—waters and clouds, silence and the night; the vast green sea, the water that is formless and multiform; the place where thou shalt never be; the lover thou shalt never know; the flowers that are monstrous and the perfumes which are madness; the cats that swoon upon pianos, and moan like women with a hoarse sweet voice.
>
> "And thou shalt be beloved by lovers, courted by my courtiers. Thou shalt be the queen of those green-eyed men whose breasts I have also pressed with my nocturnal caresses,—of all those who love the sea, the vast green sea, the water that is formless and multiform, the place where they shall never be, the Woman they shall never know, the sinister flowers

that seem the censers of a religion unknown, the perfumes which weaken the will, and the animals, voluptuous and untamed, which are the symbols of their own madness."

And, therefore, hath it come to pass, thou dear accursed spoiled-child, that I am now lying at thy feet, seeking to find in all thy person some reflection of the awful Divinity, of the fatidical godmother, of that poison-giving nurse who nurseth all *lunatics*.[14]

Besides Hearn's translation, which is one of the early English versions of the Baudelaire piece, there are a few more done by Arthur Symons, Louise Varèse, and others.[15] Without comparing all these versions in full, let us concentrate on three immediate questions: how far Hearn's translation is literal, how his paraphrase begins, and what his peculiarity is.

First, his literalism: Hearn's persistent use of the second singular of the personal pronoun may indicate an effort to reproduce the tone of the French original. More probably he had in mind the poetic and archaic solemnity of the Biblical usage. For a similar reason perhaps, he rendered "la redoutable Divinité" into "the awful Divinity" (cf. Symons' "fearful goddess" or Varèse's "dread Goddess"). In the same vein he clings to his "fatidical" for "fatidique," instead of Symons' "prophetic" or Varèse's "fateful." We may wonder, though, whether he would be still partial to his "deposed her colors" for "déposa ses couleurs," compared with Symons' "painted" or Varèse's "left." He must concede, in any case, that his "in the expansion of her joy" for "dans l'expansion de sa joie" does not go so well as Symons' "in the flood of her joy" or especially Varèse's "in the fullness of her joy." In spite of all this, he would insist that Baudelaire's "tous les *lunatiques*" should be "all *lunatics*," of course italicized, certainly not "all the moonstruck of the world" (Symons') or "all *moon-mad men*" (Varèse's).

Second, his paraphrase: This method becomes effective whenever Hearn exercises good judgment. Such is the case with his close attention to the French sense of time, especially its imperfect tense. Also notable is his discriminating translation of the ambiguous French "gorge" by either "throat" or "breast," depending on which fits Baudelaire's intention. But his zeal for improving the original runs to an extreme as soon as he indulges in "that *strange* visitor" for "cette visiteuse," "a *vast* desire to weep" for "l'envie de pleurer," or "their *own* madness" for simple "leur folie." The rendering of "herself the embodiment of caprice" for "le caprice même," and the interpolation of "hath it come to pass" are difficult to justify; Hearn goes a little too far here.

Third, his peculiarity: Hearn's "weirdly" for "bizarrement" is worth mentioning. It is the word he would use so fondly all his life. His repeated use of emphatic inversion is also understandable, considering the general mood he is intent upon conjuring; and "a religion unknown" for "une religion inconnue" may be more evocative than "some unknown religion" or simply "a strange religion." But why his repeated use of that encompassing *all*—"all that" for "ce que" and "ce qui," and "all those who . . ." for "ceux-là qui . . ."? "The place where they shall never be, the Woman they shall never know" for "le lieu où ils ne sont pas, la femme qu'ils ne connaissent" is arresting, since Hearn is so meticulous about tense in the rest of the poem. Could this be another case where Hearn goes too far on his own? He must be well aware of what he is doing; in all likelihood he believed he was improving Baudelaire in spirit. Take also his capitalization of "the Woman" for the French "la femme." Here, it seems to us, Hearn attempts to recreate what Baudelaire must have meant. In doing so, he comes to lend a very personal twist to the material. "Woman" here suggests even more than what the French call "la femme fatale." We may perhaps detect here the germ of his philosophical concept, the Eternal Feminine. As we shall see later, it is in her image that Hearn came to find the manifestation of the Western man's aspiration for the Impossible. Perhaps this suggestion explains why he shifted the tense from the present to the future, implying thus that they *can* never know her. What happens, then, is that the translation becomes Hearn's interpretation of Baudelaire's "Les Bienfaits de la lune." As a result of this contact between Baudelaire and Hearn, it assumes the spirit of both.

As all these examples indicate, Hearn's art of translation possesses maximum latitude; his approach is highly mobile and flexible, ranging from literalism to paraphrase. Within this range fall all the translations, more than two hundred in number, which Hearn made for three New Orleans newspapers, the *Item,* the *Democrat,* and the *Times-Democrat,* and also his translation of Anatole France's *Le Crime de Sylvestre Bonnard,* which, despite his customary objection to hurried work, he had to make in a few weeks to defray the expenses of his expected voyage to Japan. Hearn's New Orleans translations have certain characteristics worth special mention. His subjects cover a variety of nationalities and races, French, Spanish, German, Russian, Jewish, Chinese, and so on, all of which but the Spanish are rendered from French originals or French translations. While these are short stories for the most part, there are many sketches, brief excerpts from various novels, and some miscellaneous pieces of literary and scientific interest. That the great majority of them, moreover, are drawn from contemporary literature is indicative of Hearn's artistic tastes and ambition.

In the *Item* translations Gautier still takes the lead, understandably enough; in the *Democrat* group, on the other hand, Zola dominates, followed by Loti. In the last, *Times-Democrat,* group Hearn introduces new figures, Coppée, L'Isle-Adam, Daudet, and others. While Zola recedes, Maupassant and Loti come to the fore, together with new subjects, Jewish, Arabian, and Chinese. The increasing frequency of Oriental topics runs parallel with Hearn's increasing interest in literary exoticism, which culminates in the publication of *Stray Leaves from Strange Literature* (1884) and *Some Chinese Ghosts* (1887). These two books may be described as free adaptations or imitations; that is to say, examples of Hearn's art of translation in its widest application.

One more thing to be said here is that, while working on these translations, Hearn made it a rule to write short, incisive critical notes on the works and their authors. As a result we have comments on Gautier, Nerval, Baudelaire, Zola, Maupassant, Loti, Heine, Dostoevski, Bourget, and others, all of which constitute a valuable portion of his criticism. At the end of this period Hearn emerged as translator, critic, and stylist.

Whether Hearn himself knew it or not, cultivating translation as art led him directly to his later work in Japan. Without his ten-year-long preparation as a translator, he could hardly have achieved his later fame as an interpreter of Japan. While in Japan (1890–1904), Hearn not only transmitted to the Western world the essence of Japanese culture but also made many translations of those innumerable legends and poems which are scattered all over his Japanese books. There is no question that Hearn did not know much Japanese. Nevertheless, his Japanese translations cannot be rejected by anyone who is fully aware of what translation meant to him. Those legends in which he attempted to probe into the soul of Japan may not be translations in the most rigid sense, but they are still translations in the same sense that his *Stray Leaves* and *Some Chinese Ghosts* are. In particular, the poems he chose in order to illustrate a world unfamiliar to his Western audience are authentic translations in every sense. Being acutely aware of his handicaps as well as his forte, Hearn took every possible precaution in tackling this nearly impossible task. Within his reach he had people, native and foreign, willing to offer help in one way or another. Also, he would often resist dealing with Japanese poems, formal or popular, old or

new, until he believed he could confidently feel their spirit and emotionally re-experience their subtle meanings. That is why the majority
of these legends and poems did not appear until in his later, more
mature Japanese books.[16]

A translation from "Songs of Japanese Children," the lullaby sung to
the child of a *daimyo,* gathered from Izumo, is a perfect example of
Hearn's literalism in its primary sense:

> Augustly rest, augustly rest! Soon this evening augustly sleep! Early at
> daybreak, at the august awakening, what, what honorable gift shall be
> presented at the august awakening? Flower of honorable milk shall be
> presented. If the flower of honorable milk be augustly disliked, then the
> fighting of the cocks will be honorably displayed. If the fighting of the
> cocks will be honorably disliked, then will not honorable cake be augustly
> accepted? [17]

As Hearn himself admits, this is meant to convey the most intriguing
part of Japanese to foreigners. As an experiment with the peculiarities
of the native speech it is interesting indeed, but this sort of translation
is too heavy-handed to catch the delicacy, grace, and tenderness of the
original.

Hearn also translates a poem by Chiyo of Kaga, the beloved Japanese
woman poet:

> Tombō-tsuri!—
> Kyō wa doko madé
> itta yara!

(Catching dragon-flies! . . . I wonder where *he* has gone today!)

The original is typical of the studied simplicity of Japanese *haiku*
(*hokku*) form. Only that which is absolutely necessary may be kept,
so that into the minimum utterance may be compressed the maximum
force of emotion; hence, all pronouns are omitted in the original. As
Hearn explains, the poem is intended "to suggest, not to express, the
emotion of the mother." Accordingly, he keeps as close to the original
as possible. In order to catch the spirit of the poem, a mother's sorrow,
with immediacy and intensity, Hearn restores but two pronouns "I"
and "he." But fearing his reader's failure to understand what is unsaid
in the poem, Hearn supplies an explanation: "She sees children running
after dragon-flies, and thinks of her own dead boy who used to join
in the sport—and so finds herself wondering, in presence of the infinite

Mystery, what has become of the little soul. Whither has it gone?—in what shadowy play does it now find delight?"[18]

The English version alone is so bare, so literal that some may suspect it to be the very evidence of Hearn's deficiency in Japanese, though his explanatory note suggests the contrary. But a third selection should help to dispel this sort of suspicion:

> Mi ni shimiru
> Kazé ya!
> Shōji ni
> Yubi no ato!

With the caution, "in literal translation probably more obscure," Hearn offers his own version: "Oh, body-piercing wind!—that work of little fingers in the shōji!" As if to answer those who might accuse him of mere literalism, he then footnotes: "More literally: 'body-through-pierce wind—ah!—shōji—in the traces of (namely: holes made by) fingers!'" What he has gained by retouching this crude version is too obvious to be mentioned. Hearn adds an explanatory note:

What does this mean? It means the sorrowing of a mother for her dead child. Shōji is the name given to those light white-paper screens which in a Japanese house serve both as windows and doors—admitting plenty of light, but concealing, like frosted glass, the interior from outer observation, and excluding the wind. Infants delight to break these by poking their fingers through the soft paper: then the wind blows through the holes. In this case the wind blows very cold indeed—into the mother's very heart;—for it comes through the little holes that were made by the fingers of her dead child.[19]

The setting may be Japanese, the situation could be considered limited. But as an expression of a mother's deep-felt sorrow over her dead child, the poem is universal. This seems to be what Hearn is driving at in his note.

At first glance, our last two examples may seem merely descriptive of daily situations. They will remain no more unless we realize that these descriptive elements are poetic equivalents to the human emotion completely controlled. As Hearn rightly observes, the poetic virtue of *haiku* is "only to stir imagination without satisfying it." What he terms "ittakkiri," signifying "all told" or "any *completeness* of utterance," is abhorred as the worst lapse in the *haiku* form. Of this aspect Hearn is well aware, as evident in the passage following his explanatory note above: "The impossibility of preserving the inner quality of such poems in a literal rendering will now be obvious. Whatever I attempt in this direction must of necessity be ittakkiri;—for the unspoken has to be expressed." Every artistic translation, let us admit, tends to be the translator's interpretation of the original. This is especially true of the kind of poetry Hearn is dealing with. The ultimate value of translation in this instance depends entirely on whether it succeeds in revealing the "inner quality" or expressing the "unspoken" essence of the original. What the translator must always guard against is the conscious and unconscious interjection of unwarranted subjectivism, of the sort that we find occasionally in Hearn's renderings of Gautier, Flaubert, and Baudelaire. Perhaps because he knows less Japanese than French, ironically enough, Hearn often fares better with these Japanese poems.

One final example will be useful, the celebrated frog poem by Bashō, an inimitable master of *haiku*:

> Furu iké ya,
> Kawazu tobikomu,
> Midzu no oto.

(Old pond—frogs jumping in—sound of water.) [20]

Here, in one of the best examples of Hearn's deliberately literal approach, nothing is added to the original. More or less than this would only lessen the highest intensity that is the spirit of the poem. Along with Hearn's translation, it is illuminating to read some other English renderings.[21] One version reads: "The old pond./A frog jumps in—/ Plop!" The translator defends his onomatopoeia, objecting to the English "sound of water" on the ground that it is "too gentle, suggesting a running stream or brook." There is some truth in this, but at the same time his own substitute "plop" leaves no room for the imagination. Once the rendering becomes too specific, this sort of poetry loses the wholeness of its multiple implication. The point is well illustrated in a second version which reads: "A lonely pond in age-old stillness sleeps . . ./Apart, unstirred by sound or motion . . ./Suddenly into it a little frog leaps." Neither a mere paraphrase of the original nor a mere explanation of what happens in the poem makes a good translation. Here, since the essence of the original slips through a net of rhyme, the translation is anything but poetic. On the other hand, a third version, the nearest to Hearn's, reads: "The ancient pond/A frog leaps in/ The sound of the water." This is as literal a translation as is possible in English. What is peculiar about Hearn's is that, unlike the others, it refers to more than one frog. Is this, we may wonder, owing to Hearn's deficiency in Japanese? Or is it perhaps due to his awareness that the sense of number is usually absent in the Far Eastern mind? That the latter is more probable is suggested, indirectly, in his deliberate omission of all articles, a fact thoroughly consistent with the original language, which has no such equivalents. In view of the last translator's persistent use of articles, this is not insignificant. In presenting Bashō's original with his own version Hearn observed, in passing, that the Japanese master's feat is the creation of "one complete sensation-picture." Then he confessed that it is difficult, if not impossible, to repeat the feat in English. Does this imply that he has succeeded in the attempt? The question is less important than Hearn's conviction that his double strategy,—his seemingly literal but deliberately simple rendering along with his explanatory note, may effectively meet the difficulty.

Aside from this general method of approach, there is one more point to be made. It is that Hearn rarely pretended to render Japanese poems in conventional English verse form, except for those pieces whose heightened emotion would best be expressed in blank verse. This we may be tempted to explain away either by his admitted deficiency in Japanese or by his oft-mentioned lack of gift for versification.[22] It is more likely due to his belief that prose translation can be as good as verse translation. Through dealing with Japanese poems he came once again to the conviction that great poetry remains the same *"even when it is translated into the prose of another language."* To explain further: ". . . poetry which cannot be translated is of no use whatever in world-literature; and it is not even true poetry." What makes true poetry is not the sound values of words but fancies, emotions, and thoughts—those elements which contribute to its universality. In this belief he ventured to denounce as a waste of time all poetry which must depend for existence on the peculiarities of one language, for the reason that it "can never live in people's hearts."[23] Disagreeing freely with Schopenhauer over the issue, Hearn would resort to some notable examples, such as the English translation of the Bible, Nerval's prose translation of *Faust*, and other French prose translations of Byron and Heine.

Hearn's argument is far from convincing, but his attitude toward poetry could only be expressed by one who would sacrifice almost anything to transfer every possible shade or peculiarity of one language to its equivalent in another. It was in this vein that he advised his Japanese students to attempt translation of Shakespeare "into the living speech of today, into the ordinary language of conversation."[24]

Although he once said that "all verse translations are useless," [25] he did not hesitate to laud the English translation of the *Rubaiyat:* "Fitzgerald was probably the best translator that ever lived. He did not make literal translations; he translated only the spirit; the ghost of things." [26] Hearn's self-contradiction here is only seeming; it disappears once we realize his actual standard,—that the ultimate quality of translation depends on how well it transfers the "spirit" or "ghost" of the original, whether in verse or prose. He is really talking of translation in its widest and most fundamental sense, the only sense in which it can become creative art. Great literature, in his opinion, hardly deserves the name if it loses its essence in the process of translation. Hence his insistence that only an artist, not a mere linguist, should be entitled to practice that particular art.

In summing up Hearn's art of translation we may well recall what George W. Cable said of his friend Hearn's translations, referring specifically to his Gautier collection:

> There is in New Orleans a man of letters who has already made his mark, Mr. Lafcadio Hearn, who has managed to translate the body and soul of Théophile Gautier's writing into English. Indeed I am inclined to think that Mr. Hearn has imparted to his translations a sensitiveness, a delicacy, a spiritual essence not to be found in the originals. A ten minutes' talk with Mr. Hearn is among my most vivid recollections of a brief stay in New Orleans. He struck me as a man capable of putting versatility to new uses. He is a specialist in almost every branch of information. I hope to hear that he is writing a book which shall be a translation of the mysteries of his own mind and imagination.[27]

In Cable's "hope" there is something of prophecy. As Cable rightly saw, Hearn considered translation still as "only the first step of the literary ladder," even if "the best preparation for original work." It was through translation that young Hearn dreamed of creating a new literary style. Those French masters chosen deliberately for his own exercise came to nurture not only his style but his literary attitudes. Later on, as he worked on "a translation of the mysteries of his own mind and imagination," he produced *Stray Leaves* and *Some Chinese Ghosts,* created *Chita, Youma,* and "Karma," and finally completed a series of travel books of his own kind.

Hearn's translations have a historical significance of which he was probably unaware. As the first English translator of Coppée, L'Isle-Adam, Maupassant, and Loti, he introduced contemporary French writers to the New Orleans audience. His translations of Flaubert, Gautier, and Anatole France remain English classics never surpassed by those of his successors. Also, through his translations and reviews of Zola and his naturalist group, he eventually gravitated to the center of the Victorian controversy over naturalism. Though his voice was never well heeded, his position in the history of French naturalism in America is secure and undisputable. As a translator from the Japanese he anticipated the modern literary and cultural contact between the East and the West. And it was translation that he suggested as one most feasible method of realizing our dream of a world literature. Thus all of his work in this area became part of the body of Victorian translation, which played a vital role in the formation of modern cosmopolitan literature.

Finally, we must consider one more and perhaps the most fundamental significance of Hearn the translator: with him translation was more than only the first step of his literary career; throughout his life Hearn remained a translator in one way or another. As we have seen he always started with literalism when translating but did not hesitate to make free with the original, bordering on paraphrase or adaptation. In his entire literary career as well, Hearn moved between these two poles—between literalism and free adaptation, finally maturing into an interpreter of life.

As an act of interpreting "the body and soul" of the original, translation is indicative of Hearn's aesthetic approach to reality. For this reason it becomes incomparably more important in dealing with Hearn's art of translation to understand that the essence of it lies in his intuitive approach to his subject rather than in a particular technique of translation. Dr. Gould justly called this gift "innate and spontaneous" with Hearn, given him by "the inscrutable, illogical, and fantastically generous-niggard Fates." The same biographer continues, "His was almost a unique expertness of entering into the spirit of his models, refeeling their emotions, reimagining their thought and art, and reclothing it with the often somewhat hard and stiff material of English weaving." [28] Whatever his implication, Dr. Gould is perfectly right in attributing this faculty to Hearn's intuitive approach. It is indeed emblematic of his mode of vision, the vision of a seer rather than a maker, a discoverer rather than an inventor. Hearn himself must have been aware of this. Perhaps that is why he came to attach a highly personal significance to the ancient fable of Salmacis and Hermaphroditus, an unmistakable symbol of wholeness and completeness. In this sense translation is the beginning and end of Hearn's career, as we shall see in the following chapters.

II

"My Long-Cherished Dream"

A Stylistic Experiment

The general reaction to *One of Cleopatra's Nights* was sharply divided. The *Observer,* for instance, attacked both the original and the translation on moral grounds. "Now," as Hearn put it, "the holy *Observer* declared that the *Cleopatra* was a collection of 'stories of unbridled lust without the apology of natural passion'; that 'the translation reeked with the miasma of the brothel.'"[1] On the other hand, the volume won him a few new admirers over the country, such as Jerome A. Hart and Wayland D. Ball. To Ball, a Congregational divinity student, Hearn wrote, duly thanking him for his enthusiasm:

> I am beginning to feel considerably encouraged. The "lovers of the antique loveliness" are proving to me the future possibilities of a long cherished dream,—the English realization of a Latin style, modelled upon foreign masters, and rendered even more forcible by that element of *strength* which is the characteristic of Northern tongues. This no man can hope to accomplish; but even a translator may carry his stone to the master-masons of a new architecture of language.[2]

Hearn would like to see translation in terms of his favorite theme, a fusion of the north and south. There is no way of dating the inception of this dream, though he declares it to be "long cherished." It is probably as old as his first work, *One of Cleopatra's Nights,* since this declaration coincided with the one of his artistic ambition. As his formal tone suggests, he adopted translation as the best means of realizing his dream of "English in splendid Latin attire."[3] What he attempted in his Gautier collection was to reproduce in English "a perfection of melody, a warmth of word-colouring, a voluptuous delicacy," the qualities for which, in his opinion, Gautier's style was noted.[4] As he explained in his letter to Ball, the Gautier collection was only the first fruit of his attempt to "translate a series of works by the most striking French authors, each embodying a style of a school." Thereafter, leisure and health permitting, he planned to do the same for about five others.[5] The whole attempt is somewhat reminiscent of his early Cincinnati effort to establish an English system of punctuation, the only result of which was his humorous nickname "Old Semicolon." But this time his dream became a reality; all the reviews, favorable or not, agreed on one point at least, that the translator not only was faithful to the original but even improved on it.

Yet translation, he felt, was only the first step of the literary ladder. It was but part of the blueprint then outlining itself in his mind. It was time to take the next step, to create his own style, even in the light of his own quaint belief that it is impossible to master a good literary style before thirty. Like the twentieth-century scholar who has to be a specialist or nothing, he felt the need of "a fixed purpose and plan" for literary study. In order to nurture imagination and fancy, he was going to explore mythology, history, romance, and poetry, in all of which he planned to seek the extraordinary, the monstrous, the terrible, the fantastic, and the sensuous. To these four subjects he added science, astronomical, geological, ethnological, etc., as an "absolutely essential study in the formation of a strong style."[6] As for classical English literature, he wrote to W. D. O'Connor: "I now find life too short to study it,—except for style."[7] While boasting of his two-thousand-dollar private library, in which every single volume was *"queer,"* Hearn declared: "Knowing that I have nothing resembling genius, and that any ordinary talent must be supplemented with some sort of curious study in order to place it above the mediocre line, I am striving to woo the Muse of the Odd, and hope to succeed in thus attracting some little attention."[8] This rather pathetic vow as the worshipper of "the Odd, the Queer, the Strange, the Exotic, the Monstrous," calls to mind that Bohemian self-portrayal he had made a decade earlier in Cincinnati, and his deliberately Poesque nom de plume, "The Raven."[9] Without giving a second thought to its possible consequence, Hearn set out to forge a style ideally suited for the literary altar of the Extreme. Out of this self-imposed discipline and single-minded devotion came his *Stray Leaves from Strange Literature* (1884) came, the language of which he called all his own.[10]

Not until the end of his New Orleans period did Hearn come to see clearly the real nature and direction of his stylistic experiment, or more strictly speaking, where his whole-hearted enthusiasm had finally landed him. In April 1886, after sending off the manuscript of *Some Chinese Ghosts,* he confided to O'Connor that the volume was "an attempt in the direction I hope to make triumph some day: *poetical prose.*"[11] As he explained, these Chinese tales, each having cost him "months of hard work and study," would represent "a much higher attempt than anything in the *Stray Leaves.*" Writing to another friend a little later, as if to sum up what he had learned from his own stylistic experiment Hearn said: "A man's style, when fully developed, is part of his personality. Mine is being shaped for a particular end."[12] The statement seems confused and does not clarify the actual relationship between personality and style.

In his autobiographical letter to an early admirer, written after the publication of *Some Chinese Ghosts* (1887), Hearn supplies something like a clue to the matter. There he first refers to Baudelaire's observation: *"Quel est celui de nous qui n'a pas, dans ses jours d'ambition, rêvé le miracle d'une prose poétique, musicale sans rhythme et sans rime."* It is this observation, Hearn continues, that "haunted me and inspired me to attempt something in another direction, after having made various translations which never found a publisher because they never deserved it."[13] The reference to Baudelaire may remind us of those numerous dream pieces called "Fantastics," which Hearn had already created "out of [his] own head" for the *Item* and the *Times-Democrat.* In these pieces, most of which antedate his stylistic declaration, he was attempting prose poetry with considerable success—more or less in the manner of Baudelaire. There he is definitely close to Baudelaire, indeed closer to him than to any other French master. All these pieces weave one common romantic theme of love and death, and his piece "Spring Phantoms" (*Item,* April 21, 1881) is virtually a free adaptation of Baudelaire's prose poem, "Les Bienfaits de la lune." Many of these pieces, such as "A Dream of Kites" (*Item,* June 18, 1880), indicate that Hearn is quite at his ease, and that his style and thought are in harmony, flowing as naturally as his master's. In these there is little of Hearn's later addiction to word-coloring; yet, they can appeal to our mind's eye because there is more movement. Considering their potential value, we may wonder why Hearn was dissatisfied with what he had already achieved and why he felt it necessary to abandon freedom of style and thought, making instead that grandiose stylistic declaration of intent to venture into another, obviously unprofitable enterprise.

In the statement quoted above, the reference to more than one master, makes it clear that Hearn had others than Baudelaire in mind. Dr. Gould believes Flaubert in particular to be Hearn's "literary deity," alleging parallels in phrase-building, sentence-making, and word-choosing.[14] Though there is much truth in this, Hearn's immediate model was Gautier rather than Flaubert. In all probability Hearn had Baudelaire as his starting point, but attempted nevertheless to combine Baudelaire and Gautier. This seems to be corroborated by his new enthusiasm with Loti and the more than a score of translations he made of Loti during this period of experimentation. One main reason for Hearn's enthusiasm was that Loti, in his opinion, "combines the rich strength of Gautier with the tropical fantasticality of Baudelaire, and something more,—a profound pantheistic philosophy which tints every page of his book." [15] When he recommended Loti's style as one to be "studied and imitated by a new school of romanticism," it was because of his conviction that Loti was "perhaps the only living writer combining the artistic perception of a painter and musician with the scientific knowledge of a nineteenth century scholar." [16] Speaking of his projected "little book of sketches," Hearn averred that the whole plan would be "philosophical and pantheistic," his style "largely inspired by the new style of Pierre Loti." [17] In Loti, Hearn saw the possible realization of his own dream, a synthesis of Baudelaire and Gautier; that is, of Baudelaire's melodious harmony and Gautier's pictorial ornamentation.

A history of Hearn's stylistic experiment during the 1880's is in a sense a history of his oscillation between Baudelaire and Gautier, or more specifically a style for the ear and a style for the eye. But this oscillation existed only in theory. The fact is that throughout his experiment Hearn remained closer to Gautier than to any other masters, including Baudelaire. This we may attribute to overcompensation for his poor sight and to his color sensitivity; but most probably it was due to his own flattering success with those "lovers of the antique loveliness." Whenever he touched on the question of style, especially word-work and ornamentation, Gautier was always his ideal. For instance, in his introductory note to the Gautier collection we read the following significant statement: "As a writer he [Gautier] remained the artist still. His pages were pictures, his sentences touches of color; he learned, indeed, to 'paint with words' as no other writer of the century has done."[18] Gautier was in his opinion "the mightiest of modern artists";[19] he might be Lancelot if Hugo be the Arthur of the French Romantic movement. Compared with Hugo, Gautier excelled in "word-chiselling," "goldsmithry," and the creation of "mosaics of word-jewelry without equals."[20] Gautier was his model for ornamentation, too. "What troubles my style especially is ornamentation," he wrote to a friend in 1884. "An ornamental style must be perfect or full of atrocious discords and incongruities; and perfect ornamentation requires slow artistic work." He could never hope to be like Gautier, but would certainly improve.[21]

Although he says, "Mine is being shaped for a particular end," he explains neither to himself nor to us why this should be so. One thing is certain: he has come to the conviction that a literary style of his kind should be ornamental and therefore for the eye alone. Taking this for granted, he remains completely deaf to other possibilities. Once in a while he runs to the other extreme of a style for the ear alone; and interestingly enough, this happened near the end of his New Orleans period. In October 1886, he wrote to H. E. Krehbiel, his musician friend in Cincinnati, as though he had made a new discovery: "Well, you remember my ancient dream of a poetical prose,—compositions to satisfy an old Greek ear,—like chants wrought in a huge measure, wider than the widest line of a Sanscrit composition, and just a little irregular, like Ocean-rhythm."[22] Whether or not he had in mind Baudelaire's *"le miracle d'une prose poétique, musicale sans rhythme et sans rime,"* Hearn's statement here is too hyperbolic to be convincing.

Despite the evidence of Hearn's increasing attention to the musical quality of literature, he has, nevertheless, remained a word painter rather than a word musician. In order to create art, "a *durable* thing," Hearn wrote in 1886, one must write every line "at least twice, if possible *three* times." While noting the difficulty of achieving "new ideas of grace, force, and harmony," Hearn never could rid himself of the Gautierite obsession. "My imagination and enthusiasm," he continued, "have to be kept in control; my judgements to be reversed or mended; my adjectives perpetually sifted and pruned. But my work is ornamental—my dream is a poetical prose: a style unsuited to literature of the solid and instructive kind." [23] His willingness to go through this hard labor is very fine, but he does not yet see that a purely ornamental style can never achieve genuine literary value. What is new, however, is that he is vaguely aware of the narrowness in his literary style, in poetical prose for its own sake. Even in the moment of triumph, when he touched on the musical quality of his new style, a feeling of doubt was lurking in his mind. "I really think I will be able to realize it at last," he wrote to Krehbiel, "And then, what? I really don't know. I fancy that I shall have produced a pleasant effect on the reader's mind, simply with pictures; and that the secret work, the word-work, will not be noticed for its own sake. It will be simply an eccentricity for critics; an originality for those pleased by it." [24] What an anti-climax after all his efforts to shape his style for a particular end! He was incapable of any distinction between an artist and an artisan; he could not believe that all along he had been striving for artificial perfection at the expense of what is fundamental.

The first phase of Hearn's stylistic experiment presents an extraordinary case, a case which is highly, though negatively, instructive for all style-conscious artists. The age in which he lived, the trade which he followed, the tradition which he inherited, and the audience which he courted—all of them tending to cherish his kind of florid style— may have been in part responsible for driving his excessive zeal to the point of obsession. Yet the fault is largely Hearn's own, since he himself would not listen to his artist's instinct. From the start his attempt was bound to fail, not because his stylistic fusion of northern strength and southern warmth was an impossible dream but because his concept of style lacked solidity and soundness. Equating a literary style with an artificial style, he was oblivious to the essential point, that style must be functional. In this sense his concept of style was not even narrow or superficial; it was confused, indeed so confused that he failed to recognize the organic relationship between style and subject, that they are one and the same, constituting an inseparable whole. What made the matter worse was his failure to pause in moments of self-doubt and misgiving to re-examine his foundation and direction more objectively, a task by no means impossible for lesser minds than his.

At any rate, it was along the line of poetical prose that Hearn did all his serious writing prior to his Japanese period, and it is worth looking at examples of the results to determine the functionality of his poetical prose. Our examples are chosen, therefore, from his more ambitious works rather than those early prose poems where his poetical style is at once justifiable and functional.[25] We may well begin with *Some Chinese Ghosts* (1887), a work in which Hearn attempted to realize his "ancient dream of a poetical prose":

> And while they talked the long shadows of the evening slowly blended into one violet darkness; the great citron-light of the sunset faded out; and those starry beings that are called the Three Councillors, who preside over life and death and the destinies of men, opened their cold bright eyes in the northern sky.[26]

This is an exotic Chinese love-scene between a young poet, Ming-Y, and the ghost of Sië, the ancient beauty—at her dreamy abode among blooming orchard trees. Yet, it could also be used as an ideal background for Gautier's hero and heroine. There are shades of violet, citron-light, twilight shadows, sunsets, and stars—all of which we remember as Gautier's favorite colors and details for decoration. Even for star-crossed lovers like Ming-Y and Sië the setting is excessively exotic; moreover, it is ineffective because Hearn is more interested in coloring the evening sky than in dramatizing the fate of his lovers.

Some may still accept such ornateness on the ground that it adds to Hearn's legend an atmosphere of weird beauty; however, our second example should illustrate how pointless the style becomes when applied to a situation which is wholly human. It is from *Youma* (1890), Hearn's West Indian romance:

> . . . Sunset yellowed the sky—filled the horizon with flare of gold;— the sea changed its blue to lilac;—the mornes brighted their vivid green to a tone so luminous that they seemed turning phosphorescent. Rapidly the glow crimsoned—shadows purpled; and night spread swiftly from the east—black-violet and full of stars.
> Even as the last vermilion light began to fade. . . .[27]

The passage appears near the end of the romance, at the very moment when the tension between the white colonists and their native slaves is mounting to the point of explosion. Though Hearn may insist that the tropical setting demands and justifies his technique of multi-coloring, the luxuriance indicates his weakness. He is no longer attending to the human drama, his real concern. Lacking function, the passage is out of place.

These two examples, which happen to be nature descriptions, may lead us to one vital question: can his approach possibly penetrate the world within and beyond, those mysterious layers of the human mind which have only invisible colors? Perhaps Hearn might say that that is not what he tried for, that he only tried to realize his "ancient dream of a poetical prose." At the same time, however, we cannot but ask, as Hearn himself did, "And then, what?"

Hearn carried his dream with him to Japan. It persisted as late as 1893, when he came to another more crucial turning point in the evolution of his style. As many of his letters to B. H. Chamberlain show, Hearn had to solve at least two problems, the literary value of word work and the limitations of a poetical prose. Now he came to admit that every important word has three qualities: form, sound, and color. What is interesting, compared with his old color-craze, is that he was now more concerned with the second quality, the rhythmic aspect of a sentence. Relating rhythm to emotion, he said that it may come close to blank verse, "at the termination of paragraphs, if a strong emotion be expressed." With the admonition that "all this is never done by rule,—only by instinctive feeling, half-unconsciously," he continued, "In the body of a paragraph, too much flow and rhythm seems to hurt the effect. Full force is best reserved for the casting-throw of the whole thought or emotion. I should like now to go through many paragraphs written years ago, and sober them down." [28]

While defending his use of Japanese words in his writings, he came back to the function of word work. He conceded that, practically speaking, foreign words should be used sparingly or at least made clear; but because of his artistic and romantic viewpoint he would not hesitate to use them where he felt it necessary. "For me," he said, "words have colour, form, character; they have faces, ports, manners, gesticulations; they have moods, humours, eccentricities;—they have tints, tones, personalities." It makes little difference if they are unintelligible, since he was writing for those "beloved friends who can see colour in words, can smell the perfume of syllables in blossom, can be shocked with the fine elfish electricity of words." [29] In reply to Chamberlain, who had suggested that he try an article on words, Hearn continued to express his love for the "physiognomical beauty" of words. Defending once again the artistic use of foreign words in his writing, he wrote: "Long ago I said that words are like lizards in their power of changing colour with position. But they change much more than colour,—tonic value and force and psychology." [30] Here for the first time a sense of context became apparent, so to speak, as a result of his long study of word value with all its ramifications, chromatics, music, dynamics, cosmetics, physiognomy, and psychology. He could now value the personality of every word primarily as part of the literary organism.

On the other hand, his admission of the fallacy inherent in poetical prose came more abruptly. By now he had learned the stylistic force of Sir Thomas Malory's *Morte d'Arthur,* which after all excels the "over-delicate" artificiality of Tennyson's *Idylls of the King,* in which Hearn had delighted twenty years before. "After for years studying poetical prose," he finally confessed,

> I am forced now to study simplicity. After attempting at ornamentation, I am converted by my own mistakes. The great point is to touch with simple words. And I feel my style is not yet fixed,—too artificial. By another year of study or two, I think I shall be able to do better.[31]

This marks his return to those northern writers whose style of "great, huge, smooth, frank strength" he had once admired, despite his love for stylistic Latinism. "They are my despair!" Hearn wrote to his friend toward the end of 1893, "I could *never* write a page like Björnson though I studied for a century. But I could imitate in English a Florid Romantic. Ornamental luxurious work isn't the hardest. The hardest is perfect simplicity." [32]

Probably, several new factors made him realize the limitations of his style, limitations which had become more and more conspicuous since the late eighties: first, his renewed admiration for northern writers; second, his discovery of Kipling and Stevenson, especially the former, of whose work Hearn said: "I despair when I read"; [33] third, his growing appreciation of Japanese aesthetics, which in point of suggestiveness resembles the northern genius; and fourth, the scope of his projected Japanese books, which demanded more variations in style than his poetical prose allowed. All of these indicate that his intellectual and artistic maturity caused him to question the narrow artificiality of his single style, poetical prose.

In his Japanese lecture on French Romantics, Hearn made a revealing comment on Flaubert's stylistic experiment, which seems to shed some light on his own.[34] As he explained, Flaubert's endeavor to combine the ornate prose of Gautier and the melodious prose of Baudelaire was only partially successful. In holding Flaubert's so-called *mot juste* theory responsible, Hearn reminds us especially of his own agonizing experience. Flaubert, Hearn continued, attempted "the study of words in themselves, classing them according to colours, tones, qualities of hardness or softness," and combined them into "a musical mosaic of a new sort." The result was nevertheless not wholly regrettable, for his experiment helped to break down conventional forms, thus enabling him to command three different styles. They are the "plain prose" of *Madame Bovary,* "suited to the novel of real life"; the "irregular, fantastic, highly coloured prose" of *Salammbô,* "best suited to romance of an exotic character"; and the Baudelairean poetic prose of *La Tentation de Saint-Antoine,* which can best treat "dreams, visions, speculations, notions of the supernatural world."

There are at least two points to which we should pay special attention: One is Hearn's comment on Flaubert's *Tentation,* one of Hearn's earliest translations: "This is a wonderful book, in dramatic form; all the gods, all the religions, all the philosophies that ever existed in the world appear in it, each being described in an utterance of a few lines, like a strain of music." And here Flaubert's style, Hearn points out, was based on the style of Baudelaire's prose poetry. The other is Hearn's emphasis on the literary virtue which demands a discriminating use of a style according to each subject. This aspect Hearn further elaborates in respect to Maupassant as representative of "the purest realism and the simplest style." Noting the struggle between these two styles, ornate and simple, for supremacy, Hearn remarks that "with a simple style all the effects of an ornate style can be produced." In conclusion, he refers to Flaubert's advice to Maupassant: "Change your style to suit your subject," as "the ultimate truth, which Englishmen must accept at a later day." This seems to be the plain truth that he has come to learn in such a tortuous way. The phrase "converted by my own mistakes" should be taken, therefore, as the relinquishment of his narrow and confused concept of literary style, and as recognition that his theoretical adherence to a single style, regardless of the subject before him, resulted in artificiality.

The admission of his error came in 1893, which was also the year that preceded the publication of Hearn's first Japanese book, *Glimpses of Unfamiliar Japan,* so that his widening concept of style concurred with his final struggle for the completion of *Glimpses.* At that time he was confronted with a particular problem, "a very important one," namely the stylistic problem of the travel book. That the solution is connected with stylistic freedom Hearn suggests once again in his Japanese lecture:

> Everything depends upon the character of the book. If the book be composed of different kinds of material, it seems to me quite proper that it should be written in different styles to suit the differences of subjects. You can not do this, however, except in a book which is a miscellany, a mixture of reflection and fact. Combinations of the latter kind are chiefly possible in works of travel. In a book of travel you can not keep up the tone of poetical prose while describing simple facts; but when you come to reflect upon the facts, you can then vary the style. French books of travel are much superior to English in point of literary execution, be-

cause the writers of them do this. They do it so naturally that you are apt to overlook the fact that there are two styles in the same book.[35]

As a personal account of how Hearn came to cope with his immediate problem, nothing could be more enlightening—especially for the reader of his Japanese books. Hearn's success, moreover, was not limited to *Glimpses* alone; its significance was a far-reaching one, since at the time he was entering upon his mature period.

The dozen books he published while in Japan are the fullest expression of Hearn the man and Hearn the artist. Into this life diary he poured everything possible and impossible—poetry and truth, dreams and facts. Here we find Lafcadio Hearn in his totality. All his Japanese studies may be sorted into four major genres: prose poems, sketches, legends, and essays.[36] Freed from his narrow concept of style, he can now vary his style according to his subject; or, rather, his style follows the dictates of his subject. He does not hesitate to use his old poetical prose if the occasion demands and justifies it. In his "Fantastics" he finds the proper use of his poetical prose. In his legends and sketches, on the other hand, Hearn uses pure, simple colloquial style, the virtue of which he has finally learned. If one is objective, the other is subjective; and that which is common to both styles is suggestiveness. He also adopts a sort of middle style in his essays. Hearn has become an artist of more than one style, but the traditional attitude toward him, even when it shows admiration for his style, seems ignorant of his variety. The importance of the point justifies a close examination of his style in relation to the three major genres, sketch, legend, and prose poetry, which we are considering here.

Revolting against what he termed the "tyranny of fiction," Hearn consciously upheld the dignity of sketches and essays, in which genres he found England far inferior to France. The basic difference between these two genres is that the value of the essay, unlike that of the sketch, depends on "scholarship" or "philosophical capacity." The sketch is, generally speaking, "any brief study in prose which is either an actual picture of life as seen with the eyes, or of life as felt with the mind," or "only a record of something seen, but so well seen that, when recorded, it is like a water-color." Anecdotes are different in that they are mere narrative, not psychologized. The sketch ought to deal with "psychological impressions."[37] His definition of the sketch suggests that it is either a visual or psychological record. A quotation from "From Hōki to Oki," one of his early Japanese travel sketches, will demonstrate how Hearn makes an exact visual observation:

But I saw a marvelous effect of color under those formidable cliffs of Omorishima. They were lighted by a slanting sun; and where the glow of the bright rock fell upon the water, each black-blue ripple flushed orange: I thought of a sea of metallic violet ink.[38]

His "marvelous effect of color" may at once lead us to expect those gorgeous word-paintings familiarly associated with the Hearnesque style. There are still some of his old favorite details and colors. But his water-color technique, or more precisely his Oriental brush technique, is effective enough to arrest nature in its simple immediacy. This sketch was presumably completed sometime between his 1892 summer trip to Oki and the publication of *Glimpses,* and it may be quite proper to detect in these lines the consequence of his stylistic conversion. Noteworthy too is the abrupt way the impersonal tone is broken in the last line, only to be resumed: "I thought of a sea of metallic violet ink." The unexpected introduction of his personal mood adds a new dimension to the picture. On the whole the passage can profitably be compared with an earlier gaudy description of the tropical sea found in his travel sketch of 1887:

Morning: the second day. The sea is an extraordinary blue,—looks to me something like violet ink. Close by the ship, where the foam-clouds are, it is beautifully mottled,—looks like blue marble with exquisite veinings and nebulosities. . . . Tepid wind, and cottony white clouds,—cirri climbing up over the edge of the sea all around. The sky is still pale blue, and the horizon is full of a whitish haze.[39]

In this tropical sketch Hearn is still at the mercy of his own palette; his use of "like" shows that all depends on the mechanism of analogy. In the Japanese sketch, on the other hand, he has good control over the material. Accordingly, his style can now be appreciably objective and yet suggestive, even when applied to nature description.

Hearn believed that the sketch of the future should be "the sketch of psychological impressions," a record of "life as felt with the mind." This is actually realized in some of his writings, which border on the sketch and the *conte.* One of the most notable examples is "On a Bridge," a piece which appeared in *A Japanese Miscellany* (1901):

"Twenty-two years ago," said Heishichi, wiping his forehead—"no, twenty-three years ago,—I stood here, and saw the city burn."

"At night?" I queried.

"No," said the old man, "it was in the afternoon—a wet day. . . . They were fighting; and the city was on fire."

"Who were fighting?"

"The soldiers in the castle were fighting with the Satsuma men. We dug holes in the ground and sat in them, to escape the balls. The Satsuma men had cannons on the hill; and the soldiers in the castle were shooting at them over our heads. The whole city was burned."

"But how did you happen to be here?"

"I ran away. I ran as far as this bridge,—all by myself. I thought that I could get to my brother's farm—about seven miles from here. But they stopped me."

"Who stopped you?"

"Satsuma men,—I don't know who they were. As I got to the bridge I saw three peasants—I thought they were peasants—leaning over the railing: men wearing big straw hats and straw rain-cloaks and straw sandals. I spoke to them politely; and one of them turned his head round, and said to me, 'You stay here!' That was all he said: the others did not say anything. Then I saw that they were not peasants; and I was afraid."

"How did you know that they were not peasants?"

"They had long swords hidden under their rain-cloaks,—very long swords. They were very tall men. They leaned over the bridge, looking down into the river. I stood beside them,—just there, by the third post to the left, and did as they did. I knew that they would kill me if I moved from there. None of them spoke. And we four stood leaning over the railing for a long time."

"How long?"

"I do not know exactly—it must have been a long time. I saw the city burning. All that while none of the men spoke to me or looked at me: they kept their eyes upon the water. Then I heard a horse; and I saw a cavalry officer coming at a trot,—looking all about him as he came. . . ."

"From the city?"

"Yes,—along that road behind you. . . . The three men watched him from under their big straw hats; but they did not turn their heads;—they pretended to be looking down into the river. But, the moment that the horse got on the bridge, the three men turned and leaped;—and one caught the horse's bridle; and another gripped the officer's arm; and the third cut off his head—all in a moment. . . ."

"The officer's head?"

"Yes—he did not even have time to shout before his head was off. . . . I never saw anything done so quickly. Not one of the three men uttered a word."

"And then?"

"Then they pitched the body over the railing into the river; and one of them struck the horse,—hard; and the horse ran away. . . ."

"Back to the town?"

"No—the horse was driven straight out over the bridge, into the country. . . . The head was not thrown into the river: one of the Satsuma men kept it—under his straw cloak. . . . Then all of us leaned over the railing, as before,—looking down. My knees were shaking. The three samurai did not speak a single word. I could not even hear them breathing. I was afraid to look at their faces;—I kept looking down into the river. . . . After a little while I heard another horse,—and my heart jumped so that I felt sick;—and I looked up, and saw a cavalry-soldier coming along the road, riding very fast. No one stirred till he was on the bridge: then—in one second—his head was off! The body was thrown into the river, and the horse driven away—exactly as before. Three men were killed like that. Then the samurai left the bridge."

"Did you go with them?"

"No: they left immediately after having killed the third man,—taking the heads with them;—and they paid no attention to me. I stayed on the bridge, afraid to move, until they were very far away. Then I ran back to the burning town;—I ran quick, quick! There I was told that the Satsuma troops were retreating. Soon afterwards, the army came from Tokyo; and I was given some work: I carried straw sandals for the soldiers."

"Who were the men that you saw killed on the bridge?"

"I don't know."

"Did you never try to find out?"

"No," said Heishichi, again mopping his forehead: "I said nothing about the matter until many years after the war."

"But why?" I persisted.

Heishichi gave me one astonished look, smiled in a pitying way, and answered,—

"Because it would have been wrong;—it would have been ungrateful."

I felt properly rebuked.

And we resumed our journey.[40]

The piece is presented as a casual conversation between Hearn and his native rickshaw-puller, Heishichi. A simple setting, a minimal number of characters, a straightforward action, and a rapid alternation of violence and silence—all these factors gather a force which is doubled by the studied naïveté and clarity of his style. In this highly suggestive technique Hearn almost anticipates the modern masters of the short story, say Hemingway. At the end we are suddenly confronted with the peculiar mentality of the Japanese, his unconditional acceptance of life. Heishichi's unexpected answer to the question makes Hearn confess: "I felt properly rebuked." Our shock of recognition, the intended effect of this piece, we may agree, owes much to Hearn's functional style, which fits both the situation and the characters involved.

In dealing with Japanese materials Hearn's task is doubly difficult; he must both convey the native spirit in the material itself and enable his piece to stand on its own. Another example, "Diplomacy," is from *Kwaidan* (1904), a collection of "weird" tales:

It has been ordered that the execution should take place in the garden of the *yashiki*. So the man was taken there, and made to kneel down in a wide sanded space crossed by a line of *tobi-ishi,* or stepping-stones, such as you may still see in Japanese landscape-gardens. His arms were bound behind him. Retainers brought water in buckets, and rice-bags filled with pebbles; and they packed the rice-bags round the kneeling man—so wedging him in that he could not move. The master came, and observed the arrangements. He found them satisfactory, and made no remarks.

Suddenly the condemned man cried out to him:

"Honored sir, the fault for which I have been doomed I did not wittingly commit. It was only my very stupidity which caused the fault. Having been born stupid, by reason of my karma, I could not always help making mistakes. But to kill a man for being stupid is wrong—and that wrong will be repaid. So surely as you kill me, so surely shall I be avenged;—out of the resentment that you provoke will come the vengeance; and evil will be rendered for evil." . . .

If any person be killed while feeling strong resentment, the ghost of that person will be able to take vengeance upon the killer. This the samurai knew. He replied very gently—almost caressingly:

"We shall allow you to frighten us as much as you please—after you are dead. But it is difficult to believe that you mean what you say. Will you try to give us some sign of your great resentment—after your head has been cut off?"

"Assuredly I will," answered the man.

"Very well," said the samurai, drawing his long sword;—"I am now going to cut off your head. Directly in front of you there is a stepping-stone. After your head has been cut off, try to bite the stepping-stone. If your angry ghost can help you to do that, some of us may be frightened. . . . Will you try to bite the stone?"

"I will bite it!" cried the man, in great anger—"I will bite it!—I will bite"—

There was a flash, a swish, a crunching thud: the bound body bowed over the rice sacks—two long blood-jets pumping from the shorn neck;—and the head rolled upon the sand. Heavily toward the stepping-stone it rolled: then, suddenly bounding, it caught the upper edge of the stone between its teeth, clung desperately for a moment, and dropped inert.

None spoke; but the retainers stared in horror at their master. He seemed to be quite unconcerned. He merely held out his sword to the nearest attendant who, with a wooden dipper, poured water over the blade from haft to point, and then carefully wiped the steel several times with sheets of soft paper. . . . And thus ended the ceremonial part of the incident.

For months thereafter, the retainers and the domestics lived in ceaseless fear of ghostly visitation. None of them doubted that the promised vengeance would come; and their constant terror caused them to hear and to see much that did not exist. They became afraid of the sound of the wind in the bamboos—afraid even of the stirring of shadows in the garden. At last, after taking counsel together, they decided to petition their master to have a *Ségaki*-service performed on behalf of the vengeful spirit.

"Quite unnecessary," the samurai said, when his chief retainer had uttered the general wish. . . . "I understand that the desire of a dying man for vengeance may be a cause for fear. But in this case there is nothing to fear."

The retainer looked at his master beseechingly, but hesitated to ask the reason of this alarming confidence.

"Oh, the reason is simple enough," declared the samurai, divining the unspoken doubt. "Only the very last intention of that fellow could have been dangerous; and when I challenged him to give me the sign, I diverted his mind from the desire of revenge. He died with the set purpose of biting the stepping-stone; and that purpose he was able to accomplish, but nothing else. All the rest he must have forgotten. . . . So you need not feel any further anxiety about the matter."

And indeed the dead man gave no more trouble. Nothing at all happened.[41]

To the highly disciplined samurai, the above incident is insignificant, ordinary, and purely ceremonial. They must be aware of what they are doing, and they must act with serene and alert conviction. It is their version of measure for measure. Hearn captures their spirit perfectly when he describes: "There was a flash, a swish, a crunching thud: . . ." It is realistic and intense; there is nothing bloody. The story itself creates its effect even if we are not familiar with those intricate Buddhist notions of the human mind that frame the situation, not only because what happens here is psychologized, but even more because of Hearn's style, which is capable of sustaining its intensity to the last. His last line, "And indeed the dead man gave no more trouble. Nothing at all happened," puts an end to our feeling of suspense as well as of fear. Every factor in the story contributes to Hearn's purpose of recreating a sense of weirdness.

In his prose poetry, Hearn returns to Baudelaire. In expounding his theory of the genre he heavily depends on the French poet's *Petits poëmes en prose* (1869).[42] Although he accepts Baudelaire's professed indebtedness to Aloïsius Bertrand's *Gaspard de la nuit* (1842), he nevertheless likes to minimize Bertrand's influence as merely suggestion or impulse. He points out that only with the publication of *Petits poëmes en prose* was the new poetical prose fairly established. In his opinion, it is more probable that Baudelaire owed his inspiration to Poe, though there is no mention of this in the French poet's own preface. Assuming the joint influence of Bertrand and Poe, Hearn seeks to synthesize two prose poetical traditions, French and Anglo-American. That is to say, in Baudelaire he saw the meeting of the French tradition of Bertrand and Nerval, and the English-American tradition of Blake, Coleridge, De Quincey, and Poe. His opinions suggest that Hearn regarded himself as legitimate heir to the Anglo-French tradition of poetical prose.

As for the unique value of poetical prose, too, Hearn goes along with Baudelaire. Obviously with Baudelaire's preface in mind, Hearn said: "Baudelaire believed that prose could be made quite as poetical as verse or even more so, for a prose that could preserve the rhythm of poetry without its monotony, and the melody of poetry without rhythm, might become in the hands of the master even more effective than verse." As we recall, it is this musical quality of poetical prose that Hearn has come to seek, unsuccessfully, along with his Gautierite coloring. In this sense Hearn's stylistic experiment was his own attempt to realize the traditional romantic urge, to unify poetry and prose so as to produce the effects of both. As for the application of this poetical style, Hearn is more cautious, remembering his youthful error: "But such prose was not adapted to the writing of novels and long stories. It could only be used for very short studies of a highly emotional character." Its use must, he suggests, be confined only to "reveries," "dreams," "philosophical fancies." These words rightly characterize Baudelaire's prose poems, and define the ideal function of poetical prose, to record the lyric moments of a poetical soul.

In Baudelaire, Hearn discovered the rationale of the genre which occupies the emotional and imaginative center of his Japanese studies. If we call this particular genre "fantasies" or "fantastics," instead of prose poems, it is because of the very continuity between these Japanese fantasies and his early "Fantastics" group for the *Item*. It will be useful to read two examples. One is "The Eater of Dreams," from *Kotto* (1902), which deals with the Baku, a mythical creature whose particular function is to eat dreams.

It was on a very sultry night, during the Period of Greatest Heat, that I last saw the Baku. I had just awakened out of misery; and the hour was the Hour of the Ox; and the Baku came in through the window to ask, "Have you anything for me to eat?"

I gratefully made answer.

"Assuredly! . . . Listen, good Baku, to this dream of mine!—

"I was standing in some great white-walled room, where lamps were burning; but I cast no shadow on the naked floor of that room—and there, upon an iron bed, I saw my own dead body. How I had come to die, and when I had died, I could not remember. Women were sitting near the bed—six or seven—and I did not know any of them. They were neither young nor old, and all were dressed in black: watchers I took them to be. They sat motionless and silent: there was no sound in the place; and I somehow felt that the hour was late.

"In the same moment I became aware of something nameless in the atmosphere of the room—a heaviness that weighed upon the will—some viewless numbing power that was slowly growing. Then the watchers began to watch each other, stealthily; and I knew that they were afraid. Soundlessly one rose up, and left the room. Another followed; then another. So, one by one, and lightly as shadows, they all went out. I was left alone with the corpse of myself.

"The lamps still burned clearly; but the terror in the air was thickening. The watchers had stolen away almost as soon as they began to feel it. But I believed that there was yet time to escape;—I thought that I could safely delay a moment longer. A monstrous curiosity obliged me to remain: I wanted to look at my own body, to examine it closely. . . . I approached it. I observed it. And I wondered—because it seemed to me very long—unnaturally long. . . .

"Then I thought that I saw one eyelid quiver. But the appearance of motion might have been caused by the trembling of a lamp-flame. I stooped to look—slowly, and very cautiously, because I was afraid that the eyes might open.

" 'It is Myself,' I thought, as I bent down—'and yet, it is growing queer!' . . . The face appeared to be lengthening. . . . 'It is not Myself,' I thought again, as I stooped still lower,—'and yet, it cannot be any other!' And I became much more afraid, unspeakably afraid, that the eyes would open. . . .

"*They* OPENED!—horribly they opened!—and that thing sprang from the bed at me, and fastened upon me—moaning, and gnawing, and rending! Oh! with what madness of terror did I strive against it! But the eyes of it, and the moans of it, and the touch of it, sickened; and all my being seemed about to burst asunder in frenzy of loathing, when —I knew not how—I found in my hand an axe. And I struck with the axe;—I clove, I crushed, I brayed the Moaner—until there lay before me only a shapeless, hideous, reeking mass—the abominable ruin of Myself. . . .

"Baku kuraë! Baku kuraë! Baku kuraë! Devour, O Baku! devour the dream!"

"Nay!" made answer the Baku. "I never eat lucky dreams. That is a very lucky dream—a most fortunate dream. . . . The axe—yes! the Axe of the Excellent Law, by which the monster of Self is utterly destroyed!

. . . The best kind of a dream!" My friend, *I* believe in the teaching of
the Buddha.

And the Baku went out of the window. I looked after him;—and I
beheld him fleeing over the miles of moonlit roofs—passing, from house-
top to house-top, with amazing soundless leaps—like a great cat. . . .[43]

Although at first glance one might dismiss this piece merely as a
vagary of the writer's fancy, the factors that make it so singularly suggestive deserve a closer look. Its basis is the native belief, which Hearn
explains in his introductory note, that whenever you have a nightmare
or an unlucky dream, you should quickly repeat the invocation three
times, whereupon the Baku or Hakutaku will come to eat the dream
and change the misfortune or the fear into good fortune. Within this
framework, the dream itself seems to be a highly personal experience;
yet its mechanism, the separation of two selves and their antagonism, is
quite commonplace in literature. One may recall Stevenson's classical
study of double personality or Poe's tale, "William Wilson." The
burden of man's conscience may remind us of Baudelaire's prose poem,
"Chacun sa chimère." Seizing on the suggestiveness inherent in this
common psychical experience, Hearn twists it, in terms of Buddhism,
so that it assumes another larger significance.

Hearn's language is not like that which we have come to expect of
his heightened poetical pieces; it is plain enough to be rather close to
that of "On a Bridge," which it further resembles because both are
dialogs. As a whole, this piece is a prose poem rather than a sketch
because it belongs to the category of "reveries," "dreams," and "philosophical fancies." The Baku not only interprets the dream (this is after
all his particular function) but dramatizes the whole piece. Note how
transformation takes place—the "shapeless, hideous, reeking mass—the
abominable ruin of Myself" becomes "the monster of Self" as the axe
in the dreamer's hand turns out to be "the Axe of the Excellent Law."
Through the Baku, as agent of dramatization, the piece is elevated
from the psychological to the philosophical level. It signifies the annihilation of our last illusion, the Phantom Ego, as a promise of spiritual
salvation. In the process of metamorphosis, "The Eater of Dreams" has
no element of monstrous horror but yet maintains the ghostliness and
mystery of the experience.

The above can be taken as an example of Hearn's attempt to create
through a simple style the same emotional effect as through his poetical

prose. We turn to our second example, "Noctilucae," from *Shadowings* (1900):

The moon had not yet risen; but the vast of the night was all seething with stars, and bridged by a Milky Way of extraordinary brightness. There was no wind; but the sea, far as sight could reach, was running in ripples of fire—a vision of infernal beauty. Only the ripplings were radiant (between them was blackness absolute);—and the luminosity was amazing. Most of the undulations were yellow like candle-flame; but there were crimson lampings also—and azure, and orange, and emerald. And the sinuous flickering of all seemed, not a pulsing of many waters, but a laboring of many wills—a fleeting conscious and monstrous—a writhing and a swarming incalculable, as of dragon-life in some depth of Erebus.

And life indeed was making the sinister splendor of that spectacle—but life infinitesimal, and of ghostliest delicacy—life illimitable, yet ephemeral, flaming and fading in ceaseless alternation over the whole round of waters even to the sky-line, above which, in the vaster abyss, other countless lights were throbbing with other spectral colors.

Watching, I wondered and I dreamed. I thought of the Ultimate Ghost revealed in that scintillation tremendous of Night and Sea;—quickening above me, in systems aglow with awful fusion of the past dissolved, with vapor of the life again to be;—quickening also beneath me, in meteor-gushings and constellations and nebulosities of colder fire—till I found myself doubting whether the million ages of the sun-star could really signify, in the flux of perpetual dissolution, anything more than the momentary sparkle of one expiring noctiluca.

Even with the doubt, the vision changed. I saw no longer the sea of the ancient East, with its shudderings of fire, but that Flood whose width and depth and altitude are one with the Night of Eternity,—the shoreless and timeless Sea of Death and Birth. And the luminous haze of a hundred millions of suns—the Arch of the Milky Way—was a single smouldering surge in the flow of the Infinite Tides.

Yet again there came a change. I saw no more that vapory surge of suns; but the living darkness streamed and thrilled about me with infinite sparkling; and every sparkle was beating like a heart—beating out colors like tints of the sea-fires. And the lampings of all continually flowed away, as shivering threads of radiance, into illimitable Mystery. . . .

Then I knew myself also a phosphor-point,—one fugitive floating sparkle of the measureless current;—and I saw that the light which was mine shifted tint with each changing of thought. Ruby it sometimes shone, and sometimes sapphire: now it was flame of topaz; again, it was fire of emerald. And the meaning of the changes I could not fully know. But thoughts of the earthly life seemed to make the light burn red; while thoughts of supernal being—of ghostly beauty and of ghostly bliss—seemed to kindle ineffable rhythms of azure and violet.

But of white lights there were none in all the Visible. And I marveled. Then a Voice said to me:—

"The White are of the Altitudes. By the blending of the billions they are made. Thy part is to help to their kindling. Even as the color of thy burning, so is the worth of thee. For a moment only is thy quickening; yet the light of thy pulsing lives on: by thy thought, in that shining moment, thou becomest a Maker of Gods." [44]

It is not difficult to detect Hearn's old characteristics: his technique of coloring; his peculiar fondness for inversion; his perennial twin subject—sky and sea; and his sustaining power of language. But there is little sign of riot among them; they seem to know their assigned function and place. The colors, once subdued in the context, become symbols of flickering lives against the enormous background of "blackness absolute." Hearn's personal habit of juxtaposing sea with sky endows the piece with a sense of change and movement. Eternity resides only in this endless cycle of life and death.

Only by following the changes of Hearn's vision can we come to accept what the Voice says. The colors thus become fires; and when their sparklings turn out to be the beatings of our hearts, the fires become the flames of those candles which we all dedicate to the altar of Eternity. The piece has no trace of Hearn's old "sweet pantheism," for it has been resolved into a cosmic vision of sublimity. Setting "the White" against the "blackness absolute," the Voice reaffirms the humble yet genuine significance of a colored atom called individual which would otherwise be hopelessly lost in the vastness of its field.

"Noctilucae" is Hearn's poetic record of what man feels but seldom can prove, the unity of man and the universe. It is also an attempt to impregnate his emotional lyricism with universal thoughts, without losing its emotional immediacy. The piece exemplifies the highest function Hearn assigned to his prose poetry, that of expressing the sublime and ghostly of the cosmic emotion. In this sense he aligns himself with Poe rather than Baudelaire. Referring to Poe's fable, "Silence," he said in one of his Japanese lectures: "Here Poe has surpassed even the French—even Baudelaire,—who dreamed of prose more perfect than poetry, and who wrote a book of prose-poems in imitation, perhaps, of the style of Poe." That is to say, "in the melody, the sonority, the melancholy beauty" of Poe's piece there is "something altogether foreign to the French language,—and Baudelaire could not repeat the effect of Poe." [45] The difference to which Hearn points is more than linguistic. It is the kind of difference one feels between *Les Fleurs du Mal* and

Eureka, and more readily between "Les Bienfaits de la lune" and "Silence." What pervades Poe's fable is a sort of cosmic chill, a metaphysical horror, a feeling alien to Baudelaire, who is profoundly moral and human. In "Noctilucae" Hearn finally comes back to his old master by way of Baudelaire, and this fact points to the general direction of his later prose poems.

In 1898, when one of his American admirers mentioned his "old ambition," Hearn readily admitted that at one time it had led him far in the wrong direction. But he qualified this admission by saying that whatever he had learned of style was certainly due rather to French and Spanish studies than to English ones. "I have now dropped theories, nevertheless," he added, "and I simply try to do the best I can, without reference to schools."[46] He was no longer an artist dreaming of "English in splendid Latin attire"; awakened from his old obsession, he was now willing to follow the dictates of his artistic instinct. Undoubtedly with his own experience in mind, Hearn called his young students' special attention to the question of style. In his lecture, "On Composition," Hearn proposed to prove that "there is no such thing as style," that what was once called style no longer exists. Setting aside the conventional notion of "general" style, which is "simply rhetorical," he turns to what he calls "individual" style. As he defines it, ". . . style, in the modern meaning of the word, is character." This Buffonesque definition, like his earlier one, "A man's style, when fully developed, is part of his personality," may still be too vague; but this vagueness, Hearn believes, is the inevitable result of any attempt to define an artist's style as the manifestation of his personality. Since "no two minds think and feel in exactly the same way," their approaches, more strictly their styles, should naturally differ, even when they deal with the same subject. There are various ways of showing the stylistic difference between one writer and another, Hearn continues, but there still remains much in a writer's style that refuses to be defined by any devices as ingenious as those advanced by George Saintsbury and Sidney Lanier. Their attempts to define style are, in his opinion, questionable; still more questionable are those fashionable attempts to differentiate among writers simply by tabulating their vocabularies. What pseudo-scientific methods ignore is the plain truth that every word as part of the organic whole is chosen "not by rule, but by feeling, by what is called the literary instinct." "Words are," as Hearn puts it, "very much like lizards; they change colour according to position"; hence his warning against the so-called study of style which usually "mistakes results for causes," the very mistake he made in his own wild stylistic experiment. What he likes to say, therefore, is this: "If any writer does his best to perfect his work, the result of the pains that he takes will be style in the true sense." He now insists that any literary style must start from its most enduring source, the language of the common people, or it is bound to degenerate into artificiality. Beyond this, he says, everything is up to our sincerity, honesty, and labor.[47]

One may recall here the implied pledge Hearn made in 1882: "But without the sacrifice can we hope for the grace of heaven?" The sacrifice, which he made by wooing the "Muse of the Odd," was after all something much more simple and natural, if, strangely enough, harder than he imagined. Only after his long experiment, full of blind confusions and bitter failures, did he come to realize the paradox that style can be achieved by mastery of thought, not style. He was now mastering what he had once called the first way, "to force thought by concentration," the way "fatiguing beyond all expression," and even "injurious," because he had become aware of the insufficiency of his second way, "to force *work* only, and let the thought develop itself."[48] With death just a few years ahead, he finally learned that only this double strategy, form and thought, could realize the ideal that style is character.

III

Many-
Colored
Ghosts

The
Twice-
Told
Tales

No flamboyant declaration regarding Hearn's stylistic experiment accompanied the publication of his second book, *Stray Leaves from Strange Literature,* in June 1884. His reticence is strange, in view of the fact that at the time he was searching for what he had once termed a medium of utterance, and that his new volume signified the beginning of his long cycle of twice-told tales, one of the main sources of his later literary fame.

Stray Leaves, which Hearn himself called "a little mosaic work of legend and fable," was the unified product of his diverse interests and concerns at that time: his ambition for artistic translation; his ancient dream of a poetical prose; his study of mythology, one of the four subjects chosen for his literary pursuit; and above all his passion for things ghostly. In the "Explanatory" there is a sense of modest confidence, when Hearn reflects upon his intention and performance: ". . . their colors were so weird, their luminosity so elfish, that their intrinsic value could not be wholly destroyed even by so clumsy an artificer as I." [1]

It is this something "so weird" that separates *Stray Leaves* from all his previous attempts as a teller of tales. Take for instance "The Cedar Closet," a ghost story written ten years before, the earliest story of his yet known.[2] Presented as a reminiscence by the lady of an ancient English manor, it tells of a recurring ghostly apparition which first troubled her on the eve of her wedding day. As the story unfolds, we become aware that the apparition is the revengeful ghost of Lady Draye, a love-hungry ancestress of the narrator's husband. Two centuries before, this deformed and jealous woman had cruelly put an end to the love triangle in which she had been involved. The pattern of execution, setting, atmosphere, plot progression, and denouement is unmistakably Gothic. In developing the story in a leisurely manner, using the bliss of domestic love as the framework, and providing the end of the story with a rational explanation, "The Cedar Closet" follows Lytton's ghost stories, especially his "The Haunted and the Haunters," which Hearn admired along with *A Strange Story,* another by the same author. While retaining Lytton's mellow fullness, it lacks both Poe's psychic intensity and Gautier's ghostly fascination. Neat and complete as it is, the story is still an imitation full of Gothic machinery. There is little distinctly Hearnesque in it, except for a human warmth that one does not usually find in the ghost story.

"The Cedar Closet" is the only ghost story of its kind ever attempted by Hearn. His rapid departure from conventional Gothicism we can hardly fail to note even in those other stories he tried in the several years following.[3] As all these pieces indicate, Hearn set out to explore the basis of psychic reality in terms of local ghost stories, folk superstitions, and mythological subjects. Among these, "Nightmare and Nightmare Legends," one of his early *Item* contributions, seems to show sufficiently that Hearn was approaching the world of *Stray Leaves.*[4] While examining the psychic reality of Poe's horror stories, Hearn defines nightmare as the supernatural or collective psychical basis of legend, folk tale, and myth. After tracing the etymology of the word "nightmare" as far as its origin, "Night-Mara" or "Mara of the Night," he reminds us of the Scandinavian belief that "this Mara was a female specter, not hideous or fantastic of aspect, like the hollow Ell-women or witch-wives, but fascinatingly beautiful." As an example Hearn recounts a curious story about a Norseman who managed to possess this nocturnal enchantress as wife only to lose her, to his mortal despair. After Hearn has explored the meaning of nightmare in terms of the Mara motif or spectral lover theme, he finds the psychic horror of ghost stories changed into something entirely different. It comes to assume a "weird beauty." Hearn would have accepted Poe's famous dictum that terror is not of Germany, but of the soul, but he would have expanded it too. For him terror, interchangeable with beauty, is universal; but it is also tied down to a specific locality. From this point to *Stray Leaves* there are only a few steps to take.

In *Stray Leaves* Hearn pretends to be thorough in scholarship, as shown in his "Explanatory" and "Bibliography." But there is little doubt that all these twenty-seven pieces are his imaginative reconstruction of the English and French sources found in his private library, the library which, as he once boasted, numbered "nearly five hundred volumes—Egyptian, Assyrian, Indian, Chinese, Japanese, African, etc." [5] Having passed through his hands, they are no longer translations. They have all become twice-told or even thrice-told tales. Accordingly, the degree of freedom Hearn takes in rendering varies: The third group, "Runes from Kalewala," consists of three "veritable translations" from Léouzon Le Duc, whereas the last group, "Traditions Retold from the Talmud," is executed on the principle of condensation. "A Legend of Love," of the fourth group ("Stories of Moslem Lands"), is Hearn's artistic alloy of an Arabian fragment and Stendhal's theory of love. The second group, on the other hand, presents eleven tales from Indian and Buddhist literature; and three legends, Egyptian, Polynesian, and Eskimoan, comprise the opening group, "Stray Leaves."

These legends and fables could be called translations only in the sense that they recreate the emotions and thoughts peculiar to the lands, races, and faiths whence they originate. The worlds they represent are largely those of folklore, legend, and myth. If *Stray Leaves* as a whole appears to be only a kaleidoscope of many colors, shapes, and meanings, it is because we stand too close to it. If we keep our distance, there will be no difficulty in discerning what is common to all the tales and controls their individual variations. The central theme of the volume is the perennial human dichotomy between passion and wisdom. Although wisdom is the only antidote to human craving for everything material and immaterial, man is always too conceited, clumsy, or shortsighted to glimpse the subtle faces wisdom assumes. Human wisdom, furthermore, can become divine if it blends into faith. So we have Solomon, who, for the sake of humanity, refuses to "drink of the waters of youth and know the bliss of earthly immortality" ("Boutimar, the Dove"); Rabbi Eliezer, whose prophecy is fulfilled in the martyrdom of Rabbi Akiva ("The Dispute in the Halacha"); and the Bodhisattva, who can reach salvation only through his faith ("The Lotos of Faith").

While this is the central theme of *Stray Leaves,* the emphasis is not so much on wisdom as on passion, and it might perhaps be better called a book of passions. Everyone here is a slave of his passion, whether for power, knowledge, immortality, or woman. Everyone burns with passion, tormented in its whirlwind. This is true of Emperor Titus, who must die completely powerless because of the gnat put into his head by the God of Jerusalem ("A Tradition of Titus"). Again there are four Brahman brothers together on a journey to seek fame and fortune, the three older ones superior in the art of magic and the last posssessing but horse sense, which saves his life when the others are devoured by a lion, their own magic creation ("The Lion"). Prince Satni too, despite his possession of the Book of Thoth, the secret of knowledge and immortality, is helpless before the bewitching beauty of revengeful Thoutboui ("The Book of Thoth").

The stories move through various passions to the ultimate one, love. In the volume love is double-faced; it can be destructive as well as life-giving. Prince Satni, in his infatuation with the enchantress, takes the pledge: "Be it so; were I ruler of heaven, even heaven would I give thee for a kiss." Unable to forget "the beautiful dead face and the slender dead feet and the golden throat" of his young wife, an old Brahman prays in his misery: "Yes, O Narayana, half of my life will I give unto her gladly" ("The Brahman and his Brahmani"). There is also a youth who, in his vision of a beauty, makes a strange vow: "And if by thy favor I be enabled to marry that loveliest of women, O Devi, verily I will make a sacrifice of my own head to thee" ("The Corpse-Demon"). Because of this same mortal weakness the Khalif is lured by his fair prisoner to have his most faithful general beheaded ("Natalika"). Through love Brahma makes Tilottama, his own creation, the cause of destruction of two evil princes: "Descend, good Tilottama, into the world of men, and display the witchcraft of thy beauty in the sight of Sounda and Oupasounda, so that the Daiteyas may be filled with hatred, each against the other, because of thee" ("The Making of Tilottama").

Love triumphs, however, whenever it ceases to be mere infatuation or passion. It becomes instead the source of divine life. The love between a Christian maiden and a Moslem youth transcends the difference of their creeds, as in death both abandon their faiths to be together in the world beyond. The irony implied here is only human ("A Legend of Love"). As one love leads to heaven, so does another cause a descent from heaven. In spite of Indra's wrath, Bakawali, an immortal virgin, chooses to reincarnate herself on earth for the sake of her mortal lover Taj-ulmuluk ("Bakawali").

Beyond its destructive and divine power, love assumes another and perhaps more peculiar aspect in the form of love for supernatural beings. This is the case with Bakawali, Tilottama, Thoutboui, etc., whatever their respective motivations. To this group belong also both "The Fountain Maiden" and "The Bird Wife." One is a story of a Polynesian's love for the maiden of the Vaipiki fountain; the other a story of an Eskimo ivory hunter's union with a bird woman. Common to both is that the maiden and the bird wife are sooner or later to return to their own worlds, leaving their human husbands in despair. It is significant that these two stories are joined to "The Book of Thoth," which also deals with a mortal's infatuation with a ghostly being, to form "Stray Leaves," the opening group. What ties the three together is the Mara motif, or spectral love theme. Hearn seems finally to have found here what he considered the universal theme—under stories of different faces and colors, whether Egyptian, Polynesian or Eskimoan.

Some Chinese Ghosts (1887), Hearn's next book, naturally contains the interests and concerns noticed in *Stray Leaves*. But in this collection of six Chinese legends Hearn is no longer experimental and diffusive; instead he displays power of concentration as well as taste for selection. At the time it was published, Hearn, remembering the "months of hard work and study" each piece cost him, said that the collection represented "a much higher attempt than anything in the *Stray Leaves*." [6] His confidence in the accomplishment remained such that later, while in Japan, he suggested that the work be included in the proposed *Juvenilia*. [7]

As in *Stray Leaves*, Hearn's sources for *Some Chinese Ghosts* are well known. In both notes and glossary he is as thorough as he can possibly be, citing more than a dozen eminent Sinologists whose works provided him with materials and also with linguistic and philosophical information about those Chinese expressions altogether untranslatable. With all this scholarly preparation, Hearn did not call his book something "reconstructed." As he said in the preface, he set out to seek "especially weird beauty" in those materials and recreate it in his own versions. As if to justify his continuous interest in and his present treatment of the supernatural, he repeated Sir Walter Scott's observation: "The supernatural, though appealing to certain powerful emotions very widely and deeply sown amongst the human race, is nevertheless, *a spring which is peculiarly apt to lose its elasticity by being too much pressed upon*." [8] Here we have something of Hearn's strategy: one must be artful, if weird beauty is to be presented as universal, as the essence of the supernatural. His strategy having been thus defined, he is now able to concentrate on developing the materials without sacrificing their ultimate authenticity. By recreating their weird beauty he can still remain a veritable translator; by reading his own themes into them at the same time, he can be an artist, too. Largely because of Hearn's success in this double role, *Some Chinese Ghosts* is far superior to its predecessor.

Let us see, first, to what extent his art can be authentic in translating the soul of China. The traditional Oriental belief that in spirit man can be immortal is quite convincingly recreated in "The Return of Yen-Tchin-King." [9] In it a loyal warrior is sent by the emperor to put down a rebellion and is murdered by traitors. Hearn's real interest lies in the fact that the patriot "died, striving even in his death to bow his head toward the South—toward the place of the Emperor's palace— toward the presence of his beloved Master." Accordingly the warrior's spirit appears before his master to make his humble report—at the very moment of his death, and finally assumes immortality in the dust-crumbled coffin. Hearn shows insight into the core of the legend, that by sincerity man can move the will of Heaven.

In "The Soul of the Great Bell," which heads the collection, Hearn deals more fully with a similarly familiar theme, filial piety.[10] Under the imperial command the worthy mandarin Kouan-Yu must cast a bell of enormous size whose sound can be "heard for one hundred *li*," whose voice is "strengthened with brass, and deepened with gold, and sweetened with silver," and whose face and great lips are "graven with blessed sayings from the sacred books." He and his crew toil night and day to carry out the command, but to no purpose, because the metals will not fuse. Upon his second failure Kouan-Yu receives an imperial message: *"Twice thou hast betrayed the trust we have deigned graciously to place in thee: if thou fail a third time in fulfilling our command, thy head shall be severed from thy neck. Tremble, and obey!"*

It so happens that Kouan-Yu has a daughter of "dazzling loveliness" named Ko-Ngai, "whose heart was even more beautiful than her face." Having discovered her father's plight she sells some of her jewels secretly and hastens to an astrologer, who prophesies: "Gold and brass will never meet in wedlock, silver and iron never will embrace, until the flesh of a maiden be melted in the crucible; until the blood of a virgin be mixed with the metals in their fusion." She must sacrifice herself so that her father's success in the last attempt may be assured. Hearn closes the story with a pathetic episode, all the more telling, that the virgin leaping into the molten metal left her "tiny, dainty shoe" in her maid's clutching hands. Whenever the bell, now perfectly blended, rings the name Ko-Ngai, all the Chinese mothers whisper to their children: *"Listen! that is Ko-Ngai crying for her shoe! That is Ko-Ngai calling for her shoe."*

In point of filial affection, the story is a good companion piece to "The Legend of Tchi-Niu." Briefly stated, it is about a Chinese youth, Tong-Yong, who offers himself as a slave in order to build a handsome tomb in memory of his deceased father.[11] From morning to night he labors until he falls victim to "the fever of the rice-fields." The Master of Heaven, taking pity on him, sends the Goddess Tchi-Niu to restore his strength and be his wife. With her divine craft she weaves a great piece of marvelously figured silk each day, thereby helping her mortal husband to fulfill his dream and buy his freedom. But as soon as she gives him a son, "not less wonderful than his wonderful mother," she reveals her identity and returns to the Master of Heaven.

Needless to say, Tong-Yong's filial piety and heavenly rewards, such as Tchi-Niu, their son, etc., well exemplify the traditional Chinese concept of family succession. The moral of the story is still present in Hearn's retelling; but what is curious is that as the story goes on, the emphasis shifts from the original moral to the beauty of passion. Hearn must have felt guilty about this, even if vaguely. In the notes he refers to one of Giles's books as his authority and not only denies that "the details of the apparition, the cure, the marriage ceremony, etc." are a figment of his imagination, but also asserts that his narrative is "at least conformable to Chinese ideas." [12] The point, however, is not that "The Legend of Tchi-Niu" is inconsistent with the Chinese spirit, but that in it there is something more than Chinese.

The tendency becomes more conspicuous in "The Tradition of the Tea-Plant," a story about an Indian pilgrim's final conquest of Mara—on his way to China.[13] As an account of an ascetic struggling with Mara, the last of all human illusions, it is as Buddhistic as can possibly be, the purest pattern being that of the Buddha's own Enlightenment. Alternating holy prayer and invocations with a never-ending chain of illusions, Hearn makes this drama of the soul highly realistic and convincing. Nevertheless, it is not difficult to notice that more than once Hearn's mind is drawn to Mara rather than to the protagonist. No matter how justifiable in the context, Hearn's elaboration of her bewitching qualities is excessive. Indeed, when he twists *"O the Jewel in the Lotus"* into *"O the jewel in her ear!"* we cannot but recall Flaubert's description of the Queen of Sheba.[14] Perhaps Hearn was subtly influenced by the resemblance of his subject here to *The Temptation of St. Anthony.*

On the other hand, "The Tale of the Porcelain-God," the last in the collection, best illustrates what can be achieved if an artist successfully reads his own theme into a legend before him.[15] The hero of the story is the master-artisan Pu, who must sacrifice his own life for completion of his art. It is again an emperor who bids this "matchless artificer" produce an impossible vase, "a vase having the tint and the aspect of living flesh"—"*of flesh made to creep by the utterance of such words as poets utter,—flesh moved by an Idea, flesh horripilated by a Thought.*" The Oriental despotism suggested in Father d'Entrecolles' original version is transformed into something entirely new.[16] In Hearn's tale the imperial command becomes symbolic of the rage and conscience which possess all great artists.

Pu tries everything humanly possible—without success. He has no daughter like Ko-Ngai, an embodiment of heavenly grace, who as we know helped to complete the great Bell. Alone he has to face the furnace. In despair he hears the mysterious voice of the Spirit of the Furnace: "Canst thou give ghost unto a stone? Canst thou thrill with a Thought the entrails of the granite hills?" At the fifth and last attempt the voice is more demanding: "Canst thou divide a Soul? Nay! . . . Thy life for the life of thy work!—thy soul for the soul of thy Vase!" And on the ninth night Pu yields up "his ghost in the embrace of the Spirit of the Furnace." Thus the vase is created, not only "seeming to be flesh moved by the utterance of a Word, creeping to the titillation of a Thought," but also uttering, whenever tapped, "a voice of a name,—the voice of its maker, the name of its creator: PU." Art means more than a perfect mastery of technique; it demands the spirit or ghost of an artist, thereby assuming its own life. The motif itself is very commonplace in the Far East, but out of Hearn's imagination it emerges as a story of the artist.

In a book as ambitious as *Some Chinese Ghosts,* it is not surprising to find Hearn taking up his favorite theme of spectral love. To what extent his Mara threatened to dethrone his protagonist we have already seen in "The Tradition of the Tea-Plant." And in what manner the Goddess Tchi-Niu descended from her heavenly abode to be a wife to Tong-Yong long enough to reward his filial piety we have also seen in "The Legend of Tchi-Niu." In both stories the original moral tends to be obscured by Hearn's partiality for his heroines. Hence his feeling of discomfort. In "The Story of Ming-Y," however, this sense of guilt no longer exists, for the beauty of spectral love is the very spirit of the legend.[17]

Ming-Y is a young poet-scholar engaged as a private tutor to a great family. Permitted to make his first visit of respect to his parents, he takes a journey through dreamy vernal scenery. On the way he can hardly resist sitting down "among the young blossoms, under the branches swaying against the violet sky, to drink in the perfume and the light, and to enjoy the great sweet silence." This is the place where he falls in love at first sight with a lady named Sië, "the fairest and sweetest being" he has ever seen. From then on Ming-Y keeps hurrying to their nocturnal rendezvous under the pretence of returning home, and his life of bliss continues until it is accidentally discovered by his father and employer. At the last meeting Sië predicts his great future by presenting him with "a lion of yellow jade" and "a brush-case of carven agate" as a parting gift. Sië is actually the ghost of Sië-Thao, favorite mistress of Kao-pien, an ancient poet. As she foresaw, Ming-Y later obtains high dignities and honors by reason of his talents and his learning. Indeed, she has said to him, ". . . you will not be able to forget me while you live," and this proves to be true. He could never forget Sië-Thao even after his marriage to "an illustrious house," nor could he speak of her—"not even when his children begged him to tell the story of two beautiful objects that always lay upon his writing-table."

Within the general framework, which is quite Chinese, there is much of Hearn. His "you will not be able to forget me while you live" is reminiscent of Baudelaire's "The Moon's Blessings," where the moon whispers of "the lover thou shalt never know." When we come to know that the ghostly lover's parting gift, the brush-case and the paper-weight, once belonged to the mighty poet, Kao-pien, the two themes of the artist and the spectral love tend to fuse into one single theme of love. In the broadest sense, love is an act of creation in life. Love is art in the sense that it gives form to life. In *Some Chinese Ghosts* Hearn has reached the point from which to unify the manifold passions he glimpsed in *Stray Leaves*. His discovery that the essence of passion is love of weird beauty therefore becomes the unifying theme of *Some Chinese Ghosts*.

Not by *Stray Leaves* and *Some Chinese Ghosts* but by his Japanese legends do we remember Hearn the story-teller best. For this there are many good reasons, one of which is the simple fact that these Japanese legends, which number more than fifty, constitute a quarter of his total production in Japan. Beginning with *In Ghostly Japan* (1899), they definitely increase as Hearn goes through *Shadowings* (1900), *A Japanese Miscellany* (1901), and *Kotto* (1902), until they take up most of *Kwaidan* (1904) and *The Romance of the Milky Way* (1905). With few exceptions, they all belong to the last five years of his career in Japan, when he knew more about the country, which may also help to explain why his reputation as a writer of Japan depends so much upon these legends.

Most of them were drawn from old and well-known native materials, and for the most part retold by his Japanese wife, Setsuko. This advantage of working from oral sources, coupled with his stylistic conversion, helped to free him from his obsession with a poetical prose, and his handling of the materials is much better than in *Stray Leaves* and *Some Chinese Ghosts*. After living for years in a world which accepts the supernatural as an integral part of its daily life, after exploring the Buddhist theory of karma in terms of evolutionism, Hearn became convinced of the validity of his early presentiment, that the ghostly is not the periphery of the human, but the very center of it, the very spirit of it. To him it was no longer something impossible. As an artist who believed that "every man is haunted by ghosts," he saw a priceless value in those native legends then "passing or likely to pass away." Furthermore, he knew how to use them.[18] In these tales he becomes a master raconteur in English, comparable to Hans Christian Andersen or the brothers Grimm, as Malcolm Cowley has recently observed.[19]

Unlike these masters, however, Hearn is seldom interested in fairies. His concern is decidedly with the domain of ghosts.[20] His Japanese legends as a whole can best be called "Weird Tales," the term which he applied to *Kwaidan*. Everything he sets out to recreate is weird, or ghostly, whether it be horror, beauty, or laughter.[21] The variety of his subjects and their qualities is such that one finds it impossible and perhaps useless to treat each tale adequately. It is more important to discover the center of Hearn's interest, the Buddhist doctrine of karma, upon which he could readily base the popular native belief in two sorts of ghosts: the *shiryō* and the *ikiryō*. As Hearn himself explains in *Out of the East* (1895), the *shiryō*, merely the ghosts of the dead, follow their universal habit of coming at night only, whereas the *ikiryō*, the ghosts of the living, may come whenever they will, exercise their dreadful power upon other people, and frequently cause the death or survival of those concerned.[22] Against this background we can better understand why all his Japanese legends are invariably haunted by ghosts of both the dead and the living, and why the overall tone is profoundly Buddhistic.

In *Kotto,* for instance, there are two stories, "Ikiryō" and "Shiryō," which make a good pair. The one is about the ghost of a late district governor which returns to protect his family, property, and reputation. His medium is a maidservant in the household who, following a series of physical convulsions, assumes the voice of her late master to expose the villainy of his former subordinates. The other is about an able clerk at a famous porcelain dealer's, who is ceaselessly tormented by the shadow of a woman. It turns out to be an *ikiryō* of the dealer's wife, who hates the clerk, suspecting that he will someday delude her simple-minded son so as to take possession of the family business. Her hatred alone is sufficient for an *ikiryō* to detach itself from her body.

The moral of both stories is that the ghostly is not only self-sufficient but also supreme. In one way or another, most of Hearn's legends center on this principle. "Of a Promise Kept," from *A Japanese Miscellany,* tells about a samurai who commits harakiri, so that at least his ghost may fulfill his promise. The theme could be taken as an example of the triumphant samurai spirit, but the underlying belief is that one may will his ghost or soul to act for him in the performance of a duty. In the same way, if the gods are willing, one may even transfer his own life to another person or living thing. In "Ubazakura," from *Kwaidan,* a milk-nurse dies willingly, taking the place of her charge. In "Jiu-Roku-Zakura," from the same book, an old man saves the life of a withering cherry tree.

It is one's desire or will that turns the wheel of karma. In Hearn's Japanese legends, as in human life, there seems to be no stronger human desire or will than love. For the sake of love many a ghost returns to its former human world, either visibly or invisibly, and fulfills its original wish. There is a girl who is reborn in another human being to be finally wedded to her lonely betrothed, thanks to their mutual pledge ("The Story of O-Tei," *Kwaidan*). There is a dead wife whose ghost, returning as soon as her samurai husband breaks his promise to remain faithful to her memory, tears off the new bride's head ("Of a Promise Broken," *A Japanese Miscellany*). There is also a girl who pines, sickens, and dies in her longing for a handsome youth she saw only once. Her ghost still clings to a robe she had made after his. Whoever wears it but once dies much in the same manner—haunted by the vision of the unknown youth ("Furisodé," *In Ghostly Japan*).

These three ghosts are all female; and, to be sure, none of Hearn's tales recounts a male ghost's return for love. There are, however, two pieces which suggest that love is creative, regardless of its agent's sex. They are "The Screen-Maiden" and "The Sympathy of Benten," both of which appear in *Shadowings*. The first story tells the strange manner in which a young scholar's daydream comes true. Tokkei, bewitched by Hishigawa Moronobu's full-length portrait of a young girl on an old screen, falls sick—so sick that he believes himself about to die. But following the ritual prescribed by an old friend, he succeeds in conjuring her out of the screen with his whole-hearted prayer. As the friend explains, it is because Moronobu painted her mind as well as her form, and thus her spirit lives in the picture.

The situation is a little more complicated in the second story, since a young poet-scholar here has to marry the spirit as well as its original. At a temple of the goddess Benten, Hanagaki Baishū picks up a *tanzaku* or fancy paper tablet blown to his feet by a sudden gust of wind. Soon he finds himself in love with the unknown girl who so wonderfully wrote on the tablet the famous poem on first love. In reward for his prayer and seven days' religious service, the goddess of lovers has the god of marriage arrange his acquaintance with the writer herself. Another wonder happens when a rich stranger, inspired by the same goddess, asks him to be his son-in-law. So he has to marry twice *"the same—yet not the same,"* that is, first the soul of the beloved and now her body. The miracle is explained by one of Hearn's Japanese friends: The spirit-bride is the double of the writer and was evoked from the *tanzaku,* while the real girl probably remains unaware. It was when she wrote those beautiful characters upon the paper tablet, that something of her spirit passed into them.

Both stories point to the same moral: A work of art, if genuinely executed, may not only exercise a magical power upon its beholder, but may also enable its spirit to detach itself from the work, thereby becoming alive in its own right. This is the sense in which art can be considered divine. The theory, highly indicative of Far Eastern aesthetics, is nothing novel to those who remember Hearn's previous treatment in "The Tale of the Porcelain-God," where Pu the master-artisan gave his own soul for the soul of his vase. But the artist theme is only one side of these two Japanese stories. From another point of view, they carry forward his earlier concern, the spectral love theme. It is more than probable that Hearn prized the stories for their double theme. Take, for instance, Tokkei's murmuring before the portrait: "How gladly would I give my life—nay, a thousand years of life!—to hold her in my arms for a moment!" It clearly echoes the wretched lovers in *Stray Leaves*. It is also significant that Hearn adds his own themes to a legend like "The Sympathy of Benten," "an interesting mingling of Shintō and Buddhist ideas," as he noted. All in all, there is good evidence that his Japanese legends, apart from their intrinsic merits, constitute a thematic continuation and development of their predecessors, notably *Some Chinese Ghosts*, by giving fuller treatment to his earlier double theme, art and love.

Two later stories also center on the problem of art, "The Story of Kwashin Koji" and "Kōgi the Priest," both in *A Japanese Miscellany*, an immediate successor of *Shadowings*. Evidently they were meant to complement each other. Oguri Sōtan's famous Buddhist kakemono, now in Kwashin's possession, constantly changes according to its temporary owners. It becomes blank if possessed unlawfully; otherwise it represents exactly what was paid for. The full value of the painting reveals itself only to those purely motivated, for it is a painting beyond all price. Pressed further, Kwashin explains thus: "In any picture of real excellence there must be a ghost; and such a picture, having a will of its own, may refuse to be separated from the person who gave it life, or even from its rightful owner. There are many stories to prove that really great pictures have souls." Then he cites a few examples like some painted sparrows which flew away from a sliding-screen, and a painted horse which used to go out to eat grass. Trying to convince those present of his point, he turns to the screen representing a lake view, and waves his hand toward a painted boat. To their surprise, as the water of the lake begins to overflow—"out of the picture into the room," a real fishing-boat glides forth, fetches Kwashin away into the distance, and disappears forever.

Kōgi's story may be not so weird as Kwashin's, but it is still interesting since it indicates the secret of artistic creation. Of all Kōgi's famous paintings of fish, the best, "Dream-Carp," is "not drawn from life," but "made from the memory of a dream," in which he was playing with the fish under the water. Although willing to part with his drawings of other subjects, he would not sell a picture of living fish to anyone cruel enough to kill or to eat fish. In reward for his kindness he is turned into a golden carp, whose aquatic freedom he has so long envied. Returning from his soul's journey, he finds his funeral service has been performed. The story ends: "It is related that, long after his death, some of his fish-pictures once happened to fall into the lake, and that the figures of the fish immediately detached themselves from the silk or the paper upon which they had been painted, and swam away!" The crux of the whole story is that the secret of art is not to copy the object realistically but to capture its soul, and that in order to achieve this feat an artist must first of all be one with his object. This view of artistic creation, it may be said, is singularly similar to the psychic union which is the essence of Hearn's favorite fable, Salmacis and Hermaphroditus. Together with Tokkei and Baishū, Kwashin stands for the approach one should take to a work of art, whereas Kōgi suggests the approach an artist should take to his subject or his reality. And yet Kwashin the beholder and Kōgi the creator meet on the same ground where art is fundamentally magical and divine.

All this leads to one final question, the relation of the artist to life which provides the central theme for "The Boy Who Drew Cats," one of Hearn's few fairy tales, and "The Story of Mimi-Nashi-Hoïchi," the opening piece of *Kwaidan*. The former is about an acolyte of a village temple who is dismissed because of his excessive fondness for drawing cats on walls, screens, and holy scriptures. That night, when he takes shelter at a deserted temple, he cannot resist drawing cats before falling asleep. Ironically, the cats he has drawn save his life from "a goblin-rat, —bigger than a cow." [23] The latter, known to have been Hearn's own favorite, is also called "The Story of Hoïchi-the-Earless." A blind biwa-player is a renowned reciter of the tragic geste of the Heike and Genji, medieval Japanese military clans. His chanting of the song of the Battle of Dan-no-ura is so truly magnificent that even the goblins weep. Trouble begins, however, when Hoïchi is nightly led away somewhere by a ghostly voice to appease the lost souls of the ancient warriors. This occurs only during the patron-priest's absence. When the matter finally comes into notice of the priest, he writes down the text of the holy sutra all over the stripped body of Hoïchi—except his ears. That night Hoïchi is for the first time free from the ghostly power, but the angry spirit tears off his ears, which fact, needless to say, boosts his professional success all the more.

With these stories Hearn completes the artist theme which originated long before in "The Tale of the Porcelain-God," "The Soul of the Great Bell," and even further in "The First Musician" (*Stray Leaves*), a tale of Wainamoinen, whose divine musical art moved all hearers to tears. All of these legends, despite their varying colors, are in one way or another concerned with the question of art and life. Some deal with the sacrifice the artist has to make for his art, and others with the salvation of an artist through grace. Hearn has now come to realize the absolute necessity of heavenly grace for any real artist to survive and perfect his art. Grace is necessary because, as "a being cursed with the gift of song," an artist must constantly expose his own fragile existence to the menacing power of the ghostly.[24]

The spectral love theme offers another evidence for an artistic continuity between Hearn's Japanese legends and his early works, *Some Chinese Ghosts,* for example. Besides those we have already touched upon, there are a few more, all falling between "A Passional Karma" (*In Ghostly Japan*) and "The Story of Itō Norisuké" (*The Romance of the Milky Way*). There are "The Story of Chūgoró" (*Kotto*), a story about a poor retainer who dies in love with a beautiful woman at the bridge, actually a great and ugly frog; "Yuki-Onna" (*Kwaidan*), a story about the Woman of the Snow who melts into a bright white mist as soon as her human husband reveals their secret; "The Story of Aoyagi" (*Kwaidan*), a story about the spirit of a tree which marries a good young samurai only to return to its own world; and others.

"A Passional Karma" retells Enchō's romance, *Botan-Dōrō* (or *Peony-Lantern*), Japanese in setting, though inspired by a Chinese tale. Hearn's version begins with a situation very similar to that of "Furisodé." A young samurai, Hagiwara Shinzaburó, and O-Tsuyu fall in love with each other at first sight. The girl dies in her longing for the youth, since he somehow fails to come back again. When her ghost, attended by her maid O-Yoné, begins to visit him nightly, he no longer belongs—at least in spirit—to this world. In their strange nuptials, their love is consummated with an everlasting vow. Soon alarmed by the seriousness of his situation, Hagiwara follows the advice of the high-priest Ryōseki and fixes the holy texts over all the apertures of his house. The measures thus taken seem to be successful against the two ghostly visitors in their desperate supplication. But Hagiwara's servant Tomozō, persuaded by his shrewd wife, treacherously removes the holy texts and even steals his master's amulet, thus enabling the ghostly bride to approach her human groom and choke him to death.

As it is, the story is a bit too close to the actual human predicament, but it does meet the essential requirements of a spectral love story. What is interesting is the comment on Hagiwara's character, presented in the form of dialog between the author and his Japanese friend. Here Hearn says that in every way Hagiwara proves himself contemptible. Compare him with those true lovers of Western ballad literature, all "only too glad to follow a dead sweetheart into the grave," in spite of their Christian belief in only one human life to enjoy in this world. As a Buddhist, Hagiwara has "a million lives behind him and a million lives before him"; yet he is "too selfish to give up even one miserable existence for the sake of the girl that came back to him from the dead." Also as a samurai he is even more cowardly than selfish when he begs of a priest to protect him from ghosts. All in all, he is a despicable creature worth O-Tsuyu's death treatment. To this the Japanese friend makes no objection.

Hearn must have remembered this comment when he took up the theme again—five years later. This time he worked it out to his own heart's satisfaction. The result is "The Story of Itō Norisuké" (*The Romance of the Milky Way*), the piece which, significantly enough, winds up the long cycle of his ghost stories. Beyond question, he fashioned the story very closely after the versions of the perhaps most celebrated Far Eastern legend of the astral goddess Tanabatatsumé's annual union with her mortal husband.[25] Yet, the general situation of "The Story of Itō Norisuké" is strangely reminiscent of many of his early spectral love stories, particularly "The Story of Ming-Y."

Itō Norisuké, a young samurai and a devotee of letters, is a poor offspring of the Heike clan. One autumn evening he is led by a strange girl messenger to a remote village, "densely shadowed by a grove of young trees," and introduced to his bride-to-be, the noble daughter of Shigéhira-Kyō, the great Heike general and statesman. He wonders at her beauty, asking himself whether he is before the very person of that astral goddess Tanabatatsumé. After their wedding feast, which immediately follows, the bride reveals her ghostly identity and the mystery of their karma-crossed love: their first meeting took place not in his present life but very, very long ago. After seeing him, the world was no longer the same to her; because of her great wish for him, she could not "obtain another body, nor enter into another state of existence." It has been a waiting through many ages of men.

Itō is fully aware that "who weds a ghost must become a ghost." He is now "ready to die, not once, but many times, rather than betray by word or look one thought that might bring a shadow of pain to the brow of the beautiful illusion before him." He desires "nothing more in life, or in all his lives to come, than to feel her arms about him, and to hear the caress of her voice." When morning dawns they exchange gifts for remembrance—a little *suzuri*, or ink-stone for the *kōgai* of his sword. The lovers, though now husband and wife, are destined to meet only every ten years. The groom departs from the ghostly region, dreaming of their next reunion ten years ahead.

Itō is no longer the same person. His health gradually fails. When the tenth year comes around at last, the little girl messenger arrives with the summons from the ghostly bride. Then for the first time he relates to his mother the story of his ghostly bride and dies, asking that the ink-stone should be placed in his coffin. There ends the story. There are many echoes in it: Their reunion every decade is another intensification of the annual rendezvous of the astral lovers in "The Romance of the Milky Way" in the same volume; the bride's gift, the ink-stone, was already foreshadowed in Sië-Thao's parting gift to her human lover: a lion of yellow jade, and a brush-case of carven agate. Unmistakable, also, is Hearn's delight to see in Itō a foil to Hagiwara Shinzaburō, whose selfishness and cowardice he so thoroughly despised, and Itō Norisuké is in this sense the archetype of all Hearn's ideal lovers. Even Buddhism, previously an effective barrier between the human and the ghostly, now is used to reconcile the two realms. The spectral love theme, which has so persistently fascinated Hearn, now becomes something like a hymn of the immortality of love, human and ghostly.

Whether or not Hearn's idiosyncrasy or personal obsession may have originally motivated his interest in the spectral love theme, he is safely free from his own shadow in these stories, which are his best.[26] In order for us to do him full justice, the theme of spectral love must be considered along with his artist theme. To what extent each blends with the other we have already noted in "The Story of Ming-Y." Lovers such as Ming-Y, Tokkei, Baishū, and Itō Norisuké are all artists as well, in one way or another. For Hearn, all artists ought to be lovers at heart, the lovers dreaming of their ghosts which are also emblems of the Impossible. Why this should be so, Hearn seeks to explain in one of his poetical rhapsodies, "The Eternal Haunter." A Japanese color-print representing the spirit of the cherry tree provokes his thought:

> You ask what is the use of drawing the Impossible? Your asking proves that you do not feel the charm of this vision of youth—this dream of spring. *I* hold that the Impossible bears a much closer relation to fact than does most of what we call the real and the commonplace. The Impossible may not be naked truth; but I think that it is usually truth—masked and veiled, perhaps, but eternal. Now to me this Japanese dream is truth—true, at least, as human love is. Considered even as a ghost it is true. Whoever pretends not to believe in ghosts of any sort, lies to his own heart. Every man is haunted by ghosts. And this color-print reminds me of a ghost whom we all know,—though most of us (poets excepted) are unwilling to confess the acquaintance.[27]

Only in their pursuit of the Impossible can all artists become lovers. Their prizes are not the Impossible but her parting gifts, such as Ming-Y's paper-weight and brush-case, and Itō's ink-stone, all symbolic of their craft. Therefore, it becomes their mission to unveil, by whatever their art, the image of the Impossible for the sake of their inarticulate fellow men, who can only dream of her.

When Hearn came to discover the same pattern recurring in the world of folk tales, legends, and myths, and when he saw therein not only the colorful differences of those various lands, peoples, and their cultures, but also the common root from which they have grown spontaneously, he did not fail to accept them as the manifestation of man's aspiration toward the Impossible. After all, they are but versions of dream truths that are ever the same the world over, as he explains in his lecture on the supernatural in fiction.[28] They are the cherished prizes of humanity in its quest for the Impossible, just as the paper-weight, brush-case, and ink-stone are those of the artist-lovers. Folk tales, legends and myths, as records of these dream truths, demand some one to render them in human terms, some one who is not only a translator but also an artist. It is as if Hearn was born to meet this demand, for he succeeded in fulfilling the double role of translator-artist. In approaching his many-colored legends he could be at once Kwashin the beholder and Kōgi the creator. Like Kwashin, he absorbs the soul of his object; like Kōgi, he lets the object absorb his soul. Like Pu, he gives his soul in order to possess the soul of his object. Once Hearn advised his young students of literature: "Trust to your own dream-life; study it carefully, and draw your inspiration from that. For dreams are the primary source of almost everything that is beautiful in the literature which treats of what lies beyond mere daily experience." [29] The same seems to apply to him. Trusting his own dream life, he could also trust the dream life of humanity; for with him they are one. Herein lies the perennial charm of Hearn's art as a storyteller.

IV

Romances
Born
and
Unborn

Hearn's
Ambition
in
Fiction

The period intervening between *Stray Leaves* (1884) and *Some Chinese Ghosts* (1887) was a trying one for Hearn. Neither *One of Cleopatra's Nights* nor *Stray Leaves* satisfied him. The former, he thought, was only the first step, and even the latter was little more than an attempt to apply his art of translation more liberally to myth, fable, and legend. His ambition lay elsewhere,—in fiction, the ruling passion of the age. It was indeed with this in mind that he had so single-heartedly undertaken his stylistic experiment. Sometime in 1883, the year before the publication of *Stray Leaves,* he confided to John Albee, an admirer of his Gautier translations:

> It has long been my aim to create something in English fiction analogous to that warmth of colour and richness of imagery hitherto peculiar to Latin literature. Being of a meridional race myself, a Greek, I *feel* rather with the Latin race than with the Anglo-Saxon; and trust that with time and study I may be able to create something different from the stone-grey and somewhat chilly style of latter-day English or American romance.[1]

Recalling his youthful dream of creating "English in splendid Latin attire," we may question the merit of this attitude. He himself must have had some doubts, for he added immediately: "This may seem only a foolish hope,—unsubstantial as a ghost."

His ambition grew persistently as time went on. "Fiction," he wrote to W. D. O'Connor in July 1885, "seems to be the only certain road to the publishers' hearts, and I shall try it, not in a lengthy, but a brief compass,—striving as much as possible after intense effects." [2] In October, he wrote to H. E. Krehbiel:

> I have become considerably disgusted with what I have already done. But I have not yet abandoned the idea of evolutional fiction, and find that my ethnographic and anthropologic reading has enabled me to find a totally new charm in character-analysis, and suggested artistic effects of a new peculiar description. I dream of a novel, or a novelette, to be constructed upon totally novel principles. [3]

From these letters it is possible to surmise what "a novel, or a novelette, to be constructed upon totally novel principles," should be. It should be brief but with "intense effects"; it should obtain its peculiar charm through an authentic study of folk subjects; and it should draw its philosophic inspiration from evolutionism. Here we cannot but suspect that Hearn is intent upon attempting the impossible; even if he is not, we may rightly wonder if this sort of synthesis can produce valuable results. While attempting to combine all these elements in fiction, Hearn could not rid himself of certain misgivings. As he admitted in his letter to Krehbiel, ". . . the outlook is not encouraging. Years of very hard work with a problematical result!" He felt "pretty much like a scholar trying hard to graduate and feeling tolerably uneasy about the result." But in order to go beyond *Stray Leaves,* Hearn had to overcome these doubts. *Chita: A Memory of Last Island,* was the first result of Hearn's attempt to do so.

The genesis of *Chita* is more than complicated. According to one biographer, Hearn got the story about the tidal disaster at Grande Isle from G. W. Cable, as early as 1882. [4] Later, when Hearn vacationed at the Louisiana resort in the summers of 1884 and 1886, he must have remembered it. His fresh enthusiasm for the Gulf went duly into "Torn Letters," a series of prose poems about his undeclared love for a Basque girl (*Times-Democrat,* September 14, 1884). [5] The whole plan came along very slowly. Shortly before the summer of 1886 Hearn was still uncertain about his projected novelette. His "tiny book" was going to be "all divided into microscopic chapters of a page or half-a-page each," and every one of these was to be "a little picture, with some novel features," and of course with some "touches of evolutionary philosophy."

At any rate he would make "something altogether odd, novel, ideal in the best sense." The theme was ready for his use, but he was not quite sure how to arrange the main part. All he could tell was that "there will be much more of *suggestion* than of real plot." [6] On his second vacation he made good progress. "My work progresses," Hearn wrote to Mrs. Marion Baker, "I have most of my scenario done, but have not yet decided what drama to use. I have three admirable plots, and shall use them all sooner or later. A whole series of projects have been evolved for me." [7] By October the manuscript had been completed and delivered to Henry Alden, editor of *Harper's*.[8] It finally made its way to the reader, first as a magazine feature, in 1888, and then in book form in the following year.

Unfortunately, there is no way of knowing exactly what his "three admirable plots" were; but we have Hearn's own explanation of the original episode which provided a basis for *Chita*:

> Chita was founded on the fact of a child saved from the Lost Island disaster by some Louisiana fisher-folk, and brought up by them. Years after a Creole hunter recognized her, and reported her whereabouts to relatives. These, who were rich, determined to bring her up as young ladies are brought up in the South, and had her sent to a convent. But she had lived the free healthy life of the coast, and could not bear the convent;—she ran away from it, married a fisherman, and lives somewhere down there now,—the mother of multitudinous children.[9]

With this in mind, it is illuminating to read Hearn's final version, which consists of three parts. The first one, "The Legend of L'Île Dernière," has little direct bearing on the action of the story itself, being mostly descriptive of the eve of the tidal cataclysm of August 10, 1856. The section is Hearn's sonorous proem to the main action. As it opens, the tempo is leisurely, freely interrupted with the author's meditative utterances. The tempo soon increases. Parallel with the roaring rhythm of nature, the gay melody of Weber's "L'Invitation à la Valse" from the resort hotel accentuates a sense of dramatic irony and intensifies our apprehension. In its maddening mirth and confused excitement there is a sense of impending doom; this whole part becomes an invitation to Death. Glancing alternately at the glittering hotel windows and the stormy sea, Captain Smith of the *Star* mumbles: *"The Wind waltzes tonight, with the Sea for his partner!"* At the finale the ocean sweeps over the entire island.

The second part, "Out of the Sea's Strength," opens with an account of the following morning at the cottage of a Spanish fisherman, Felieu, and his pious wife Carmen. They have found two tidal victims afloat, a mother drowned and her child still alive. To this child, four years old or so, they give the name Chita, after their dead child Conchita. Days later a rescue party arrives and attempts in vain to establish the child's identity. The suspenseful interview between Chita and Laroussel, a Creole member of the party, is too brief to produce anything definite; all it suggests is a sense of mysterious affinity. The scene shifts to New Orleans, where Dr. Julien La Brierre mourns over the fate of his wife Adèle and their only child, Euralie. He recalls old memories of gay Paris, and above all his love for Adèle, over whom he fought a duel with his friend Laroussel. Both friends have been estranged ever since. This coincidence explains the affinity drawing Chita and Laroussel together in their encounter. Laroussel could hardly manage to remove his black gaze from Chita. "Her eyes, too, seemed to be all for him—to return his scrutiny with a sort of vague pleasure, a half-savage confidence. . . ." "Was it," Hearn muses at this point, "the first embryonic feeling of race-affinity quickening in the little brain?—some intuitive, inexplicable sense of kindred?" In "the embryonic feeling of race-affinity," there is much of the Spencerian doctrine of race memory; and somehow Hearn must have felt this to be the place for his "evolutional fiction." Even though he dramatizes the child's special fondness for Laroussel by having her play with his watch-chain, Hearn the storyteller becomes obtrusive. Much is dramatized, but too much is explained.

"The Shadow of the Tide," the last part of the romance, resumes the drama ten years after the incident related above. By now Chita, the child of nature, has grown into a beautiful maiden. Laroussel is dead, after a battle-field reconciliation with Dr. La Brierre, who has survived the horror of the Civil War. The doctor is summoned to Viosca's Landing by the ailing Henry Edwards, a friend of his father. Arriving only to find his patient dead, La Brierre, in exhaustion, falls mortally ill. Glimpsing Chita, he feels that she must be his own child, Euralie, lost long ago; but he cannot be sure of it. On his death-bed he is intermittently haunted by the inscrutable resemblance between Chita and his dead wife, Adèle, by Chita's birthmark, and by the dying Laroussel's unfinished account of his meeting with a Creole child in a remote fishing village years ago.

In many ways, *Chita* represents Hearn's situation during the mideighties. It demonstrates his mastery of the so-called local color technique, to which, as he later admitted, it owed "a great literary success,—

contrary to expectation."[10] Having written previously on folk subjects in *Gombo Zhèbes* (1885) and *La Cuisine Créole* (1885), Hearn could thoroughly recreate the primitive folkways, the crude though deeply humane workings of the folk mind, and the exotic rhythm of out-landish dialects, especially Creole and Spanish. His handling of these details has been said to be authentic; it is also consistent with the design of the story.

In *Chita* Hearn missed no chance to exercise his poetical prose. The third chapter of the opening part is a good example. The emotional tone is suggested by the first sentence: "On the Gulf side of these islands you may observe that the trees—when there are any trees—all bend away from the sea; and, even of bright, hot days when the wind sleeps, there is something grotesquely pathetic in their look of agonized terror." Hearn does not stop here:

> A group of oaks at Grande Isle I remember as especially suggestive: five stooping silhouettes in line against the horizon, like fleeing women with streaming garments and wind-blown hair—bowing grievously and thrust-ing out arms desperately northward as to save themselves from falling. And they are being pursued indeed;—for the sea is devouring the land. Many and many a mile of ground has yielded to the tireless charging of Ocean's cavalry.

The tone of the chapter, heightened with a series of elaborate meta-phors, is sustained until the end: ". . . the Voice of the Sea is never one voice, but a tumult of many voices—voices of drowned men—the mut-tering of multitudinous dead—the moaning of innumerable ghosts, all rising, to rage against the living, at the great Witch-call of storms. . . ." He must have especially delighted in this Tennysonian alliteration.[11]

Hearn's ability to sustain a poetic tone throughout the story may de-serve admiration; but in his enthusiasm he seems oblivious to the truth that a lofty style, like everything else in a work of art, must be func-tional. In *Chita,* the style tends to be an exercise for its own sake. Years later in Japan—at about the time of his stylistic conversion—Hearn said he was ashamed of *Chita,* and added, referring to his poetical style in particular, that the work was overdone.[12] What weakens the story, however, is not so much his poetical prose as his failure to develop both plot and characters fully. In fact, there is scarcely any development of the plot, and the characters all appear only in profile. There is no human drama, although there is dramatic tension of another kind.

In a sense Hearn succeeded in his original hope, that "there will be much more of *suggestion* than of real plot." His aim, as he explained elsewhere, was "only to reach and touch that kindred *something* in another which the Christian calls Soul,—the Pantheist, God,—the philosopher, the Unknowable."[13] It was an attempt to treat "modern Southern life in the same spirit of philosophic romance" that was exemplified in his *Some Chinese Ghosts*.[14] In creating what he termed a philosophic romance Hearn was naturally concerned with the relationship between the human and the natural world. But the result was an unbalanced emphasis on natural force, which can be seen even in his epigraph from Emerson: "But Nature whistled with all her winds,/ Did as she pleased, and went her way." It may be true that Hearn is not so much concerned with the insignificance of man in the vast force of the natural world, by contrasting the dancing music with the roaring ocean, as with the way of nature by which the primitive folk can survive. This intention is quite obvious in his juxtaposition of the summer vacationists from New Orleans and the inhabitants at Viosca's Landing. Perhaps it is because he remained faithful to his intention that Hearn does not depict the later part of Chita's life, as outlined in the original episode, and contents himself only with "much more of *suggestion* than of real plot," as in his poetical description of Chita now well acclimatized to her new world:

> . . . losing herself at the conclusion of desperate efforts to run races at night with the moon, or to walk to the "end of the world." If she could only once get to the edge of the sky, she said, she "could climb up." She wanted to see the stars, which were the souls of good little children; and she knew that God would let her climb up.[15]

Though there is something ethereal about her that may lift her above the state of nature, Chita is still nature's child.

From Hearn's letter to Mrs. Marion Baker and from the original episode already quoted, we can conjecture his additions to the tale: the varying degrees of character relationship between Conchita and Chita, Laroussel and Chita, Julien and Laroussel, Julien and Chita, etc. There is a hint of karma in this cycle of human characters, a sense of irony in their relationship, an irony intimating the mystery of the cosmos. Perhaps for this reason Hearn parallels Emerson's lines with Hugo's in the opening of the romance: "Je suis la vaste mêlée—/Reptile, étant l'onde; ailée,/Étant le vent,—/Force et fuite, haine et vie,/Houle immense, poursuivie/Et poursuivant." The ultimate pantheistic identity of the natural and the human in the cosmic scheme, then, is the basic theme of *Chita*. Hearn's hymn to nature was meant to be also his hymn to man, as is obvious in the following passage:

All, all is blue in the calm,—save the low land under your feet, which you almost forget, since it seems only as a tiny green flake afloat in the liquid eternity of day. Then slowly, caressingly, irresistibly, the witchery of the Infinite grows upon you: out of Time and Space you begin to dream with open eyes,—to forget the past, the present, the substantial,—to comprehend nothing but the existence of that Blue Ghost as something into which you would wish to melt utterly away forever. . . .[16]

It is small wonder that all the characters, including Chita, appear only as silhouettes against such a vast cosmic background. We may have no objection to Hearn's philosophy as such, but still be justified in asking what human episode, unless fully dramatized, could possibly balance the naked force of philosophy, especially when it is a romantic pantheism like his.

Hearn's second romance, *Youma,* as shown in its subtitle, "The Story of a West-Indian Slave," is one of the two works growing out of his two-year stay in the West Indies. Its theme concerns the heroic career of the Creole nurse, Youma. Bereft of her mother, a personal servant in the Peyronette household in Saint Pierre, the child Youma remains as playmate of Aimée, daughter of Mme Léonie Peyronette. When Aimée is married to a planter at Anse-Marine, Youma follows her young mistress. Soon Aimée dies, leaving her daughter Marie or Mayotte to Youma's care. The child is as delicate as her mother. She often envies the slave children, who, like Chita, are free to "run and roll in the sun." Foreshadowed in Youma's nursery tale of Dame Kélément, which lulls the nervous Mayotte to sleep, a serpent incident occurs. One night Youma discovers a venomous reptile in the child's dark bedroom, and succeeds in checking its advance by her bare foot, despite its reflex attack: "The foot of the half-breed, never deformed by shoes, retains prehensible power,—grasps like a hand;—the creature writhed in vain to escape." Gabriel, a Negro *commandeur* of the plantation, answers her call for aid. One result of this incident is that Youma emerges as the object of popular veneration. Another result is that Youma and Gabriel are involved in a drama of passion. Since his rescue of Youma, this "sullen, incorrigible, and dangerous" *commandeur* feels a growing attachment toward her. After obtaining her consent, he approaches his white master and implores him to intercede with Mme Peyronette on their behalf. But their union is refused on the ground that he would make a rough mate indeed for a girl brought up as Youma has been. Gabriel then suggests to the nurse their elopement to Dominica, the neighboring island of freedom. After much hesitation, she rejects her lover's advances, choosing to remain loyal to her benefactors. In the meantime there are rumors of emancipation or uprising, and finally a revolt of the colored natives breaks out against the white rulers. Though her master begs her to leave for the people of her color, Youma stays with Mayotte among the whites. She does not falter even when the rebels set fire to the house-fortress where the colonists are gathering. Rejecting repeated entreaties by Gabriel, now with the rebels, Youma shares calmly the fate of her child-mistress' race in the midst of the all-destroying flames. The concluding passage is Hearnesque in its twist: "At the same hour, from the other side of the world,—a ship was running before the sun, bearing the Republican gift of liberty and promise of universal suffrage to the slaves of Martinique."

By Hearn's own account *Youma* is based on an incident which actually occurred during the 1848 uprising of the natives in the French colony, and the story is "substantially true." [17] Nevertheless, there are certain similarities and continuities between *Chita* and this work. First, in *Youma* Hearn makes use of the same local color technique. Martinique dialect is one of the six major Creole dialects he has already treated in *Gombo Zhèbes*. As usual he takes pains to recreate the colorful shades of the Creole world, its quaint customs, peculiar racial traits, plantation system and life, and the relations between the white masters and their slaves. Second, Hearn's favorite method of antithesis recurs throughout the romance, and with greater intensity, as exemplified in the contrast between the white and the colored, the city-bred and the country-bred, the civilized and the primitive.

But there are crucial differences between the two works, with the later one developing themes of the earlier. In both, which have similar tropical settings, Hearn depicts two types of storm, natural and human; in contrast with the tidal disaster which sets *Chita* in motion, the revolt of the natives in *Youma* signifies the author's new emergence out of the natural into the human world. So too with the heroines: Youma is in some sense the continuation of Chita, but nature is Chita's point of return and Youma's point of departure. This shift from the natural to the human indicates Hearn's own departure from his early romantic pantheism. Hearn himself probably referred to his shift of emphasis when he wrote to Elizabeth Bisland in 1889 shortly after his return from Martinique. Regarding her "pretty eulogy" of *Chita* as a timely encouragement, Hearn said: "I don't think I shall write another story in the same manner,—feel I have changed very much in my way of looking at things and of writing." [18] Although it is believed that *Youma* was mostly written in the West Indian period, Hearn's feeling of having "changed very much" is quite evident in this romance, too. *Chita* delineates man as an episodic atom in the vast force of nature; *Youma* is distinctly a human drama.

Structurally considered, *Youma* is far more complex and dramatic than its predecessor. As a whole it may be divided into five acts of dramatic progression: exposition (I–II), amplification (III–IV), intensification (V–VII), conflict (VIII–X), and resolution (XI–XIV). As for its plot, the romance combines three different sources: the Youma episode as the basis of the romance, the serpent episode drawn from the historian Rufz de Lavison, and the Gabriel episode. These three elements meet in the serpent scene in the fourth chapter, a dramatic peak which is adeptly prepared for by the nursery tale of Dame Kélément in the preceding chapter. In the serpent scene Youma for the first time gains heroic stature. As a consequence she becomes involved with Gabriel, tragically obliged to choose between her new-born love and her sense of loyalty and responsibility. The conflict within her mind is thus psychologized, again with Spencerian flavor: "At his [Gabriel's] advent into her life, something long held in subjection within her,— something like a darker passionate second soul, full of strange impulses and mysterious emotions,—had risen to meet him, bursting its bonds, and winning mastery at last: the nature of the savage race whose blood dominated in her veins." [19] But she has a promise to keep with her dead Aimée: "Youma, O Youma: you will love my child?—Youma, you will never leave her, whatever happens, while she is little?—promise, dear Youma!" From this point on, the romance turns into drama which runs with simplicity and intensity toward the denouement.

As this well-knit dramatic structure indicates, Hearn is quite sober. Seldom is he lost in philosophic meditations and lyric outbursts like those in *Chita*. He is more interested in his characters, Youma and Gabriel. At the outset of the story Youma is described: "Her tint was a clear deep red;—there was in her features a soft vague beauty,—a something that suggested the indefinable face of the Sphinx, especially in profile." But in the serpent scene she comes to appear in heroic dimensions: "She stood like a bronze." The moment may symbolize the tragic nature of her race, its silent suffering and endurance. When their love is rejected, Gabriel reasons with the hesitant Youma: "Do you believe slavery is a good thing,—a right thing, Youma?" Even this overly propagandist tone is not inconsistent with the character of Gabriel, who soon joins the mob besieging the fortress of the white colonists and yet is able to defy it to save his lover. Neither Youma nor Gabriel is determined by external forces, since both have chosen their own ways. Primitive nature, losing its control over the hero and heroine, recedes into the background and has meaning only in relation to the human action. In the final scene they are triumphant: Gabriel standing "alone—colossal, menacing, magnificent—daring the hell about him for her sake. . . ." and Youma with Mayotte in her arms—remaining at the window. "There was now neither hate nor fear in her fine face: it was calm as in the night when Gabriel had seen her stand unmoved with her foot on the neck of the serpent."

It is important to note that Hearn makes a Negress and a Negro the central characters of his romance. They are treated in a very serious way, unlike their contemporary brethren in many humorous local color stories. Unlike other propaganda writers of the time, Hearn is never interested in painting either character or race simply black or white. Although their racial peculiarities add further complexity to the story, their struggle against the world within and without is thoroughly human and universal. Consider for instance the direction each one takes to solve their common problem. Gabriel resorts to the socio-political pattern, whereas Youma chooses the more personal. As to these two levels of morality, Hearn makes no partisan judgment in the work itself. There is only a heightened sense of irony in the ending, which brings to them too late the news of emancipation. The thematic balancing of these elements keeps the romance from degenerating into propaganda.

The position Hearn has taken in this story is unmistakably idealistic although he never visualizes Youma or Gabriel as the so-called "noble savage." He is equally idealistic in handling those colonists who remain paternalistic in the midst of the racial turmoil. An extreme form of this idealism underlies "Karma," his third and last romance. This somewhat Hawthornesque story of moral purgation, which Hugh Walker extravagantly called "one of the noblest moral tales in the language," [20] and which another critic believes to be "the most personal product from Hearn's pen," is also perhaps the most elusive one he ever wrote.[21] It presumably was written sometime between May and October of 1889 while Hearn was a guest of Dr. George Gould in Philadelphia. A letter addressed to Miss Bisland during this period divulges what was on his mind:

> It seems to me that with this century the great novel will pass out of fashion: three-quarters of what is written is unnecessary,—is involved

simply by obedience to effete formulas and standards. As a consequence we do not read as we used to. We read only the essential, skipping all else. The book that compels perusal of every line and word is the book of power. Create a story of which no reader can skip a single paragraph, and one has the secret of force,—if not of durability. My own hope is to do something in accordance with this idea: no descriptions, no preliminaries, no explanations—nothing but the feeling itself at highest intensity. I may fail utterly; but I think I have divined a truth which will yet be recognized and pursued by stronger minds than mine. The less material, the more force;—the subtler the power the greater, as water than land, as wind than water, as mind than wind.[22]

There is little doubt that "Karma" is Hearn's attempt to realize his hope. There are indeed "no descriptions, no preliminaries, no explanations—nothing but the feeling itself at highest intensity." As a result we have a story of mind, a story which should be considered in its entirety.

One may loosely call "Karma" a love story, though it lacks the essential paraphernalia of love. There are only two characters, a young man and a young woman, but we know little about them, not even their names. The story is not so much concerned with their love as with the suffering of one who has found his ideal love and yet may have to forsake it because of an old sin. Thus dealing with the theme of love and suffering, "Karma" is fundamentally a moral tale.

Despite her high intelligence, the heroine is a lady of artless simplicity and sincerity, whose presence inspires the hero with a strange mixture of awe and admiration. "In her beauty is the resurrection of the fairest past; in her youth, the perfection of the present;—in her girl-dreams, the promise of the To-Be." When he finally summons up the courage to ask for her hand, she demands: "as soon as you feel able to do it properly,—write out for me a short history of your life;—just write down everything you feel that you would not like me to know. Write it,—and send it. . . . And then I shall tell you whether I will marry you."

This austere command compels him to face the past squarely. He is no longer an exalted lover dreaming of the future. One may deceive his ladylove, but never his own heart. What is more, in this instance the heroine stands for "his higher self." It is also she who asked, "Would you do what you thought or felt to be wrong to please me?" So the past, now alive with his ancient sin, begins to gnaw his body and soul. To accept the past, he realizes, is to acknowledge the sin. In his dark despair the confession is sent off. Days later he finds himself before his beloved, who asks if he wishes the manuscript to be burnt: "He stood before her as before God,—morally naked as a soul in painted dreams of the Judgment Day." Dropping it into the flames, she now bids "in God's name":

> —You will go, my friend, to that man whom you wronged,—that man who still lives and loves under the delusion of your undying lie,—and you will tell him frankly, plainly, without reserve, what you have dared to confess to me. You will ask him for that child, that you may devote yourself to your own duty; and you will also ask how you may best make some reparation. Place your fortune, your abilities, your life, at that man's disposal. Even should he wish to kill you, you will have no right to resist. But I would rather,—a thousand times rather you should find death at his hands, than to know that the man I might have loved could perpetrate so black a crime, and lack the moral courage to make expiation. . . . Oh! do not let me feel I have been totally deceived in you!—prove to me that you are only a criminal, and not a coward,—that you are only weak, not utterly base. . . . But do not flatter yourself with the belief that you have anything to gain:—I am not asking a favor;—I am simply demanding a right.[23]

He obeys, and also continues to write to her, without response. A year later he is allowed to visit her, with his child. Here for the first time she receives him with open arms, as would "the Angel of his dream":

> —Suffering is strength, my beloved!—suffering is knowledge, illumination, the flame that purifies! Suffer and be strong. Never can you be happy; the evil you have wrought must always bring its pain. But that pain, dearest, I will aid you to endure;—I will shield your weakness;—I will love your boy. . . .

Thus summarized, "Karma" would seem to be either a lover's fantasy or a literary burlesque of Victorian didacticism; yet, in 1918, when it was reprinted, one reviewer went so far as to comment: ". . . typically Hearn—a sensitive, flowing, idealistic bit, with a sustained analytic tone." His only complaint was about the conclusion: "There is, however, disappointment at the end, where Hearn has sagged into sentimentalism."[24] This reviewer has missed the point entirely. He seems to expect the manipulation of the love plot to its familiar tragic denouement. But Hearn would have rejected the contrived situation for the reason that it would possibly make a conventional novel, but never the kind of romance he was really interested in creating. The reviewer regards "Karma" merely as a love story, thereby separating its two elements, love and sin, from each other. In this story, however, love comes to assert its purity in the very process of moral redemption. Love is neither what is born when sin is expiated, nor what is beyond moral

purgation. It is another side of moral awakening. In this sense love becomes inseparable from sin. Therefore, the conclusion of "Karma," it
seems, is immune to the charge of sentimentalism, being the only possible solution of the central question, love and sin. The double problem can be answered in terms of one's acceptance of the past, and this
seems to be suggested in the title itself.

The theme of "Karma" also refutes Dr. Gould's claim that it is he
who gave a soul to the romance and to its author as well. In *Concerning
Lafcadio Hearn* Dr. Gould presented his case in this manner:

> To the world and without the knowledge of its making, "Karma" must
> have seemed an illogical and even impossible thing for Hearn to have
> written. It is apparently the sole work which he ever wrote, created *de
> novo* and without the data having been found or brought to him from
> without. But it was only a seeming creation. It was only the telling, the
> coloring, that was his, as in his other tales before or after. In our long
> walks and talks in the Park at night, we wrought out the title, the datum,
> and the whole trend of the story. He rebelled, but I held him to the task,
> which he finally executed with frank and artistic loyalty. . . . I do not
> think there is exaggeration of the importance of the story, and what led
> up to its writing, in saying that it was the greatest of the turning-points
> in his life, and that directly because of it the magnificent works of the
> Japanese period were profoundly influenced through the attitude of mind
> thereby gained.[25]

In some respects the above contention seems indisputable. True,
Hearn was about this time standing at the crucial turning point in his
life; as a man of humility, he would entertain uncommon respect for
those whose minds seemed to be larger than his; and certainly, during
this period of intimate friendship, Hearn was to some extent under the
influence of his puritanical friend. But the spirit of the story is still
Hearn's own on several counts. First, its intensely moral tone con-
summates rather than contradicts the basic sentiment which has become more and more pronounced from *Stray Leaves* on, especially in
Chita and *Youma*. Second, in dealing with the lost mother theme,
"Karma" is still a continuation of *Chita* and *Youma,* whether or not
it relates to the author's own experience. Like Chita, Youma, and
Mayotte, the child in "Karma" loses his mother. For that matter, in
"Karma" the hero's love could be compared to a child's longing for his
lost mother. In his dark midnight despair he is haunted by a dream of
marriage to his beloved: ". . . Angel!—but with a woman's heart! . . .
For she only smiled at his words, at his fears, with compassionate
lovingness,—with tenderness, as of maternal indulgence for the follies

of a child. . . ." At the same time we may also note that "Karma," like *Chita,* treats of a father's search for his lost child.

To support his contention, Dr. Gould quotes a letter from Hearn which seems to concern the heroine of "Karma":

> Your objection to my idea is quite correct. I have already abandoned it. It would have to be sexual. Never could find in the tropics that magnificent type of womanhood, which in the New England girl, makes one afraid even to think about sex, while absolutely adoring the personality. Perfect natures inspire a love that is a fear. I don't think any love is noble without it.[26]

Even this sexual idealism is by no means novel to the reader who has been familiar with the heroic stature of Youma or more specifically with Hearn's persistent interest in the spectral love theme. In one sense the heroine of "Karma" is not so much a human character as a human embodiment of divine femininity. This may account for that dreamlike, haunting atmosphere of "Karma" as a whole, an atmosphere which, we have observed, surrounds many of his tales of spectral love. Note how the heroine of "Karma" is transformed, toward the end of the story: "For the first time their lips touched. . . . She had become again the Angel of his dream." Hearn's goddess-like heroine, as we shall see later, in his version of the Eternal Feminine. She personifies what he termed the age-old Western tradition of the Eternal Feminine, and she is the literary descendant of those celebrated, unearthly beauties of Homer, Dante, Petrarch, Spenser, Goethe, and many others. Ideationally too, then, "Karma" is quite Hearn's own, contrary to Dr. Gould's contention.

In reference to Hugo's romances, Stevenson once wrote: ". . . the moral significance, with Hugo, is of the essence of the romance; it is the organizing principle." [27] The statement, with little modification, also holds true for Hearn's three romances. It seems to be no mere coincidence that upon publication of *Chita,* one reviewer called its author "the American Victor Hugo." [28] In *Chita, Youma,* and "Karma," Hearn attempted to concretize idealism, that which he considered the highest function of art, "only to reach and touch that kindred *something* in another which the Christian calls Soul,—the Pantheist, God,— the philosopher, the Unknowable." No matter how nobly inspired, it must be said, Hearn fell far short of his high ideal. Indeed his life ambition to create romances of this kind was never altogether realized. Many of his romances, indeed, remained unborn. It is said that "Lys," the last chapter of *Two Years in the French West Indies,* hardly retains what was in the original form, "170 pages of minutely written MS." When *Harper's* rejected this original, which supposedly deals with a girl from the Tropics dying in the northern climate, it also killed off "Nini," its companion piece about the northern mind's capitulation to the tropics.[29] In the vein of "Karma," which was first turned down by *Harper's,* and subsequently accepted by *Lippincott's,* Hearn also planned two more pieces, "Ruth" and "The Mother of God," neither of which had the luck of "Karma." [30]

So "Karma" has remained the last of Hearn's romances. In spite of his dreams, in spite of all his efforts, no romance was created out of his Japanese years. The wider his reputation as a writer on Japan, the more painful his sense of failure grew. In his fifth year in Japan, Hearn confided to his friend Chamberlain:

> I must do better some day with something, or acknowledge myself a dead failure. I really think I have stored away in me somewhere powers larger than those I have yet been able to use. Of course I don't mean that I have any hidden wisdom, or anything of that sort; but I believe I have some power to reach the public emotionally, if conditions allow.
>
> One little story which would never die, might suffice,—or a volume of little stories. Stories, fiction: that is all the public care about. Not essays, however clever,—nor vagaries, nor travels,—but stories about something common to all life under the sun. And this is just the very hardest of all earthly things to do. I might write an essay on some topic of which I am now quite ignorant,—by studying the subject for the necessary time. But a story cannot be written by the help of study at all: it must come from outside. It must be a "sensation" in one's own life,—and not peculiar to any life or any place or time.[31]

In another letter to the same friend, written a few months later, Hearn was still clinging to his old dream, "evolutional fiction." "Unfortunately," said he, "poor I have not the constructive art necessary to attempt anything of the kind—not yet! Perhaps in twenty years more." [32] Again in 1897, when his good friend Mitchell McDonald suggested that he try his hand at fiction, Hearn gave two reasons for his inability to do so. They are, first, his "little knowledge of life," an obstacle to his understanding of the "artificial and complex growth of modern society," and second, his alienation from the source of his artistic material, life itself. In the same letter Hearn made a counter suggestion; his friend, a man of the world and a foreigner living in a Japanese open port, should furnish him with "six little stories,"—in the course of three years —about the life of the open port in the era of Meiji.[33]

Within a few years death came and carried him away with all his dreams and projects. To explain his failure one may as well begin with Hearn's works themselves. As his three romances indicate, because of his growing subjectivity he is incapable of creating a variety of characters, of weaving the complex structure that his theme demands, and of dramatizing what he has to say. What Hearn lacks is the dramatic faculty vital to any writer, whether in fiction or romance. This seems to be what he meant in the above letter when he said that "I have not the constructive art necessary to attempt anything of the kind." Although he added hopefully, ". . . not yet! Perhaps in twenty years more," it is something one is born with, certainly not to be acquired. This none knew better than Hearn. Years before, in Martinique, he had touched on the issue. He said then, "I am convinced I have no *creative* talent, no constructive ability for the manufacture of fiction. I cannot write a story. Even *Chita* was not a story: it was a mere crystallization of sensations into symmetrical shape. . . ." [34] Still, he could not accept his own verdict. Perhaps this is a vanity every artist must have, and Hearn was but one of many similar cases in the world of art. It is only pathetic that in his ambition there is more of resignation than of confidence.

There remains one singular fact—that despite all his dreams no romance was created out of his Japanese years. Granted that constructive imagination was absent in him, Hearn might still have produced something in the manner of *Chita, Youma,* or "Karma." There may be many possible ways of explaining his failure to do so, but every one of them must get down to three fundamental points. First, there is Hearn's increasingly exclusive concept of the romance itself, namely "only the essential," which not only narrowed his total perspective of modern fiction but also hindered the natural flow of his own creative urge. Any attempt to grasp directly only the essential or the ultimate will inevitably result in dissolving the very stuff of fiction. Second, Hearn's mentality is essentially sensitive, and responds exceedingly to his changing physical and cultural milieu. Note his frequent qualifications, such as "if conditions allow" or "I think, under certain conditions I can find power to please,—just as a certain wind instrument will play of its own accord if placed in a fitting current of air." [35] Of course, Hearn is not merely responsive to his milieu, but always intent upon transmuting his own sensations or impressions into some significant philosophical themes. Hence his master-passion, the problem of the influence of environment on the human mind, manifest in *Chita* and *Youma,* and admittedly the central theme of those unborn romances like "Lys" and

"Nini," and probably also of his projected stories about the life of the open port in Japan. It is highly possible that, as a result of his being engrossed in philosophical study, this master-passion was sublimated in his concern with the question of man and nature, one of his major philosophical themes.

Third, there is Hearn's typically romantic attitude toward life and art. As art was to him always the completion of life, so was life the starting point of his art. Whenever the reciprocity between life and art was established he was still capable of producing *Chita, Youma,* and "Karma." From this point of view it could be said that Japan helped to curb the natural flow of his creative mind. His fourteen-year-long sojourn in Japan meant a fatal blow to the further realization of his ambition in fiction. Against his will, but because of his love, Hearn became a settler in that lotus land. Many letters he wrote from Japan to his friends there and elsewhere record his nostalgic outcry for his own world, where, so far as he was concerned, art and life could be reciprocal, if not in complete harmony. In his letter to McDonald already mentioned, Hearn laid bare his heart: ". . . there is nothing in this world nearly as wonderful as life itself. All real life is a marvel— but in Japan a marvel that is hidden as much as possible—especially hidden from dangerous characters like Lafcadio Hearn." [36] It must be for this reason that he called himself a "caged cicada."

Complete harmony between art and life is usually the artist's dream. Many a time he must sacrifice life if he is to remain an artist. Of art's austerity Hearn was not unaware even in that moment of exuberant ambition when he made his holy pledge nearly twenty-five years before: "I should feel also that the Unknowable had selected me for a mouth-piece, for a medium of utterance, in the holy cycling of its eternal purpose." When writing from Martinique, too, he did not lose confidence: "I am not yet discouraged into the belief that my mind has no value whatever." [37] After his long period of groping for the will of the Unknowable, he finally concluded that the romance was not his medium of utterance, and that his old ambition in fiction was a sad chapter in his career. But Hearn might well have been grateful for what made him a caged cicada, because as a result he was driven back to his destined role of translator or discoverer rather than of artificer, and was forced to explore all the more intensely that seemingly narrow but unfathomably dark and deep world of the human psyche. What he created out of this caged life seems, ironically, of more permanent value than his dreamed-of "little story which would never die."

V

"To
Be
a
Literary
Columbus"

Hearn's
Literary
Exoticism

Hearn's New Orleans period came to an abrupt end early in June 1887 with his departure from that city, to which he had come aboard the *Thompson Dean* almost ten years before. As his immediate motivation Miss Bisland points out the success of *Chita,* that enabled him to "realize his long-nourished dream of penetrating farther into the tropics." [1] But to those who have followed him since his birth on a coastal isle of Greece, his departure from New Orleans is but another chapter in his long series of wanderings. Not long after his arrival in New Orleans, Hearn wrote to H. E. Krehbiel, his old friend in Cincinnati:

I have become weary of this Southern atmosphere with its lazy heat and voluptuous odours, and have a vague desire to see something else,—to do something else.

I am certainly going somewhere. But when? I don't know. I only know that there are many ships sailing to and fro; and that some day I shall creep under the shadow of a sail and lie down on a coil of rope, and sail away. And when they shall ask me, saying, "Whither, O stranger, dost thou desire to go?—and at what port dost thou desire to disembark?"—then I shall only answer in a dreamful way, "Sail on, O Mariner, anywhere, everywhere;—I don't know!" [2]

These words may echo Baudelaire's prose poems, "Le Port," "L'Invitation au voyage," and especially his "Any where out of the world," which ends, "N'importe où! N'importe où! pourvu que ce soit hors de ce monde!" But it is important to remember that poetic exoticism comes naturally to Hearn. More important still is the fact that he accepted his "insatiable wanderlust" as hereditary and attributed it to the gypsy blood reputedly running in the family. Or, as he put it more symbolically in his prose poem, "A Ghost," he believed himself to be

> . . . the civilized nomad, whose wanderings are not prompted by hope of gain, nor determined by pleasure, but simply compelled by certain necessities of his being,—the man whose inner secret nature is totally at variance with the stable conditions of a society to which he belongs only by accident.

This kind of nomadism has no rational source, he says. It may be traced back to some ancestral habit—"self-evident hereditary tendencies," whether or not they be "some pre-existent larval aspiration." So he must wander from one place to another. When "the first vague charm, the first sunny illusion of some fair city" is overshadowed by "some slow solid sharpening of details," he becomes once again the captive of another wave of wanderlust. Finally a day comes when there is no consolation for the pain of monotony, ". . . and you feel that in order to live you must decide,—regardless of result,—to shake forever from your feet the familiar dust of that place. . . ." [3] Nothing could better explain Hearn's sudden departure from New Orleans—at least psychologically. Symbolically speaking, however, it was his continuation of the previous journey to the "Gate of the Tropics" (so Hearn called New Orleans), for the destination of this southward journey was the West Indies. In this fulfillment of his "long-nourished dream of penetrating farther into the tropics" there is something of inevitability.

It is no wonder that Hearn entertained his own theory of travel. In one of his early *Item* editorials he pondered on the significance of travel in American literature. Travel, he suggested, must have a "Bohemian" touch, first of all. Undertaken not for material gains but for artistic purposes, it could be profitable both for one's self and for the land and the people visited.[4] Indeed, behind him there was a horde of French Romantics from Chateaubriand down to Loti, all enthusiastic travelers, each contributing to the tradition of modern French literary exoticism. Also behind him there was a series of travel sketches from his early work, those thirteen "Ozias Midwinter" letters, to his latest, "Floridian Reveries." Even in his Ozias Midwinter letters Hearn no longer pretended to be a political reporter from the Cincinnati *Commercial.*[5] His interest was really literary, as may be seen in the pseudonym, Ozias Midwinter, borrowed from Wilkie Collins' *Armadale,* and in the fact that the last two pieces of the series touching on Louisiana politics were written only under a virtual ultimatum from Cincinnati. The remaining letters deal with the beauties of the great river, the glorious Southern sunsets, New Orleans legends, Creole lore, and the like. In the funeral of the great Confederate general, N. B. Forrest, Hearn noted the sad procession of the old to the new South. It seems that he could not get rid of this new dimension of time itself. In the Crescent City, wrote Hearn upon arriving there, the foreign traveler never fails to find "some memory of his home—some recollection of his Fatherland—some remembrance of something he loves." "I never beheld anything so beautiful and so sad," he wrote to Henry Watkin,

> When I saw it first—sunrise over Louisiana—the tears sprang to my eyes. It was like young death,—a dead bride crowned with orange flowers,—a dead face that asked for a kiss. I cannot say how fair and rich and beautiful this dead South is. It has fascinated me. I have resolved to live in it.

The same feeling he did not hesitate to repeat in one of his news letters: "O, fair paradise of the South, if still so lovely in thy ruins, what must thou have been in the great day of thy greatest glory!"[6] His "Ozias Midwinter" letters are therefore the letters home from an artist-traveler's exploration into the paradise of the South, under the shadow of time. Indeed, his journey down the Mississippi seems to suggest the double direction of his exoticism, not only into space but also into time, in search of their common origin.

Only in a general sense could *Leaves from the Diary of an Impressionist* be called a book of travel, being a collection of sketches about Florida, essays on Creole women in New Orleans and the West Indies, and Arabian subjects. Nor would it be appropriate to deal with it as such, since Hearn for some reason failed to carry out his initial plan.[7] Yet, there is no doubt that the four sketches, "To the Fountain of Youth," "A Tropical Intermezzo," "A Name in the Plaza," and "Vultur Aura," were intended to form the center of this projected book. They are mostly the product of Hearn's journey to Florida, undertaken in the early summer of 1885—with Charles Johnson, his old Cincinnati colleague. Yet, it is evident that Hearn has no intention of attempting any ordinary type of travel sketch. His motto, the quotation from Eugène

Delacroix, makes this clear: ". . . Jeune artiste, tu attends un sujet? Tout est sujet; le sujet c'est toi-même: ce sont tes impressions, tes émotions devant la nature. C'est toi qu'il faut regarder, et non autour de toi."

Each of these four pieces has its central concern. But when they are taken together we may discover the continuation of Hearn's old theme, the search for paradise in the heart of nature under the shadow of time, and something of its consequence. "To the Fountain of Youth" is a hymn to the divinity of nature and the holiness of beauty, a hymn recited by a pilgrim in search of the legendary Fountain of Youth—in the sanctum of nature. It is Hearn's version of man's eternal quest for the garden of Hesperus, as he aptly named it. Its logical sequel, so to speak, "A Tropical Intermezzo," is a tale told in the form of confession by a dying wanderer from the Spanish Americas. As a young warrior, he wanders one night alone into "the dale of fountains," where he becomes a lover of the woman of the dale. "Verily," says he, "it was the Eden-garden, the Paradise of Eve." Yet, unable to resist "the sound of the trumpet summoning him," he strays, in spite of her previous warning (*"Lest the shadows lay hold upon thee"*), beyond the dale of bliss only to lose it and its apotheosis as well. Then begins his long futile search for her. In both pieces there is seen the fate of man seeking "sweet pantheism." The lost Eden symbolizes the fate of every Rip van Winkle who returns to the human world, the world of time.

Time remains supreme in "Vultur Aura." Through the eyes of a divine vulture circling high above Saint John of the Pines, the ancient Spanish fort, Hearn muses on the passing caravan of races, nations, and civilizations. Man may, Hearn seems to suggest in "A Name in the Plaza," transcend time only by discovering where time begins. In quest of the mystery of a "blonde name" on the white stone in the plaza Hearn wanders "from the Present into the Unknown," the unrecognizable past, and feels "the presence of its ghost." This dream-piece is concerned with the mystery of our memory, whose origin must be traced back beyond our human realm. It anticipates his later belief that time crosses many bournes of existence. The center of "Floridian Reveries" has as its theme man's search for the Garden of Eden, where man and nature are one, and his tragedy when they are divorced. That which both harmonizes and divorces them is the mystery of time. In this, "Floridian Reveries" already foreshadows his *Two Years in the French West Indies*.

As we know, Hearn's *Two Years* (1890) grew out of his two sojourns in the West Indies, one brief, from July to September 1887, and the other much longer, from October 1887 to May 1889. The volume consists of the head piece "A Midsummer Trip to the Tropics" and the fourteen seemingly independent pieces, comprising "Martinique Sketches." Some of these chapters appeared in *Harper's*, and the book itself was not completed until after his return to the United States.[8] In spite of this the book has a unity of impression and thought, as he indicates in the preface:

> During such hasty journeying it is scarcely possible for a writer to at-
> tempt anything more serious than a mere reflection of the personal experi-
> ences undergone: and, in spite of sundry justifiable departures from
> simple note-making, this paper is offered only as an effort to record the
> visual and emotional impressions of the moment.[9]

These words could also be applied to his previous project; but what separates *Two Years* from the earlier book is its appreciable degree of structural unity. The book begins and ends in New York Harbor, the voyage coming full circle. As expectation yields to ecstasy, and then to apprehension, the whole voyage turns out to be a sort of pilgrimage. Besides this cyclic pattern, there is structural grouping among the chapters. The early ones are altogether concerned with descriptions or sketches, whereas the narrative quality comes to dominate the later chapters, such as " 'Ti Canotié" (VIII), "Ma Bonne" (XI), " 'Pa combiné, chè!' " (XII), "Yé" (XIII), and "Lys" (XIV). The gradual shift from the descriptive to the narrative or dramatic corresponds with that from the "visual" to the "emotional." As this change develops, the narrator also emerges from that impersonal realm, and now more personally weaves sketches, legends, and episodes into one fabric of his own reflection. The tropical world steals into the mind by way of the five senses. The whole process is much as we might expect: "Tropical nature is indeed an enchantress; but she does more than bewitch, she transforms body and soul."[10]

Structurally, the initial piece, "A Midsummer Trip to the Tropics," a complete account of Hearn's first West Indian voyage in 1887, serves the total effect of the book by contrast with the ensuing "Martinique Sketches." A travel sketch done by a sensitive observer, it is open-eyed but never emotionally involved. Certainly this is one way of writing travel sketches, but Hearn seems sceptical of its merit. We almost suspect that it is his real intent to demonstrate what a travel sketch could be without one's growing awareness and emotional commitment. Hearn seems to believe that the emotional approach must complete the intellectual, if travel writing is to be genuine art. In this respect "Martinique Sketches" is the main part of the drama, whereas the opening piece serves as a prolog. Their combined effect is that of appearance and reality juxtaposed.

Chapter VII, "La Pelée," functions as the structural center or peak of the entire volume, and the two groups of chapters mentioned above stand at either side of the very summit of Mt. Pelée. The six chapters up to this point are largely descriptive, while the ensuing seven are basically dramatic. The first group is concerned primarily with the natural, in the sense that nature and man are in harmony, or that man is merely part of nature; and the second, with the human, in the sense that a conflict develops between nature and man. This is another indication that the basic theme of the book progresses along the structural line. The parallel between the structural and the thematic can be illustrated in several sharply distinct treatments of Mt. Pelée. At first it is described this way:

> The semicircular sweep of the harbor, dominated by the eternally veiled summit of the Montagne Pelée (misnamed, since it is green to the very clouds), from which the land slopes down on either hand to the sea by gigantic undulations, is one of the fairest sights that human eye can gaze upon.[11]

The mountain is presented as the center of the island scene. There is nothing personal in this objective description. Later, however, Mt. Pelée assumes the pose of a native woman:

> . . . This evening, as I write, La Pelée is more heavily coiffed than is her wont. Of purple and lilac cloud the coiffure is,—a magnificent Madras, yellow-banded by the sinking sun. La Pelée is in *costume de fête,* like a *capresse* attired for a baptism or a ball; and in her phantom turban one great star glimmers for a brooch.[12]

The approach has become more human; yet his light touch and volatile simile connote nothing serious. All is in a holiday mood.

In contrast with these two scenes, typical of "A Midsummer Trip," the chapter, "La Pelée," begins in an ominous tone, describing how the first attempt at colonization of the island had to be abandoned due to those features "too rugged and too mountainous," and also the "prodigious number of serpents which covered its soil." Gradually we are drawn nearer to reality as Hearn scales the mountain and makes a thoroughly impersonal observation of the volcanic lake near its summit:

> The committee of investigation in 1851 found the temperature of the lake, in spite of a north wind, 20.5 Centigrade, while that of the air was

but 19 (about 69 F. for the water, and 66.2 for the air). The depth in the centre is over six feet; the average is scarcely four.[13]

We are now at the point of emotional zero. But the total effect is all the more tremendous, when immediately after this flat understatement, the meaning of the drama suddenly unfolds at the moment when Hearn and his party conquer the summit:

> At the beginning, while gazing south, east, west, to the rim of the world, all laughed, shouted, interchanged the quick delight of new impressions: every face was radiant. . . . Now all look serious;—none speak. The first physical joy of finding oneself on this point in violent air, exalted above the hills, soon yields to other emotions inspired by the mighty vision and the colossal peace of the heights. Dominating all, I think, is the consciousness of the awful antiquity of what one is looking upon,—such a sensation, perhaps, as of old found utterance in that tremendous question of the Book of Job:—*"Wast thou brought forth before the hills?"* . . . And the blue multitude of the peaks, the perpetual congregation of the mornes, seem to chorus in the vast resplendence,—telling of Nature's eternal youth, and the passionless permanence of that about us and beyond us and beneath,—until something like the fullness of a great grief begins to weigh at the heart. . . . For all this astonishment of beauty, all this majesty of light and form and color, will surely endure,—marvellous as now, after we shall have lain down to sleep where no dreams come, and may never arise from the dust of our rest to look upon it.[14]

Where heaven and earth meet, man finds his peace in the cosmic symbolism for which the height of the mountain stands,—far beyond the tragic schism between nature and man, and even beyond their primitive harmony. Then in the closing chapter where we leave behind the "Pays des Revenants," Mt. Pelée reappears:

> Even Pelée wears only her very lightest head-dress of gauze; and all the wrinklings of her green robe take unfamiliar tenderness of tint from the early sun.[15]

We are back to the earlier position, but no longer the same after our voyage to reality. This series of descriptions of Mt. Pelée, geographically the center of the island, serves as the basic pattern of a slow though deliberate approach toward what is real and ultimate.

On the surface, the theme of *Two Years* is predominantly sociological, being concerned with the tragic contact between the colored natives and the white colonists, and also between the primitive and the civilized worlds. But going a step further, we recognize something more fundamental. Hearn's ultimate interest centers on the antipodal relationship between nature and man. One approach is represented by the natives; the other by the whites. The first half of the book is primarily a study of the native approach toward nature, whereas the second half presents a dramatic conflict between nature and the civilized race. Quite contrary to our expectation, Hearn becomes more and more hesitant about judging between these two approaches. Having come to know something of nature's destructive force, he seems to feel no longer comfortable with his earlier romantic pantheism. His new awareness is adumbrated in the third chapter, "Un Revenant," a story about the heroic missionary struggle of Père Labat. Of the outcome of Père Labat's futile efforts in the face of nature, Hearn writes: ". . . all that ephemeral man has had power to change has been changed,—ideas, morals, beliefs, the whole social fabric. But the eternal summer remains." [16] The eighth chapter, " 'Ti Canotié," on the other hand, relates a pathetic story of two native divers, Maximilien and Stéphane. After a long drift on the sea Maximilien is dying:

> A breeze was rising;—Maximilien felt it blowing upon him. All at once it seemed to him that he had ceased to be afraid,—that he did not care what might happen. He thought about a cricket he had one day watched in the harbor, drifting out with the tide, on an atom of dead bark,—and he wondered what had become of it. Then he understood that he himself was the cricket,—still alive. But some boy had found him and pulled off his legs. There they were,—his own legs, pressing against him: he could still feel the aching where they had been pulled off; and they had been dead so long they were now quite cold. . . . It was certainly Stéphane who had pulled them off. . .
> The water was talking to him. It was saying the same thing over and over again,—louder each time, as if it thought he could not hear. But he heard it very well:—"*Bon-Dié, li conm vent . . . li ka touché nou . . . nou pa save ouè li.*" (But why had the Bon-Dié shaken the wind?) "*Li pa ka tini zié,*" answered the water. . . . *Ouille!*—He might all the same care not to upset folks in the sea! . . . *Mi!* . . .[17]

This passage focuses on the peace-in-death where the dying boy identifies himself with a cricket. It is the peace promised only in passivity, a kind of bliss, no matter how enviable, which Hearn can no longer share with the native. They may be able to bypass time to be in harmony with nature, for time means too little to their world, where only "the eternal summer remains." The tropical time is indeed the present eternal, void of shadow and depth. Where time stands still, they are free from the perennial conflict between life and art, nature and society, emotion and thought. But for one born into the world of time, escape from it is the greatest possible sacrifice. Just as time is human, Hearn is human—perhaps too human, or too Western, to forsake his own birth-right.[18] This tragic possibility, escape from the world of time at the sacrifice of his own heritage, is what Hearn has discovered at the equatorial terminus of his southward flight.

The struggle between man and nature cannot be so easily won; for it is at heart the drama of temptation, which, as usual with Hearn, must come in the guise of a Circe rather than a Mephestopheles. All his senses, one after another, become inert before her mesmerism. He becomes oblivious to his burden of knowledge and his world of civilization. This final moment of temptation is personally and yet symbolically dramatized in the twelfth chapter, " 'Pa combiné, chè!' " To Hearn's friend Félicien, an ailing white youth, his native lover whispers: *"Si ou ainmein moin, pa combiné—non!"* Hearn comments:

> And in her strange exotic beauty, her savage grace, her supple caress, the velvet witchery of her eyes,—it seemed to me that I beheld a something imaged, not of herself, nor of the moment only,—a something weirdly sensuous: the Spirit of tropic Nature made golden flesh, and murmuring to each lured wanderer:—*"If thou wouldst love me, do not think!"* [19]

Earlier she had implored Hearn ". . . you are his friend! why do you let him think? It is thinking that will prevent him getting well." The youth's illness is a familiar symptom accompanying his total conversion to the world of nature. It is a soul's struggle for all or nothing, a struggle which knows no compromise. Once out of this drama of temptation, one has no choice. He must return to the world he is destined for. This seems to be the real meaning of Hearn's own flight from the tropics.

The very fact that the whole drama reaches its climax near the end of *Two Years* may suggest the book's thematic design and Hearn's climatic obsession. In the closing chapter, "Lys," both combine so as to create a sense of dramatic irony. There the author's return home coincides with Lys's visit to New York. This West Indian maiden is leaving her homeland forever to be a governess! No matter how absurd the whole situation sounds, it is going to be surely another rehearsal of that bitter dilemma from which he has narrowly escaped. Foreseeing her future full of tragic possibilities, Hearn cannot resist deep compassion toward her. The last paragraph of *Two Years* is the author's mental address to Lys, a child of nature, standing alone in the mighty perspective of New York:

> Thou knowest it not, this gloom about us, little maiden;—'tis only a magical dusk we are entering,—only that mystic dimness in which mir-

acles must be wrought! . . . See the marvellous shapes uprising,—the immensities, the astonishments! And other greater wonders thou wilt behold in a little while, when we shall have become lost to each other forever in the surging of the City's million-hearted life! . . . 'Tis all shadow here, thou sayest?—Ay, 'tis twilight, verily, by contrast with that glory out of which thou comest, Lys—twilight only,—but the Twilight of the Gods! . . . *Adié, chèl—Bon-Dié ké béni ou!* . . .[20]

Hearn's irony is unmistakable in the juxtaposition of these two figures, and also in the coinciding of Lys's arrival and with his own return.[21] His southward flight finally proved to be a pilgrimage, but when this pilgrimage terminated as a drama of temptation, Hearn had to bid farewell to the heart of the tropics. His farewell, however, was no more than a gesture of flight, because it meant simply the beginning of another flight. In his "twilight only,—but the Twilight of the Gods! . . ." there is already a shadow of uncertainty. As his truce with his own world turned out to be only temporary, his presentiment came true also. To settle in America, Hearn must have felt, would be a compromise, not a reconciliation. He had to continue pursuing the destined pattern for "the civilized nomad." No sooner was *Two Years* published (March 1890) than he was on his long journey to the East across the Pacific.

One thing likely to be forgotten is that Hearn never intended to remain long in Japan. His original plan was to stay there just long enough to write a series of articles on "The New Civilization in Japan," as proposed by *Harper's*. After contemplating the general scheme of this new project, Hearn wrote to William Patten, art editor of *Harper's*:

> In attempting a book upon a country so well trodden as Japan, I could not hope—nor would I consider it prudent attempting,—to discover totally new things, but only to consider things in a totally new way, so far as possible. I would put as much *life* and *colour* especially into such a book, as I could, and attempt to interpret the former rather through vivid sensation given to the reader, than by any account or explanations such as may be found in other writers, whether travellers or scholars. Such a book would therefore be essentially a volume of Sketches brief for the most part,—each one reflecting a peculiar phase of life. Until one is upon the ground, it would not be possible to lay down a decided plan of work; but I have drawn up a tentative list of subjects which I think should form part of such a book,—several of which have not been, to the best of my belief, previously treated in any *popular* book on Japan.

Then Hearn lists "First impressions: climate and scenery; the poetry of nature in Japan," and fifteen other possible subjects. The letter continues:

But the titles of the real chapters, I would make altogether romantic—possibly Japanese; and would attempt nothing really in the shape of essays. A subject would be considered solely in the relation of personal experiences bearing upon it, from which relation anything bordering upon commonplace narrative would be carefully excluded. The studied aim would be to create, in the minds of the readers, a vivid impression of *living* in Japan,—not simply as an observer but as one taking part in the daily existence of the common people, and *thinking with their thoughts*. Whenever possible a narrative would be made at least as entertaining as a short story.

I would also expect to prepare a novelette, toward the latter part of my stay, depicting Japanese feeling.

This is about the best suggestion I can at present offer regarding the plan of the book.

And Hearn's postscript is:

I should expect to make a volume containing quite as much text as the West Indian book—in the neighbourhood of five hundred pages. In another form, this amount of text would, in larger type and a different setting, suffice for a very much handsomer volume.[22]

As he did in New Orleans and Martinique, Hearn stayed longer than initially intended—this time until his death, in spite of his recurring wanderlust. Of the Land of the Rising Sun he wrote some dozen books, instead of one like his West Indian volume. Or perhaps it is more appropriate to say that the one grew into the dozen. The development is essentially organic, and it is possible to treat all his Japanese books as a unit. Taken as a whole, his Japanese books show a singular parallel to his *Two Years,* though they are incomparably superior in quantity and quality. *Glimpses of Unfamiliar Japan,* in two volumes, is the "one" that Hearn originally proposed to write on Japan, as "A Midsummer Trip to the Tropics" was the one he had intended on the West Indies. The relationship between this collection of twenty-seven sketches and the rest of his Japanese books is similar to that between "A Midsummer Trip to the Tropics" and "Martinique Sketches," which together comprise *Two Years.* This suggests the necessity of considering each individual work as related to a whole composed of all the Japanese books.

Glimpses (1894), which Hearn called only an introductory book, is a record of the traveling artist's self-initiation into the island country, old and yet so new, during the period of 1890–94. As his letter to William Patten indicates, Hearn was determined to note down anything Japanese "solely in the relation of personal experiences." There is little attempt "in the shape of essays"; instead, *Glimpses,* for the most part, consists of sketches with varying degrees of detail and a few legends. The further he moved from his original plan to describe the new civilization in Japan, however, the more deeply he ventured into the ancient inland region. This process of deviation renders *Glimpses* an account of Hearn's personal involvement with the intricacies of native life. Nor does it lack the familiar mood of the traveler, a sense of excitement and exhilaration. For this reason, perhaps, *Glimpses* retains the vivid realism and irresistible charm rarely found together in globe-trotters' reports from Japan.

Although *Glimpses* is highly successful as an artist-teacher's sensitive chronicle of impressions and observations of things, places and people, it does lack rich variety, original reflections, and intellectual depth, all so characteristic of its successors. Between *Glimpses* and even *Out of the East* (1895), his second Japanese book, there is a sharp change. Here, for the first time, Hearn is taking a decisively inward turn. Beginning with "The Dream of Summer Day," where he weaves his own feelings into the celebrated legend of a Japanese Rip van Winkle, we go through an alternation of dark disillusionment and ecstatic illumination. A passage near the end of the book indicates the beginning of another cycle:

> Five years, all spent far away from treaty ports, slowly flitted by before I saw the Jizō-Dō again. Many changes had taken place both without and within me during that time. The beautiful illusion of Japan, the almost weird charm that comes with one's first entrance into her magical atmosphere, had, indeed, stayed with me very long, but had totally faded out at last. I had learned to see the Far East without its glamour.[23]

By this time Hearn's involvement with the life of Japan has become too complicated for any easy, irresponsible withdrawal. He has now ceased to be a mere traveler gathering sundry impressions and observations on the surface. It is a renewal of his old pattern, a conflict of life and art, which we have already seen in his prolonged sojourn in New Orleans and Martinique. The best he can do now is to create art out of the inevitable that is life. The volumes that followed *Out of the East* are, with no exceptions, the letters home from his inward voyage into the heart of Japan.

Hearn's attempt to synthesize his art and thought and to express the totality of his existence in contact with Japan is evident in the thoroughness of his approach. He makes free use of four genres: sketches, essays, legends, and prose poems or fantastics. This is the most basic structural characteristic that distinguishes Hearn from other writers on Japan. Sketches of his quality could have been written by Kipling or Loti; essays of equal excellence might have been done by Chamberlain or Lowell; legends and tales of the same exquisiteness might also have been rendered by other hands. But in creating those highly personal prose poems and blending all these four genres into one organic whole, Hearn is unique.

The titles of the three books following *Glimpses*—*Out of the East: Reveries and Studies in New Japan* (1895); *Kokoro: Hints and Echoes of Japanese Inner Life* (1896); *Gleanings in Buddha-Fields: Studies of Hand and Soul in the Far East* (1897)—reveal the general trend of Hearn's thought. The singular charm of Shinto finally surrendered to Buddhism. His essays on Buddhism, such as "The Stone Buddha," "The Idea of Preëxistence," and "Nirvana," amply document the steady progression of his mind, which was seeking intensely the meaning of the past, as suggested in "Jiujutsu," "A Conservative," and "Some Thoughts on Ancestor-Worship." The union of evolutionism and Buddhism, foreseen long before, came to its fruition in *Exotics and Retrospectives* (1898), the theoretical zenith of all his Japanese books. In its preface Hearn wrote:

> To any really scientific imagination, the curious analogy existing between certain teachings of evolutional psychology and certain teachings of Eastern faith,—particularly the Buddhist doctrine that all sense-life is Karma, and all substance only the phenomenal result of acts and thoughts,— might have suggested something much more significant than my cluster of *Retrospectives*. These are offered merely as intimations of a truth incomparably less difficult to recognize than to define.

The volume, divided into two parts, each dealing with Buddhism and evolutionism, is the best refutation of the popular notion that Hearn is but a writer of Japanese travel sketches.

The opening piece, "Fuji-no-Yama," not only illustrates the way he can fuse thought and emotion into a seemingly simple sketch, but also reveals something of a growing awareness in all his Japanese books. To the distant observer, he writes, Mt. Fuji appears with

> . . . a symmetry of beautiful bending lines with a curve like the curve of a cable stretched over a space too wide to allow of pulling taut. (This comparison did not at once suggest itself: the first impression given me by the grace of those lines was an impression of femininity;—I found myself thinking of some exquisite sloping of shoulders towards the neck.) [24]

To the climber, on the other hand:

Fuji has ceased to be blue of any shade. It is black,—charcoal-black,—a frightful extinct heap of visible ashes and cinders and slaggy lava. . . . most of the green has disappeared. Likewise all of the illusion. The tremendous naked black reality,—always becoming more sharply, more grimly, more atrociously defined,—is a stupefaction, a nightmare. . . . Above—miles above—the snow patches glare and gleam of white teeth I once saw in a skull,—a woman's skull,—otherwise burnt to a sooty crisp.[25]

To Hearn, entering Yokohama in the spring of 1890, the mountain revealed still another aspect:

Then with a delicious shock of surprise I see something for which I had been looking,—far exceeding all anticipation—but so ghostly, so dream white against the morning blue, that I did not observe it at the first glance: an exquisite snowy cone towering above all other visible things—Fujiyama! Its base, the same tint as the distances, I cannot see—only the perfect crown, seeming to hang in the sky like a delicate film,—a phantom.[26]

The whole process, dramatically staged in these three examples, corresponds with that of Hearn's previous experience with Mt. Pelée. Apart from the ultimate significance of his recurring mountain symbolism and femininity reference, the irony implied in the difference between appearance and reality seems to have at least two levels of meaning. First, it reflects the alternation of expectation and disappointment which Hearn actually underwent in relation to Japan. But more than this, it suggests something of his own metaphysical quest. In this sense even the Japanese proverb which heads the Fuji-no-Yama chapter: "Kité mirébe, Sahodo madé nashi, Fuji no Yama!" ("Seen on close approach, the mountain of Fuji does not come up to expectation") signifies more than it seems to at first. With Hearn, disillusionment was always the point of another departure and another cycle of pilgrimage; the process of disillusionment itself was the intimation of enlightenment. While on the summit of Fuji, noting that Shinto and Buddhism were in a timeless marriage, he once again felt the familiar sense of sublime peace: ". . . and there is a silence that I remember from West Indian days: the Peace of High Places." From all this we may infer that Mt. Fuji, thematically as well as structurally, assumes the same role in Hearn's Japan as Mt. Pelée does in his West Indies.

Winding up *Out of the East, Kokoro,* and *Gleanings in Buddha-Fields,* which constitute the first group, *Exotics and Retrospectives* marks the best of Hearn's theoretical approach. Yet, how intensely personal his vision could become even at that moment, we have observed. In the second group, *In Ghostly Japan* (1899), *Shadowings* (1900), *A Japanese Miscellany* (1901), and *Kotto* (1902), his doctrinal method, whether Buddhist or evolutionary, is conspicuously absent. In these books Hearn has reached the point where retrospection vies with introspection. The tone is clearly suggested in the Japanese poem he quotes at the outset of *In Ghostly Japan:* "Yoru bakari Miru mono narito Omou-nayo! Hiru saë yumé no Ukiyo nari-kéri" ("Think not that dreams appear to the dreamer only at night: the dream of this world of pain appears to us even by day"). Although now and then Hearn dwells on miscellaneous human subjects, his vision passes beyond the human realm and tries to probe into the world beyond. As a result we have, on the one hand, an increasing number of Japanese legends invariably haunted with ghostly shadows, and on the other, a series of insect studies with bizarre speculations about their symbolic bearing upon human existence. Against this background his fantasies seem full of psychic shock and horror.

Nowhere is this sense of *frisson* expressed more powerfully than in "Fragment," the first piece of *In Ghostly Japan.* It is a story about a young pilgrim who, under the guidance of the Bodhisattva, tries to reach the mountain-top, "the place of the Vision," through the dark, desolate night hours. He progresses, now frightened by a dim glimpse of "the cheekless gibe of death," and now encouraged by the guardian's voice: "Do not fear, my son! only the strong of heart can win to the place of Vision!" When the day finally dawns they find themselves among nothing but skulls of men. Even more frightening is the Bodhisattva's shocking revelation: "A mountain of skulls it is. But know, my son, that all of them ARE YOUR OWN! Each has at some time been the nest of your dreams and delusions and desires. Not even one of them is the skull of any other being. All—all without exception —have been yours, in the billions of your former lives." [27] It matters little that the story originally was provided by Mrs. Ernest Fenollosa. The point is that Hearn seized on this suggestion as "a find only by the rarest and most unexpected chance." [28] In "Fragment" he has driven the theme of his previous chapter on Fuji-no-Yama to its logical end. At that time Hearn wrote, after referring to a "gleam of white teeth I once saw in a skull—a woman's skull—otherwise burnt to a sooty crisp":

> So one of the fairest, if not the fairest of earthly visions, resolves itself into a spectacle of horror and death. . . . But have not all human ideals

of beauty, like the beauty of Fuji seen from afar, been created by forces of death and pain?—are not all, in their kind, but composites of death, beheld in retrospective through the magical haze of inherited memory? [29]

Compared to this ultimate point of pilgrimage, Hearn's early descriptions of the Fountain of Youth and the dreamy dale of fountains, if beautiful, are superficial; and compared to the horror of this vision, his youthful self-portrait as a worshipper of the grotesque and arabesque and as a believer in the "Revoltingly Horrible" and "Excruciatingly Beautiful" has too much self-consciousness. Now Hearn's vision has become that of metaphysical horror and he has traveled spiritually as far as he can go.

In this sense *Kwaidan* (1904) could be considered a point of transition between the second and the third group. Hearn's interest in things beyond the human world culminates here, while at the same time he manifests the intensely human quality characteristic of his last period. As *Kwaidan* is the culminating point of his legends, so his next book, *Japan: An Attempt at Interpretation* (1904) is the apex of his essay writing. The book, originally prepared for the prospective Cornell lectureship, exemplifies Hearn's formal approach to Japan. Most scholarly of all his writings, it owes its merit and fascination to Hearn's systematic probing into the cult of ancestor-worship as the essential key to the soul of Japan. If this essay is the façade of his Japanese studies, *The Romance of the Milky Way* (1905), his posthumous collection, is the dome of that edifice. " 'Ultimate Questions' " is Hearn's final reflection on evolutionism, whereas other legends, such as "The Romance of the Milky Way" and "The Story of Itō Norisuké," are his hymns of lovers' reunion in the realm both heavenly and ghostly. "Stranger than Fiction," originally entitled "Forgiveness," is a short story about a West Indian Negro, a wizened old man who killed his white master in the revolt of 1848 and yet, strangely enough, returned to beg the mistress' pardon, thereafter continuing to serve her. Whether or not it is intended to be a sequel to *Youma,* Hearn's West Indian romance, the main point is the old slave's reconciliation with those he once antagonized. This sense of love and mercy suffuses the entire volume, giving it a tone of finality; and the fact that Hearn's subject is no longer confined to Japan may indicate that his Japanese studies are nearing the end of their long cycle.

In his Japanese lecture, "The Prose of Small Things," Hearn makes a comparison between English and French practice in travel literature.

English formalism demands that the whole volume center around the basic theme or have some relation to it, whereas the French approach insists that each piece in the volume should be "a complete work of art in itself." [30] From this point of view Hearn's approach in each of his Japanese books is undoubtedly French; yet, taken as a whole, they tend to form certain groups and center on kindred genres. This suggests that his approach, ironically enough, becomes more and more English. He even goes further, as the essays develop more basic motifs along with their individual variations. These are Japan as symbol of Hearn's earthly paradise; the conflict between two Japans, one old and the other new; the contrast between the East and the West; their ultimate union by way of Buddhism and evolutionism, and the reconciliation of religion and science. Some of these themes, as we know, have grown out of his early interests and preoccupations. Japan in transition possibly reminded him of the South he had seen during the eighties; and the contrast between the East and the West could be regarded as a further variation of that between the native and the white in the West Indies.

Beyond all this is one fundamental motif that really unifies all phases of his work—the relationship between man and nature. The Japanese studies are a direct continuation of *Two Years,* the essential difference being that in Japan Hearn finally became aware of the possibility of harmonizing man and nature. In other words, Japan seemed to Hearn to suggest a possible solution for his West Indian dilemma, the incompatibility of civilization and nature. Since the whole question is essentially a philosophical one, it cannot be discussed in full detail until we come to the last part of this study. For the present purpose it suffices to point out Hearn's final realization: the conflict between man and nature may best be resolved in terms of his aesthetic concept of reality. Of the function of art as mediator between man and nature Hearn wrote in *Exotics and Retrospectives:*

So far as I have been able to judge, Japanese poetry usually ignores the inferior qualities of sensation, while making the subtlest of appeals to those superior qualities which we call aesthetic. Even if representing nothing else, this fact represents the healthiest attitude toward Nature. Do not we Occidentals shrink from many purely natural impressions by reason of repulsion developed through a morbid tactual sensibility? The question is at least worth considering. Ignoring or mastering such repulsion,—accepting naked Nature as she is, always lovable when understood,—the Japanese discover beauty where we blindly imagine ugliness or formlessness or loathsomeness. [31]

As to whether such a generalization is philosophically tenable or not we must reserve our judgment for the moment. What is significant is that in search of the Far Eastern mind Hearn came to discover the truth about himself and his own world, thus completing his inward voyage.

This brings us back to Hearn's point of departure, Delacroix's advice: ". . . Jeune artiste, tu attends un sujet? Tout est sujet; le sujet c'est toi-même: ce sont tes impressions, tes émotions devant la nature. C'est toi qu'il faut regarder, et non autour de toi." Starting with the Romantic cult of ego, Hearn was then drawn toward the cult of nature, only to realize the dangerous lures of his so-called "sweet pantheism." Herein lay the real meaning of his West Indian drama of a temptation demanding his total surrender. Emerging from this intellectual and spiritual crisis, he was still unable to accept either an easy compromise or an uncertain truce; with his questioning mind torn between those narrow cults, he had to travel further into the heart of the East. Only at this last stage of his voyage could Hearn see the possible reconciliation of man and nature on their common original ground. In registering the paradoxical truth that one's self-discovery is possible only through his discovery of others, Hearn's travel lore thus comes to take root deep in the age-old tradition of the philosophical voyage, that allegorical search for the nature of man which has haunted many of the thinking minds of the Western world.

"I would give up anything to be a literary Columbus," Hearn wrote in 1883, "—to discover a Romantic America in some West Indian or North African or Oriental region,—to describe the life that is only fully treated of in universal geographies or ethnological researches." [32] As it turned out, the adventurous voyage proved to be something far more fascinating, significant, and profitable than he himself had imagined because he discovered that "Romantic America" not only in regions far from home, such as Martinique and Japan, but also within his own heart, hidden under many layers of time. In exploring the nature of man he also had to trace back the very origin of man. Of this double direction of exoticism Hearn was not unaware when he wrote on his trans-Pacific voyage of 1890:

> Thus, by mechanical suppression of time, the planet is ever being made smaller for us. Perhaps, when it shall have begun to seem too small, man will turn more readily to the study of that vaster world within himself, —whose deeps are yet unsounded and untraveled, whose only horizon is the infinite. . . . [33]

Although in the past decades those deeps have been much sounded and traveled, we are still groping in the dark for the mystery of that vaster world within called the psyche. If such an approach to the world of psyche by means of time exemplifies Western man's time-consciousness, it would follow that Hearn is, in his approach, unquestionably a son of the West.[34]

II Criticism

VI

*"To
Strive
after
Truth"*

*A
Critic
in
the
Making*

Hearn's career as a critic began with the review of
Tennyson's *Idylls of the King* which secured him a post with the Cincinnati *Enquirer* in 1872. In the years that followed, he dealt with many
literary topics and events, local and national, at home and abroad; but
it was only during his New Orleans period (1877–87) that his critical
power found its outlet in important issues of contemporary American
letters.

Hearn entered upon this most versatile period of his career as as-
sociate editor of the New Orleans *Item*. Since one of his multiple jobs
was to write book reviews, he was led almost immediately to consider
the function of the reviewer as critic. In one of his early *Item* editorials,
he lamented that few newspapers could afford to keep a professional
book or drama critic on their editorial force. "Fair" newspaper critics,
he pointed out, being well aware of their fallibility, make it a rule to
play safe, that is, "rather to speak favorably than otherwise," and in
any event "to strive after truth without pretending to be oracular."
That is why book notices are "rather advertisements than criticisms."

No doubt, he admitted, this may be one of their functions, but they can be criticisms, too, if the reviewers be "capable" and "candid."[1] This last point is especially revealing since the two virtues of capability and candor, coupled with artistic aspiration, drove Hearn to his zealous commitment to some of the major issues of American literature during the 1880's—only to emerge therefrom as a critic.

Of his critical activities during the decade Albert Mordell remarked that Hearn touched on almost every phase of American letters in the eighties. Asserting that his critical utterances are "curiously similar to those of the most advanced critics in America today," the same commentator warned: "No literary historian should be unfamiliar with Hearn's work as a critic of American literature."[2] Despite a testimony such as this, little recognition, generally speaking, has been accorded to Hearn as a critic. For this there are several reasons—all plausible: first, Hearn's activities were locally limited to the post-Civil War South; second, his French literary background, though congenial to New Orleans, was far from palatable to the Eastern, predominantly Anglo-Saxon literary world; third, his romantic mentality, nurtured by Flaubert, Gautier, Baudelaire, and others, opposed rather than accepted the current trend toward realism; fourth, his cosmopolitan outlook further helped to fortify the general impression that as an émigré writer he was more or less isolated from the main stream of American letters; fifth, the major issues he tackled so passionately have been acclimatized to the American soil completely, so completely indeed that they are no longer issues of any consequence to us today.

Yet Hearn was there. By virtue of his literary ambition, critical sensibility, and personal candor, he was compelled to go beyond his modest determination to strive after truth without pretending to be oracular, and to become involved with important literary issues of the decade, such as Southernism, the local color movement, aestheticism, realism, and, especially, French naturalism. Through his active participation in the formative period of modern American literature Hearn not only made a significant contribution to literary opinion but also gained his maturity as a critic.

First of all, Hearn was familiar with the contemporary publishing world. Whatever he had to say about various literary topics is both accurate and interesting to us. On one occasion, much in the manner of Poe, he pointed out the necessity of international copyright laws for the promotion of many a native genius.[3] On another occasion he observed the waning vogue of the so-called cheap, paper-covered, quarto

editions on both sides of the Atlantic, and concluded that, however un-
favorable the business situation, there was some likelihood that such
books would bring in a sizable profit.[4] This sort of foresight makes
many of his newspaper articles, though at times wrong-headed, highly
entertaining for the modern reader. A case in point is one called "Dime-
Novel Wickedness." There he argued that law should ban all juvenile
literature that glorifies robbery, murder, and burglary, contrary to its
assigned function to "please the fancy quite as strongly," and to "excite
the nobler rather than the baser sentiments." We are made aware that
the modern comic-book problem is by no means peculiarly our own.
Perhaps even more interesting is his suggestion that we may have to
establish something "corresponding to that old Parisian organization
whose members were known as *agents des moeurs.*" Literary censorship
of any kind is dangerous; and yet its possible danger, Hearn believes,
"might be averted by having the text submitted to literary experts—men
without mawkish respectabilities or exaggerated prudery." The work in
question, Hearn once again insists, ought to be judged from the point
of view of juvenile readers.[5] One more example is his remark on the
universal fashion of illustrated publications. This he condemns on the
ground that any literary work of merit should be able to win its way
without aid of illustration. "Fine literature," as he put it, "has about as
much chance of attracting public notice while surrounded with sensuous splendors of illustration, as an exceedingly aged and learned philosopher has of monopolizing attention in a ballroom full of beautiful
women." [6]

As a veteran journalist Hearn had something to say about American
journalism, too. Although his curse on journalism as such was only
too well-known, he was objective in diagnosing the general situation
and constructive in suggesting the ideal course for modern journalism
to take. First of all he would like to see the future newspaper become
essentially an artistic production which would combine "the piquant
humor of the Parisian gazette," "the logical force of English editorial
opinion," and "the newsgathering enterprise of the American journalism." This would be "one magnificent creation," in his humble opinion,
"certain of realization." [7] Hearn's picture may sound like an artist-
journalist's wishful dream, but few could object to the possible merit
of his suggestion. In any case, his cosmopolitan thinking can already be
seen here.

As a literary aspirant, Hearn naturally saw greater opportunity in the
magazine world than in the newspaper; hence his more extensive and

more positive criticism about contemporary periodical literature. In his general survey of 1878, Hearn first regretted the decline of the *Atlantic,* once reputed as "a first-class magazine" and "a great monthly," under Howells' leadership. Other major magazines received his commendation; he found *Scribner's* "attractive," noted that *Harper's* was sustaining its "character," and praised the "excellence" of *Lippincott's.* Hearn believed the *Atlantic's* decline to be due largely to the recent change in its managing policy.[8] Two months later he touched on the same point, attacking the *Atlantic,* which had lately adopted a policy of publishing contributors' names. This new policy, he feared, was very likely to demoralize the best magazines, because the traditional "impersonal" policy alone could provide the best talent with the opportunity to enter "into doubtful competition with famous names." [9] The remark seems to have a special personal implication, for Hearn was at the time eager to establish his literary reputation through these Eastern magazines. For this reason, undoubtedly, he took up the issue again, four years later. Standing by his old position, he insisted that major magazines should adopt an impartial policy in order to encourage native genius.[10] Toward the end of 1883 he made another survey: the *Atlantic,* still "poor"; the *Century,* "fourth-class"; *Harper's Magazine,* "hardly critical"; the *Nation,* failing in "maintaining an independent existence"; the *Critic,* with all "its many excellencies," scarcely comparable with the *Westminster.* He found only the *New York Sun* to be worth a year's subscription. By and large, Hearn complained, modern criticism is "conducted rather in the private interests of publishers than in the interest of literature." [11]

Here we might as well note that 1883 marked the appearance of Hearn's first magazine article, "The Scenes of Cable's Romances,"—in the "fourth-class" *Century.* (From this time on until his departure from New Orleans in 1887, he was to entertain the readers of both *Harper's Weekly* and *Harper's Bazar* through more than a score of articles on various topics. Even after he left America he could never wholly sever himself from Northern magazines like *Harper's* and the *Atlantic.*) [12] His dream now fulfilled, Hearn became conciliatory. His editorial of 1884, "Eclecticism in Periodical Literature," shows the change in his tone. Here he stressed the introduction of foreign literature, European and Oriental, into the States, and thereby proposed "a really *eclectic* periodical," naming the *Revue des Deux Mondes* as a ready model. At the same time, he added, "No such periodical exists today—not even in Paris." On this genuinely cosmopolitan scale the proposed periodical should welcome the "best" contributions from many writers of opposite schools:

> An absolutely perfect magazine—an eclectic periodical *par excellence,*— should, it seems to us, allow the largest liberty to opinion and the greatest possible range to diversity of style,—at the same time encouraging certain forms of treatment of certain subjects. Such a literary medium ought to be conducted by a committee of men loving art for art's sake, and fully conscious of the fact that beauty is not necessarily confined to any one style of expression or any particular school of *belles-lettres.*[13]

Here, needless to say, Hearn virtually envisions an ideal medium for his stylistic ambition, his artistic recreation of many-colored legends, and his dream of world literature. Yet, the significance of his proposal is more than personal. It is something we still dream of today.

From the start Hearn saw the world at large as his only proper stage. Very probably because of his inborn cosmopolitanism, he was often able to see beyond his immediate ken. This faculty Hearn displayed best in dealing with Southernism, one important literary issue of the decade. Politically, he was sympathetic about the painful dilemma of the South and did not hesitate to expose the political practices of notorious Northern carpetbaggers; emotionally, he was nostalgic toward its fading glory. While reviewing a recent biography of General Grant, Hearn openly defended the position of the South. "The South," he wrote, "will do well to remain solid as granite,—solid not against the North, but the rings,—solid, not against a sentiment, but against the men who would 'corner' in politics even as they once before 'cornered' in gold." But the *raison d'être* of the South, as he saw it, was not in its sentimental opposition to the North.[14] To his credit, Hearn was capable of drawing the line between politics and literature. His concern was with literature, not with politics; for he was convinced that in the former alone the Southern genius could outshine the Northern and create something genuine and durable.

His initial assault was aimed at the so-called Southern novels, all playing upon one theme, "like school compositions by members of the same class." Ridiculing the growing Southern parochialism in literature, he said: "Southern writers of real talent do not write for a district or State, but for the country at large; they are not shoddyites; they do not write books advertised 'Southern novels.'"[15] When a Southern magazine was proposed, he seized the opportunity to drive home his point. Though he favored the project in principle and went on to suggest that such a magazine be issued by a Southern publishing house, he nevertheless demanded that it should be free of all Southernism and sectionalism, and "conducted impersonally in most respects." Its standard must be intrinsic and cosmopolitan. "A Southern magazine must be an American magazine, a United States magazine, an English magazine, if it be worth supporting." For this to be achieved, the editors must be guided only by one principle, the religion of art.[16]

As it stood then, the literary situation in the South was deplorable, Hearn admitted, but at the same time he was confident about the bright future of the South when he said: ". . . the good time for Southern literature is yet to come." He had no intention of condoning the general feeling that the North was either malicious or indifferent to the South. This is no time for "bragging about what we *can* do," he reminded his readers; what is really important is that "it must be *done*," and the sooner the better. So saying, he wrote in "Southern Literature," a *Times-Democrat* editorial of 1883:

> We must learn that the literature or the art, which has no better claim to recognition than the fact that it is Southern, can never maintain its claim to recognition at all. It must be able to stand on its merits and to challenge comparison with what is produced elsewhere, independently of any reference to sectional origin.

Literature and art, he continued, are "eminently catholic—not sectional or provincial." To value literature or art for its own intrinsic merits is no denunciation of the so-called local color school. In his opinion, the subject material is one thing and the achieved form is quite another. Furthermore, sectionalism is in many cases merely a political expression in the guise of literature.

Another weakness, Hearn pointed out, is the South's general sensitivity to criticism. Here the South is mistaken about the true function of criticism. Itself a department of literature and a very essential one, criticism should play its vital role; it may at times be ignorant, incompetent or unfair; but intelligent and impartial criticism, he believed, is "absolutely necessary to the formation of a sound and healthy literature." Therefore, it is really better for the author, as well as for the public, that the critic should "err on the side of severity than on that of over-indulgence." After having said this, Hearn urged the South not to blame, but to learn from the North, where publishers, critics, and authors were unitedly working for what was better to come. As he said: "They have *built each other up*."[17] Whether or not this picture of the North is too roseate is another matter. When the *Observer* castigated his stand, Hearn did not hesitate to declare that Southern authors remain unknown and obscure essentially because of the indifference and neglect on the part of the Southern public; and that the critics' formal praise or extravagant eulogy makes the situation worse. What is really responsible for the state of Southern literature is the lack of genuine appreciation and critical spirit.[18] In delineating a critic's primary function in the formation of a new literature, Hearn has departed considerably from his early determination to strive after truth without pretending to be oracular. This indicates how rapidly he has come to involve himself with the issue and, at the same time, to realize the complex role of a critic. Throughout his discussion he both pointed out the potentiality of Southern belles-lettres and upheld the catholicity of art. There is good reason why Jay B. Hubbell, while surveying the South in American literature, has recently said: "There was much truth in Hearn's shrewd diagnosis." [19]

The second issue, essentially an extension of the first, centers on the local color movement, which was then sweeping the whole continent, from Maine to Georgia, from the Mississippi to the Pacific. To the artistic use of local subjects "for the exercise of high art," Hearn saw no good objection. In fact, as one who was later to write *Chita* and *Youma,* he defended some and encouraged others in this trend. His interest in the movement showed itself as early as 1873, when he wrote a review of Thomas Bailey Aldrich's collection of short stories, *Marjorie Daw and Other People.* With specific reference to "Père Antoine's Date-Palm," a story based on a New Orleans legend, he noted a certain resemblance in "rich humor" and "witty method" between the author and Bret Harte.[20] Still later, when a *New York World* reviewer spoke rather harshly of Harte's *Drift from Two Shores,* Hearn came to his defense. In reply to the reviewer's observation that the real merit of the volume depends "not upon the ability of the writer so much as upon the extraordinary experience he had undergone," Hearn said:

> . . . that experience of the most extensive and unusual character is not so necessary to the success of the modern novel and poem, as that mental power of winnowing out the precious wheat from the chaff of common life, that heart sympathy with all that suffers and hopes and loves in the poorest conditions of society.

These two virtues, mental power and heart sympathy, he continued, Bret Harte so eminently possesses. Although his recent works show some decline of his artistic power, he is still capable of fulfilling his early promise.[21] What is interesting is Hearn's contention that the merit of literary art rests on the artist's powerful execution rather than the peculiarities of his characters and their experiences, namely the local color artist's stock in trade. The irony is that in defending Harte, Hearn exposed the basic weakness of Harte's school.

Both as artist and critic Hearn took uncommon interest in the artistic exploration of Southern subjects. He was firmly convinced that the utilization of local subjects was a native artist's birthright. This may account for his laudatory review of Père Rouquette's *La Nouvelle Atala* as an example of literary success in evoking "the spirit of a life,—a most unique and strange life." [22] Hearn also suggested that the South might be able to contribute something valuable to American literature through the use of native, rather than Old World materials in historical fiction. In an *Item* editorial, "Successful Literature," he cited Cable's romances as notable examples.[23] On the same basis, Hearn praised Mark Twain's *Life on the Mississippi* as an "absolutely unique" piece, a creation far more serious than his previous *Innocents Abroad*. The author's humor especially, he said, is "of the most typically American sort," and compared with him, Artemus Ward is already "old-fashioned." [24]

What Hearn had to say about George Washington Cable is interesting in view of their literary friendship, which began promisingly but ended abruptly.[25] Hearn's early enthusiasm, already touched off in Cincinnati by Cable's bizarre tale, "Jean-ah Poquelin," continued to grow after their first meeting in New Orleans. Beginning with a *Century* article, "The Scenes of Cable's Romances," Hearn wrote several commendatory reviews of Cable's work. "Mr. Cable's *Dr. Sevier*" is typical of Hearn's attitude. Cable's descriptive style is called "literary aquarelle." In Hearn's view, *Dr. Sevier* is superior to Cable's previous *Grandissimes,* but the author's real forte is in his "short, bright, graceful stories," as he lacks the kind of force indispensable to larger works. At the same time Hearn chides those Southerners who unjustly criticize Cable's works for his known biases, social, political, and religious.[26]

It was over another local colorist, Charles Egbert Craddock (Mary Noailles Murfree) that Hearn clashed with Howells. Hearn questioned Howells' advice that she should "abandon her romantic ideals" and "give us her mountain-folk as she saw them *before her fancy began to work upon them.*" The controversy had larger implications, however, in Hearn's defense of the local color school itself, more specifically, its "artistic possibility." Accusing Howells of being "color blind" and exhibiting a "spirit of neo-Puritanism," Hearn wrote that the artist grasps immediately the artistic possibility, with its various details of color, form, and suggestiveness. He branded Howells' doctrine false realism because it "adopts its own imperfect ways of seeing and thinking as a universal standard whereby to judge all literary work." What does Mr. Howells mean by "truth"? Hearn demanded. As far as he could see, it was but "The Opinions of William Dean Howells." Howells, he admitted, was "absolutely correct" in condemning Miss Murfree for the kind of sentimentalism which, to some degree, contaminated the majority of local color writers; but because of his own doctrine of realism Howells failed to see an artistic possibility in the local color method.[27]

Hearn saw an ironic discrepancy in Howells—although Howells denounced Miss Murfree's "romantic ideals," he also insisted that the critic's function should not be praising or blaming but only "classifying and analyzing the fruits of the human minds." [28] To Hearn, it is clear, the critic is also an artist, a truth-seeker, a discoverer, a guide, a taste-maker, a participant, and, when necessary, a judge. In short, a critic is anything but the scientist or quasi-scientist seemingly demanded by Howells' method. Hearn showed the revealing aspect of an artist-critic when dealing with the question of local color literature. Recognizing the potential of the local color school, he wrote in his editorial, "Southern Literature":

> The history, manners, customs, usages, language, scenery, and other incidental peculiarities of particular countries, races, and sections, may furnish materials for the exercise of high art, pictorial or literary; . . . the art itself must be founded upon catholic principles—upon those touches of nature, which make the whole world kin. It must be independent of the nativity or nationality of the artist, whether he be Jew or Greek, Nubian or Patogonian.[29]

The statement should clarify Hearn's stand. Life is not identical with art, though one ought to be always open toward the other. The local color school, and Howells' school for that matter, seem to err in equating art and life.

Because of his conviction about the fundamental relationship between art and life, Hearn violently opposed the judgment of art by any standard not absolutely intrinsic and cosmopolitan. The artist must be motivated internally, not externally, for the purity of a work of art can be created only out of the genuine drive he finds within himself; it must, Hearn believed, come as a result of "the irrepressible love of the beautiful, the simple desire to share a pleasure or communicate an esthetic discovery—the anticipation of kindling new sympathies and giving an impulse to large ideas." [30] The love of the beautiful is no doubt the prime mover, but it is not the object that the artist should pursue. His duty is to give form to his innermost creative urge. In emphasizing beauty, the cult of beauty is thus reaffirming the autonomy of art. Here Hearn is at one with the aesthetes of his day, but at the same time he was well aware of basic differences between himself and the followers of art for art's sake. He might well have agreed that the fallacy of both realism and aestheticism was their singularly similar confusion of art and life: realism was an attempt to transplant life into art; aestheticism, an attempt to transplant art into life; and beauty was something either to avoid or to embrace.

Hearn's third issue was directly concerned with the art for art's sake movement, which was beginning to cross the Atlantic. As a disciple of Gautier, that arch-champion of the cult of beauty, Hearn devoted two articles in 1882 to Oscar Wilde, then rising as the self-named apostle of aestheticism.[31] At first he offered genuine brotherly sympathy for the rough fate that might befall this lover of beauty, as it had his predecessors, Hugo, Gautier, and other French Romantics. Hearn welcomed Wilde as a new classicist of Victorian neo-Romanticism, even though he detected a weakness in the lack of "physical magnetism and aggressive force sufficient to effect a reformation by himself." In so saying Hearn also made his position on beauty plain: "there is holiness in it [beauty]." Its influence not only "purifies" but also "moralizes." Chiding the public ridicule of Wilde, he then advised the reader to estimate the issue "with American fairness."

Soon Hearn must have grown sceptical about Wilde's crusade as he came to note that Wilde's success "with the female society of London" had become more and more like that of "a designer of new dress patterns or new spring bonnets." With "the great point gained," Hearn suggested, Wilde should now attempt "a very different system of propagandism"; otherwise he might have to submit to the dismal fate of the hero of *Patience*. Hearn believed that few would question the worthiness of Wilde's cause but that it ought to be "sustained by something less ephemeral than the love of novelty and less femininely fickle than fashion." Wilde's famous knee-breeches must have reminded Hearn of Gautier's legendary red waistcoat, a symbolic declaration of the French Romantic Revolt. He seemed to have sensed almost instinctively that the resemblance between Gautier's revolt and Wilde's fashion was no more than superficial, and that there was a paucity of substance in Wilde's attempt to fashion life after art. This seemed to Hearn the reverse of the way Gautier and his comrades actually battled against odds. Wilde's novelty-hunting, he suspected, came from an artificial concept of the relationship between life and art.

Hearn considered this one question—what is the relationship between life and art?—paramount in all three issues, Southernism, the local color school, and aestheticism. He came to the conclusion that art is not identical with life, and that there should be no confusion between them. Art demands its autonomy, but without forsaking its relationship with life; for their relationship is basically organic. Hence the important function of criticism as mediator between life and art. For this reason he criticized Southernism and the local color movement, though well aware of their artistic possibility. Here his objection was an aesthetic one. Similarly, he commended the cult of beauty and even championed it, as we remember; yet, this did not prevent him from pointing out Wilde's immaturity. Here his criticism was a philosophical one. In both instances he displayed his critical faculty for going straight to the root of the matter.

There is one more issue about which Hearn had to be at once aesthetic and philosophical, the French naturalism of Zola and his school. One of the major literary topics of the decade, it engaged the minds of many of the makers of modern American literature, thereby marking an important chapter in the history of American realism. Over the issue Hearn more than once crossed James and Howells. Hearn led the battle in a way that seems strange to us, fought it with a strategy of his own, and wound it up in such fashion that few have suspected his direct participation. That he participated in it at all is only a recent discovery.[32] One of the reasons why his position on this issue has remained obscure is that he rejected Zola and his naturalism, a rejection likely to be interpreted as a futile gesture of romantic reaction or Victorian prudery. But his rejection, as we shall see, has little do with either of them. The controversy, which lasted longer than any in which he had yet been involved, helped to complete Hearn's apprenticeship as a critic.

Hearn's involvement was deliberate from the start. As a newspaper book reviewer he introduced Zola to the reading public; as a translator he made English renderings of Zola's works for the New Orleans papers; as an artist he scoffed at other American translations of Zola; and as a critic he exposed the fundamental nature, aesthetic and philosophical, of Zola's art. With a sketch from *Nouveaux Contes à Ninon* under the title "My Two Cats" (*Item,* September 28, 1878) Hearn became one of the earliest American translators of Zola. The piece was soon followed by Hearn's review of Zola's *Hélène*. There he presented Zola as "a realist—the chief of the new and daring school," and the novel as "one of the least objectionable" of his works, certainly better than *L'Assomoir*, "a marvel of indelicacy and filthiness." With all its "moral errors," Zola's new book, Hearn remarked, is "exquisite." It is "the work of a master." [33] The following year, 1879, was noteworthy for American literature and for Hearn as well. That year witnessed the publication of the first American translation of Zola. A Philadelphia firm, T. B. Peterson and Brothers, with an eye on the Zola vogue, issued a series of Zola translations done by "John Stirling" (Mary Neal Sherwood). According to the preface to her version of *L'Assomoir*, the translation was "toned down with literary ability combined with taste, delicacy and refinement to suit the American public." [34] This touched off Hearn's blunt assault on Stirling as a Zola translator. "A purified version of Zola is not Zola. Zola is nothing if not impure"—this was the gist of the argument he made, in spite of his objection to the nature of Zola's art.[35]

But Hearn viewed the issue of naturalism in a larger framework of realism. In 1879, while noting that modern fiction was "obliged to seek realism for novelty's sake," he described its new theory: "The more perfect the novel of today the more truthful must it be as a reflection of actual life." The old conflict between the Classical and the Romantic schools, as he saw it, was now replaced by that between "the harsher realism" and "the conservative realism." The latter school was, in his opinion, "perhaps the most truly artistic." "Art is," he said, rejecting the realistic doctrine of *vraisemblance*, "not the minute imitation of nature, but the power to render the agreeable impressions created by nature." He believed this to be as true in literature as in painting and sculpture.[36] But what did he mean by these two types of realism, harsher and conservative? The best answer seems to be found in his editorial, *"The Abbé's Temptation,"* a piece called forth by Stirling's translation of Zola's work, *La Faute de l'Abbé Mouret*. In this review Hearn designated Zola as "one of the greatest novelists who ever lived." He does not question the fascination of Zola's world, "artfully wicked,—magically immoral," which seems to embody a sort of evil in its "materialistic benevolence toward vice." As far as he knows, none of Zola's novels is "commonplace or uninteresting," none is "devoid of artistic beauty." But he also added that none of them could be considered "a good wholesome book." In spite of his admiration for Zola's artistic stand, Hearn never could be wholly satisfied with him. As his own seemingly conflicting epithets indicate, Hearn's enthusiasm was far from whole-hearted. He also questioned the oft-mentioned similarity between Zola and Balzac. Though admitting the common bond between the *Rougon-Macquart* series and the *Human Comedy,* he could not overlook the basic disparity between Zola and his master: ". . . there is at least no shadow of resemblance as to methods of execution. There was in Balzac much of the Romanticist,—a poetical enthusiasm for the extraordinary, and tendency to idealism." [37]

From this point on, the antithesis between the harsher and the conservative realism, still vaguely outlined, became Hearn's basic theme of naturalism *versus* idealism. By this time he must have known of Zola's manifesto of 1880, *Le Roman expérimental.* The issue was treated more explicitly in another editorial, "Naturalism," of October 12, 1881. As his article suggests, Hearn was not unaware of the historical role this school was going to play: "That Naturalism has a great historical role to fill, an important place to occupy in the literature of the nineteenth century, it would be vain to deny." But this recognition did not ease his objection to naturalism itself, which seemed to him to be "literary photography," however scientific, positive, and analytical. To this new school Hearn contrasted what he termed "idealism." "The highest art," he said, "does not consist in the faithful copying of living models, but in the idealization of the best peculiarities and characteristics of those models." The basis of such a high art as this must be imagination, the force which does synthesize rather than photograph or dissect life.[38]

The more Hearn came to know of Zola's art the more he became convinced of this fundamental inadequacy of naturalism, aesthetic as well as philosophical. He clearly expressed his attitude in a review of Zola's *Au Bonheur des Dames* (1883). This new novel, a sequel to *Pot-Bouille,* failed, he thought, to show any further spiritual growth on Zola's part. Focusing on Denise, the heroine, "almost the only really moral person," Hearn pointed out that Zola, after having created her as a noble and pure soul, now refuses to do her justice, "as though she were an illegitimate literary offspring." Being "no believer in free agency," Zola fashions his character after his "philosophic positivism," though all evidence in the novel indicates that she should be otherwise. Thus Denise is made virtuous "by necessity rather than choice, by dint of hereditary tendencies rather than by ethical reasoning." All this, Hearn concludes, suggests "how much the French mind of the nineteenth century needs the invigorating and purifying force of that idealism which the Zolaites would banish from the world." [39] From these remarks it is obvious that Hearn does not argue the point from the standpoint of conventional morality. He attacks Zola's scientific determinism as well as the aesthetic distortion resulting from it.

In 1884, when he reviewed *La Joie de Vivre*, his attitude became even more positive. Under the title "Idealism and Naturalism," he first observed that what could be said about this novel could also be applied to the whole *Rougon-Macquart* series. Zola, in Hearn's opinion, has not written novels; he has only created "a pseudo-literary museum." With reference to Zola's early prediction of the triumph of naturalism over classicism, romanticism, and idealism, Hearn said that this would be tantamount to the denial of imagination as the very basis of art. What has resulted from Zola's crusade for "sober facts and solid truth," he found, is nothing more than the contraction of the realm of human experience. What Zola has failed to see is the plain fact that spirit is as indispensable to humanity as matter. Idealism is no mere literary fashion; it is the manifestation of man's aspiration for "the unreal, the impossible, the unattainable," or more simply for, "the Impossible." On this ground Hearn could afford to be more optimistic about the future of idealism: "So long as humanity endures, Idealism shall guide men to higher things;—and the Impossible will continue to dominate the intellectual aspirations of mankind." [40]

Here it must be noted that the mid-eighties marked a period of prime importance in the history of naturalism in American literature. In 1884 James and Howells stood up at last to champion the cause of Zola's school through respectable Northern periodicals. James wrote to Howells that Zola, Flaubert, Daudet, and their contemporaries "do the only kind [of writing], today, that I respect; and in spite of their ferocious pessimism and their handling of unclean things, they are at least serious and honest. . . . Read Zola's last thing, *La Joie de Vivre* . . . the work is admirably solid and serious." [41] Now freed from his early Puritan heritage, James is upholding the autonomy of art. But it is as artist rather than as critic that James expresses his new admiration for Zola's artistic sincerity and integrity. And 1886 saw a change in the general opinion in favor of French naturalism. The publication of *Germinal* in the preceding year was a propitious sign for those Zolaites who, now abandoning their passive defense, singled out the humanitarian purpose of Zola's new novel. Their rank was reinforced by Professor J. W. Davidson's timely Concord School lecture, in which he likened the significance of Zola's crusade to those of Aristotle, Jesus, and Goethe in the history of mankind. [42] Howells also, through his

Harper's columns, "The Editor's Study," for the following six years (January 1886–March 1892), continued to support the cause of realism in general. "We must," he sermonized, "ask ourselves before we ask anything else, Is it true?—true to the motives, the impulses, the principles that shape the life of actual men and women."[43]

Undoubtedly Hearn, then literary editor of the New Orleans *Times-Democrat,* kept a close watch on this trend in American letters. Soon he resumed his attack on the doctrine of art as truth. In "Realism and Idealism," an editorial of early 1886, he examined the method of Howells and James in the light of their French masters. The American school, he pointed out, while free of "the coarseness of vice" so peculiar to the French, lacks "the deep interest which the works of the French masters possess for the student of morbid anatomy." That is, the American followers are merely mediocre, with no psychological depth. "What our age really needs," Hearn then suggested, "is not more realism, but more of the pure idealism which is founded on a perfect knowledge of the essential facts of human life." After all, realism should be "the means, not the absolute end, of the writer of fiction." The more scientific, the farther modern fiction departs from its highest function, "the recreation of minds that are weary of the toil and strife of the world." It would be a serious error on the part of novelists to expect their readers to be keen about a medical treatise or an essay on political and social economy. Once again he expressed his hope for idealism:

> So long as the world endures there will be no lack of heartrending realism; so long as human nature remains unchanged there will be an unappeasable yearning for the idealism without which men have neither the courage to struggle nor the power to enjoy.[44]

As Hearn understood, realism was the result of the artist's suicidal surrender of imagination to the "over-scientific spirit." Because realists fail in their primary mission, they usually run to the so-called tendency novel. Hearn reminded them that literature is "never intended to expound schemes of philosophy and wire-drawn theories concerning the organic structure of the social fabric." "It is better," he insisted, "that philosophy and fiction should dwell apart." Whenever art is consciously based on philosophy rather than on imagination, it fails to achieve its assigned function, the completion of life.[45]

For this reason Hearn welcomed *L'Oeuvre,* Zola's recent work. In spite of Zola's intent to make it "a colossal satire on artistic idealism," the work appeared to Hearn to be highly suggestive of the self-contradiction inherent in the doctrine of naturalism. The limit of its aesthetic stand has finally betrayed itself in the suicide of the hero-artist, who, torn between two women—the one "a Woman of Flesh" and the other "a woman of canvas and paint," exhausted his art and life in "efforts to portray the latter with the aid of the former as a model." In attempting to "paint flesh," realism overreached itself, thereby turning into "an Idealism wilder than aught which the old Romantic school could ever have been charged with." With all his avowed intention, Zola has been forced in the process of his creation to recognize the reality of idealism as a motive for human conduct, the very thing that he and his school have refused to accept, owing to their limited view of human existence. In this work, it is clear, the naturalist school quite unconsciously divulged "the secret of a New Idealism." Hearn believed that Zola achieved this feat only because he rose above his own theories. Ironically, Hearn found the genius of Zola precisely where Zola failed to practice his gospel of naturalism.[46]

Whatever the justification for its effective revolt against romanticism, Hearn felt that naturalism had now fulfilled its self-appointed mission. The time had come for it to be replaced by idealism. This sense of urgency dominated Hearn's reviews of Maupassant, a disciple of both Flaubert and Zola. When he became interested in Maupassant, it was in the Maupassant who "belonged to no school." [47] But his expectation soon turned to disillusionment with the publication of Maupassant's *Bel Ami* (1885). Though expressing his admiration for the author's superb workmanship, Hearn had to reject the philosophical pessimism underlying his "false positivism," another name for the *fin de siècle* malady. Hearn was shrewd enough to identify this pessimism with the one expressed in "Lazare's fear of death," an episode from Zola's *La Joie de Vivre*.[48] But the kinship of Zola ended there, Hearn found, because Maupassant was rapidly moving from his master's orbit. Toward the end of 1886, the year that recorded the new favorable attitude toward French naturalism in America, Hearn went still further to suggest the necessity of "a legal net" to halt naturalism's rapid degradation into sensationalism.[49] Hearn's desperate expedient was undoubtedly the result of critical exasperation.

It must not be assumed, however, that Hearn ultimately returned to the point from which many of his prominent contemporaries, including James and Howells, departed so determinedly. Hearn was not a belated romantic nor a reactionary anachronist, as so often alleged. His philosophical revolt against realism in general differs from that of many moralists whose voices are now muffled in the history of modern literature. The difference hinges on what Hearn termed "idealism," and this highly ambiguous term requires a closer look.

In 1883, when Hearn for the first time introduced Loti to the American audience, it was his belief that a revolt against naturalism was setting in within its own fortress. Even as Maupassant, though negatively, hinted at the logical impasse of Zola's doctrine, so Loti seemed to usher in a new literary school. What Hearn discovered in this new luminary of the Parisian literary world is quite clear in "A New Romantic," his first review of Loti, written that year. Loti's phenomenal success seemed to offer positive evidence that true art can prevail in spite of naturalistic innovations. In Hearn's opinion, Loti's melancholy was distinctly different from the sickliness of the French naturalists; it was an artistic expression of something higher, nobler, and more spiritual, including evolutional tendency.[50] His joy of discovery was such that he subsequently produced a series of articles on Loti, in addition to his translations.[51]

His faith in idealism increased during the mid-eighties, when he noted the sudden success of Russian literature in Paris as well as a new trend in French fiction itself. His sense of confirmation is well recorded in his *Times-Democrat* editorial, "Russian Literature Abroad." Let us admit the tremendous impact of naturalism upon future literary schools, he suggested. Naturalism has been surely "a monstrous extreme," but its historical significance is worth remembering as "the death-blow to many literary extravagancies, many theatrical idealisms, many laborious affectations." As *Germinal* indicates, Zola himself has departed from his initial position. Maupassant is "daily further and further away from it." Once Zola's reign is over, because of the aberration of his followers, there is "a magnificent return of fine artistic feeling," as evident in Bourget, France, and others. To Hearn it seems to be no mere coincidence that Russian literature has achieved a "sudden and immense popularity" in France. Indeed, he welcomed it as "a good influence of Gothic blood into anemic veins—a restoration of literary virility." There is no one either in England or elsewhere—except for Scandinavian countries—really comparable in this matter to the Russian masters, like Pushkin, Gogol, Tolstoi, Turgenev, and Dostoevski. Their two main artistic virtues are naked simplicity and a sense of chastity. Hearn pointed out that no Russian writers would seem to entertain our common notion, that "to be interesting one must be lascivious."[52] Citing *Crime and Punishment* in particular, Hearn blessed the continuing influence of Russian fiction: ". . . it deals only with possibilities and realisms;—but the possibilities are the extremes of suffering that a human mind may endure, and the realisms are pictures of a soul in living agony." Dostoevski is just one of many Russian examples. "What," Hearn asked, "is the secret of this immense superiority of the semi-barbaric Russian novel?" It must, he suggested, be a "closer contact with mighty nature." [53]

At the same time Hearn called attention to Paul Bourget among the recent French Academy winners, a young talent "absolutely unknown two years ago," the author of that "magically written" book, *Cruelle Enigme* (1885). Bourget's profound understanding of human nature shows that he "belongs to the new school altogether,—the School of the Future." [54] His next novel, *Crime d'Amour* (1886) called forth another review, "The Religion of Suffering." As "a magnificent sermon" the work is "a surprise unequalled in recent French fiction." The essence of the novel is the sublime sentiment of pity, which Bourget called "Virtue of Charity," and its closing pages singularly echo those of *Crime and Punishment*. From this Hearn concluded that the general trend is indeed "a beneficial one" and will eventually exert a great influence on the rising generation. [55]

All these factors Hearn once again attempted to consider in proper perspective, as his editorial, "The Future of Idealism," indicates. While realism still persists, the world clamors for "pictures of *real* life." In this era of rampant positivism, scepticism, and "esthetic barrenness," paradoxically, we need "unreal life." "Unreal life, ideal life," he wrote, "—anything a little too beautiful to exist, too much spiritualized to be tangible,—too exquisite to be believed in,—too pure for refined appreciation, belongs merely to the realm of nonsense, and can obtain no serious consideration." Our age has done away with "all inclination to sacrifice at the shrine of the Impossible." The only way of restoring man's innermost rage for the Impossible is to return to "the soil of imagination." In commenting on the obvious antithesis between northern spiritualism and southern sensualism Hearn advanced his favorite theory of climate. Turning once again to the salubrious influence of Russian literature, he stated: ". . . while it promises to renovate idealism, it has also given the world some of the strongest realistic work ever done, without descending into impropriety." This, he believed, is highly suggestive of the future of idealism. [56]

It is thus plain that Hearn's concept of idealism is basically spiritual. In "The Spiritual Sense in Literature," an editorial written shortly before his departure from New Orleans, Hearn put it in unmistakable terms: ". . . the idealism which has heretofore inspired all the greatest creations of man, and which is assuredly, in some vague and eternal way connected with the religious sentiment, can never be thrust out of poetry or fiction by new false prophets or pseudophilosophers." [57] This may not be so complete as we should like it to be, but what he implies is sufficiently clear. Idealism is that which emanates from "the religious sentiment," which mankind has maintained, while abandoning "one *form* of religion for another." It is idealistic in the sense that it directly or indirectly points to man's instinct for eternity, an instinct which forms at once the root of his existence and the basis of all his religions. Only with this sentiment can art represent the human aspiration for the Impossible, man's deepest dream; and to inspire man with this dream is the highest function of art.

Hearn's aesthetic revolt against realism has become philosophical in proportion as it has probed into the basis of naturalism as the logical outcome of realism; and this revolt has terminated in his recognition of man's spiritual nature. Idealism for him, then, refers to man's fundamental attitude toward his own existence, man's whole-hearted acceptance of life. Far beyond either escapism or didacticism, Hearn's position is one which unconditionally affirms the value of human life and resists any sort of theoretical opposition. There is no doubt that this concept of idealism has grown out of his study of myths and legends, and developed further with his later conversion to evolutional monism. It is also the foundation of his concept of romance, even though in *Chita, Youma,* and "Karma" his performance fell far short of his high ideal. In *Stray Leaves, Some Chinese Ghosts,* and his many Japanese legends, however, Hearn explored the reality of idealism more successfully; and, as we shall see later, idealism becomes the guiding principle of his literary study, the basis of his concept of world literature, and a premise of his philosophy.

In 1880, while defending Sarah Bernhardt against those moralists who demanded that the authorities ban her stage appearances, Hearn scoffed at their stupid confusion between art and morality, a confusion which, in spite of pious intention, would only fan the general curiosity.[58] Six years later he took the same position when he questioned Howells' criticism of Goethe's treatment of women. "Nothing must be forgiven to a man's genius," Hearn quoted Howells, "The greater his power, the greater his responsibility before the human conscience, which is God in us." To this oracular voice of the Dean of American letters the then still obscure New Orleans editor retorted: "Goethe's vices were never so accepted, nor Byron's;—the great influence of those men in literature was the influence of their strength and truth, not of their weakness or moral obliquity." Any reference to "the private character" is quite irrelevant in good literary criticism. Howells' philosophy, Hearn then wrote,

> seems to be that of a school-boy, and his power of criticism limited to Sunday-school standards,—good and respectable standards in their way, but never intended for the measurement of centuries and civilizations. It is no use for Mr. Howells to pose as a Converted Idealist: his early work, now resuscitated, shows that he never possessed the imaginative faculty to any remarkable degree.[59]

But this should not be taken as Hearn's categorical rejection of moral criticism as such. As he stated later in relation to Dr. Johnson's, moral criticism is not a bad system, but simply a narrow and small one.[60] Ironically, because of his faith in the inseparability of art and life Hearn never denied the value of either moral or aesthetic criticism.

Hearn's critical stand, once placed in perspective, re-emerges intact with the passage of time. The substance of his critical argument over these various issues of the eighties in American letters is valid today because of his conviction about the organic relationship between life and art. Despite his constant stress on their reciprocity he was able to keep himself from falling into the familiar confusion of his time. His critical career started with an aesthetic revolt against Southernism, the local color movement, and others. It was his Gautierite passion for form that was responsible for his ostentatiously severe criticism of Whitman's poetry, which centered on one vital point, the lack of form in his art.[61] As a declaration of the autonomy of art, Hearn's aesthetic revolt, it is true, had much in common with those of Wilde's aestheticism and Zola's naturalism. Yet, in rejecting the former's puerility and the latter's scientific determinism, Hearn came to insist on our return to life as the source of art. His philosophical revolt resulted in what he termed "idealism," and included aesthetic as well as moral criticism. If there is much insight, consistency, and integrity in his critical utterances on the major issues of the decade, it is because Hearn fulfilled his early determination, to strive after truth, and also dared to be oracular whenever necessary.

VII

Literary
Study

The
Japanese
Lectures

In December 1895 Hearn accepted the chair of English literature at the Imperial University of Tokyo. In the years following his arrival in Japan (1890), he had taught at government schools, first in Matsue, and then in Kumamoto,—with impressive success.[1] From this teaching experience he had come to know a great deal about Japanese students, their dreams, desires, despairs, their weaknesses and fortes. He knew what kind of students he would have at the university. He had already started a systematic study of English literature, partly as pedagogical duty and partly for his personal benefit. With *Glimpses of Unfamiliar Japan* (1894) he had proved to the world his sympathetic understanding of Japan; now he was entering on the second phase of his Japanese study. In his philosophical study he was reaching the point from which to attempt a synthesis of evolutionism and Buddhism. It was at this time that he was persuaded by his friend Professor Basil H. Chamberlain to accept the offer from the university. Hearn's stated hope was to teach literature emotionally and historically upon the principles of evolution.[2]

Hearn's stint of teaching at the Imperial University of Tokyo, and later briefly at Waseda University, extended from the fall of 1896 until his death in September 1904. It was far from a labor of love. Being well aware of his lack of formal academic discipline, he must have felt quite uncomfortable in the post. A man of humility, he naturally tended to underestimate his own caliber as a teacher of literature. Two years later, when his friend Mitchell McDonald suggested that his lectures be printed, Hearn flatly said no. He wrote,

> They are only dictated lectures—dictated out of my head, not from notes even: so the form of them cannot be good. Were I to rewrite each of them ten or fifteen times, I might print them. But that would not be worth while. I am not a scholar, nor a competent critic of the best; there are scores of men able to do the same thing incomparably better.

The only merit he could think of was that his lectures might be "good for the Toyko University," being "adapted, by long experience, to the Japanese student's way of thinking and feeling."[3] Toward the end of his teaching career he was still harping on the old complaint. About his subject, he said, he knew very little and "never could learn very much." He had learned just enough, he said, to talk about the general history of English literature, and about the major poets and prose writers of the later periods, without the use of notes or books. "But," he continued, "I have not the scholarship needed for the development and exercise of the critical faculty, in the proper sense of the term." He knows "nothing of Anglo-Saxon"; and his knowledge of the relation of English literature to other European literature is "limited to the later French and English romantic and realistic periods." All he could do was to make the most of this situation, to stick to his "illegitimate" approach to literature, namely to teach literature as "an art of emotional expression"—on the basis of imagination.[4]

Yet, ten years after Hearn's death, when many selections made from his former students' verbatim notes began to appear one after another, it turned out that he was by no means the best judge of his own achievement. His misgivings about the lack of form in his lectures were groundless; many actually preferred the notes to an improved version Hearn might have made for publication. To these readers Hearn endeared himself by virtue of his originality, spontaneous response, and unguarded candor. In fact, few would take issue even with his occasional indulgence in superlatives. In introducing Hearn's lectures, John Erskine said: "In substance if not in form they are criticism of the finest kind, unmatched in English unless we return to the best of Coleridge, and in some ways unequalled by anything in Coleridge."[5] In the controversy that followed this statement, Erskine would neither modify nor retract his initial stand.[6] Norman Foerster, reviewing *Interpretations of Literature,* the first of these posthumous collections, found "many traces of their impromptu presentation," denied any distinction to Hearn as "a judge of literature," but conceded that Hearn must have been "an illuminating teacher." [7] Somewhat more sympathetically, S. P. B. Mais, author of *Books and Their Writers,* observed: "I have proved by experience that the best books of criticism on English literature for beginners are Lafcadio Hearn's *Interpretations of Literature,* and *Appreciations of Poetry.*" [8] Again, when Hearn's *A History of English Literature* appeared, the *Times Literary Supplement* greeted it with the following comment: "Few lecturers in English, in England, can afford to leave this tribute from Japan unstudied." [9]

The status of Hearn's lectures is still uncertain, especially in relation to the rest of his work. Some dismiss them lightly as if they were a waste of time; some can find in them no other value than that they are Hearn's lectures; some, while accepting their value, conclude that their existence is merely accidental in his career and quite extraneous to his work; still others feel a certain correlation between these lectures and the rest of his work, and yet fail to determine what it is. Such negative views as these can be found even among Hearn's admirers. But I should like to assign a far more positive value to the Japanese lectures not only as a direct continuation but also as the consummation of Hearn's American newspaper writings, notably those dealing with literature and philosophy. In his Japanese lectures there is the same critical spirit, with greater maturity, that made possible his emergence as a critic on the American literary scene. In them, also, he entertains more definite thoughts about criticism, aesthetics, and world literature. In Japan, as in America, Hearn had to have an outlet for his critical intelligence, and his lectures served the purpose well.[10]

Evidence for this continuity in Hearn's criticism may be found in his brief survey of American literature. That there is no mention of Herman Melville, Mark Twain, Emily Dickinson, and other major figures is understandable in view of two facts; Hearn, now thousands of miles away from America, was no longer in touch with its literary situation, and there was still a generation before any serious study of American literature was to be contemplated even at home. But whatever he had to say about his chosen figures is worth noting. Does American literature as such exist? So Hearn asked in "Notes on American Literature," one of his special lectures delivered in the fall of 1898.[11] It does, he answered, though "in a very small quantity." Take American poetry, for instance: Bryant is but "a pale shadow" of eighteenth-century literature, and his good work is so small in quantity that he can hardly be said to have done more than attempt to maintain tradition. Whittier managed well "only the very simplest forms of verse." Long-fellow, Hearn's old favorite, is "beyond all question the greatest American poet"; but even he ranks "at his best scarcely above what English critics would call the third class." There is indeed Poe, one American poet who shows "a really noteworthy mastery of verse." Though he wrote "very little," his poetry has proved to be influential, especially abroad. Lanier, as his poem, "The Marsh Song," indicates, was promising. He might have become "one of the very best of poets," had he not died young. Hearn concludes: "There is going on in America a sort of poetical incubation which promises well; but which will scarcely produce anything great for two generations to come."

With prose, Hearn says, the situation is different. American prose has made its impact on English prose. There is first Irving, who has become "a classic which *must* be read." There is little doubt about his "immense importance" in the literature of the English-speaking world. Opposing critics and popular judgment, Hearn regards "The Adalantado of the Seven Cities; or the Phantom Island" as the best of all Irving's short stories. Cooper, "the greatest novelist of pioneer life in the American West," has little to offer "in the way of pure literature." He ranks high "only as a story-teller, not as a stylist, nor as a man of letters in the truest sense of the word." To Poe and Hawthorne as an interesting pair, Hearn devotes much space. Poe is as much "unmoral" as Hawthorne is "moral." Poe's international and perennial fame owes much to two important qualities of his short stories—their imaginary realization of all human wishes and the pleasure of fear, that is, dream fear. With this general observation Hearn attempts a detailed analysis of Poe's stories. He calls special attention to Poe's poetical prose—the highest effect of which even Baudelaire failed to emulate; the *raison d'être* of the ghost story in terms of the sublime; and, finally, Poe's lack of a sense of humor. All these points can be applied to Hearn as well. Singularly enough, he thinks very little of Poe's metaphysical writings. Because of his philosophical objection to Poe's position, Hearn finds them likely to become obsolete. While Poe's imagination is "entirely his own," Hawthorne's is "recognizably the imagination of Puritan New England"; hence his profound moral sense and dark imagination. Of the romances, *The Scarlet Letter* is "the most gloomy"; *The House of the Seven Gables,* "a very remarkable book"; and *The Marble Faun,* full of "that dark moral tone so peculiar to Hawthorne—the awful sense of responsibility and conscience, characteristic of the Puritan mind, insufficiently brightened by the brightest atmosphere of the 19th century feeling." Concerning the short stories Hearn agrees with Gautier that "Rappaccini's Daughter" is "a very great bit of art." "At all events," says Hearn, "if you read this story, you have read the very best pages of Hawthorne."

Hearn's partiality is unmistakable in his dealing with Holmes and Lowell. Holmes's *Breakfast-Table* Series is "good." His "delicate touch of mockery" leaves no room for "religious nonsense." The series is full of "moral tonic," nevertheless. *Elsie Venner* is, in Hearn's opinion, "not only the most extraordinary book that Dr. Holmes wrote," but also "one of the most extraordinary novels of the 19th century." As an evolutional novel the book is "not so well known, as it deserves to be." About Lowell, on the other hand, Hearn seems to have little good to say. He would certainly not question the significance of Lowell as editor of various magazines in promoting American literature, but he suspects that Lowell's position has been much exaggerated.

Though calling Emerson "one of the greatest figures in the history of American thought," Hearn, to our disappointment, affords little space to this giant, whose genius he had once called "irregular, strong" —as early as 1882 in his obituary note of Emerson.[12] This is probably because of the limitations of the lecture itself, as Hearn himself apologizes. "Great" as Emerson can be in his philosophical poetry and in his emotional style, Hearn is reluctant to recommend him to his students as a model of either of prose or verse. His style is "inimitable; it is Emerson himself," though it may teach "the value and the strength of very short sentences." But "from the artistic point of view," in his natural eloquence "a great deal of ore remains crude." From this comment it is not difficult to see why Hearn was so unreasonably harsh and severe about Whitman's poetry that he made a separate lecture on the poet, as he explains, "not to praise him, but to warn you against him, as far as I am able."[13] As regards Whitman's philosophical monism and artistic integrity, Hearn shows an insight and generous sympathy. His real complaint is Whitman's lack of form: ". . . when a composition has no form at all, it is nonsense to call it poetry." Whitman's tremendous influence is due to two qualities, his "literary protoplasm" and his "great temptation to the lazy and to the incapable." His poetry possesses "certain merits of coarse strength and excellent sincerity," but it is not poetry; it is not "literature in the true sense." There is no hint of compromise in Hearn's conclusion: "He is worth reading for the sake of his honesty, his simplicity, his real innocence; but he is not worth reading twice. I imagine that he may have had some lesson to teach—the lesson of being true to oneself in literature." This judgment is obviously the result of Hearn's Gautierite obsession with form as the basis of art.

With the American local color movement in general Hearn is disappointed. Bret Harte, once known for his work, "rough work, but very strong," has exhausted the subject which made him famous. There are, besides, writers like Marion Crawford, Aldrich, Cable, Craddock, and Woolson—all of whose works have "a delicate flavour of romance." At this point Hearn ventures one of his most interesting predictions about Howells and James. Both, it is true, belong to realism, but they work in entirely different manners. Those critics who believe Howells' success to be only temporary are quite right, Hearn suspects. His style is "simple and strong, highly polished, and of the first class," but his characters and scenes are "invariably commonplace." There is "perfect realism." *The Rise of Silas Lapham,* his "first great novel," will remain "the best." James, however, is "never commonplace." He is "always realistic" and yet "always extraordinary." "In my opinion," declares Hearn, "Henry James is by far the greatest of living American writers, —although his greatness is not to be measured by his popularity." He is "too refined in his art to be popular." On the whole, James is "the only writer of English novels possessing the same kind of psychological art as distinguishes the great modern novelists of France—such as Daudet or Bourget." Furthermore, James is "capable of an astonishing variety of work." As an artist of social chronicle he can take his reader to all corners of the known world; but also he is "a moral fabulist." He takes his reader "out of the known world of fact into the unknown world of psychological fact." "Almost anything that he has written is worthy of study," Hearn tells his Japanese students, adding, "I must warn you that he is very difficult, perhaps the most difficult of all novelists of the time." In view of our recent James revival Hearn's observation seems prophetic.[14]

Other evidence for the continuity in Hearn's criticism can be found in his remarks on nineteenth-century French literature. Here he commands a distant, and therefore more objective, view of major figures, in three groups: Hugo, Musset, Sainte-Beuve, Gautier, Dumas, Balzac, Mérimée, and Sand; Nerval, Louis Bertrand, Baudelaire, and Flaubert; and finally Maupassant, the brothers Goncourt, Daudet, and Zola. As we see in his special lecture, "Note on Some French Romantics," Hearn still retains his wild enthusiasm for Hugo, Gautier, Nerval, and

Flaubert, and his fair appreciation for Balzac, Daudet, and others.[15] His emphasis falls on the development of nineteenth-century French prose, especially the contrast between Gautier's "myopic" style and Mérimée's "presbyopic" style; the significance of Baudelaire's poetical prose in the Anglo-American-French tradition; Flaubert's attempt to combine both Gautier's ornate prose and Baudelaire's melodious prose; and Maupassant's simplest yet very powerful style.

By now Hearn has grown tolerant of Zola's art, if not of naturalism as such. He eases his early philosophical objection to what Zola stood for, and stresses the obvious discrepancy between Zola the doctrinaire and Zola the artist. Now he has come to appreciate the historical and even aesthetic significance of Zola's efforts: "No matter what critics may say—justly say—about Zola's immorality, filthiness, shamelessness, there can be no question of his genius." He is "a very great artist." Referring to the inevitable inconsistency between Zola's theory and practice, or between his conscious intention and actual achievement, Hearn continues:

> . . . he is a great artist not because he is a realist, or a naturalist, as he wished to be called; he is a great artist because in spite of all his theories, he is really a romantic—a man whose imagination is enormous and lurid, and perceives in exaggerated form all the horrible side of human existence.

"His realism," Hearn suggests, "lies only in the fact that he uses notes as they never were used before." Like his other references to Zola, this one indicates that Hearn has not compromised. In fact, he is firm in his idealistic stand, but he also has insight into the nature of artistic creation. Hearn possesses two important qualities for a critic, the capacity of perceiving the genuine merit of any given artist, regardless of his known literary tags, and the capacity of appreciating the genius of a writer whose nature is alien, contrary, and repugnant to his own.

That Hearn came to recognize Zola's artistic genius, although rejecting his scientific determinism, is indeed significant because it followed his enthusiastic acceptance of evolutionism. As will be seen elsewhere, evolutional philosophy came to provide Hearn's early idealism with a philosophical foundation, his aesthetics with a theoretical structure, and his concept of world literature with an intellectual endorsement. There is clear indication that his philosophical study was not detrimental to his critical sensibility, and that each in fact complemented the other. Primarily as a student of literature, Hearn continued to widen his view by exploring further English, German, Scandinavian, and Russian literatures. When he came to conceive of them as a European literature he also came to the logical point from which to anticipate the meeting of the West and the East. Both by fortifying his philosophical foundation and expanding his literary horizon, Hearn for the first time reached the point from which to envision the world at large—not only philosophically but also literarily. As a teacher of literature he now had the task of translating his own vision into a language comprehensible to his student audience, without distorting its ordered scale of values, overstressing the one at the expense of the other, or sacrificing its concrete immediacy. It was a task always familiar to Hearn, the "transformation de la volupté en connaissance," to use Baudelaire's phrase.

His lectures as a whole consist of two distinct groups: first, there are two consecutive historical surveys of English literature, each covering three academic years; then there are also special lectures on subjects directly and indirectly related to literature which appealed to his fancy and which students needed—in his judgment. Both groups are a result of his double strategy, literary history and criticism, to use our modern terminology. In the former, where he felt his own scholarly deficiency, he traces the evolution of English literature, with frequent references to many contemporary authorities, through its major stages and periods. In the latter, however, Hearn is very much his own master, grouping poetry by subjects of interest, expounding fundamental laws of artistic composition, offering a veteran craftsman's practical advice, and evaluating individual writers and their important works.[16] Whether aware of it or not, he also came to tackle one of the most important questions in literary study, where and how to reconcile literary history and criticism.

As his library catalog indicates, Hearn, especially after accepting the university post, set out to purchase the major English classics, most of which he studied assiduously and stored well in his prodigious memory. There seems to be little doubt that, in preparing an historical survey of English literature, he made a special study of contemporary scholars, such as Hallam, Symonds, Taine, Gosse, Dowden, and Saintsbury, and attempted to incorporate into his own observation the result of their scholarship and the best of their criticism. Although he entertained uncommon respect for Saintsbury, Gosse, and Dowden, Hearn freely opposed their views on many points.

His survey possesses its own distinct personality. As he said in the postscript to his first series, it is intended to familiarize students with representative figures and significant movements. It may be only "the skeleton or frame of a plan which includes all that is important," but that will do, since students, if they desire, can fill up the gaps through private study. In Hearn's opinion, however, "familiarity with a single great author is infinitely better than a superficial knowledge of even a thousand second or third-class authors." After all, literary study ought to begin "from the solid parts—the greatest work—never from the work of small or curious writers." While admitting the possibility of occasional errors, he is confident about the essential value of his survey. His hope is that he has succeeded in his objective, "to awaken your interest in particular directions."[17] Upon this foundation Hearn makes it a rule, wherever and whenever he can, to present the development of English literature from three points of view which he considers all-important for his students. First, his persistent application of evolutional philosophy to certain issues makes the whole survey both dogmatic and consistent. In applying it to Berkeley's idealistic opposition to eighteenth-century materialism, Byron's widely known but much misunderstood Satanism, the philosophical error of G. H. Lewes and other followers of Comte's positivism, and Meredith as a representative poet of evolutionism, Hearn apparently overreaches himself. Even when clearly wrong, as he often is, he is amusing rather than annoying. Second, his constant reference to the contribution of foreign elements to English character and literature is intended to make his students aware of the salutary effects of foreign influences on a particular national literature. He emphasizes, for example, the importance of pre-Christian elements in molding English character and literature, and the impact of Gautier and Baudelaire on English poetic sensibility. Third, his frequent reference to parallels and contrasts between the West and the East enable him to visualize English literature in terms of what his students have experienced in their own culture. The Scandinavian religion of courage, identified as one of the contributing factors in the formation of English character, is compared to the guiding principle of Japanese feudalism.

Hearn's evolutionism, taken alone, might be considered only his personal bias; so, too, his romantic stand against classicism, neo-classicism, or realism. Yet, when combined together, they no longer appear personal biases. They enable Hearn to write his own version of the literary history of England, wholly from the point of view of his generation. While pausing on the significance of the eighteenth century as the starting point of modern literature, he said: "After all has been said and done, our study of English literature must be essentially a study of living literature, contemporary literature."[18] Evidently he is not contented with chronicling literature as something accumulated in the dead past; he is intent on interpreting literature in terms of the modern literary conscience. For this reason he devotes half of his time and space to a comprehensive survey of the nineteenth century, roughly two-thirds of which is reserved exclusively for the Victorian period. His approach, contrary to the traditional practice in literary study, made F. L. Pattee, in 1937, epitomize Hearn's Japanese lectures in general as "a brilliant introduction to the literary period we are studying now." [19]

As a Victorian, Hearn regarded the whole nineteenth century as a continuation of Romantic expression that started with the pre-Romantic revolt against the classical school. His standpoint is that of a Victorian when he designates the Romantic poets of two generations as "Pre-Victorian Poets." In dealing with the nineteenth century Hearn is at his best. His approach to the period in three major genres, poetry, fiction, and non-fiction (including essays, histories, and criticism), is generally twofold. Within the historical context he makes an overall survey of English literature, and at the same time undertakes in his special lectures a close study of individual authors in the light of their major works. In these special lectures Hearn discusses almost all the major figures from Blake to Robert Bridges, remarks briefly on whatever in their artistic personality or character he considers pertinent to their achievements, and then moves on to elucidate their individual works in terms of intrinsic and extrinsic values. Often he makes a comparative study of several poets—not to determine their rank by any arbitrary standard, but to sharpen some basic difference in their artistic qualities. He also deals with those figures, minor and otherwise, who are likely to be sacrificed because of the generalizations inevitable in an historical survey of literature. In either case Hearn refrains, as a rule, from venturing generalizations or speculations about his subjects until he can amply explicate their works. In his analyses of writers, and especially of their works, Hearn shows us the best of his critical performance.

What he attempts to do in his historical survey is to indicate the general relationship of the major figures to significant literary movements, and their indebtedness and contribution to their tradition. To him literary scholarship means this kind of correlated knowledge; hence his profound respect for it. Once scholarship claims to be more than this, Hearn seems to believe, it becomes injurious to literary study. He is convinced that the core of literary study, which makes it a genuine literary experience, is not scholarship but criticism.[20] It is in this light that we must understand him when he speaks of his own want of "the scholarship needed for the development and exercise of the critical faculty, in the proper sense of the term."

In his special lectures Hearn not only offers the best specimens of his critical performance but also delineates the nature of criticism, its function, and the primary virtues that make a critic.[21] Discussing Sainte-Beuve's impact on his three English followers, Saintsbury, Dowden, and Gosse, Hearn defines criticism in this manner: "To state it as simply as possible, criticism is the art of discovering and of stating what is good and what is not good in a book." It has little to do with the classical school of criticism, which uses prescribed methods and rules, especially in treating new works. In the same essay, he ventures another definition: "A great criticism should be equally true in all times and countries, for the highest criticism should not concern itself with any question except those of beauty and of truth—nay, I should add, eternal beauty and eternal truth." These two definitions do not contradict each other. As the former points to the beginning of all criticism, the latter suggests the universality toward which the highest form of criticism should tend.

As he sees it, there are three qualities which a critic must possess in order to perform his proper function: first, he must be free from any sort of bias, prejudice, and narrowness; second, he must have the kind of scholarship that is at once wide and profound; and third, he must be born with "a certain kind of genius," or "intuitive and perceptive faculties of an extraordinary kind." Education can give us scholarship and help us free ourselves from all sorts of prejudice; but we must be born with the third quality. For this faculty of intuition or perception Hearn uses the term "soul sympathy." Through this inborn faculty a critic is able to perceive the "character," or "face" of his subject. It is of prime importance to do this, because criticism is essentially our character judgment of a given subject, whether it be an author or a book. Like many of his contemporaries, Hearn regarded Sainte-Beuve as "the greatest critic that ever lived" because of "his genius, his infinite sympathy, his irreproachable tolerance, his profound humanity." To read Saint-Beuve is therefore "an education," since his criticism is biographical, historical, philosophical, and artistic. Few of us today would go this far. The statement is important, however, in what it reveals of Hearn rather than of anyone else. At least two of these virtues, a cosmopolitan outlook and the faculty of sympathy, Hearn himself possessed to a remarkable degree.

In designating soul sympathy as one of the critic's essential virtues,

Hearn points to the common ground between the critic and the artist. The artist, owing to his faculty of artistic seeing, is capable of perceiving the "character," "face," or "physiognomy" of things, animate and inanimate. He perceives the emotion of a tree, for example, if a tree is what he is observing.[22] The critic must have the same inborn faculty of seeing the character, face, or physiognomy of the object recreated by the artist. As the artist recognizes the essence of reality, so the critic must recognize the essence of the work he is considering. From this standpoint Hearn defines criticism as "the art of discovering and stating what is good and what is not good in a book." Thus, in reading or seeing the face of their object, both the artist and the critic are much the same: their art is that of discovery, translation, or interpretation. For this reason Hearn defends his kind of criticism against the academic criticism whose primary concern is judgment usually by some extraneous rules and standards. With Hearn, judgment is not the main function of criticism but its logical consequence. Because of his stress on this primary stage of criticism, Hearn's interpretations have a freshness of insight and perception that grips our imagination anew, whether or not we agree with his final judgment.[23]

The art of criticism is, in this sense, the art of reading. By reading properly one recognizes the face or character of the work of art. This art of reading as the basis of literary study Hearn took seriously enough to prepare a special lecture on the subject.[24] In his opinion, reading is the most difficult of all human disciplines. It has nothing to do with amusement, though many of us often confuse one with the other. "Nothing is more difficult in this world," Hearn says, "than to read a book and then to express clearly and truly in a few lines exactly what the literary value of the book is." To achieve this by no means small feat we must have experience as well as capacity. He urges us to study any literary work worth reading "in precisely the same way" that we study a scientific book—not simply for amusement. A good literary work should have the same amount of value in it that a scientific book has, though the value may be "of a totally different kind"; for a good work of literature is indeed a scientific book in the sense that it has been composed "according to the best principles of more than one science, but especially according to the principles of the great sciences of life, the knowledge of human nature." Genuine literary appreciation is possible only when we master the art of reading in relation to an individual work; likewise, judgment is meaningful only when we set literature against the background of life. That is why a great book, as we all know from our own experience, "grows exactly in proportion to the growth of the reader's mind." From this Hearn concludes: "The test of a great book is whether we want to read it only once or more than once." This seemingly naïve and yet most practical advice must be understood as applying only to those who have mastered the art of reading.

Owing to his special stress on the art of reading, Hearn fell neither into historicism, the kind of criticism which plays safe by relying on raw "facts" and conventional judgments, nor into impressionism, the kind of criticism which indulges in sheer subjectivity. His stand that literary study must begin with our understanding of an individual writer or work is well illustrated by many of his special lectures in this category. But the question itself was not new with Hearn; it was already suggested in his Cincinnati article, "That Old Painter," a record of his interview with Mr. Aubrey, a prominent local painter:

Reporter— Then you think that the art of a great artist is only to be felt, not to be described.
Aubrey— Yes.
Reporter— But it is an acknowledged truth in the literary world that there's no feeling which cannot be verbally expressed—as Edgar Poe took pains to observe.
Aubrey— I don't believe that is a truth.
Reporter— But I have read elaborate art criticisms in which the style of an artist—his peculiar characteristics as an artist—were technically described.
Aubrey— I never knew anybody to try to describe the style of an artist without making fools of themselves.
Reporter— But that is what the critics are for—to describe such things.
Aubrey— I think, of all people, critics are the most soulless, unappreciative, materialistic, unfeeling.[25]

This dialog reveals something of Hearn's early awareness of the familiar hostility between the artist and the critic. With his reference to Poe, Hearn may have had in mind his avowed master's essay, "The Philosophy of Composition." Whatever the accuracy of this conjecture, he was too conscious a craftsman either to play safe or to remain with his impressions alone. As an artist he was convinced of the autonomy of art; as a critic he was aware of the anatomy of art; and more important, as an artist-critic he had to demand both.

In his special lectures Hearn's criticism, as essentially extensive application of the art of reading, groups around three dominant concerns: literary works; literary situations; and literary issues. In each he attempts to find in what terms his particular subject can best be approached. In the first group dealing with individual works Hearn sets out to unveil the face or character of each work and thereby illuminate its unique quality. In approaching Poe's verse, for instance, he focuses on the poet's primary poetic virtues, mastery of language and novelty of fancy.[26] Taking "The Bells" as an example of Poe's musical device "repetend" carried to the highest point, Hearn illustrates Poe's highly selective and deliberate method through which four different kinds of mood and atmosphere are created by four different kinds of bells—"merriment and sparkling brightness," by means of sleigh bells; "rapturous joy, pleasure, softness, sweetness," by means of wedding bells; harsh fear and violent confusion, by means of firebells; and "ghostliness" and "terror" by means of church funeral bells. Hearn's analysis reveals how, as the poem progresses, merriment evaporates into death, light recedes into darkness, and finally we are thrust into the domain of strange and horrid fantasy. Likewise, in his critical analysis of "The Haunted Palace," Hearn stresses the originality of Poe's fancy in the shadowy and the fearful, a quality common to most of his poetry. Designating the palace as "the mind of man, or perhaps of a beautiful woman—long radiant with happiness, then helplessly wrecked," Hearn follows in detail the way the poem, by its inextricably knit imagery, depicts "a mind becoming insane." After explicating the piece at length, Hearn likens Poe's technique to that of Paganini playing "any tune upon one string," "ghostly fear" in this case.

With Browning's "colossal attempt in psychology," *The Ring and the Book,* Hearn fares as well, but this time by concentrating on its structural peculiarity, namely its point-of-view method, which makes possible the poet's dramatic study of the complexity of life, and which creates a sense of ambiguity by intensifying the fallibility of human judgment and the impossibility of the absolute truth.[27] With equal dexterity Hearn elucidates Meredith's Arabian fable, *The Shaving of Shagpat,* which in his estimation, is "the greatest fable imagined during the nineteenth century." [28] Hearn feels that, in spite of Gosse's "charming" essay on it, the fable remains obscure, owing to "want of critical appreciation." Although there is perhaps "no particular purpose" on Meredith's part, Hearn believes that we can still seek a symbolic meaning. The fable can be taken as an allegory of a familiar human situation,—conflict between radical reformism and reactionary conservatism. As Hearn analyzes it, Bagarag the barber-hero stands for the "reformer who is not allowed to reform anything—threatened with death if he persists," and the "single hair" on Shagpat's head, for "any social illusion, any great popular error." The metamorphosis of Noorna, the bride of Bagarag, from a shriveled old woman to a young lady of divine beauty is symbolic of our mastery of science, "the most delightful mistress." And the sword of Aklis, found by her assistance, represents the sword of science, "the power of exact scientific knowledge, wielded against error, superstition, humbug, and convention of every injurious kind." Hearn admits that "this bit of interpretation" cannot reveal the whole of its meaning. Whether or not we agree with Hearn's high estimate of the fable, his reading does not contradict the position we know Meredith to have on the issue. These examples suggest something of Hearn's intuitive faculty of responding to the essential quality of his subject. His closeness to his subjects is such that there is little intrusion of his personality. It is undoubtedly for this reason that Hearn is at his best in the first group of special lectures.

In the second group Hearn's criticism goes beyond its primary stage, a study of individual writers and works, in order to grasp literary situations. His survey of Victorian poetry is a good example of the more comprehensive approach. Hearn considers the Victorian poetic situation as the meeting of diverse poetical traditions with the all-pervading new science; he pairs Tennyson, "the supreme perfection" of the Romantic movement, with Browning, who had "gifts greater than any possessed by Tennyson"; and Rossetti, who furthered Tennyson's tradition in the domain of medieval sentiment, with Swinburne, who "carried the art of English verse to the highest point ever reached in the direction of musical effect." Only after these two pairs of major poets come Meredith, Arnold, and other minor figures.[29] Hearn then devotes special lectures to individual discussion of these poets, and of their important works. In these close-ups he attempts to settle many questions: where the poets stand in relation to their predecessors; how they further their poetic tradition; where they can claim their originality; where they meet each other in the general poetic milieu; where they differ from each other; and the like.[30] In his conclusion, Hearn considers all of them in much larger perspective, first raising the question: How many of these poets are entitled to the office of world poet?

None, it seems, to his disappointment, though their failure may be due to the unsettled state of the Victorian world itself. Tennyson, Browning, Meredith, and Swinburne, it is true, represent the metaphysical directions of Victorian poetry.[31] Referring to *In Memoriam* and other works, Hearn declares his old love, Tennyson, to be "rather a reflector, a mirror, of ideas of a class than an original voice," the quintessence of his poetry being not its newness, but the extreme beauty of his poetic language. Compared with him, Browning is "very much deeper," as his dramatic monolog, "Rabbi Ben Ezra," exemplifies. His contribution to the metaphysical poetry of the Victorian period is his psychological method, which becomes "philosophical in the best sense" by exploring ways of life. On the other hand, Swinburne and Meredith are far more explicit than either Tennyson or Browning. Their position is unmistakably pantheistic, but their similarity ends here. Taking "Hertha" as representative of Swinburne's philosophical poetry, Hearn suggests that its core, Hertha, should be understood as the combination of three conceptions of nature: the scientist's "Force," the scientific philosopher's "the Unknown," and the religious thinker's "God." Thus Hertha embodies the unity of life. But the poet's assertion of the religion of human love is still "very much open to discussion." Hearn concludes: "As a poem, 'Hertha' is beyond praise; as philosophy and morality it is unquestionably thin and disappointing." When Meredith comes to deal with the meaning of life in relation to ourselves, he has more to say than Swinburne, Hearn thinks. "Earth and Man" is a case in point. It suggests that the real purpose of nature is "to force man to develop himself until he reaches the divine condition." By accepting "the moral order of the universe," Meredith becomes more positive than Swinburne.

Hearn deals with these poets exclusively from the philosophical point of view; but in general, he believes, there are two ways of approaching poetry, either by its form or by its thought. Since two kinds of poetic perfection are seldom united in any one individual poet, Hearn suggests that we value a poet by the quality in which he excels. Rossetti's lack of a philosophy explains Hearn's silence concerning the thought in his poetry. Indeed, Rossetti rarely concerns himself with the great problems or mysteries of life, although he is "perhaps the very greatest of our emotional poets" of the century and "nearly as great as a master of form as Swinburne." So with Tennyson, who, as a thinker, is "much below" Meredith. Arnold, on the other hand, should best be studied as a thinker of "a very peculiar kind." The fact that Hearn devotes nearly forty pages to a study of Arnold's "gray, colourless, but very curious poetry," may be a puzzle if we recall his early disparagement of Arnold as "one of the colossal humbugs of the century," or "a fifth-rate poet and unutterably dreary essayist." [32] In his special lecture Hearn still thinks little of Arnold's essays and his literary style. After having done justice to many of Arnold's poems, Hearn comes to the poet's philosophical position. Arnold's, he believes, is "not the value of an expositor of new ideas, but the value of the man himself, a personal value, a value of character." His character and therefore his way of thinking do "faithfully represent hundreds of thousands of similar characters and similar ways of thinking during the middle of the present century, the thought of cultivated minds." Here is the weakness of Arnold's poetry. He remains a faithful mirror of his own age; his vision fails to go beyond it. This, in Hearn's view, is due to Arnold's philosophical dilemma, such as may be found in his poem, "In Harmony with Nature." Pointing specifically to the lines, "Man must begin, where Nature ends;/Nature and man can never be fast friends," Hearn cites Shakespeare's: "Nature is made better by no means, but Nature makes that means," which is in accord with the evolutional concept of the essential harmony between man and nature. "Dover Beach," as an expression of the poet's narrow philosophical position, does not satisfy Hearn, either. As he sees it, the poem depicts no drama of thought, being simply "the presentation of thoughts awakened by the sound of the sea in the mind of a scholar and a doubter." In conceiving nature and man in mutual distrust and animosity, Arnold remains a victim of philosophical scepticism, torn between the old and the new world.

In surveying the Victorian poetic situation, too, Hearn begins with close reading, but as he goes on to probe into the philosophical foundation of particular poems he is driven to the point of passing judgment, a partisan attitude which is hardly unavoidable in any sort of philosophical enquiry. This tendency becomes manifest in the third group of his special lectures, where Hearn deals with literary issues of controversial nature. In general, he is not willing to await the verdict of history, as, for instance, when he deals with Tolstoi's *Resurrection*.[33] He begins by saying that it is the duty of the literary student to acquaint himself with those great literary issues of his own day which appear to have important moral or social significance. When Hearn speaks of Russian literature he continues his early fight against Zola's scientific naturalism. Russian literature may be small in quantity, but its quality has "not been surpassed by any other literature, not even by the French." Russian writers are not masters of form as the French are, but in depicting human life, "so as to bestir the best emotions of the reader," they really stand "almost alone." Next to Turgenev, Tolstoi represents the highest literary art of Russia; but Hearn suspects that Tolstoi "will eventually be judged even greater than Turgenev" for his dramatic faculty. With this introductory note he comes to consider Tolstoi's recent work, *Resurrection* (1900), in the light of the controversy it has created in Europe. It is "a religious novel,"—religious not "in relation to dogma or doctrine of any kind," but in relation to the moral sentiment. The offense of this religious novel "only happens to be that it is more Christian than Christianity." In it the author attempted to express "essentially the Christian doctrine—the doctrine of human love as held by the ancient Christians, and after a manner antagonistic to the modern doctrine and political Christianity of Russia." Though the alleged cause of Tolstoi's excommunication is that he spoke of Christ as being only a man, Hearn thinks that the resentment on the part of the Church authorities is something else. It is "the manner in which the great machinery of the Church, is quite as often used to uphold injustice as to make for justice," and that "there is, even among the aristocracy of the Church, a kind of political indifference to the essential duties of that Church." Although defending Tolstoi, Hearn does not fail to detect something defective in "this very terrible and wonderful book." As a follower of Spencer he cannot but point out the naïveté in Tolstoi's social application of the doctrine of brotherly love. As he sees it, this doctrine is "beautiful" and there is a great deal of truth in it, but by no means all the truth. "The existing characters of men," Hearn explains, following Spencer's social conservatism, "cannot be so changed, either by religious teaching or by education or law or by any other means, as to render such a policy of life even thinkable." Then he concludes: "But the defects which I have specified are after all, on the noble side; they do not really spoil the work in the least; and they make even men who cannot accept such teaching, who cannot help smiling at it, think in a generous way about matters which deserve the most careful consideration." As Hearn qualifies it, this sort of personal objection has little to do with the artistic virtue of *Resurrection* itself.

In approaching literary works, literary situations, and literary issues, Hearn's criticism ranges from explication to evaluation, from interpretation to judgment, from appreciation to remonstration; but he always begins with the art of reading as the foundation of criticism. If this fact were kept in mind, few would accuse his criticism of being merely dogmatic from start to finish. His criticism is in fact anything but a closed system. This is due to his belief that a critic should not forget his primary function, the function of instilling in his reader the pleasure of discovering something fresh and the desire of confronting it; the reader must be drawn to the original rather than repelled by it. Hearn does not believe that criticism must or can exist for its own sake; only in relation to the primary work of art can criticism claim its legitimate place in our literary study.

Following his own conviction that "a great book grows exactly in proportion to the growth of the reader's mind," Hearn did not have the slightest intention of imposing his own interpretations upon his young students. As all his lectures indicate, he merely attempted to demonstrate his way of reading and interpreting. Believing that criticism as the art of reading is basically practical, he attempted to show his students how to approach a subject, rather than what to look for. In the lectures there are indeed many weaknesses, but they are a result of his unguarded effort to discover the core of his subjects, instead of playing safe. There are many more virtues. He was never afraid of making mistakes. That is why he said, opening his discussion of Tolstoi's theory of art: "One of the most important things for a literary student to learn is not to allow his judgment to be formed by other people's opinions." His own opinion should be treated in the same way. "Do not think," said Hearn, "that something is good or bad, merely because I say so, but try to find out for yourself by unprejudiced reading and thinking whether I am right or wrong." [34]

Hearn repeated this advice in his lecture, "On a Proper Estimate of Longfellow." It is quite true that Longfellow is "only a second class poet," but a student should remember that second-class poetry may "often be quite as important in its way as" first-class poetry, and that it may "possess emotional beauty that the first class poetry cannot show." Warning his students against some recent English criticisms of the poet, Hearn said: "If we listen to the critics only, we should very soon believe that there is nothing in the world which is good." [35] Or as he said of Keats's unwitting substitution of Cortez for Balboa in his Chapman sonnet, these critics are "very fond of picking out little faults and dwelling upon them." They should first try to see what Keats gained by the error.[36] What Hearn suggests is not critical anarchy but critical tolerance. Art can survive the passage of time only through its merits, not through its faults. It is also naïve to be monistic about literature. Art is as many-sided as life. As the artist creates art out of life, so does the critic interpret art in terms of life. Thus art and criticism do not exclude each other; they should and can complement each other. Yet, there should not be a confusion of art and criticism, or of artist and critic. The artist should mind his own search of the beautiful, whatever it may be; and the critic, his unprejudiced evaluation of his object in the light of life's complexity. The duty of the former is concentration and that of the latter is expansion.

Throughout his Japanese lectures Hearn encouraged his students to form original ideas about whatever book they read. They should not be afraid of doing this, for, he observed, we all know too well that even the greatest critics are liable to strange errors, misjudgments, and misreadings. Therefore, one should, through his own art of reading, cultivate his own critical power. If there is one authority that he can trust as "the greatest of critics," it is the public—"not the public of a day or a generation, but the public of centuries, the consensus of national opinion or of human opinion about a book that has been subjected to the awful test of time." This human opinion, Hearn admits, may be not so articulate as the opinion of a trained critic, since it is based upon feeling rather than upon thinking. It only says "we like this." Yet, there is no judgment so sure as human opinion for the simple reason that it is "the outcome of an enormous experience." [37] Although criticism is basically empirical, it has at least this foundation, which is vague but solid, inarticulate but unerring. What we today call great books should be able to serve as the main background against which a literary student may test his own judgment of a given author or work. In doing so, he can make this human opinion less vague and more articulate, and thereby adjust anew his own outlook. This is far from merely following conventional opinions to play safe. The human opinion of which Hearn speaks is the greatest of critics because it is most impartial. Against the body of impartial opinion a literary student should all the more willingly try to judge a new author or a new work, as Hearn demonstrated with his evaluation of Tolstoi's theory of art, and of *Resurrection*. While introducing James Thomson (B. V.) as typical of the *fin de siècle* pessimism, Hearn said: "Many lecturers on English literature would at this day refuse to consider him in a university lecture; but he has fairly forced his way in the face of all obstacles to a very high place among the minor poets." Hearn did not see "any reason to be silent about him merely because he represents the blackest quality of despair." Since literature is the reflection of all human forms of thought and feeling, the dark should be as great in moral value as the bright.[38] In sum, if the student of literature wishes to be creative in his criticism he must meet two requirements: he must be versed in the art of reading, and he must be open-minded toward new literary works.

In his Japanese lectures Hearn still remains at heart an artist-critic, even when theorizing as a thinker and communicating as a teacher. It is not difficult to depict his faults. His excessive praise of Kipling, Stevenson, and Meredith, and his disparagement of Howells, Whitman, and Arnold are illustrations of them. But there is an essential soundness in many of his critical judgments, as well as in his "illegitimate" approach to literature. He possesses two cardinal virtues as a critic, capacity and candor. If his Japanese lectures can survive the enormous changes in the climate of opinion, it is mainly because there is an essential sanity in his method of literary study. Hearn always comes to grasp the root from which all branches out. Exploring criticism to its primordial function, he has reached the point where it is creative as mediator between art and life. He stands at the basis of criticism, where the artist and the critic can complement each other, and where criticism and literary history can benefit each other. With his lectures, we are always returning to "the infancy of criticism," as Gosse so aptly characterized them.[39] Indeed, our literary study would mean very little should it lose this main source of literary values, that is, our personal response.

VIII

Aesthetics
of
Organic
Memory

Literature
as an
Art of
Emotional
Expression

To teach literature emotionally and historically upon the principles of evolution—this was Hearn's intent as a university teacher in Japan.[1] Perusing his lectures, we are struck by his repeated definition of literature as "an art of emotional expression." A letter to Ellwood Hendrick, written toward the end of his teaching career, expresses in a few lines his belief as interpreter and teacher of literature:

> . . . you might well ask how I could fill my chair. The fact is that I never made any false pretences, and never applied for the post. I realised my deficiencies; but I soon felt where I might become strong, and I taught literature as the expression of emotion and sentiment,—as the representation of life. In considering a poet I tried to explain the quality and the powers of the emotion that he produces. In short, I based my teaching altogether upon appeals to the imagination and the emotions of my pupils,—and they have been satisfied (though the fact may signify little, because their imagination is unlike our own).
>
> Should I attempt to lecture on literature in America, I should only follow the same lines—which are commonly held to be illegitimate, but in which I very firmly believe there are great possibilities.[2]

His teaching experience seems to have fortified his initial stand that literature as an art of emotional expression be taught on the basis of imagination. As he realized the intrinsic value of his "illegitimate" approach, his attitude grew less apologetic and more positive. In his discussion of the highest art, too, Hearn attempted to apply the same definition to art in general. As he sees it, all the arts are "so related to each other, and to some form of highest truth, that each obeys the same laws as the others, and manifests the same principles." In a word, art should signify "the emotional experience of life in some form or other." [3]

This definition of literature as an art of emotional expression is, however, so vague that it is likely to raise more questions than it answers. Some may suspect that it is but Hearn's hazy version of the popular emotive theory of art. If it is not, where does he differ from his fellow theorists? What significance does his professed evolutional philosophy have in relation to this emphasis on emotion? How does his definition relate to his life-long fealty to the cult of the beautiful? And what has become of both his artist-lover theme, the central theme of his retold legends, and his concept of idealism, the concept upon which he attacked Zola's naturalism? With these questions we are really enquiring into the foundation of Hearn's aesthetic thought.

Hearn's aesthetics, if rightly understood, is capable of integrating all these questions into its doctrine of emotion. If his appears to us to be an eccentric or at best esoteric system without clear reasoning and logical basis, it is mainly because Hearn concerns himself with the human psychical structure, a subject which is bound to remain obscure, and because he approaches his subject intuitively and speculatively, though freely using Spencer as his point of reference. In spite of his occasional incoherencies, his inadequate and oft-confusing terminology, and his poetical language, his observations on some major problems of modern aesthetics show much insight, not only into his own art, criticism, and philosophy, but also into the aesthetic tradition shared by Poe, Baudelaire, and others. Furthermore, in exploring the meaning of emotion to its primitive and mythical core, Hearn anticipates Freud and, especially, Jung.

First of all, Hearn's definition of literature as an art of emotional expression stemmed from his conviction about the universality of emotion as the basis of literary art. For this reason he rejected eighteenth-century neo-classicism in general, and questioned the genius of Pope: "Could he write poetry in the highest sense?" Hearn does not think so. Take for instance the *Essay on Man:* It is "supremely perfect proverbial literature put into rhyme—that is all"; but this is not "poetry" in the highest sense. The implication here is obvious—that form, the poet's chief poetic merit, can scarcely amend his lack of emotional quality; hence Hearn's conclusion: "Great verse or emotional verse he never did write." [4] This suggests Hearn's belief in the organic reciprocity between life and art, but he was also aware that there is a difference between the natural and the aesthetic emotion. So he criticized Byron's art: "Passion is not poetry. To utter one's feeling in verse is not poetry. That is only the beginning, the foundation, of a poem." [5] By the same token he chided the Victorian Spasmodics for their failure to "compress" emotion "to get the power." [6] In his opinion, art is not an escape from emotion, but its transmutation, a transmutation of the natural into the aesthetic emotion, the personal into the superpersonal. Artistic creation must therefore be the artist's conscious impersonalization of the natural and the personal. Only when the artist can think of his personal grief, for instance, "as representing only one little drop in the great sea of the world's pain," can art become universal—through its "beautiful and impersonal form." "Nobody," Hearn warns, "should allow himself for a moment to imagine that his own particular grief, that his own private loss, that his own personal pain, can have any value in literature, except in so far as it truly represents the great pain of human life." [7]

How, then, should the artist go about this task of perceiving his personal passion as representative of the universal phenomenon? Hearn's special lecture, "On Composition," is his attempt to answer this question. [8] As might be expected, the lecture is by no means a formal treatise; it is an artist's shop talk, a fact which may make it all the more interesting. At the outset he introduces himself as a workman—"only as a practical man-of-letters, as one who has served his apprenticeship at the difficult trade of literature." In dealing with literature as the kind of trade that can only be acquired by practice, Hearn rectifies certain common errors among literary students. Education, he says, may teach you theories about literature, but this has nothing to do with literature as a practical art. To put it simply, education does not make an artist. That is, the poet is born, not made. This romantic theory Hearn no doubt accepts, though he adds that no great work is possible without painful effort. Yet, in literature as a practical art there are certain rules, not rules of composition, not rules of grammar or prosody, rhetorical at best, but "higher rules" which are universal and applicable "equally well to every language under the sun, no matter what its construction." "For," he continues, "these universal rules have to do only with the truth; and truth is truth everywhere, no matter in what tongue it may be spoken." The kernel of this special lecture is therefore Hearn's exploration of that which constitutes the universal rules of literature as an art of emotional expression.

First he defines emotion by distinguishing it from sensation. Then he theorizes on its value, "its fugitive subtlety," and "the extreme difficulty of getting hold of it." The sensation always precedes the emotion; the sensation is "the first impression received from the senses, or the renewal in memory of such an impression"; the emotion, on the other hand, is "the feeling, very complex, that follows the sensation or impression." More accurately stated, the result of a certain sensation would be "something like a photograph, nothing more"—"a coloured photograph" which would record "almost exactly a visual impression." But photography is not art; its mechanical realism, no matter how accurate, has no worth, at least from the artistic point of view. "To describe sensations," as Hearn puts it, "would be no more literature in the higher sense, than a photograph could be called art in the higher sense." He suggests, returning to his point of departure, that literature is "not a picture of sensations, but of emotions." At the same time it would be a serious mistake to jumble emotions with "tears," "sorrow," and "regret."

What is this emotion, then? This he illustrates by the simplest kind, say "the emotion of a tree." "Two things happen," Hearn reminds us, "when you look at a tree." First there is "the picture of the tree reflected upon the brain through the medium of sight," or "a little card picture," "a little photograph of the tree." But almost as quickly there will come "a second impression, very different from the first." It is "a peculiar feeling of some kind." This is because the tree has "a certain character." The perception of the character of the tree creates the feeling or the emotion of the tree. And that is what the artist looks for.

Hearn then explains that everything, animate or inanimate, causes a certain feeling within its observer—by virtue of its "face," "physiognomy," or "character." If the example of the tree does not convince, he suggests another, namely our most common daily experience, our so-called facial impression of a stranger. Hearn asks: Is it not true that such an impression is immediately followed by some kind of feeling? If this is a familiar experience, it is simply because the object happens to be a human face. The difference between the artist and the rest of the world is that the artist is capable of perceiving the face of things, whether animate or inanimate, whereas the common people are incapable of such an artistic perception, for they are long conditioned by their practical concern or educational bias to see these objects always in terms of the ideas and the languages of other men. That is why they do not know how to describe their own feeling, a habit which is "contrary to every principle of art."

In this regard the child is incomparably superior to the average man. Because of its absolute innocence, the child is capable of artistic seeing. It is not too much to say that the artist sees like the child. This point Hearn further elaborates—much in the manner of Baudelaire:

> To the child's imagination everything is alive—stones, trees, plants, even household objects. For him everything has a soul. He sees things quite differently from the man. Nor is this the only reason for the superiority of the child's powers of observation. His instinctive knowledge, the knowledge inherited from millions of past lives, is still fresh, not dulled by the weight of the myriad impressions of educational and personal experience.[9]

This instinctive power of the child is also that which constitutes the power of the artist, a faculty completely independent of education. Education has not made great poets. "On the contrary," Hearn says, "they have become great in spite of education." Education necessarily tends to "deaden and dull those primitive and instinctive feelings upon which the higher phases of emotional art depend." Knowledge, which is the purpose of our education, as a rule demands the sacrifice of "certain very precious natural faculties." Standing by his obvious analogy between the child and the artist, Hearn then states that the artist is one who is able to keep "the freshness of the child in his mind and heart, notwithstanding all the knowledge he absorbs."

Hearn's emphatic distinction between sensation and emotion thus becomes empirically clear; but on what theoretical basis can such a distinction as this be acceptable? In the above quotation he merely hints, without further satisfying our curiosity. Hearn attempted to explain this more fully by his evolutional doctrine of organic memory —not in his lectures, but in *Exotics and Retrospectives,* one of his Japanese books. In its second half, which we might call Hearn's treatise on aesthetics, he applies the doctrine of organic memory in exploring the physiological, psychological, and metaphysical basis of aesthetic experiences. Especially in the three essays, "First Impressions," "Beauty is Memory," and "Sadness in Beauty," Hearn first offers us an overall theory of emotion, and then explains beauty as the core of that theory.

In "First Impressions" Hearn takes up one of the most common human experiences, the subject already touched upon in his lecture on composition, in order to contrast emotion and sensation.[10] Here he examines first impressions in the light of evolutional psychology, especially its theory of psychical inheritance, which accepts "the superindividual—preëxistence revived in compound personality." In our so-called first impressions, Hearn points out, we really do not read faces, but only feel the impressions they create. The reasons for their remarkable accuracy and for their mystery we never can find in the narrow range of our personal experience, because they are in reality superindividual. "It is not the individual eye that perceives everything perceived in a face," he argues. "The dead are the real seers." Here is the most convincing explanation of why we many a time refer to "physiognomy"—which is quite independent of minute, superficial facial characteristics. Implicitly, we all accept the reality of superindividuality, especially when we use phrases like "force of character," "moral force," "personal fascination," "personal magnetism," etc., meaning that "the influence exerted by man upon man is known to be independent of mere physical conditions." The dead are the real seers, because "the flesh-and-blood man is only the visible end of an invisible column of force reaching out of the infinite past into the momentary present—only the material symbol of an immaterial host." Those fugitive subtleties of expression are "the ebb and flow of life ancestral—under-ripplings in that well-spring unfathomable of personality whose flood is Soul." Every human face is really "a living composite of countless faces—generations and generations of faces superimposed upon the sensitive film of Life for the great cosmic developing process." But the trustworthiness of this verdict of the dead, though greater than that of any external facial manifestation, is "limited to the *potential* relation" of the one seen to the one seeing. The same features make different impressions upon different minds, according to "the delicate balance of personality," or "the qualitative sum of inherited experience in the psychical composition of the observer." Because of these infinite varieties of psychical combination, a certain face will produce "nearly similar impressions only on groups of emotionally homogeneous natures."

From this point of view we can see a little more clearly what Hearn signifies by the child's faculty of artistic seeing, why he designates its instinctive knowledge as "the knowledge inherited from millions of past lives," and why he avers that its freshness is "not dulled by the weight of the myriad impressions of educational and personal experience." It is by this reasoning that he points out the fundamental analogy between the child and the artist. What is commonly called the artist's individuality is, in this sense, the sum total of his education and experience, the accumulation of which is more likely to suppress the real power vital to him, and stifle the primitive and instinctive feelings which are the source of his high emotional art. Thus, the *emotion* of the tree, not the *sensation* of the tree, corresponds with our daily experience called first impressions. The artist must deal with the emotion of the tree that is superindividual, not the sensation of the tree that is merely individual. And the superindividual, once through his hands, becomes universal, without losing its individual variety.

Psychical inheritance, as Hearn puts it, signifies "the superindividual —preëxistence revived in compound personality." This is the evolutional doctrine of organic memory. Once its mode of operation is understood, Hearn's other two essays, "Beauty is Memory" and "Sadness in Beauty," are easy to follow. In "Beauty is Memory" he narrows our so-called first impressions down to the point of love.[11] In the first part of our star-crossed love, we go through "the Period of Wonder," wonder at the power and mystery of beauty. Our power to see beauty, he believes, is as much innate as our power to perceive color. The normal person, it can be assumed, inherits some ideal of beauty, whether it be vivid or vague, which usually represents "an accumulation of countless impressions received by the race—countless fragments of prenatal remembrance crystallized into one composite image within organic memory, where like the viewless image on a photographic plate awaiting development, it remains awhile in darkness absolute." Since it is "a composite of numberless race-memories of individual attraction," this ideal form of beauty represents, "in the superior mind," that is, in the artist's mind, "a something above the existing possible—something never to be realized, much less surpassed, in the present state of humanity." To use Hearn's reasoning once again, the dead are the real lovers.

What is, then, the illusion of love? If, to the lover, the commonplace suddenly becomes "the impossible," that is because it is really blended with the superindividual and superhuman. The lover's real conqueror is not "the magic of anything living or tangible" but "a spectral snare prepared for him by myriads unthinkable of generations of dead." Therefore, beauty is fundamentally "ghostly." Beauty-in-itself is only "the name of a sensation, or complex of sensations." And this is usually mistaken for objectivity, much as sound and light and color were once believed to be "realities." Here is Hearn's complete denial of beauty-in-itself. "All the riddles and contradictions of our aesthetic systems," he declares, are "natural consequences of the delusion that beauty is a something absolute, a transcendental reality, an eternal fact." The appearance we call beauty is actually the "symbol of a fact," "the visible manifestation of a development beyond the ordinary—a bodily evolution more advanced than the existing average."

But what should beauty have to do with "a superindividual ecstasy older than all aesthetic feeling"? What is the secret of the fascination of beauty? What is the meaning of this sense of beauty? This basic question of all aesthetic systems Hearn attempts to explore. Supposing that the recognition of beauty is "a recognition of fact," the fact bears no likeness to the feeling created. That is, the fact is rather a manifestation of force. While representing higher emotion, Hearn argues, this phenomenon termed beauty also represents "a relatively superior fitness for life, a higher ability to fulfill the conditions of existence." What is responsible for our fascination is "the non-conscious perception of this representation." The sense of longing thus aroused is not for any mere abstraction, but for greater completeness of faculty as means to the natural end. From this standpoint he concludes:

> To the dead within each man, beauty signifies the presence of what they need most—Power. They know, in despite of Lethe, that when they lived in comely bodies life was usually made easy and happy for them, and that when prisoned in feeble or in ugly bodies, they found life miserable or difficult. They want to live many times again in sound young bodies—in shapes that assume force, health, joy, quickness to win and energy to keep the best prizes of life's contest. They want, if possible, conditions better than any of the past, but in no event conditions worse.

Beauty is recognition rather than cognition. It is this idea that leads to the next essay, "Sadness in Beauty." [12] First, Hearn refers us to the poet who "sang that beautiful things bring sadness," and tried to explain their sadness by their "vague soul-memories of Paradise." Old-fashioned as the idea may be, Hearn thinks, it contains a shadow of truth, since the mysterious sadness blended with the sense of beauty is clearly "not of this existence, but of countless anterior lives," namely "a sadness of reminiscence."

This explanation seems to Hearn too inclusive to serve his purpose, however. He suggests that it be further qualified, on the ground that the feeling of the sublime, the sense of vastness or permanence or power aroused by the sight of the sea, or any vision of sea-like vast space, or by the majesty of colossal ranges, is always related to fear. So is the cosmic emotion, which is vaster than any sense of the sublime, the kind of emotion that night creates in this age of expanding new science. It is nowise akin to the sadness that beauty creates. Quite unlike this cosmic emotion, including the feeling of the sublime, aesthetic sadness is related rather to desire or longing. Just as our aesthetic recognition of human beauty might be "shadowed by immemorial inheritance of pain—pain of longing, and pain of separation from numberless forgotten beloved," so is the melancholy caused by the sight of a beautiful landscape, for instance, a melancholy of longing. Longing for what? James Sully's thesis, that the aesthetic feeling for nature is modern growth—"hardly older than Rousseau," Hearn would like to qualify by calling our attention to the fact that the art and poetry of the East offer ancient proof to the contrary. Sully's contention, he points out, seems to hold true only for the West. The reason that much of the sadness evoked by a beautiful natural scene is of comparatively modern growth, Hearn suspects, is due largely to "the inherited pain of that separation from Nature which began with the building of walled cities." It is of course as possible that this is blended with "something of incomparably older sorrow," such as the primitive man experienced in the change of seasons. In any case it is a longing for "the joys of humanity's childhood." To say that "the loveliness of a scene brings tears to the eyes" is, in a sense, wrong. What is really responsible for the tears is not the loveliness of the scene but "the longing of generations quickening in the hearts of us." That is because the beauty of nature has "no real existence." It is only the longing of the dead within us that really responds to the changing face of nature. "But," Hearn sums up, "all this comes to them, filtered through the bars and veils of their rebirth, only as dreams of home to hopeless exile—of child-bliss to desolate age—of remembered vision to the blind."

The central point of the essay, "Sadness in Beauty," is Hearn's attempt to explain the mystery of those melancholy tears in the eyes, in the light of his evolutional doctrine of organic memory. The idea suggested here, no matter how poetic and fantastic it may sound, is by no means foreign to readers of modern aesthetic thought, especially aesthetic speculations of Poe and Baudelaire. In "The Poetic Principle," Poe declared that "Beauty of whatever kind, in its supremest development, invariably excites the sensitive soul to tears." He explains our weeping when we hear beautiful poetry or music as the effect of our yearning toward supernal beauty, "a certain, petulant, impatient sorrow at our inability to grasp *now*, wholly, here on earth, at once and forever, those divine and rapturous joys, of which *through* the poem, or *through* the music, we attain to but brief and indeterminate glimpses." In "The Philosophy of Composition," Poe stressed the point that beauty is "not a quality," but "an effect," and defined sadness as the tone of beauty's highest manifestation.[13] Baudelaire, in his Gautier essay, almost paraphrasing Poe's passage to the letter, added his own commentary on man's aesthetic aspiration—with a theological overtone: ". . . nature exilée dans l'imparfait et qui voudrait s'emparer immédiatement, sur cette terre même, d'un paradis révélé." [14] It is not improbable that Poe and Baudelaire, both Hearn's acknowledged masters, were on his mind when he referred to "the poet who sang that beautiful things bring sadness," and sought to explain it "by vague soul-memories of Paradise."

The significant point is that Hearn at least theoretically explored and accepted what was glimpsed by and yet remained mysterious to Poe and Baudelaire. With Hearn, this paradise, or "la patrie inconnue," if we use Proust's term, was never lost. Because of his doctrine of organic memory he was able to locate this divine, mythical realm in the very heart of man by blending time and space, unifying the natural and the human, and embracing many levels of experience, biological, psychological, aesthetic, and metaphysical. As a life-long student of myths and legends he came to the realization that the mythopoeic stage of humanity is ever-present in the primitive core of man. This is a reaffirmation of his early stand on Wilde and Zola: the artist should return to the source of his inspiration that never goes dry because it is also the unquenchable source of humanity. This source is precisely what he termed emotion as distinguished from sensation, being unable to find a better nomenclature. As evident in his illustration, the emotion of the tree, the emotion as the reservoir of psychical inheritance is at once ancestral and collective, and therefore superindividual and universal. In this Hearn singularly anticipates Jung's doctrine of primordial images or archetypes as "the most ancient and the most universal 'thought-forms' of humanity." [15]

In stressing the emotional basis of art Hearn is really concerned with the primary stage of artistic creation, the stage of man's natural vision which precedes his aesthetic vision. What we call artistic intuition or inspiration, the faculty of artistic seeing, operates at this pre-aesthetic stage. Both the artist and the child are capable of seeing the face, physiognomy, or character of everything under the sun, whether it be animate or inanimate; for their faculty of perception is fundamentally artistic. In other words, their faculty is primitive and instinctive. In both child and artist lives the primitive man, whose world vision, being free from any theoretical or practical concern, remains always sympathetic rather than analytic. What is common to both the artist and the primitive man as myth-maker is the power of personification. When Ernst Cassirer observes that the poet and the maker of myth seem "to live in the same world," he implies that their perception is mythical, namely, not objective but physiognomic.[16] This faculty of mythical perception Hearn regards as fundamental for any artist.

With this mythical perception we are still at the primary stage of artistic creation. As long as we remain there, we can hardly expect to go beyond the basic analogy between the child and the artist, the artist and the primitive man. The artist's real job, as we understand it, begins only where and when this analogy ceases. The artist must be more than what the analogy suggests. As Baudelaire said, his must be *"l'enfance retrouvée* à volonté." To recapture this state, the artist must exercise his higher and more characteristic power of creative imagination. Then only is he entering the secondary stage of artistic creation. Here the artist must face the most immediate and most demanding task, "to seize and fix" the character of the thing—by expressing through his own medium the exact feeling that the thing has produced in his mind. This, as Hearn states in his lecture on composition, is the main part of literature, very difficult, indeed beyond any child's and any primitive man's capacity.[17]

Because this feeling or emotion,—"a momentary thrill of pleasure or pain or fear or wonder" vanishes almost as suddenly as it comes, we can hardly write it down. All we are left with is the sensation or first impression of the thing and "a mere memory of the feeling." While the quality and duration of this thrill vary according to individual natures, it flees away "as rapidly as smoke, or perfume blown by a wind." To seize its fugitive subtlety and overcome the extreme difficulty of getting hold of it becomes our immediate task. From this point on there is only "arduous labour," by which alone we can revive the feeling. Comparing the artist's labor to our attempts to remember a dream after waking up, Hearn advises us "to write down immediately, as fully as you can, the circumstances and the cause of the emotion, and to try to describe the feeling as far as possible." These notes become "the seed from which the plant will be made to grow and to blossom." Their development depends entirely upon our conscious double exercise, elimination and addition. The more work the better at this stage. Despair alternates with joy, as we go from one revision to another. Soon the feeling begins to revive—"nay, revives more strongly than at first, being enriched by new psychological relations." The resulting beauty will be surprising. To others, it will give the same emotion that we ourselves felt on first perceiving the fact or the object. This whole process Hearn likens to that of "focusing with a telescope."

This process of focusing, Hearn continues, is indeed the first thing essential in any kind of literary composition. With this, the artist's job has just begun, for it is still his first inspiration. The artist never gets the whole of his inspiration at once. As a rule it comes to him "only by degrees, while he is perfecting the work." At this stage his first inspiration, no matter how complete, is "only a sudden flash of emotion," or "the sudden shock of a new idea." Considered in the light of the whole of the work he is engaged in, it only "awakens and sets into motion many confused trains of other interrelated emotions and ideas." As it is, his first inspiration may represent not the beginning of anything, but the middle of it, or the end. By seizing this first inspiration as it comes, the artist can not only solve the most common difficulty of literary work, how and where to begin, but also follow the line of least resistance, the way of imagination itself. This is the first law of composition, the architecture of the composition, as Hearn calls it.

This point Hearn further illustrates by referring to a Japanese artist who would draw horses excellently by always beginning at the tail. Hearn is surprised because this is quite contrary to the Western practice. Soon he realizes that it does not matter whether the artist begins "at the head or the tail or the belly or the foot of the horse, if he really knows his business." This suggests that the artist should work in a way peculiar to himself, a way in which he finds it easy to work. The artist, Hearn suspects, often begins at the tail. That is to say, he often writes the end of the story before he has even thought of its beginning. Hearn offers this advice: "Develop the first idea or emotion that comes to you before you allow yourself to think about the second. The second will suggest itself, even too much, while you are working at the first." If many emotions or ideas come at once, try to seize "the most vigorous of them, or the one that most attracts you to begin with, unless it happens to be also the most difficult." He suggests this way of working because of the "astonishing fact," that the different fragments, developed separately from each other, have "a tendency to grow together of themselves, and into a form different from that which you first intended, but much better." This is the inspiration of form as construction. What this literary law indicates is: "Let the poem or the story shape itself." Then

Hearn concludes, "The most wonderful work is not the work that the author shapes and plans; it is the work that shapes itself, the work that obliges him, when it is nearly done, to change it all from beginning to end, and to give it a construction which he had never imagined at the time of beginning it."

Since the lecture on composition is intended to be Hearn's practical advice to his students, there is little theoretical or systematic exploration of the two stages of artistic creation. If we get the impression that Hearn tends to overstress the importance of the primary stage, it is mainly because he believes it to entail the first qualification any beginning artist must possess, and because he examines the question in the light of his evolutionary doctrine of organic memory. This is not the case with the secondary stage of artistic creation. In dealing with the later stage as if it were too self-evident, he merely tells how the artist goes about the work that shapes itself, instead of speculating in general terms as to the nature of this particular artistic imagination. Yet, it is possible to deduce from the above illustration certain laws of the architecture of the composition which he regards as universal. First, there is a fundamental continuity between the two stages of artistic creation, that is, mythical perception and artistic imagination, as there is between the natural and the aesthetic emotion. Second, the artist works primarily in terms of images rather than in concepts. At this stage images are as much emotions as ideas. With these concrete particulars the artist must work. Third, the competent artist can let them "grow together of themselves" into one coherent form; that is, he can let the work shape itself. As explicit in Hearn's special emphasis—"if he really knows his business"—this inspiration of form as construction should mean not passivity on the part of the artist, but his more positive and complete collaboration with the given material.

It now becomes clear why Hearn defines the artistic genius in terms of the primary stage rather than the secondary stage of creative process. As a student of evolutionary psychology, Hearn once declared himself to be "a profound, earnest believer" in genius. How that works may be mysterious, he admits, but he ventures this speculation: "Seeing in lightning flashes. Perhaps it also means remembering—*seeing retrospectively,* through rifts in the curtain of the past. The faculty is, of course, explainable only by the ancestral hypothesis." Referring to Spencer's illustration of ancestral memory, he then called attention to the effect of superimposing "a number of coloured negatives." "Only vague suggestions," he added.[18] Later, when he set out, in his essay "First Impressions," to formulate his aesthetics of organic memory, Hearn returned to the same point, suggesting "the emblematical significance of the Composite Photograph." There for the first time he came to view genius as a product of our psychical inheritance, and, much like Jung later, attempted to evaluate it. At least from the ethical viewpoint, Hearn cautions, the superindividual that is our psychical inheritance is "a lower manifestation." The power in itself is of evil, "brutal in its origin," and still "allied to those malignities and ferocities shared by man with lower predatory creatures." It really indicates not "a recognition of higher moral energy," but "a higher *mental* energy signifying larger evolutional experience of wrong, deeper reserves of aggressive ingenuity, heavier capacities for the giving of pain." But there is another side to it, too, namely its beauty. Its beauty, Hearn states, reveals itself "in that rarer power which the dead lend the living to win trust, to inspire ideals, to create love, to brighten whole circles of existence with the charm and wonder of a personality never to be described save in the language of light and music." [19] Here is the birth of an artistic genius and his mission.

Here Hearn seems to accept the Romantic belief in genius as born, not made. He has no means of explaining why genius is born, but now he can at least account for what constitutes this power and how it manifests itself. Every being, human or otherwise, comes into existence with a certain quantity of what Hearn calls life-force. Though its manifestation fluctuates according to one's psychical inheritance, there must be a general average. Genius is one whose life-force exceeds this general average to an inconceivable degree. Since the mystery of life-force lies in the superindividual, whose energy is not moral but merely mental, genius is constantly exposed to its power. Only from this point of view, Hearn believes, can we understand the strength of an artistic genius, and even defend the moral weakness that often characterizes him.

Hearn deals with this issue in his short fragmentary lecture, "Literary Genius." [20] First, he believes the evidence that genius has "some relation to moral weakness" to be "certainly very large." He cites Coleridge, Byron, Shelley, Villon, Baudelaire, and Nerval as weak characters. Hearn suspects, nevertheless, that the proportion of men of genius who have been either insane or bad has been greatly exaggerated, especially so in view of the prejudice that can always be found in this sort of thinking. So warning, he turns to Cesare Lombroso's controversial book, *The Man of Genius.* The gist of this fellow evolutionist's study, as Hearn sums it up, is that genius means "a kind of insanity," "usually accompanied with physical and moral weakness," that men of genius show in the general pattern of behavior "not an advance upon the morals of their time, but a reversion to the morals of a former stage," and that, as the criminal represents "the original savage men, the survival of instincts of a former age," so is the man of genius "in some degree related to the criminal rather than to the moral type of mankind." While accepting Lombroso's "facts," Hearn resorts to Spencer's *Psychology* for an explanation of them. Unlike Lombroso, who is opinionated to the point of one-sidedness, Spencer is more convincing when he points out that the eccentricity of genius means two things, "higher developments" and "degeneration,"—two opposites. In other words, the man of genius tends to be superior to other men in one faculty, and inferior to other men in other faculties. That is because genius can "only be produced at a tremendous cost to the vital energy of the being in whom it exists."

Applying this principle to literature, Hearn observes that the artistic genius must possess and, to a high degree, develop those inborn qualities, such as a love of the beautiful, great capacities for sympathy, a certain gentleness of disposition, and so on, the qualities which usually belong to "the softer side of human nature." [21] A high degree of cultivation of one such faculty can usually be expected at the cost of other faculties. Since the conduct of artists is generally swayed "by feeling rather than by cold reason," Hearn believes, they are often likely to make unfortunate mistakes. Byron is an example: no mere religious or social condemnation of his character should influence us to ignore his "deeper" nature, essentially "generous and sympathetic." It is the inspiration of his deeper nature that enables him to give us "the best of what he has." In this sense alone, Hearn suggests, we should understand a Persian poet's observation, that "no bad man could possibly become a poet,"—*i.e.* he cannot be bad according to the consensus of human experience, although he might offend particular conventions. And this kind of genius we should call weak rather than bad, for it is the weakness of his deficient or ill-balanced personality that keeps him out of harmony with his surroundings. At this point Hearn parts company with fellow Romantics who tend to glorify the myth of the accursed poet. It is true, as he admits, that many artists of genius in our literary history have been subjected to this sorry fate, but it is also true that being accursed is not a sort of prerequisite for literary genius. The highest type of genius, Hearn thinks, should be able to escape this fate; and he points to Shakespeare as an example of the ideal.

Most probably because of this conviction Hearn returns to Shakespeare time and again. In his lectures on Shakespeare all the crucial points of his aesthetics, such as genius, organic memory, and poetical personality, are interrelated to each other and treated as one coherent whole.[22] The best possible way of approaching this "greatest figure in all human literature," he suggests at the outset, is to regard him not as a common man or author, but as "a phenomenon" in literature corresponding to the more recent phenomenon of Napoleon as "a political, military and economic force." Shakespeare is "not only the greatest, but also the most difficult of authors to understand"—that difficulty being neither in his language nor in his thoughts, but in the comprehension of the depths of his characters, the depth of his knowledge of human nature.

Compared with Shakespeare's hundreds of characters, those of other dramatists are at best something like "phantoms" which become the less real the more we come to know them. What is the secret of the force of Shakespeare's characters? There may be many possible answers to this question, but Hearn thinks that the real key is his power of memory, memory of that special form called the representative faculty. Imagine, he suggests, a man who can draw a cat in any position, from memory. This illustration must be expanded infinitely if we try to understand Shakespeare's way of creating characters. It would be absurd to attribute his knowledge of character to his purely personal experience. The real answer is intuition, "imagination in the form of instinct," that which we call inherited knowledge. "I shall say therefore," he continues, "that the faculty of Shakespeare represents something very much resembling the memory of thousands of experiences in hundreds of anterior lives, as man and woman, in different conditions of civilization, and different parts of the earth." Thus Shakespeare is genius as multiple personality, supremely gifted with "a kind of organic memory" or "a kind of inherited memory." In defining genius as "a multiple personality," Hearn virtually exemplifies Coleridge's phrase, "myriad-minded." Only in this light can we adequately explain the major traits of Shakespeare's characters: their intense vitality, capable of infinite variety affecting so many minds in so many ways; their "comparative immortality," made possible by reason of their unchanging humanity; and their distinct individuality that resists any sort of general grouping.

Shakespeare possessed not only this primary quality of artistic imagination, which is responsible for his profound knowledge of human nature, but also a complete mastery of his trade. By virtue of these two qualities essential to any great artist, Shakespeare could free himself from all sorts of rules, thereby reaching the point of artistic unconsciousness. There was of course one limit which he had to obey, "the limit imposed by the dramatic necessities of the stage"; and this limit he obeyed "magnificently." Hearn rejects the commonly held theory of a fundamental idea in all of Shakespeare's works. If he had anything in mind, Hearn believes, it was to "make them as close to truth as he possibly could." In other words, "to portray truth—not as a philosopher, but as a play-writer." In this sense Shakespeare is one prime example of the artistic genius who "does not work by theory, but by feeling and by direct perception."

His estimate of Shakespeare enables us to see why Hearn took so lightly what we call constructive imagination, or the inventive faculty. Shakespeare, it seems to him, confirms his own stand, that this faculty in itself does not necessarily constitute the artistic genius, or at least is not as essential as the primary qualifications. Our study of the sources of Shakespeare's dramatic works is therefore rewarding in one sense only. Better than anything else, it convinces us of "the enormousness of Shakespeare's genius," and also "how little genius needs to trouble itself about original invention." While many artists often fail because of their single ambition to contrive something novel, Shakespeare freely takes up an old subject to make it new, or a beautifully told story to tell it infinitely better. If one is sure of his own artistic power, Hearn says, the question of a new subject matter would never even occur to him. With Shakespeare, the plot is nothing more than the frame of a picture. As a matter of fact, this is the method used by nearly all great artists in literature. "Genius," as Hearn states, "does not need to invent, because it re-creates anything which it touches."

Hearn stresses this point again while dealing with Defoe in comparison with Shakespeare. Defoe possessed two great qualities, an enormous power of factual observation and a particular faculty of constructive imagination. The second especially is a power of a very high order which makes fiction "so dramatic that it appears to be truth." More important, however, is the way this power is used and the composition of the mind that uses it. Had Defoe been "as sincere a man as Shakespeare" and possessed a sense of beauty and a knowledge of proportion as well developed as Shakespeare's, he might have created magnificent dramas. The implication is that Defoe, despite his great qualities, had "no sense of beauty, and no sense of truth, in the higher meaning of the phrase." [23] But what does Hearn mean by "the composition of the mind," "as sincere a man as Shakespeare," "a sense of beauty," "a knowledge of proportion," and "a sense of truth"? Most of his answers to these by no means clear questions are to be found once again in his Shakespeare lectures. Here Hearn really approaches Shakespeare's personality as genius, as a complete artist.

What most fascinates Hearn in considering Shakespeare's mature years is "proof absolute that his faculties were not one-sided; and that a more perfectly balanced character is not possible even to imagine." One thing unusual about Shakespeare is that he is at once a supreme artist and a supremely good man of business. He is thus a remarkable exception to Spencer's observation regarding the eccentricity of genius, to the general fact that "genius can only be produced at a tremendous cost to the vital energy of the being in whom it exists." The story of Shakespeare's life, Hearn says, should make for us "a very important revelation, the moral revelation." How should we account for this fact, that he was generous and yet economical, that he loved pleasure but never allowed his feeling to drive him into any extremes, and finally that in middle age he was able to retire to private life with a comfortable fortune? From all that has been known to us, there is in Shakespeare little trace of the so-called accursed poet. What is the secret of the ideal balance of force and delicacy so supremely exemplified in this man? The only explanation Hearn can think of is what is physiologically called inhibitory power, an extraordinary power which enabled him "to endure the experiences of his career." This power might also be called self-control. But while self-control means only the regulation of outer action, the inhibitory power is the control of imagination and intellectual operations, a control "infinitely more difficult" than mere self-control.

In this strength of personality, Hearn believes, lies the impersonality of Shakespeare's art, which was also in Keats's opinion the secret of Shakespeare's poetical character. Here Shakespeare stands far above Goethe. When Hearn says that Shakespeare's genius is "essentially moral," he means simply that it is superior to weaknesses of any sort, that is, "immoralities." Shakespeare can be impersonal because of his "immense way of looking at life." In his art there is "something of the vast indifference of Nature herself, always producing, producing, producing,—evil and good in ceaseless alternation,—yet never preaching, never pitying, never making mistakes." In a religious sense his art is neither moral nor immoral; it is "altogether real." His art was never created "for a moral purpose," both because life itself is multi-colored, and because Shakespeare was "too much like a god for that." Shakespeare's morality is a god's morality, which must be distinguished from any theological morality. It is "a morality of superior self-respect, superior knowledge of life, superlative perception of the proper relations of things—perhaps especially of the proper relations of the individual to the family and of the family to the state." Because he was so deeply convinced of impersonality as the ideal of poetic character, Hearn had his say about the controversial question of Shakespeare's sonnets. He wonders why we must say that the poet's "marvellous intuition may not have enabled him to paint and to animate all the sorrows of a passion never indulged in by him except in imagination." It is very possible, Hearn suggests, that the person addressed in the sonnets existed only in Shakespeare's dream. In view of the fact that throughout his plays Shakespeare never shows us his own personality, but always appears in other personalities, Hearn asks, ". . . why then should we suppose that he chose to be less impersonal in his poems?"

When Hearn writes that "the sources of Shakespeare's plays exist only nominally in other books and dramas; their real place was in his heart and brain," this statement can be understood only in relation to Hearn's definition of emotion as the basis of art in general. The emotion for which the artist's heart and brain stands is indeed the very point that unifies the artist and the rest of humanity, his audience. The artist's primary responsibility both to himself and to his audience is to develop the best and strongest qualities of his heart and mind. Since this signifies self-culture on his part, artistic creation ought to be especially "a moral exercise." It ought to be the source of "the chief pleasure" and "the constant consolation of life." [24] His art is born in the process of this moral exercise, this self-culture, an attempt to deepen his personal vision, wherein to discover the mystery and beauty of the superindividual that is timeless and placeless. Only when he succeeds in this attempt does his vision become distinctly his own voice, and yet at the same time the voice of humanity. It must be in this sense that Hearn declared: "Assuredly the road to all artistic greatness is the road of sincerity—truth to one's own emotional sense of what is beautiful." [25] When the concept of beauty is enlarged to mean also the "truth of feeling," the most crucial question, the relation of the beautiful, the good, and the true, begins to resolve itself; and their reunion takes place on the level which Hearn defines as the emotion.

Through the medium of emotion, nature always demands to be completed in art; and art in turn always tends to be related back to its source of origin. Because of his faith in the fecundity of nature as the soil of art Hearn could never accept the Romantic cult of art for art's sake nor the Romantic glorification of the artist as an Ishmaelite alienated from the rest of humanity. Art must be kept in constant contact with nature. In 1886, Hearn said of the appeal of art, referring specifically to music:

> . . . its appeal to the esthetic sense remains incomplete so long as its effect does not unite with a series of natural emotions that existed before it. It does not itself create these emotions; but simply enhances them: it should form the ultimate and supreme expression of utterance for those, who, while capable of much feeling, may be incapable of much artistic execution. A master-piece is, in this sense, a mouthpiece;—representing not merely the emotion of a master, but the emotion of a race or of an epoch.[26]

Going even further than this, Hearn now ventured to assign to the artist a function more positive and nobler. Since the artist represents in the highest degree what is emotional in man, it is his duty to help "to keep alive the more generous impulses of human nature." His office is therefore as holy as that of the priest.[27]

IX

*Toward
World
Literature*

*For a
Literature
of
Humanity*

Questioning his old friend Hearn's qualifications as a professor of English literature, Dr. Gould wrote in 1908:

> There is not a hint in all he did that he had read a line of the great creators of literature,—the Greek dramatists, Goethe, Shakespeare, and a hundred more; he could not give time to read, much less study them. His pretension of ability to teach English literature was soon recognized even by the Japanese, and it is well that over-zealous friends did not secure him a lectureship at Cornell University. To be sure, he never had time to study even the history of his science and art,—but he never would have done so, it is plain, if leisure and opportunity had been offered him. The ideal and the rewards of scholarship never entered his mind.[1]

We need not take it upon ourselves to answer most of these charges, which can be taken care of by the volumes of Hearn's Japanese lectures. There are, however, two points to be set straight. First, it was not for English literature but for Japanese subjects that Cornell University approached Hearn, whose fame as a writer on Japan was then becoming world-wide. Second, and more important, no Japanese has gone on record as questioning Hearn's ability to teach English literature. On the contrary, Japanese writers about Hearn consistently mention his hold on his students' minds. We have, for instance, Yone Noguchi's account of how Japanese students reacted to Hearn's half-forced resignation from the Imperial University:

> . . . when his resignation from the University was known, with what sympathy and honesty those students protested against the attitude of the University; how they tried to keep him with them. Their hearts were wounded terribly to think that even the biggest school of Japan could not afford to keep one Hearn. . . . They thought at once that there was no greater teacher of literature than Hearn in Japan.[2]

Decades later, when making an historical survey of English literature in Japan, Professor Takeshi Saito of the same University also noted Hearn's contribution as a teacher:

> Though he was not an academical scholar or critic, his lectures are said to have had the magic power of transforming the lecture-room into a fairyland where poets and novelists of olden days and new came and went, and each lecture disclosed to students some hidden corners of their hearts. Hearn attracted his pupils with his penetrating insight into others' minds as well as with his unworldly character and love of Japan.[3]

These are but two of many Japanese tributes to Hearn's stature as an inspiring teacher, which is now part of the Hearn legend. The Japanese are in a better position to pass judgment on this matter than is Dr. Gould, for instance, because they can see it in proper perspective. Indeed, to view the matter in this light, I believe, will not only settle the question of whether Hearn was the best possible foreign teacher of literature Japan could hope for at the time, but also clarify Hearn's view of world literature.

Let us first take a brief look at the particular historical situation of the Japan which welcomed Hearn. In politics, the Restoration of 1868 paved the way for Japan to emerge as a modern state out of the Tokugawa feudalism. Abandoning traditional isolationism and using advanced Western democracies as models, her determined statesmen managed to steer through the perilous period of transition from the old Japan to the new. With the establishment of constitutional government, New Japan won two wars, the Sino-Japanese War (1894–95) and the Russo-Japanese War (1904–05), thereby making an historic debut on the world stage. In the literary world, the majority of the new intellectuals, whatever their interests and positions, were agreed over one point at least, the vital importance of accepting contemporary Western literature as a step toward creating what they called a new national literature. This task they began by introducing English literature, first, and then Continental literatures, French, Russian, German, Scandinavian, and Italian. In so doing they were compelled to digest in rapid succession romanticism, realism, naturalism, and symbolism. How well they succeeded in such wholesale imports of diverse Western literatures and the feuding literary movements which resulted are not our present concern. The point is that their acceptance of foreign literatures as the best means of literary survival was motivated by necessity rather than by leisurely interest or scholarly curiosity. In order to master in a few decades what it had taken centuries for the West to achieve, they had to accept, criticize, and assimilate foreign literatures primarily in terms of their new national literature. Few were allowed to be shut off in the ivory tower; whether by their own will or not, they all participated in the realization of their own generation's dream. They were all patriotic pioneers on the frontier of literature.[4]

Only in the light of this trend can we rightly understand the implication of Hearn's professorial appointment. As we remember, it was at the request of Dr. Masakazu Toyama, then Dean of the College of Literature, Imperial University of Tokyo, that B. H. Chamberlain sought out his friend Hearn. Dean Toyama's letter to Professor Chamberlain of December 6, 1895, reveals the motivation of the University authorities. After paying homage to Hearn's talent, the writer pointed out the paramount importance of English studies in Japan, and concluded that securing the right person for this purpose would in the long run exert a great influence upon the future course of Japanese literature itself.[5] Here it may be said that Dean Toyama, educated in America, was himself one of the leaders of a new poetry movement, an ardent evolutionist, and the first to introduce Zola into Japan. His expressed conviction was not merely a personal one, but reflected the generally accepted purpose of foreign studies in Japan—as Professor Saito explained, "first of all, to encourage undergraduates to be active in literary work either creative or critical, and *not* to lead them into mechanical and dry-as-dust work such as we frequently come across in dissertations by some German students of English." [6]

Hearn was well aware that all his pupils would be in one way or another the makers of tomorrow's Japan, and especially her national literature. Taking as an example the sudden world-wide recognition of Russian literature, he more than once reminded his students that the creation of a new Japanese literature would be "a political necessity." In order to be appreciated at all, he pointed out, Japan must create a literature which can touch emotionally the heart of peoples the world over.[7] To cultivate such a creative power is therefore the responsibility of all students of foreign literatures. For this they must turn to "the heart of all literature," its imaginative part, poetry and fiction. Hearn declared this imaginative part to be "the only part of a foreign literature which can be of real benefit" to his students.[8] All his Japanese lectures were conceived, planned, and presented with this creative function of literary study in view.

Hearn's intention of making his lectures "good for the Toyko University" is manifest in his lectures on special topics. In dealing with the subjects of his own choice Hearn is naturally at his best, and their topical variety bears witness to his versatile mind. They fall into three groups, according to their central concerns. Those in the first group, as we have already seen, are concerned with literary works and figures, literary situations, and literary issues, and are especially designed to demonstrate how to approach contemporary Western writers, analyze their individual works, and finally evaluate their art and thought in terms of one's own generation. Those in the second group examine many famous or obscure literary pieces written upon particular subjects, such as love, death, tree-spirits, the ideal woman, music, night, the moon, children, fairies, the supernatural, insects, birds, or flowers.[9] Through these studies of things, animate and inanimate, small and large, Hearn takes aesthetic or philosophic excursions to emphasize the distance or closeness between one literature and another, one race and another, and one world and another. Finally, the lectures in the third group center on some important questions that confront all students of literature. Here Hearn freely gives friendly warnings and practical advice to his young students and elucidates what he considers the secret of literary art.

Taken together, Hearn's special lectures indicate what is peculiar to his study of literature. His point of view is firmly fixed in the present from which literature can best be approached as a living whole. His interest in the contemporary stems from his belief that no study of literature will be complete without one's participation in the creation of something new and better. Because of his conviction that the secret of literary art is universal, he frequently refers to known modern instances of mutual literary influences, probing into fundamental thematic analogies or parallels between one tradition and another. This method endows many of his lectures with an air of immediacy; they are highly personal and yet do not lack universality. In Hearn's vision many-colored worlds are opened to one another, all tending toward the creation of a world larger, richer, and more beautiful.

Hearn knew that this dream, no matter how commendable, could come true only through the toil of individual talents in silence and solitude; not by talk but only by work can the dream become possible. When one of his students sought his advice for a projected literary society and a new journal, Hearn deplored the waste of time in "utterly useless" projects, pointing out that there were too many already. His fear is that as long as the "rage for wasting time," or "insane mania" for such projects continues, there will be "no new Japanese literature, no new drama, no new poetry—nothing good of any kind." *"Don't* belong to societies," he concludes, *"don't* write anything that comes into your head, *don't* waste the poor little time you have. Take literature seriously,—or leave it alone." He is troubled by his young students' confusion of means with ends. As he sees it, literary societies should exist for the purpose of editing old texts, publishing translations, encouraging literary efforts among college students, and protecting the interests of writers. Beyond this their influence is often harmful to young talents. Once again Hearn reminds his students of the real purpose of foreign literary studies: "I have small sympathy with the mere study of English literature by Japanese students and scholars. I should infinitely prefer to hear of new studies in Japanese literature. Except with the sole purpose of making a *new* Japanese literature, I do not sympathize with English or French or German studies." The only way, he suggests, is to return to "the best of all places," namely "the solitude of one's own room." [10]

In this advice, no matter how extreme, Hearn has no intention of glorifying the Romantic cult of ego; he is trying simply to be sincere and practical. As a teacher aware of the literary movements around him, Hearn could not but dread the possible consequence of his students' misdirected efforts. As a veteran artist he knew enough to show them the most practical way to serve their apprenticeship at the difficult trade of literature. The most succinct expression of this kind we find in "Farewell Address," a special lecture which Hearn said he delivered "only through a sense of duty," [11] and intended evidently as postscript to all his Japanese lectures.

At the outset Hearn stresses once again what he regards as the primary purpose of foreign literary studies. Their only value, he says, is "that of their effect upon your own capacity to make literature in your own tongue." It would be unjust to Hearn to dismiss his repeated remarks on the point simply as the result of a personal obsession. That they were meant to be his warning is made more clear if we juxtapose his view with the complaint made by Chogyu Takayama, a distinguished Japanese critic of the time, that many Japanese students of foreign literatures have come to be indifferent to their own.[12] The more foreign studies the better, however, as long as students are rightly motivated. In a mood positively optimistic, Hearn trusts that Japanese literature will be made stronger by foreign forces and able to bear finer fruits. Japanese literature is very far from this point of genuine creativity, however, as it is still going through the period of assimilation. In spite of innumerable translations, imitations, and adaptations into Japanese from Western literatures, Hearn hesitates to believe that there has been any great change in Japanese literature. Great changes come from what he calls true assimilation. They occur only when the foreign materials have been "transmuted, within the crucible of literature, into purely Japanese materials." In the sense that literature must be creative, "borrowing, or imitating, or adapting material in the raw state—none of this is creative." [13]

Then he turns to visualize the manner in which these great changes may eventually produce a new literature. Judging by "the history of literary evolutions in other countries," there will have to be a romantic movement in Japan too, "of a much more deep-reaching kind than may now appear credible." By this Hearn means something far more constructive than an iconoclastic reaction to tradition. As the best and only remedy for literary conventionalism, he believes, it may help to restore the primary function of literature as an art of emotional expression. Without it, all literature would begin to decay. In other words, it is "a frank return" to the very source of natural health, "the soil from which everything human springs." And that soil, Hearn points out, is "the life and thought of the common people." Since this return has happened everywhere else, Hearn believes that it will happen in Japan. First, however, the educated must return to the common people, sympathize with them, and conquer their prejudices against what has until now been considered as "vulgar." If they do not, the educated scholars, really the makers of future Japanese literature, will be cutting themselves off from its life source and from their own. At this point Hearn insists on the vital necessity of colloquial language as the best possible medium for a new national literature. The language of the common people should now take the place of that of scholarship, for purposes of creative art. He looks forward to the day when no scholar will be ashamed to adopt colloquial style, and make it "a vehicle of his best and strongest thought."

Having said these things, Hearn once again reminds his students of their responsibility. As one who has lived on the trade of literature, he can well imagine the hardships facing many of his students who will have to live by their pen in modern society. Despite his apprehension, Hearn suspects this to be perhaps the best way a new literature can be created out of the heart of the common people. "Even toiling through this hum-drum life," he concludes, "one must try to create a new literature, if he loves literature. There is no excuse for giving it up."

Today few would object to Hearn's stand, because much of it has since been taken for granted. But the reaction his unequivocal statement might cause in his student audience can only be understood if put in the particular historical context of modern Japanese literature. During this period the literature of the common man for the first time asserted its legitimate priority over that of aristocracy, custodian of the classical tradition. It was also during this period that conservatives and radicals clashed over the central issue of language in the creation of a national literature. No period in modern Japanese literature was perhaps more profoundly perturbed with warring "isms,"—individualism and collectivism, Nipponism and cosmopolitanism, socialism and nationalism. In view of the ideological chaos characteristic of this period, Hearn's advice was indeed timely, for he pointed directly to the most fundamental way of literary creation.[14]

Yet, when Hearn designated it a political necessity to create a new Japanese literature, his motivation was far from political. He simply re-emphasized the significance of race as a cultural unit. His insistence on national literature is not only consistent with his literary cosmopolitanism, but also indicative of his awareness of their vital relationship. While defining literature as an art of emotional expression he specified it as a collective expression of racial experience. When he urged his students to return to the "popular art" of the common people, it was in the belief that they should be reborn in the matrix of their own racial imagination. Upon this concept of racial imagination Hearn based his ideal of national literature, thereby justifying at once the *raison d'être* of a national literature in the world community and the necessity of foreign literary studies for its further development.

From this vantage point Hearn presented English literature to his Japanese students not as an isolated racial property but more broadly as part of European literature. Tracing the evolution of English literary thought, he illustrated how vigorously diverse foreign elements metabolized and vivified the native force. English literature, in this instance, best served his purpose. Using Victorian England as his *point d'appui,* Hearn called attention to foreign influences, German, French, Scandinavian, Russian, and even Oriental, all of which contributed to the making of English literature. To prove his point, he described what "a small part of world influences" English literature represents in forming the mind of the English boy, who, once past the age of the nursery songs, is more and more exposed to foreign stuff. If he is not aware of this fact, that is because foreign literature has become part of English literature—through thousands of translations, not through scholarly study. If Englishmen had studied foreign literature only in the original, Hearn commented, English literature would still have made little progress. Not only in English but in nearly every European literature, foreign influence operates mainly through translations. They are the means by which a nation can best assimilate fresh ideas from abroad; only afterwards can it expect to create an extensive new literature. The study of English literature in Japan, Hearn believes, should be extended even to English translations from other languages. In his opinion, the importance of literature in translation, as the first step of the literary ladder, is not only individual but racial or national.[15]

Largely for this reason, Hearn turned time and again to Anglo- and American-French literary relations during the nineteenth century. It seemed to him that England was still considerably behind France in practically every genre—except poetry. In criticism Saintsbury, Gosse, Dowden, and many others owed much to Sainte-Beuve. Hearn would like to see the same healthy French influence in other literary departments, such as fiction, drama, the essay, and the sketch. Even in poetry there is the same possibility. Since English poetry has excelled in form, it should now learn feeling from French poetry. As a good example, Hearn pointed to Swinburne under the combined influence of Gautier and Baudelaire. In the short story, he thought, American literature first felt the impact of France. Although he may have erred in his assessment of French influence upon Poe, his opinion is well grounded when he evaluates Baudelaire's introduction of Poe as a significant event which made the American poet part of modern French literature.[16]

The substance of Hearn's survey here, which is valid even when specific errors in literary history are admitted, is his belief that, as the Anglo- and American-French literary relations suggest, a national literature can and must profit from foreign elements for its own evolution. As he said when opening his lecture on American literature, "Every literature in the world is developed by influences from outside of itself. Left to itself a literature will die for want of food." [17] We are at once reminded of Goethe's dictum: "Left to itself, every literature will exhaust its vitality if it is not refreshed by the interest and contribution of a foreign one." [18] Consciously or not, Hearn was virtually restating what Goethe had earlier said of the national basis of his world literature. Hearn was, however, in a position to articulate more clearly in terms of world literature Goethe's dream of fusing the East and the West.[19] As Japanese literature has become part of Oriental literature through its centuries-long assimilation of neighboring literatures, he believed that it should now revitalize itself under Western influence. Only thus could it expect to become a new Japanese literature as part of world literature.[20] At the same time, Hearn pointed out that this sort of influence should be mutual, certainly not in one direction only, and called attention to the fact that the influence of Oriental literature, especially from India, has begun to show itself, and to exercise a new power in Western thought.[21]

Hearn might be said to have a view of the East and the West as hemispherical bases of world literature. Even his survey of English literary history affirms this wider view of the world as a whole. The theme of *Everyman,* the eighteenth-century Oriental vogue, the Romantics' use of Oriental material, and Fitzgerald's translations, among others, are produced as proof that Oriental literature has also been part of English literature in the same sense that Scott, Byron, and Poe have been part of European literature. In his special lecture, "Some Poems on Death," Hearn traces the Oriental influence, Indian, Chinese, and Japanese, upon Western poetry. Since it is constantly growing, Hearn says, we shall see and hear much more of it. As Tennyson's swan-song, "Crossing the Bar," shows, even the most typically insular Briton could not resist this new force.[22]

The vision of a world literature was one of Hearn's oldest dreams. Some of his American editorials, written nearly twenty years earlier, indicate that he had already envisioned the literary marriage of the East and the West. In 1882 he wrote that the future archaeological romance as antidote to realism would "probably have an Oriental basis," the vast field of Eastern literature being now fairly opened to the West through the efforts of European linguists.[23] While reviewing Helen Zimmern's free rendering of the Persian epic, *Shah-Nameh,* or *Book of Kings,* Hearn was impressed with the singular resemblance between the Persian epic and the Arthurian legend, so much so that he ventured this observation:

European literature has reached the apogee of that development given to it by its intrinsic vitality; it needs an invigorating impulse from without,—fresh blood from other sources. The ideas of the Orient are only now being fully understood and fairly appreciated;—they are certainly destined to influence Occidental thought more than superficially. The flowers of Western idealism will be marvelously improved by crossing with Eastern literary growths.[24]

Hearn was re-experiencing what Emerson and Thoreau had felt a generation earlier. At the same time he was fulfilling the prophecy in his own way in both *Stray Leaves* and *Some Chinese Ghosts.*

Now compare Hearn's statement with the one Ezra Pound made upon his discovery of Chinese poetry: "Liu Ch'e, Chu Yuan, Chia I, and the great *vers libre* writers before the Petrarchan age of Li Po, are a treasure to which the next centuries may look for as great a stimulus as the Renaissance had from the Greeks." [25] Pound's statement, made in 1915, more than a generation after Hearn's, is more sharply focused, but the two statements essentially agree that literary exoticism in its genuine sense does more than satisfy curiosity; it revitalizes a tradition. In this vein, Hearn also foresaw the future course of the Imagist movement. In his special lecture on epitaphic poetry he attempted, by referring to the *Greek Anthology,* to correct the common notion that it is peculiar to Japanese literature. He insisted that Japanese poets should not only recognize a new sense of the real value of their own short poetic form, which belongs to the genius of the language, but further cultivate it, especially since many European poets are essaying to recapture the essence of this old form. "I should like to suggest, however," Hearn said, "that it is very probable many attempts at these difficult forms of poetry will be attempted by English poets within the next few years. There is now a tendency in that direction. I do not know whether such attempts will be successful." [26] We may wonder how Hearn would have felt had he lived long enough to see what this "tendency" finally turned out to be, and also why his own name would be remembered in connection with it. As F. S. Flint said, the Imagists' initial interest was aroused by Japanese *tanka* and *haiku* forms translated by Hearn or Chamberlain. Another member of the group, John Gould Fletcher, also prized Hearn for awakening in him a feeling toward the Orient.[27] Much to their credit, the Imagist poets went beyond Hearn's immediate ken, finding Chinese poetry another enduring Oriental source of inspiration. In view of the fact that Imagism grew out of such diverse elements as Greek, French, Chinese, and

Japanese, this new poetry movement as a significant chapter of modern literature might be considered perhaps the immediate fruition of Hearn's dream of world literature.[28]

"To make a study of comparative literature," Hearn wrote in 1895, "—including Sanscrit, Finnish, Arabic, Persian,—systematizing the best specimens of each into kindred groupings on the evolutional plan. That *would* be worth doing; for it means a study of the evolutional development of all mankind." [29] The term "comparative literature" is misleading in this case; "world literature," once aptly used by Hearn in connection with Goethe, would be more faithful to his intention.[30] His interest lies not in intellectual abstraction but in concrete perception even when he sets out to "seek for *all* real good that the many-colored world of universal literature can offer him, in multitudinous shapes of pulchritude, in linguistic costumes as varied as the habits and hopes of men." It is a search for the oneness of life in the exuberant flowerings of the geniuses of many world races. This attempt to grasp unity in variety may account for Hearn's favorite metaphor of root growing into flowers. Many-colored races are to humanity what many-colored literatures are to world literature. And just as humanity is one, so is world literature one, without sacrificing its variety.[31]

Upon the organic relationship between unity and variety Hearn based his concept of world literature. Because he saw the unity he also saw that even the strongest contrasts between the East and the West were not manifestations of difference but of variety. Hearn often indicated the unity by way of parallel or analogy. When he took growing interest in a singular parallelism between the Persian epic and the Arthurian legend, and between Greek and Japanese epitaphic poetry, it was because he came to believe that this sort of parallelism was a literary manifestation of the unity of man. He neither overstressed variety with the fallacious reasoning of the literary exotic nor abstracted literature as if it were a mere history of ideas. Hearn resorted with uncommon interest to the parallel between Greek and Japanese literature, as we have already seen in his reference to Greek and Japanese epitaphic poetry. Probably the earliest example of this interest is his review in 1883 of the translation of *Si-Ka-Zen-Yo,* a Japanese anthology.[32] As his *Japan: An Attempt at Interpretation* shows, Hearn came to attach to the analogy between the Greek and the Japanese a more than literary significance. His interest in this direction is evident in his discussion of insect poetry, for example. He points out that, owing to modern science, European poets are getting rid of the traditional Christian prejudice against insects, especially musical insects, which once enchanted old Greek poets, and have always enchanted Japanese poets. In this regard Europe is ready to return "to the poetical standpoint of the old Greeks." Hearn welcomes the revival of insect poetry because, in his opinion, it marks the newer and larger age of thought, "the age that begins to perceive the great truth of the unity of life." [33]

If there is anything which sets Hearn apart from his avowed literary masters, Poe, Gautier, and Baudelaire, it is the sense of the unity of life, or the sense of humanity. His belief in the oneness of humanity prevented his romantic glorification of the artist's martyrdom in the modern world, though he was well aware that genuine art can be produced only in solitude and silence. When he criticized the "decadents," by whom he meant Mallarmé and his poetic circle, Hearn's objection was that the medium they chose was their own esoteric private language, not "the language of the *greatest* (not the *great*) majority." Their art, Hearn wrote in 1894, "seems to me a sort of alchemy in verse,—totally false, with just enough glints of reality—micaceous shimmerings—to suggest imagination of ghostly gold. I can't understand that thing at all. It pains my head, and hurts my soul." [34] Baudelaire's poetry he could accept, a fact which shows not only the limitations of his taste but also how he distinguished Baudelaire from his poetic followers. To Hearn their art seemed to have reached the point of artificiality, thereby alienating itself from its original sources of life, "the soil from which everything human springs." [35]

In this respect Hearn did not hesitate to agree with Tolstoi's view that "true art should be able to appeal to all men, not to a class only." [36] As an art of emotional expression, Hearn believed, true literature should be able to touch the true emotions of humanity that are deepest, largest, and, at the same time, universal. In the highest function of literature Hearn thus saw a fundamental agreement between the East and the West. Concluding his lecture, "The Prose of Small Things," he called attention to the ancient Chinese prophecy: "The literature of the Future will be the literature of Pity." Hearn suggests that the word "pity," in the Roman and the Greek sense, should be taken as meaning "pure sympathy with all forms of human suffering," certainly not "contempt mixed with pity." He believes that the modern word "humanity" best expresses what the ancients meant by "pity." "It is," he continues, "by giving to the world little pictures of life and thought and feeling, joy and sorrow, gladness and gloom, that the average mind can best be awakened to a final sense of what the age most profoundly needs—the

sense of unselfish sympathy." Although Hearn here is primarily concerned with the sketch genre, his words are applicable to his concept
of literature in general. Considering "the tendency of the best thought
and the best feeling of this literary age in the West," Hearn concludes,
the ancient Chinese prophecy must and will come true in the form of
the literature of pity, or of humanity.[37]

Only when it takes root deep in the heart of humanity can any literature be creative as an integral part of world literature. Similarly, only
when every literature is creative can world literature cease to be the
sum total of what has been achieved in the past, and, going beyond the
past, nurture the whole of humanity. In the sense that to exist means to
create, every literature, of necessity, tends toward world literature.
Hearn's vision of world literature as universal creation we may find in
the following passage:

> It is not the highest art, of course, this worship of beauty. We cannot
> to-day touch the skirts of Greek art,—yet we feel the realized ideal that
> one marvellous race, and only one, had a divine glimpse of, is not the
> highest *possible*. The highest must be aspirational,—like music,—aspira-
> tional with all its spirings of utterance piercing into the Future. But I
> think that every school contributes some tone, some colour—else unob-
> tainable—to that mighty future scale of emotional harmonies of which the
> depths and the heights are still invisible to us—just as the possibilities of
> colour are still but faintly guessed at by us. Sense alone—pure or impure
> love of mere beauty and light and sweetness—cannot give the highest
> tones,—nor the deepest; but they help to do something for the evolution of
> the middle lines, which the loftier and the deeper powers cannot make—
> yet without which they would remain but dimly visible.[38]

Here it should be said that Hearn is defending the cult of Beauty not
because he still blindly accepts it, but because he recognizes its limitations through his own experience. The statement as a whole seems to
suggest more than its immediate purpose. Every school, every race, and
every nation should contribute its own share to the cosmic orchestra;
world literature as such is possible only through universal cooperation
of its multitudinous members. Unity thrives only in variety.[39] Hearn's
vision of world literature reminds us of the promise he made as a
young man, in 1882, "to carry his stone to the master-masons of a new
architecture." [40] In this plea for creation of a many-colored world literature on the basis of humanity, we find the unified expression of Hearn's
aesthetics of organic memory, his conviction of idealism, and his insistence on the creative function of literary study.

III Philosophy

X

"Give Us All Japan"

Hearn on Japan

Lafcadio Hearn went to Japan as an artist and died there as a thinker, without losing the concreteness of an artist. He was not a technical or an academic philosopher; he never pretended to be one. He constructed no philosophical system; yet, the term "philosopher" can be applied to him, as it has been to lay thinkers, philosophical-minded artists, and literary philosophers. To him, as to these others, philosophy meant primarily a way of life, a way of existential quest. Because of his grasp of the actual, his imaginative speculation, his logical vigor, and, above all, his need of "intellectual health," Hearn could go beyond his personal realm, thereby exploring some of the vital questions of human culture which we today must solve to reach a unified view of the world.

Although his childhood acquaintance with the Far East was made through Chinese curios in Carnarvon, and his youthful imagination was kindled by the religion of India, it was strange that neither China nor India became the land of Hearn's heart's desire.[1] Whenever he dreamed of visiting the Orient, his destination was invariably Japan.[2] This unseen land appealed to his aesthetic sensibility.[3]

Japan was also a land which St. Francis Xavier had called "the de-

light of my soul" nearly three centuries before. It was also the gate of
Asia, which, in 1886, Henry Adams and his friend, John La Farge,
entered in futile search of Nirvana. Mingling with a horde of globe-
trotters, Loti became at once enamored of the women of this island;
in his imperialistic pride Kipling touched only lightly upon this new
and old nation; and there were many others, such as B. H. Chamberlain, Percival Lowell, Sturgis Bigelow, and Ernest Fenollosa, all of
whom for one reason or another sojourned there longer. But it was
Hearn alone who became part of Japan. In spite of his original plan,
one volume of Japanese travel grew into a dozen; and likewise, one
year into fourteen. Hearn completed the cycle of Orientalism begun
by Marco Polo and continued by Will Adams, Kaempfer, Siebold, and
others. By crossing the Pacific westward he became a symbol of the first
cincture around the world.

If Hearn's position as interpreter of Japan has been unique, it is because he was able to explore and appreciate the soul of Old Japan, the
unchanging part of Japan. For this reason, however, many have questioned whether he really saw Japan in her entirety. Even well-meaning
admirers have somewhat apologetically conceded that as a romantic
wanderer Hearn failed to do justice to New Japan. The truth is that
he did not fail to do justice to it; he simply disapproved the general
course modern Japan was taking.

In order to understand Hearn's balanced opinion of Japan, we must
take into account all his Japanese writings: his Japanese books, his correspondence, contributions to the *Japan Mail,* and editorials for the
Kobe Chronicle.[4] Indeed, his Japanese books may reconstruct one
Hearn who was enchanted by the island but never the other Hearn who
likened himself to a caged cicada. It is rather his correspondence that
divulges the inside story, if not the whole—how he felt, observed, and
thought about his adopted country. In this regard, the Hearn-Chamber-
lain letters are revealing private documents which convey in naked language those impressions, feelings, and thoughts common to thinking
Westerners in the land.

Both Chamberlain and Hearn loved the land and its people, so much
as to designate it "absolutely the most charming of all countries" to live
in; yet, their correspondence is also "the record of a disillusioned enthu-
siast," to borrow Hearn's phrase. There is a continuous oscillation between enthusiasm and disillusionment. This alternation of light and
dark they would call "the swing of the pendulum." In a letter of 1891,
for instance, Chamberlain wrote to his friend in Matsue: ". . . they

[the Japanese, emotionally and intellectually considered,] appear to me far inferior to the European race,—at once less profound, less tender, and less imaginative." With specific reference to the paucity of imaginative power in their poetry, the correspondent continued: ". . . all this is very sad to write, *and I would not write it publicly.*" And he hastened to close the letter with a customary mention of the blissful life in this lotus land.[5]

As a long-time resident of Japan, Chamberlain must have meant his remarks as a forewarning to his friend, whose fresh ardor knew no limit. When disillusionment came toward the end of Hearn's Kumamoto period (1891–94), its bitterness was all the greater, especially after his idyllic life in Matsue. "Pendulum on the left—" so saying, Hearn wrote to Chamberlain,

> To make everything that he [the Japanese] adopts small—philosophy, sciences, material, arts, machinery;—everything is modified in many ways, but uniformly diminished for Lilliput. And Lilliput is not tall enough to see far. Cosmic emotions do not come to Lilliputians. Did any Japanese ever feel such an emotion? Will any ever feel one?

"We are *Brobdingnagians!*" he summed up. "And yet, perhaps, the future is to these races!"[6] A little later he reported his tormenting hunger for the open ports.[7] That summer Hearn took a trip to Tokyo and other eastern cities; from Yokohama he wrote:

> Another day, and I was in touch with England again. How small suddenly my little Japan became!—how lonesome! What a joy to feel the West! What a great thing is the West! What new appreciations of it are born of isolation! What a horrible place the school!—I was a prisoner released from prison after five years' servitude!
>
> Then I stopped thinking. For I saw my home,—and the lights of its household Gods,—and my boy reaching out his little hands to me,—and all the simple charm and love of old Japan. And the fairy-world seized my soul again, very softly and sweetly,—as a child might catch a butterfly.[8]

One may be tempted to ascribe this mood to Hearn's secluded life in Kumamoto, especially to his unhappy social experiences there; but these alone can hardly explain it. It expresses, as Hearn himself put it, "the need of being again among men of my own race who, with all their faults, have sympathy and kindness, and who have the *same color of soul* as myself."[9] Until his last day he was not wholly resigned to his self-imposed bondage. From these it is not difficult to record the swing of the pendulum within Hearn's mind and heart, between the two poles, the apparent smallness of the native people and the irresistible charm of their land.

All this Chamberlain must have foreseen, judging from his letter. What made the situation more pathetic was Hearn's own fear that his "fire of pen," his artistic inspiration, was gone forever. At one time he was "in literary despair"; at another he complained of Japan as "a sort of psychological tropic" which dulled his mental power.[10] The lament contains, perhaps, a special kind of truth for an artist like Hearn, who was sensitive to the changing climate. Half-solacing his friend, Chamberlain responded: "The only thing I don't like is your want of satisfaction with the fame brought by your books. Japan, no doubt, is a small field. Still here you are king; and could any man be more?"[11] Soon another encouragement followed it:

> . . . you ought, I say, to be the man of all others fitted to form a just opinion,—a final opinion on this land and people. You have been under the spell, and are now disillusioned, and yet not so disillusioned as not to retain much love for that which no longer seems divine. Write another book, and call it "Illusion and Disillusion," and give us *all* Japan,—the lights and the shadows, the native and the bearded foreigners, the dear old Tempo man.[12]

Because "Hearn-san kotoba" (Hearn dialect) was his only means of communication with the native Japanese, many people doubt the authenticity of his Japanese studies. In doing so, they take too lightly the fact that as a man of a large family, all Japanese, Hearn lived long enough among the native inhabitants, seldom mingling with the people of his color in open ports. As we remember, his success as teacher of English was due largely to his awareness of contemporary Japan, and what was needed for the creation of a modern Japanese literature. Besides, he had that strange faculty he called soul sympathy, a faculty which could compensate sufficiently for his linguistic deficiency. Another fact to be noted here is that even while in Japan, he remained half a journalist with his analytical power and speculative imagination, from time to time contributing articles to the *Japan Mail,* the New Orleans *Times-Democrat,* and the *Atlantic Monthly,* and also writing editorials for the *Kobe Chronicle.*

Nonetheless, the impression that the Japan Hearn saw and idealized is only part of the whole reality is a deeply rooted one. No doubt, his honest intention was to create art, instead of reportage. He was convinced that poetry is superior to history; and yet poetry and history, we may add, are not disparate, for history, by becoming part of poetry, becomes also truth. Hearn's personal sufferings may lead us to conclude that the Japan of his books is essentially a romantic one; that his enthusiasm for Old Japan is a poet's anachronism; that his nostalgia for the past is but his incapacity to cope with the changing world; and that all he attempted was an escape from civilization. This view, however, is the result of a superficial understanding of Hearn's deliberately complex approach, especially of our failure to discern the fact that the antithesis of two Japans, new and old, is as vital to all his Japanese studies as the twofold theme of Buddhism and evolutionism.

Hearn's objection to the new Japan can be understood only in terms of his conviction as a thinker. Let us first recall that he was in a position to experience modern Japan in many dimensions. As a foreigner obliged to earn his own living, he lived in various parts of the island, such as Matsue, Kumamoto, Kobe, and Tokyo. This provided him with the opportunity to see more of the land and know more of its people than the usual foreign tourists could either afford to or would care to. Like them, he saw open ports, Yokohama and Kobe, and Tokyo, the symbols of modern Japan. Unlike them, he lived in Matsue, where railways and electric lights were still unknown, where feudalism was lingering, and Shinto was maintained intact; and then in Kumamoto, a chief city of Kyushu, "the most conservative part of Japan," the city which had been burned down by the recent Seinan rebellion of some radical nationalists.

While his mind was full of curiosity and excitement, Hearn enjoyed his Arcadian life at Matsue. Disillusionment was reserved for his Kumamoto period. His reaction was, understandably, an extreme one: "You wonder why I hate Kumamoto," he wrote to Nishida in Matsue,

Well, firstly, because it is *modernized*. And then I hate it because it is too big, and has no temples and priests and curious customs in it. Thirdly, I hate it because it is ugly. Fourthly, I hate it because I am still a stranger in it,—and perhaps because I can't get literary material.[13]

From this one infers that Hearn's hatred of the place is wholly a subjective, personal matter. Compare this with a letter to Chamberlain, written at about the same time:

. . . I detest with unspeakable detestation the frank selfishness, the apathetic vanity, the shallow vulgar scepticism of the New Japan, the New Japan that prates its contempt about Tempo times, and ridicules the dear old men of the pre-Meiji era, and that never smiles, having a heart as hollow and bitter as a dried lemon.[14]

This fear of the loss over which New Japan rather rejoiced grew more acute as Hearn moved to Kobe in 1894. Here he was able to observe more clearly what was behind the Western fashion craze in modern Japan, and to contrast its open ports with the inland region. He sensed that the future, lacking moral wisdom, would be infinitely worse when dominated by those Japanese "in frock-coats and loud neckties." [15] The old Japan was passing away, vanishing away, "like snow in sun." [16] "Oh! I am rather angry with the Gods," he wrote to Chamberlain, "I have been fighting their battles; but they don't listen to me any more." [17] Soon after, he wrote an editorial article, "A Sad Change," for the *Kobe Chronicle*. First, he noted the multiplying social evils in open ports, the general misery resulting from the increase of wealth, and the dreadfulness of the industrialized future; and he openly opposed those missionaries who would explain all this by the inherent weakness of the native people.[18] As Hearn admitted, it was a losing battle. Somewhat resigned in 1895, he wrote to Chamberlain, "I felt, as never before, how utterly dead Old Japan is, and how ugly New Japan is becoming." [19] In the ensuing year, when he settled in the capital, Tokyo, which he abhorred, Hearn confided to his old friend in Matsue: "The new generation is not promising. . . . To speak more plainly, I should state that it seems to me the spirit of study is dead: you can do nothing without heart, and the heart has almost stopped beating." [20] This feeling was never allayed, even in 1902, when he said: "Japan is changing rapidly. . . . and the changes are not beautiful." They were, he added, "ugly and sad." [21]

All his life Hearn was compelled to witness the world in transition, whether in America, the French West Indies, or Japan. As he saw two Souths, old and new, in America, so he recorded two Japans, old and new; as he noted the white invasion into the Indies, so he foresaw the peril of the Occidental encroachment upon the Orient. His sympathetic mind was capable of feeling the dire dilemma of the natives under the incoming civilizations alien to their own. The dilemma, he knew, was fundamentally tragic because it was inevitable; and it was there wherever he went. Its most telling pattern he saw in an iron-clad battleship anchoring off the shore of his kingdom of beauty, and could not help expressing his sense of storm:

> Our ten naked oarsmen once more bend to their cross-handled oars, and
> recommence their ancient melancholy song. And as we glide back, there
> comes to me the idea of the prodigious cost of that which we went forth
> to see, the magnificent horror of steel and steam and all the multiple

enginery of death,—paid for by those humble millions who toil forever knee-deep in the slime of rice-fields, yet can never afford to eat their own rice! Far cheaper must be the food they live upon; and nevertheless, merely to protect the little that they own, such nightmares must be called into existence,—monstrous creations of science mathematically applied to the ends of destruction.[22]

This imperial man-of-war, Hearn suspected, might suggest the tragic destruction toward which New Japan marched, sacrificing everything, even its own soul. Admitting that it was the only means of national survival, he was nonetheless fearful of the probable catastrophe.

At another time, during his trip to Oki, an un-Westernized island on the Sea of Japan, he was not a little shocked by a dinner in European style, a beefsteak with fried potatoes.[23] Although this may appear to us as a romantic sort of disillusionment, the incident turned his thought to the nature of his own West and its intrusion into this island country. Intrusion or invasion, the word matters little, since New Japan, after being forced to open its door, deliberately adopted the way of the West for self-protection. The more he became acquainted with his students, the more acutely he could feel how serious the situation was. Western-styled education, newly introduced, demanded the students' maximal achievements in a minimal period so that they might meet the heavy responsibility of the new nation. Under this system, Hearn saw, his students' character was changing into "something of singular hardness," or "of singular opacity." [24] Under the overloaded schedule some of them broke down mentally and physically. All this led him to doubt the sanity of the new education and further to question the value of such a mass Westernization.[25]

The task had to be carried out at whatever cost, as universally decreed by Emperor Meiji himself: "Knowledge and learning shall be sought for throughout the world." To this Hearn could not help adding his own advice. "This is an era of great and rapid change," he said in a farewell speech to his Matsue students, "and it is probable that many of you, as you grow up, will not be able to believe everything that your fathers believed before you;—though I sincerely trust you will at least respect the memory of your ancestors." [26] The dilemma confronting the new generation was how to reconcile these two phases of history, old and new, or rather how to fulfill the imperial edict even at the expense of age-old tradition. Probably time alone could do justice to both generations, passing and rising.

The issue was taken up in his chapter, "Jiujutsu," one of the most penetrating observations Hearn made on the course of New Japan. As it shows, the dilemma was, ironically enough, not only his students' but also Hearn's. Here Hearn stands for Old Japan, whereas his pupil speaks in defense of New Japan. Objecting to the foreign teacher's lavish praise of the old virtues, the youth points out the old generation's defects in "practical knowledge of the Western kind." Their conversation follows:

". . . our old society cultivated those qualities of unselfishness, and courtesy, and benevolence which you admire, at the sacrifice of the individual. But Western society cultivates the individual by unrestricted competition,—competition in the power of thinking and acting."

"I think that is true."

"But in order that Japan be able to keep her place among nations, she must adopt the industrial and commercial methods of the West. Her future depends upon her industrial development; but there can be no development if we continue to follow our ancient morals and manners."

"Why?"

"Not to be able to compete with the West means ruin; but to compete with the West we must follow the methods of the West; and these are quite contrary to the old morality."

"Perhaps."

"I do not think it can be doubted. To do any kind of business upon a very large scale, men must not be checked by the idea that no advantage should be sought which could injure the business of others. And on the other hand, wherever there is no restraint on competition, men who hesitate to compete because of mere kindliness of heart, must fail. The law of the struggle is that the strong and active shall win, the weak and the foolish and the indifferent lose. But our old morality condemned such competition."

"That is true."

"Then, Sir, no matter how good the old morality, we cannot make any great industrial progress, nor even preserve our national independence, by following it. We must forsake our past. We must substitute law for morality."

"But it is not a good substitute."

"It has been a good substitute in the West, if we can judge by the material greatness and power of England. We must learn in Japan to be moral by reason, instead of being moral by emotion. A knowledge of the moral reason of law is itself a moral knowledge."

"For you, and those who study cosmic law, perhaps. But what of the common people?"

"They will try to follow the old religion; they will continue to trust in their gods. But life will, perhaps, become more difficult for them. They were happy in the ancient days." [27]

It is enlightening to see how Chamberlain reacted to this:

The dialogue between yourself and your favorite student on the dilemma in which Japan finds herself when confronted with Western civilization seemed to me to contain almost equal truth on either side, which is surely what a dialogue ought to do if it is to sustain the reader's interest. One might almost say,—might one not?—that it is what a dialogue always ought to do if it is to represent truth; for truth has always two sides pretty nearly balanced. I don't think, though, that either you or [your] student (but of course I forgive the latter) interpret the truth fairly when you assume, without enquiry, the materialistic character of Western civilization as opposed to the ethical character of Eastern. Another half of the truth is that the Western are spiritualists, poets, philosophers, disinterested investigators of nature and speculators on and mystically rapt worshippers of Nature's God, as opposed to the matter-of-fact nose-to-the-earth Far Eastern. Yankey-dom is not the sum total of Western achievement. It is indeed a mere caricature of Puritanism, with the maxim "Work out thine own salvation" turned into "Work out thine own fortune." [28]

Except for his understandable scoff at "Yankey-dom," Chamberlain stands in a far saner position. Hearn's negligence of another side of the West, on the other hand, may be due both to his known bias against Christianity and Christian missionaries, and to the nature of the dialog itself. Even so, there is no justification for his remaining reticent about the spiritual tradition of his own West and letting his student view the West solely in terms of materialism. Yet, in fairness to Hearn, we must note that the student's concept of the West has been shared by many Far Easterners as a result of the unfortunate historical fact that Christianity made its way into the East side by side with the "black-ships," loaded with guns and many other things not related to the Gospel. Beyond all this, Hearn was right in sensing that the future tragedy of the Far East would lie in the very rejection of its own traditional values. His objection was that the new generation of Japan was importing Western materialism at the cost of Old Japan or at least of what it stood for.

Hearn was apprehensive about the efforts of this iconoclastic generation to break with its own tradition. His stand, thoroughly consistent with his regarding a new Japanese literature as part of world literature, is far from political; it is basically cultural and religious, the stand of a traditionalist. "I teach them respect for their own faiths, for the beliefs of the common people, and for their own country," he wrote to Chamberlain. "I am practically a traitor to England (eh?) and a renegade. But in the eternal order of things, I know I am right." [29] In the above dialog the teacher holds that the men of the old generations are "just like their own gods," and "almost perfect men," judged by their own standards. To the student, who retorts "In what respect?" he explains: "In kindness, in courtesy, in heroism, in self-control, in power of self-sacrifice, in filial piety, in simple faith, and in the capacity to be contented with a little." [30] By the virtues of the old school Hearn meant the importance of a sense of tradition which alone could successfully guide the new generation. He could almost foresee the future disaster into which the rising generation, with no sense of the past, would eventually plunge. Hearn rightly predicted that Japan might "stumble" not as a result of "any weakening of the national spirit" but "as a result of political mistakes,—of rash self-confidence." [31] Recent history has proved this to be true.

Hearn's notion of the men of the old generation, or "Tempo men," was nowise a theoretical one, however. He had the opportunity to know personally some living examples, such as Governor Koteda of Shimane Province; Katayama, a teacher of Chinese classics in Matsue; and Akizuki, a nationally acclaimed educator in Kumamoto. His friendship with Akizuki, it is said, was one of his most heart-warming experiences at the Kumamoto school. As for Governor Koteda, Hearn once wrote a laudatory note for the *Japan Mail*. The Governor, he declared, is "a Japanese gentleman of the old school, in the best sense of the term," and to visit his house is "to receive a lesson in taste." [32]

Through such personal experiences Hearn became more and more convinced that the future course of New Japan should be guided by the traditional principle of the "Tempo men." This matter he treated more explicitly in his chapter, "A Conservative," in *Kokoro*. It is perhaps an imaginary but nonetheless convincing story about a man caught in a dilemma. We are told of the old Spartan-styled samurai education in his boyhood, the first appearance of an English teacher hired for military training, the youth's conversion to Christianity and subsequent abandonment of it, his wandering abroad as a political exile, ever trying to grasp the relationship between Western civilizations and their religions, and his final return home with a renewed sense of the past:

Japan would have to learn the new forms of action, to master the new forms of thought, or to perish utterly. There was no other alternative. And then the doubt of all doubts came to him, the question which all the sages have had to face: *Is the universe moral?* To that question Buddhism had given the deepest answer.[33]

As a continuation of the previous essay on jiujutsu, this account is intended to portray what Hearn considers an ideal Japanese in the modern world. It describes the pilgrimage of his self-discovery through varying stages, light and dark, hope and despair. The hero of the story discovers that Western superiority is not ethical but intellectual, and that Western science must fortify the tradition of Japan. In one sense at least, the tragedy of modern Japan, not to mention that of her neighbors, is the failure to unite science and tradition. "A Conservative" is, as it were, the sequel to "Yoshida-Torajiro," R. L. Stevenson's essay about a patriot of symbolic significance at the dawn of modern Japan. With the intent of seeing the world beyond the seas, Yoshida approached the "blackships" of Commodore Perry, only to be sent home for execution. Stevenson describes how Yoshida "hoped, perhaps, to get the good of other lands without their evil; to enable Japan to profit by the knowledge of the barbarians, and still keep her inviolate with her own arts and virtues." [34] Hearn's conservative Japanese returns home with a treasure more valuable, the joy of self-discovery.

Contradicting many readers of Hearn, Chamberlain once said: "Lafcadio Hearn understands contemporary Japan better, and makes *us* understand it better, than any other writer, because he loves it better." [35] The statement is significant because it is from someone like Chamberlain, who knew intimately not only Japan but also Hearn. Note also the term "contemporary Japan." Chamberlain's "love" should not be taken to mean uncritical admiration. Rather, it means genuine appreciation, at once critical and kindly. This seems to epitomize best Hearn's attitude toward Japan, as evidenced in his editorials to the *Kobe Chronicle,* written in the midst of the Sino-Japanese War (1894–95). [36] On several occasions he ventured to defend Japan against the world criticism of her war atrocities and cruelties, and also to attack the interference by European powers. At the same time, he could not refrain from criticizing the Japanese attitude toward China. In principle, he reasoned, the war was "a cruel lesson" for China; and it would sooner or later necessitate overall reform on the part of China and Korea. He foresaw Japan's possible arrogance resulting from her victory over China and its consequences for the destiny of the Far East. For this reason he insisted that Japan be generous toward her continental rival. On more than one point she failed to come up to his expectations. Deploring a Japanese demand for dismemberment of China, he pointed out that the integrity of China would be vital for Japan's security. Japanese assistance in the administrative reform of Korea as an independent state, he then suggested, should and could be successfully carried out only with moral support from European powers; in other words, "under the joint protection and united pressure of a combination of the Powers interested."

According to Hearn, this measure would prevent Russia's southward advancement into the enfeebled peninsula kingdom, which otherwise would remain "a source of danger to the world's tranquillity." He wished to see a triple alliance of Japan, China, and Korea, "capable of preserving the integrity of the Far East against either Russian or any other Western aggression." From the vantage point of modern history, anyone familiar with the modern Far Eastern world would agree that this proposal might have been an effective means of security for the area concerned, and, consequently, for the balance of power. For some reason Japan preferred to be the sole victor, thereby contesting with Russia over the Korean problem a decade later. Although Japan emerged again as the winner of the Russo-Japanese War (1904–05), the Far East as a whole experienced rapid disintegration. Later still, Japan upheld her Messianic slogan, Greater Far Eastern Co-prosperity, not on an equal basis, but under her own leadership. This had tragic consequences for modern Japan and the whole Far East. Had the one-eyed dreamer's suggestion been well heeded, Japan and the Far East might have been considerably different from what they are today.[37] All this presents important points for consideration: First, there is a moral toughness in Hearn's challenge to the victory-glowing Japanese; second, his firm grasp of the actual is evident in his analysis of the contemporary political scene and in the accuracy of his predictions; and last, the measures that he advanced are based upon his awareness of the complexity of the Far Eastern mentality, especially the Japanese character.[38]

But Hearn was perhaps the last man who would claim to be a prophet. His characteristic modesty prevented him from pretending to understand Japan at all. As a life-long student of what he termed the race character or race soul, he was too well aware how futile and often hazardous it is to generalize and speculate about it. More than once he felt mystified by his Japanese wife (whom he called "my own little wife,") and especially by those "race-tendencies difficult to understand."[39] This barrier, which he also called the "granite wall," seemed to grow more and more formidable, so much so that he finally had to confide to his old friend: *I have learned about Japan only enough to convince me that I know nothing about Japan.*[40] In the opening pages of *Japan: An Attempt at Interpretation,* the book that could safely be his final opinion about the matter, Hearn said in the same vein: ". . . after having discovered that I cannot understand the Japanese at all—I feel better qualified to attempt this essay." [41] Human understanding always begins with such humility.

Japan, originally written for Hearn's prospective American lectures, was posthumously published (1904). His last word on his adopted country and its people, the book represents the culmination of his early observations on Japan, such as "The Genius of Japanese Civilization" and "Some Thoughts on Ancestor-Worship" (both in *Kokoro*). It has been called "a classic in science, a wonder of interpretation," and described as "the product of long years of thought, of keenest perception, or marvellous comprehension." [42] It is both persuasive because of a systematic approach based on the law of evolution, and irresistible because of a poetic charm that is entirely Hearn's. Its twenty-two chapters may well determine the stature of Hearn as interpreter of Japan.

In the preliminary chapters (I–II), Hearn examines the foundation of the Japanese soul structure, which he believes to have remained essentially unchanged throughout its historical evolutions. He attempts to discover, under the many successive layers of alien culture, the earliest ancestor-worship, or "the earliest ghost-worship," as "the root of all religions." Hearn believes Japan to be no exception to Spencer's exposition of the law of religious development. If "the history of Japan is really the history of her religion" is the guiding principle of Hearn's dissertation, it is because of his conviction that all her social institutions, not to speak of her ethics and aesthetics, are virtually what has evolved out of this moral foundation. In the ensuing chapters (III–IX) he illustrates the historical process in which this earliest ancestor-worship came to adopt and absorb alien beliefs, especially Chinese and Buddhist, and then developed into Shinto through three stages—family cult, communal cult, and state cult.

In the third part of the book (X–XVII), Hearn examines more closely Japan's contact with the older, alien civilizations. As he points out, the patriarchal society built upon these three levels of ancestor-worship, despite its exclusive nature, never could be hostile to the introduction of Confucianism and Buddhism. Although the original doctrine of Buddhism was "essentially in discord" with Shinto beliefs, Buddhism was able to meet the special needs of the Japanese because of its successful acclimatization in India, China, and Korea. It humanized and civilized the Japanese, without extinguishing the root of their indigenous ancestor-worship. If Hearn seems here to underestimate the impact of Confucianism, it is because he believes that Buddhism brought with it the whole of Chinese civilization. Thus, the elder civilization was not merely superimposed upon the Japanese social structure, but fitted into it so perfectly that "the marks of the welding, the lines of the juncture, almost totally disappeared."

By this characteristically religious conservatism constituting the basis of the Japanese soul structure Hearn explains the immense duration of her imperial dynasty as well as the relative brevity of her various shogunates and regencies. The comparatively long duration of the Fujiwara rule, for instance, is due to the fact that it represented a religious, rather than a military aristocracy, whereas the Tokugawa feudalism, under which Japanese civilization reached the limit of its development, as evidenced in its exquisite Lilliputian art and its fortified religion of loyalty, collapsed rapidly because of its merely military foundation, that is, because of its lack of the religious power of cohesion. This religious conservatism, Hearn believes, can account for the failure of the Jesuit attempt to convert Japan. Because of its monotheistic position, Christianity never could adapt itself to Japanese society, where the religion of filial piety still persisted. As this historical fact suggests, Japan would and could react in the same way to the peril of Western aggression. Under the pressure of modern Western democracies her religion could not be destroyed; it could only be diverted, transformed, and expanded to larger needs, thus becoming "the new national sentiment of trust and duty: the modern sense of patriotism." Hearn insists that, whatever the future, Japan "must depend upon the maintenance of this new religion of loyalty, evolved, through the old, from the ancient religion of the dead."

Hearn has no intention of making Japan a unique case, completely isolated from the law of universal evolution. As a matter of fact, he takes the position, throughout his discourse, that the history of Japanese social evolution is consistent with the evolutional formula laid down by Spencer. Just as Spencer is made to supply the guiding law of universal evolution, so is Fustel de Coulanges brought in to bear witness to his observation on the fundamental parallelism between Japanese and Greco-Roman society. Drawing on Coulanges' classical study, *La Cité antique,* Hearn sees the unity of the East and the West in the history of human evolution. His interest centers on one point, that Japan succeeded in maintaining its ancient patriarchal social structure while Europe lost its counterpart through the industrial revolution. In this regard Japan is "evolutionally young." Standing by this premise, Hearn muses on the present state of Japan and speculates on her possible future course in the sphere of modern international competition. In the last five chapters of *Japan* (XVIII–XXII), he expresses his apprehension, expectation, and confidence.

First, Hearn likens the evolution of the old Japanese society to those famous trees adorning many Buddhist temples, "trees trained and clipped into extraordinary shapes"—dragons, pagodas, umbrellas, etc. Although the overall reconstruction of the Meiji period has made possible her deliverance from the bonds of feudal law and her release from military rule, the foundation of Japanese society still maintains its ancient shape, following much of the original design. So far this has been possible only through tremendous triple pressure on the individual. In the new Japan, as in the old, the average individual lives under three forms of pressure: pressure from above, exemplified in the will of his superiors; pressure around him, represented by the common will of his equals; and pressure from below, represented by the general sentiment of his inferiors; all indicating "survivals of the ancient religious responsibility." Most typical of the persistent effect of the threefold social coercion is official education, which is still conducted upon a traditional plan almost the exact opposite of the Western plan, after all its Westernization. Hearn cannot but dread the possible consequence of the present policy, which has failed to give proper encouragement to cultivation of more constructive imagination. As a result "home scholarship" has been expedient, remaining indifferent to the higher emotional and intellectual life of the Western civilization.

The matter is of prime importance since Japan must now compete with the West, whose industrialization has been possible due to the four revolutionary periods which Coulanges regarded as characteristic of the history of all the ancient Greek and Roman communities. The dilemma of Japan is that, while evolutionally young enough to maintain her patriarchal society, she has been compelled to reshape herself in the course of one generation to an industrialized society. Yet, the capacity for industrial competition, as Western history testifies, must depend upon the intelligent freedom of the individual. Again accepting Coulanges' thesis that the absence of individual liberty was the real cause of the disintegration of the Greek society, Hearn comes to the conclusion that the absence of individual freedom in modern Japan is nothing less than a national danger: "Only those long accustomed to personal liberty—liberty to think about matters of ethics apart from matters of government—liberty to consider questions of right and wrong, justice and injustice, independently of political authority—are able to face without risk the peril now menacing Japan." What Japan needs desperately is therefore more freedom—"freedom restrained by wisdom," "freedom to think and act and strive for self as well as for others"— not freedom to oppress the weak, or to exploit the simple." Only if Japanese statesmen can satisfy this need will their future be secure.

As has been said, the book was originally intended as a series of lectures in America. To Mrs. Wetmore, who was then arranging his lectureship with Cornell University and Vassar College, Hearn wrote reporting its near completion:

> . . . they [the lectures] will form eventually a serious work upon Japan, entirely unlike anything yet written. The substantial idea of the lectures is that Japanese society represents the condition of ancient Greek society a thousand years before Christ. I am treating of religious Japan,—not of artistic or economical Japan, except by way of illustration. Lowell's *Soul of the Far East* is the only book of the kind in English; but I have taken a totally different view of the causes and the evolution of things.[43]

Hearn's self-confidence is unusually high, considering his professed admiration for Percival Lowell's book. But what does he mean by "a totally different view"? In order to understand Hearn's implication adequately, we must first take a brief glance at Lowell's opinions.

Lowell's Far Eastern studies are largely to be found in four books, *Choson* (1886), *The Soul of the Far East* (1888), *Noto* (1891), and *Occult Japan* (1894). Except for *Noto*, which is an ordinary travel book, they all mark this Bostonian's brilliant talent for speculation and generalization. Beyond their individual differences, the books possess one common denominator, the author's personality-impersonality theory of the distinction between the West and the East. This *"idée fixe"* of Lowell, as Chamberlain half-sceptically called it, had already manifested itself in *Choson*, a book written after his official visit to Korea. In *Choson*, Lowell formulates the "Triad of Principles" as the three basic characteristics of that hermit kingdom, recently forced to open her ports: the marked tendency of impersonality, the patriarchal system, and the low position of woman.[44] In his next book Lowell unifies this trinity in the thesis of Eastern impersonality versus Western personality. The same idea is ubiquitous even in his *Occult Japan*, a study of Shinto in particular, rather lightly treated in *The Soul*. Comparing Shinto with Buddhism, he wittily observes: ". . . while simple Shinto regards the dead as spiritually living, philosophic Buddhism regards the living as spiritually dead; two aspects of the same shield." [45] In his conclusion he examines esoteric Shinto practices, such as trance and possession, and declares that they indicate the Japanese lack of personality.

Lowell is undoubtedly at his best in *The Soul of the Far East,* where his speculation possesses the freshness of discovery, not the ugliness of distortion; and his wit exhibits playful grace, not malicious sarcasm. Much like Hearn, Lowell starts with a strange impression of topsy-turvydom, "equal but opposite," thereby developing the contrast between the East and the West. He even hopes that these two opposing mental pictures, once harmonized, would help us to understand humanity. But his argument takes a peculiar turn as soon as he designates the Far Eastern mental history as "the same story with variations" and goes on to make a sweeping statement: "We stand at the nearer end of the scale, the Far Orientals at the other. If with us the *I* seems to be of the very essence of the soul, then the soul of the Far East may be said to be Impersonality." [46] By the evolutionary law that humanity progresses from the simplicity of nature toward the complexity of individuation, it is plain that the West is in the adulthood of self-consciousness and the East in its undifferentiated childhood. Since every race, "not historically, but psychologically," goes through three stages of evolution, past, present, and future, its racial character can be best examined in its three special manifestations: ". . . in the language of a people we find embalmed the spirit of its past; in its every-day thoughts, be they of arts or sciences, is wrapped up its present life; in its religion lie enfolded its dreamings of a future." [47] Following this scheme, Lowell illustrates how in each of these three manifestations, Far Eastern impersonality "stares us in the face."

In the last chapter, "Imagination," Lowell speculates on the primary cause of this self-evident difference between the Western and the Far Eastern mentality. [48] He feels it is more likely that the soul itself possesses "the germ of its own evolution," though the environmental force must have contributed to the total process. Individuality, personality, and the sense of self are therefore only three different aspects of the same thing, a change "from a state of simple homogeneity to one of complex heterogeneity," as a result of cosmic evolution. The core of this strange force Lowell considers to be imagination, the mother of "spontaneous variety," and consequently of originality. Since it is "science rather than art that demands imagination of her votaries," the Far Orientals "ought to be a particularly unimaginative set of people," and "such is precisely what they are." As evidence of their lack of originality Lowell points to their ignorance of science. Their past achievements, no matter how marvelous to the rest of the world, are due to their taste, or delicacy of perception, which has "absolutely nothing to do with imagination."

From this diagnosis of the general cause Lowell deduces its effect. Its relative results are three: first, the Far Eastern civilization is, "not so advanced a one as our own"; second, the rate of Oriental progress has been and will be less rapid, whether in the form of the Chinese "disinclination to progress" or in the form of the Japanese proclivity to imitation; and third, the "remarkable homogeneity" of the Orientals is simply the result of "lack of divergence" or "comparative absence of genius."

It is not difficult to imagine why Hearn was horrified by Lowell's conclusions. Even in 1891, when reading *The Soul of the Far East* over again, he noted that to read it after a year and a half in Japan was quite different from reading it in America. He was still impressed by its power and charm—more than ever. "But," he added, "I am so much horrified by its conclusions—at least a few of them—that I try very hard to find a flaw therein." [49] In a sense, Hearn came closer to the spirit of Japan by scrutinizing what he considered Lowell's flaws, one after another. And *Japan,* most Lowell-like of all his Japanese books, might be considered Hearn's final attempt not only to challenge Lowell's position directly, but further to formulate his own.

Unlike Lowell, Hearn confines his scope to Japan itself, rarely venturing beyond. When he admits that Japan is evolutionally young, his intention is not to accept Lowell's view that Japanese civilization is not so advanced a one as ours, but to suggest that it is "a civilization that can be termed imperfect only by those who would also term imperfect the Greek civilization of three thousand years ago." [50]

As for the question of whether the Japanese have originality or not, Hearn cautiously opposes Lowell. To Lowell, their proclivity to imitation indicates their lack of originality, because imitation is "the natural substitute for originality." At first Hearn felt that Lowell ignored "the most essential and astonishing quality of the race: its genius of eclecticism"; [51] yet, in his first Japanese study, *Glimpses,* Hearn conceded that there is "an apparent absence of spontaneity, creative thought, original perception of the highest order," and even suspected that "this seeming deficiency is racial." [52] He soon returned to his initial position, however, and reconsidered the question in Japanese, rather than Western terms, the result being his essay, "Jiujutsu." Jiujutsu he describes as "an art of self-defense," which relies for victory "solely upon the strength of your opponent." It purports to "conquer by yielding." In Hearn's opinion, this "symbolism of Intelligence as a means to foil brute force" is basically economical, ethical, and philosophical, and above all expressive of the racial genius. Illustrating how remarkably the Japanese, in the course of history, have applied this spirit to all sorts of foreign influence, he concludes that "they are not imitative at all: they are assimilative and adoptive only, and that to the degree of genius." [53] Hence their "remarkable homogeneity" as the first prerequisite of any cultural unit is definitely something to be prized and furthered, certainly not to be thrown overboard, as Lowell suggests. It is the basis of their racial integrity and cultural tradition.

As for Lowell's theory of personality *versus* impersonality, especially his assertion regarding the Japanese lack of personality, Hearn employs a more incisive and positive strategy. As an example he calls attention to the Japanese smile, an outward expression that baffles practically every inexperienced Westerner in Japan. At first glance it seems to lack any sort of personality, but nothing could be more deceiving. In considering the question, Hearn suggests, we must take into account one thing, that "even though the heart is breaking, it is a social duty to smile bravely." From his own experience with the people and their writings he has come to the realization that their lack of personality is to a great extent voluntary. This, Hearn thinks, is a result of a traditional life that has been, from prince to peasant, regulated by the religious spirit of self-suppression for the sake of the whole, whether it be family, community, or nation. From this observation Hearn suggests that the seeming impersonality of the Japanese should be taken as signifying their "ancient moral tendency to self-sacrifice for duty's sake," not as absence of personality.[54] Referring specifically to Lowell's contention, Hearn said: "I wish he had to teach here for a year, and he would discover some of the most extraordinary individuality he ever saw." It is merely because its marks show "less quickly on the surface," and are "physiologically and conventionally" "less perceptible at first sight." [55]

Lowell seems to be a composite symbol of what Irving Babbitt termed three types of superiority complex often found in modern Orientalism: racial superiority; scientific or materialistic progress; and religious superiority.[56] The second, in particular, seems to be at the core of Lowell's speculation. According to Lowell, science is far superior to anything human, including art; science is "not even distinctively human, but cosmical." Being thus superior to man, it is "unpersonal rather than impersonal." [57] This rather dubious scientism of the later nineteenth century (as he said "perhaps the most imaginative period the world's history has ever known") makes all his argument logical, analytical, speculative, and at the same time leads him to belittle any other than scientific values. Science is the Alpha and Omega of Lowell's thought process, though his method is, as we have seen, deductive rather than inductive, and therefore dogmatic. This abstract scientism deprives him of any sense of time and space; his common scorn for myths, legends, and folklore in general indicates his inability to grasp human existence in its most concrete form. All this makes a striking contrast with Hearn.

Hearn was well aware of the fundamental difference between Lowell and himself. Despite profound respect for his distinguished contemporary, Hearn determined not to "do anything in his line." [58] Describing his own approach to the Japanese mind as psychical, he said he was "taking almost exactly the opposite ground to that of Lowell." [59] *Occult Japan,* Hearn admitted, "touches truths to the quick,—with a light sharp sting peculiar to Lowell's art"; but it is "painfully unsympathetic—Mephistophelian in a way that chills me." [60] The book strikes him "only as a mood of the man, an ugly, supercilious one verging on the wickedness of a wish to hurt." Then he turns to reflect on the reason why his own work has been spoken of as far more successful even than *The Soul of the Far East:* "Certainly not because I am his equal, either as a thinker or an observer," but rather because "the world considers the sympathetic mood more just than the analytical or critical." Hearn rightly fears that "the merely critical mood will always be blind to the most vital side of any human question," since "the most vital side is feeling,—not reason." [61] "In the psychological world a man may grow too tall to see anything near himself"—this, Hearn thinks, is Lowell's weakness. As if to sum up what has been said, Hearn contrasts his own method with Lowell's: "His standpoint of pure science is too high to allow of that intimacy which means soul sympathy. I have tried to study from the bottom what he has observed from the top." [62] For this reason Hearn, in his opening of *Japan,* called Lowell "a scientific mind." So one may say that Hearn's appreciation of Japan deepened in proportion as he ascended from the bottom to the top, while Lowell ever remained at the top. The contrast will be more clear if we compare Hearn's *Japan* with Lowell's *Occult Japan.* Both deal with Shinto as the starting point; but when they reach their conclusion, there is a world of difference between them. In *Occult Japan* there is not the "playful tenderness" of its predecessor, as Hearn indicated. There is only a completely negative attitude on Lowell's part.

If what Hearn calls soul sympathy sets him apart from Lowell, nowhere is it more succinctly expressed than in their advice to New Japan. After all his argument, Lowell closes *The Soul of the Far East* in this manner: "Unless their newly imported ideas really take root, it is from this whole world that Japanese and Koreans, as well as Chinese, will inevitably be excluded." [63] As it stands, it is absolutely just advice; but how one should transplant the strange mind-seed in the soil that cannot accept it because of its innate absence of personality, there is no way of knowing. Lowell merely voices an ultimatum. On the other hand, Hearn's advice is more practical. As he sees it, it is not the Japanese absence of personality but the absence of individual freedom that seems to be nothing less than a national danger. He suggests that more individual freedom be allowed to the Japanese, a kind of freedom restrained by wisdom, for that is the only way to maintain their ancient integrity and yet to survive in this competitive modern world. In view of the recent history of Japan it is quite obvious which advice could have been more constructive for her and for the rest of the world.

Earl Miner has recently written of Hearn as an interpreter of Japan: "The West and Japan have shared the idea that he has understood Japan as no Westerner ever had before or is likely to again and, in certain rather limited senses, this is true." [64] There are, indeed, many books about Japan written by Hearn's contemporaries; [65] unlike theirs, Hearn's books have managed to retain their original freshness and personal charm. What is then the secret of their uniqueness? The real secret, it is now clear, lies in Hearn's characteristic approach,—from the bottom to the top. Never contented with the mere surface of things Japanese, he probed into their spiritual foundation, which knows no date, and therefrom attempted to interpret those cultural phenomena as its manifestation. He could achieve this feat by virtue of his soul sympathy and his grasp of the actual, in other words, by virtue of his peculiar sense of the whole. As an interpreter of Japan his mind was a rare combination of two minds, poetic and scientific, as Chamberlain said:

> Never perhaps was scientific accuracy of detail married to such tender and exquisite brilliancy of style. In reading these profoundly original essays, we feel the truth of Richard Wagner's saying, that "*Alles Verständnis kommt uns nur durch die Liebe.*" Lafcadio Hearn understands

contemporary Japan better, and makes *us* understand it better, than any
other writer, because he loves it better. Japanese life, manners, thoughts,
aspirations, the student class, the singing-girls, the politicians, the delightful country-folk of secluded hamlets who still bow down before
ancestral gods, Japan's attitude in time of war, Buddhist funeral services
chanted by priestly choirs in vestments gold-embroidered, not men only
but ghosts and folk-lore fancies, the scenery of remote islands which
Hearn alone among Europeans has ever trod,—not a single thing Japanese, in short, except perhaps the humorous side of native life, but these
wonderful books shed on it the blended light of poetry and truth. Our
only quarrel is with some of Lafcadio Hearn's judgments:—in righting
the Japanese, he seems to us continually to wrong his own race. The objectionable character in his stories is too apt to be a European. However,
Europe is well-able to take care of herself; and if this be the price demanded for so great a gift to literature and ethnologic science, we at least
will pay it uncomplainingly.[66]

In epitomizing Hearn's approach to Japan and assessing his achievement as her interpreter, Chamberlain's tribute nowise resembles those
many partisan defenses which have only impeded our better access to
Hearn; and time has not yet proved that Chamberlain erred in his
judgment.

XI

"The Eternal Feminine"

Beyond Western Passionalism

A year and a half after his arrival in Japan, Hearn wrote to Ellwood Hendrick: "It is the hardest country to learn—except China —in the world. I am the only man who ever attempted to learn the people seriously; and I think I shall succeed."[1] Hearn succeeded in the attempt so well that we all tend to think of him solely as a writer on Japan. In refuting this common view Albert Mordell once declared that Japan gave him nothing, because Hearn "had done in America precisely what he did in Japan." In other words, "he only found in Japan the pretexts for exercising his gifts," both artistic and intellectual.[2] This is no mere hyperbole. There is much truth in it; yet, to say that Hearn can be best understood in terms of Japan is equally true. Whatever his mind-seed, it could not possibly have found a better soil than Japan. The real meaning of this figure of speech would be especially apparent if we ask what would have resulted had this mind-seed dropped elsewhere. There are certain ideas which could never have ripened but for Hearn's contact with Japan, and, more largely, the East. One of these is his thought on the question of sex in literature, which affirms Mordell's contention and at the same time modifies it considerably. It is one of those ideas which might have remained folded forever outside of Japan.

It is well known that the young Hearn held the gratification of sex as "the highest rite in Nature's temple," never concealing his interest in it. This has been repeatedly pointed out in one way or another by Hearn students. Dr. Gould, whatever his motivation, noted this tendency in his old friend's art and applied to it the epithet, *"c'est toujours femme!"* Whether form or color or the ghostly, everything, once touched by Hearn's magic wand, turned "sensual and sexual." [3] Tinker called attention to the same point in his study of Hearn: "He reached his highest point as a literary essayist in his handling of the question of sex in literature. Sex complexes completely controlled his life." It was Victorian vigilance, Tinker believed, that emasculated Hearn's sexualism and thereby diverted it to his passion for folklore and aesthetic artificiality, notably, among many other things.[4] The verdict was only to be supported rather than denied by another more competent, and more sympathetic student of Hearn, Mordell, who once observed that Hearn "anticipated many of Freud's conclusions." [5]

As a connoisseur of female beauty, it is true, Hearn wrote much on the subject; we have his articles like "Beauty Undraped" (Cincinnati *Enquirer,* October 18, 1874), "A Prize for Beauty" (New Orleans *Item,* April 25, 1881), and "Women and Horses" (*Item,* May 21, 1881). He once confided to the puritanical Dr. Gould, "Never was there a huger stupidity than the observation that 'all women are in one respect alike.' On the contrary, in that one respect they differ infinitely, inexplicably, diabolically, fantastically." [6] Through his long study Hearn came to the conclusion that all women differ not only individually but also racially. From this point of view he tried his hand at ethno-aesthetic studies of women, the result being pieces like "Fair Women and Dark Women," "Arabian Women," "Creole Women in the French West Indies," "A Woman's Diary," "Of Women's Hair," and, possibly, "The Perfume of Women," that oft-alleged yet never seen scholarly treatise.[7] In his most sober book, *Japan,* such predilection is evidently beyond his control. "For it has well been said," Hearn wrote there, "that the most wonderful esthetic products of Japan are not its ivories, nor its bronzes, nor its porcelains, nor its swords, nor any of its marvelous metal or lacquer—but its women." [8]

Hearn's interest in the question of sex is not confined to these studies alone; it knows no bounds, pervading all his admittedly more ambitious writings. Many of his legends and romances, as we remember, evolve around one central theme, love, whether human or ghostly. Besides this ever-recurring theme, practically everything, whether it be a tree or a hill or a mountain, is associated with femininity. Its omnipresence is such that we too are compelled to exclaim, *"c'est toujours femme!"* In wonderment we may ask: What is the significance of this fact? Our natural reaction is likely to be embarrassment. But the question here is vitally important for an understanding of Hearn, so important that we cannot afford to dismiss it lightly on the ground that this sort of sexualism is by no means unique with Hearn.

It is conceivable that the origin of Hearn's obsession was basically personal; and there is even reason to say that his sexualism, at least at this early stage, is almost neurotic—almost infantile and compensatory. Simply because of this, however, we must not ignore the refinement his obsession underwent. At its second stage it is already literary sexualism, though cultivated to the point of artificiality. At neither stage, to be sure, is Hearn prone to vulgar obscenity. So conceding, we may wish to close the case with a sense of relief. If we do, we are guilty of rendering disservice to Hearn, for this amounts to denying any recognition to the true significance of his sexualism at its further stage. The point is its final sublimation to the realm of thought, where it seems to assume objective validity.

This process of metamorphosis was completed only with his contact with Japan and the Far East. In exploring another race and another world Hearn discovered his own race and his own world. In this particular instance the East served as a sort of mirror for the West. To Hearn it suggested "the possibility of using it stereoptically," if we use Lowell's apt phrase.[9] With the aid of this mirror Hearn was able to see his own image in fresh perspective. It was a moment of discovery, as implied in his characteristic statement: "The East has opened my eyes." Out of this discovery came his essay, "Of the Eternal Feminine," a comparative aesthetics of the East and the West. In brief Hearn came to conceive of sex, or more strictly passionalism, as the prime mover of Western culture. "In order to fully understand Western culture," Hearn said to his Japanese students, "it is of paramount necessity to know, whether sympathetic or not, that in it woman is a sort of religion, that is, a cult, and a god."[10] Before dismissing this theory as nothing more than Hearn's personal obsession, we should glance briefly at the persistency of the Western literary genealogy of Helen, Beatrice, Dulcinea, Una, Eleonora, and their multitudinous sisters. Curiously, there is no such parallel in Oriental literature. It is rather nature that plays a similar role in Eastern culture. Sex and nature—these contrasting themes are the basis of Hearn's essay.

The term "Eternal Feminine," like others, such as "Awful Three" and "Blue Ghost," is one of the most familiar and most ambiguous phrases to students of Hearn. It is hard to tell under what circumstances he came to know the term. Did he come across it in Goethe's *Faust,* especially in its last lines: *"Das Ewig-Weibliche/ Zieht uns hinan"*? If so, it may have been through Gérard de Nerval's French prose translation, which Hearn admired for more than one reason.[11] It is equally probable that he was inspired by Gautier's essay on Baudelaire. There Gautier wrote of Baudelaire's heroines: *"Elles représentent* l'éternal féminin, *et l'amour que le poète exprime pour elles est* l'amour *et non pas* un amour, *car nous avons vu que dans sa théorie il n'admettait pas la passion individuelle, la trouvant trop crue, trop familière et trop violente."* [12] Considering the fact that in the same essay Gautier glowingly praised Baudelaire's prose poem, *"Les Bienfaits de la lune,"* and that this very piece was translated by Hearn and remained one of his lifelong favorites, this may be more than conjecture. One phrase, "the Woman thou shalt never know!" takes on a special significance, since this love for "the Woman thou shalt never know," as we shall presently see, was to be designated by Hearn as the symbolic manifestation of the Western aspiration for the impossible and the unattainable.

One of Hearn's earliest references to the term appears in his *Item* article, "The Sexual Idea in French Literature," of June 17, 1881.[13] The piece, which called forth the comment from Tinker quoted above, suggests both Hearn's recognition of the significance of sex in modern literature and the embryonic stage of his sex philosophy. In its introductory paragraph Hearn clarifies the nature of his subject, a subject which "does not appear to have been much touched upon by Anglo-Saxon critics." As he sees it, Parisian art owes its aesthetic excellence in no small degree to one dominant sexual idea peculiar to the genius of the Latin race, the *"odor di femina,"* or the Eternal Feminine. This passion for its own sake impregnates every form of modern French art, he believes, whether it be literature, music, painting, or sculpture. Love is conceived as not "spiritual or vague," but "warmly material." Yet, this fashion is not at all novel for it is in reality "the old Greek idea also in a modern garb,—Aphrodite à la Parisienne." Compared with Odin and Thor, a cult of the northern races, this *Aphrodite à la Parisienne* reflects "the warm-blooded Latins." In northern art, Hearn observes in keeping with his theory of climate, passion is rather a consequence than a motive, whereas in Latin art the relationship is completely reversed, passion being the motive rather than the consequence. In this sense, Paris should be called pantheistic, certainly not atheistic. *"L'Éternel Féminin,"* Hearn says, "is there the all in all—a veritable Alpha and Omega—a feminine Brahma." To such eyes all nature is languid with passion; everything there creates a feminine atmosphere: ". . . even inanimate objects create amorous fancies, the clouds suggest aerial love, the trees have a feminine grace, the hills own voluptuous curves 'like the hips of a woman.' " And feminine pantheism such as this, Hearn discovers to his delight, is nowise confined to the realm of sister arts alone. One "divine" example is Michelet, that "Historian of Sexual Affection," as evident in his works, *The Sorceress, Women of the Revolution, History of Rome, Bible of Humanity, History of France, Love,* and *Woman.* It is Michelet, Hearn points out, who attempted to "analyze history with the chemicals of human love," and "felt the spirit of passion impregnating all Nature like the 'Soul of the World.' "

The article as a whole may testify to the significance of Michelet in the shaping of Hearn's idea of sexualism. It is his first conscious attempt to apply a sex philosophy to literature as Michelet has applied it to history. This may account for the repeated references to Michelet whenever Hearn discussed the question in the years following. "The influence of sex and sexual ideas," Hearn wrote in 1882 to Wayland D. Ball, "has moulded the history of nations and formed national character; yet, except Michelet, there is perhaps no historian who has read history in this connection." [14] This shows that Hearn's interest was now extending beyond the Latin world. Again in 1884, when writing to W. D. O'Connor, he ventured to define love as "the creator of all the great thoughts and great deeds of men in all ages." "All the great poems of the world," he said, "are but so many necklaces of word-jewelry for the throat of the *Venus Urania;* and all history is illuminated by the *Eternal Feminine."* There exists "an ultimate relation between Strength, Health, and Beauty." For this reason, Hearn suggested, the "mad excess of love" is not injurious at all; rather it would contribute to the total progress of humanity.[15] Unfortunately, there is no way of knowing what O'Connor's reaction was, but through Hearn's own reference thereto we may guess. In his reply Hearn noted that O'Connor had "thoroughly exploded" his "fantastic idea about love"; however, instead of withdrawing his thesis, Hearn suggested that a curious article might be written on "The Amorous Epochs of Na-

tional Literature," with special emphasis on the "extravagant pas-
sionateness" of ancient and modern Eastern belles-lettres, Indian,
Persian, and Arabic.[16] This sounds as if he were trying to explain his
forthcoming book, *Stray Leaves,* the love theme of which we have already observed.

The sweetness of Japanese womanhood has been warmly pointed
out by those who have visited the island country. Hearn was no exception. It was only natural for him to find in the Japanese woman a
supreme symbol of "all the possibilities of the race for goodness." [17] In
this there is still much of his literary sexualism. Two years after his
marriage to a Japanese woman, he wrote to an American friend: "Isn't
the hunger for the eternal feminine much like the other hunger?—to
be completely exorcised in the same way. Marriage seems to me the
certain destruction of all that emotion and suffering,—so that one afterwards looks back at the old times with wonder. One cannot dream or
desire anything more after love is transmuted into the friendship of
marriage." To take this confession as Hearn's version of the time-old
theory about the incompatibility of love and marriage would be a
gross mistake. It is rather his realization of the difference between love
and passion: "It is like a haven from which you can see the dangerous
sea-currents, running like violet bands beyond you out of sight." [18]
There is no tincture of infantile disillusionment; he manifests the
serene assurance of one just out of the familiar confusion of love and
passion, and now willing to subject his own experience to scrutiny. As
a result the question of sex, now beyond literary sexualism, emerges
afresh in perspective, that is, in conjunction with Hearn's larger question of the West and the East. In this mood, he wrote to the same friend
of ". . . the sexual question in the West,—something never dreamed
of in the East," and asked, "What must be the ultimate results of this
Western worship of the Eternal Feminine?" [19]

Then in 1893, as if to accelerate this thought process, there occurred
one minor, though highly significant, incident. Sometime in April
Hearn wrote to Hendrick:

> They send me a paper—the Sunday edition, full of poetry about love,
> wood-cuts of beautiful fashion; and all sorts of chatter about women and
> new styles of undergarments. Today, after three years in the most East-
> ern East, when I look at that paper, I can hardly believe my eyes. The
> East has opened my eyes. How affected the whole thing seems! Yet it
> never seemed so to me before. My students say to me, "Dear Teacher,
> why are your English novels all filled with nonsense about love and
> woman?—we do not like such things." [20]

The phrasing of the question may have shocked the teacher with its naïveté, but it was essentially the same question he now set himself to solve with renewed interest. Soon this sex theme, doubled with his East-West contrast, dominated his thought, as recorded in all his correspondence with Hendrick and Chamberlain,—during the several months to follow. While he was developing the basic idea, one question after another, one doubt after another, passed through his mind. The work proved difficult. At one time the thesis was neatly generalized; at another time the foundation itself had to be destroyed.

In June 1893, he wrote to Chamberlain:

> And here is something else *entre nous*. I am going, in spite of considerable self-mistrust, to attempt a philosophical article on L'éternel féminin—in the West, as elucidated by the East. *Ex Oriente Lux!* This idea has encouraged me to the attempt; and I am therefore very careful of the idea,— like one having made a discovery. While cogitating it occurred to me that certain peculiarities of the art of both hemispheres can only be explained by the absence or presence of the dominant sexual idea. Not only must the Japanese remain quite blind to all in our literature, art, etc., created by that idea; but we ourselves must suffer aesthetically by the necessarily one-sided character of our own art,—or aesthetic development. I shall have to work it out before August, if possible.[21]

A comparision of this statement with his *Item* article reveals that the idea is now crossing the bounds of his private world, and thereby uniting itself to the larger theme of the West and the East. In order to understand Japan, and the East, one must carefully consider this question "as a factor in forming psychological differences." "This subject," Hearn confided to Chamberlain, "is too large for me; but a man like Lowell might do much with it. I am afraid to try. Lowell has once alluded to it; but I don't think it is a mere side issue."[22] Chamberlain in turn encouraged his friend, saying that he and W. B. Mason were immensely interested.[23] After writing one hundred pages, Hearn was still sceptical of his argument about the general absence of the love element in Japanese literature.[24] In September he felt that he might be "vaguely half right," since the difference on the matter between the East and the West could boil down to that of degree.[25] After such a prolonged period of labor the manuscript was finally sent off. "Of the Eternal Feminine" came out in the *Atlantic Monthly* for December 1893. Later, when Chamberlain reread the essay he did not hesitate to label it as "quite the best thing ever written on Japan."[26] The comment is curiously ironic since Hearn wrote in an effort to understand his own Western world.

Hearn begins his essay with the observation that every intelligent Westerner is sooner or later compelled to notice one thing: ". . . the more the Japanese learn of our aesthetics and of our emotional character generally, the less favorably do they seem to be impressed thereby." [27] Their marked indifference to what Westerners regard as the highest expression of art and thought may induce us to take it for proof of mental incapacity, the consensus of many foreign observers in Japan. But Hearn questions the appropriateness of such epithets as "a race of children" (Henry Adams also called Japan "a child's country"), "essentially materialistic," etc., when applied to the Japanese. What he has learned from his contact with the native people indicates quite otherwise, he says. The matter might well "incite us to reconsider our own estimate of those ideas, rather than to tax the Oriental mind with incapacity." One of those ideas, Hearn believes, is the Western ideal of the Eternal Feminine, the moving force of Western culture.

"Teacher, please tell us why there is so much about love and marrying in English novels;—it seems to us very, very strange." [28] As Hearn explains, this is the question put to him in his literature class by one of those young students who, though quite well able to understand Jevons' logic and James's psychology, have failed to comprehend certain aspects of a standard Western novel. Though he said "strange" for politeness' sake, Hearn thinks, his real thought could be more correctly rendered by the word "indecent." His "strange" does not mean that he is altogether ignorant about the feeling of love as such. Or when he means "indecent," it is not because the theme of these novels is love. That the Japanese are "not morbidly prudish" is plain from the fact that they have a great deal of literature about love. His question, as Hearn understands it, is directed not to the love theme in Western literature, but to the kind of indecency the Japanese find in the Scripture text: "For this cause shall a man leave his father and mother, and shall cleave unto his wife." This kind of criticism, Hearn believes, demands a sociological explanation, an explanation in terms of the whole structure, customs, and ethics of the Japanese family life.

As a general rule, he continues, the theme of passionate love in Japanese literature of the best class is not concerned with "that sort of love which leads to the establishment of family relations." It deals with another sort of love, "a sort of love about which the Oriental is not prudish at all"; it can best be described as "the *mayoi*," the "infatuation of passion, inspired by merely physical attraction" such as that felt for a professional dancing-girl. Even in dealing with this subject, the

Oriental variety of literature does not follow the fashion of sensuous literature in the West; it approaches it from a different artistic standpoint, and depicts "rather a different order of emotional sensations." The most typical heroine in Japanese romance, whether presented as a mother, a daughter, or a wife, stands for the ideal womanhood, ever willing to sacrifice all for duty, not for love. In the real life of Japan, as in her literature, there does not exist what we call society, meaning "a mingling of the sexes." In Japanese society, which still remains masculine,—"in the special sense of the word," woman is never placed on display. To speak of the general rule, Hearn says, "a refined Japanese" seldom mentions his wife, his children, or his domestic life, perhaps except his parents, no matter how proud of them he may be. With special stress on the ethical notions governing these social restraints, Hearn says this is not because he is lacking in love, but because he believes that there is a higher sentiment than love, namely duty, "first, to his Emperor; next, to his parents." He is well aware that it is his duty to love his wife, but at the same time he considers it a moral weakness to love her more than his parents, or to show her, in public, more attention than he shows to his parents. To him it would be "a proof of moral weakness to show her even the *same* degree of attention." As "an ego-altruistic feeling," love can hardly be "the loftiest of motives, however refined or spiritualized." Since for the Oriental the law of life is duty, even affection must be subordinate to duty. Compared with a sense of duty, love seems to be rather selfish, because it is personal. Having explained the matter in this way, Hearn pauses to wonder if it is now high time for Westerners to scrutinize their own moral ideals more seriously.

One of these ideals is "the moral value of the Western worship of Woman as the Unattainable, the Incomprehensible, the Divine, the ideal of *'la femme que tu ne connaîtras pas.'*" (Hearn identifies the French quotation as "a phrase from Baudelaire.") Is this moral ideal "absolutely necessary to intellectual health"? he asks. If it is essential, why is it lacking in the thought of the Far East? Is its absence due to what Westerners consider the low position of woman in Far Eastern society? Hearn does not accept this commonly shared view nor the explanation that Confucianism, Shinto, and Buddhism are responsible, pointing out the significant place of the female principle, in both tenets and practices of the major Eastern religions. Hearn believes that the absence of the feminine ideal in Far Eastern art and literature reflects tendencies "deeply rooted in racial character," incomparably older than existing social structures, older than the idea of the family, older than ancestor-worship; that is, much older than even the oldest religious beliefs and practices. He cites the Japanese language as reflecting these age-old tendencies, a language in which, as Chamberlain states, the total absence of personification is "a characteristic so deep-seated and so all-pervading as to interfere even with the use of neuter nouns in combination with transitive verbs." Citing Tennyson's line, "She is more beautiful than day," Hearn recounts his difficulty in explaining to his Japanese students psychologically the analogy between the beauty of day and the beauty of a young woman. Hearn does not think it is likely that the Western ideal of the Eternal Feminine, along with others, can be introduced and eventually take root in the Eastern mind,—even "in the remotest future." All in all, the difference between the East and the West on this matter, however subtle, is far more fundamental than commonly assumed.

In contrast with this Far Eastern lack of personification, the ideal of the Eternal Feminine is perhaps strongest evidence of the Western genius for apotheosis. This difference between the two worlds Hearn calls elsewhere "the insuperable difficulty." It is in his opinion "surely one of the greatest obstacles to intellectual sympathy between the West and the Far East." In order to overcome this obstacle, Hearn suggests, we must fully understand the immense effect upon Western life of an ideal which has no existence in the East. It has completely permeated every phase of Western civilization, and molds its life and character. Toward its historical evolution many factors must have contributed—Teutonic, Celtic, Scandinavian, classic, and medieval, the Greek apotheosis of human beauty, the Christian worship of the mother of God, the exaltations of chivalry, the spirit of the Renaissance, etc., all of which must have had "their nourishment, if not their birth, in a race feeling ancient as Aryan speech, and as alien to the most eastern East." As he speculates in his special lecture—more comprehensively and concisely:

> The idea seems to have existed that woman was semi-divine, because she was the mother, the creator of man. And we know that she was credited among the Norsemen with supernatural powers. But upon this northern foundation there was built up a highly complex fabric of romantic and artistic sentiment. The Christian worship of the Virgin Mary harmonized with the northern belief. The sentiment of chivalry reinforced it. Then came the artistic resurrection of the Renaissance, and the new reverence for the beauty of the old Greek gods, and the Greek traditions of female divinities; these also coloured and lightened the old feeling about

womankind. Think also of the effects with which literature, poetry and the arts have since been cultivating and developing the sentiment.[29]

From this standpoint Hearn conceives of the ideal of the Eternal Feminine as the most vital force in Western civilization, the enlargement and sublimation of which all its members, individual, racial, national and social, have striven toward in the centuries past. The new philosophy of evolution has proved to be no exception to this; it has added "more than all preceding influences together toward the highest possible spiritualization of the ideal of woman." In this connection, nature may serve as the final determinant. As manifest in the Western approach to nature, which is basically anthropomorphic, Western aesthetic sensibility has developed in one direction, passional, "to a degree incomparably finer than that of the Oriental." In this long process the ideal of the Eternal Feminine has become almost an aesthetic abstraction, as "through all the centuries Western fancy has been making Nature more and more feminine." This tendency toward universal feminization is limited not only to those natural phenomena usually associated with feminine loveliness or tenderness, but also to the terrible itself "if fraught with terrible beauty"—"even Destruction if only shaped with the grace of destroyers," he writes. "Thus, out of simple human passion, through influences and transformations innumerable, we have evolved a cosmic emotion, a feminine pantheism."

At this point Hearn takes another sharp turn toward self-examination, and raises a series of questions: Are all the consequences of this passional ideal in the evolution of our Western aesthetic sensibility in the main beneficial? Is it not possible that as a result of our aesthetic faculties having developed even abnormally in one direction, we are left blind to many wonderful aspects of nature? Is our predominating ideal really the highest possible? Is there not a higher, known perhaps to the Oriental soul? Hearn does not think he can answer them all satisfactorily, but he offers some suggestions. His own experience in the East, he says, has led him to the belief that there are "exquisite artistic faculties and perceptions, developed in the Oriental, of which we can know scarcely more than we know of those unimaginable colors, invisible to the human eye, yet proven to exist by the spectroscope." He finds this well indicated by certain phases of Japanese art. Coming to his main point, the treatment of nature in art, Hearn asks two questions. Are we Western artists capable of perceiving the infinitely varied aspects of nature? Are there not some serious limitations in the Western approach to nature, which is neither masculine nor feminine, but neuter or nameless? Being free of anthropomorphism, Eastern artists are able to find in nature much that for thousands of years has remained invisible to their Western confreres. Because of its anthropomorphism and because of its passional ideal, however, Western art is at heart sexual idealism, and likely to degenerate into only an indifferent realism, whenever it takes a realistic approach to nature. Eastern art, on the other hand, is "never a mere creation of fantasy, but a veritable reflection of what has been and of what is"; it is realistic through and through. The Japanese artist, for instance, with a few dashes of his brush, and "with an incomprehensible power of interpretation," can seize and recreate not only every peculiarity of an insect's shape, but every special characteristic of its motion. Even French art, which alone emulates Oriental art in its methods, seems to fall short of this height. Finally, Hearn calls attention to the rocks in his Kumamoto garden, whose great cost to their owner reflects not the expense of transporting them there but their "esthetic suggestiveness." To those who would ask what the Japanese find beautiful about a common stone, Hearn answers, "Many things; but I will mention only one—irregularity."

Once again, Lowell may help us to focus Hearn's thinking more sharply. As Hearn's reference to Lowell's femininity theme suggests, the Bostonian may have served as a springboard for Hearn's theorizing, despite their profound differences in attitude. Lowell noted with regret that the Far Eastern youth is a stranger to the feeling of passional love. "Love, as we understand the word," he continued, "is a thing unknown to the Far East." [30] Of all the higher mental and moral aspects of the feeling the Far Easterner knows nothing; "his love is hardly worthy of the name." [31] Lowell blames the peculiarity of the Far Eastern society, in which woman, because of her low position, is "not an inspiration." In his own way, Lowell regarded her as the main source of Western inspiration; and, in a reference to *hinamatsuri,* the Japanese female festival, he blessed "the advent of the universal feminine" in the Eastern world.[32]

Lowell's contention is founded on his familiar personality-impersonality antithesis. Art is to the Far Easterner what science is to the Westerner. In the Far Eastern world everyone is born artist; art is his "birthright." Although the main springs of Far Eastern art are three: nature, religion, and humor, the first is "altogether the most important" of the trio, Lowell thinks. Yet this Muse, to Lowell's dismay, appears not to the Far Eastern artist, as to the Western, "after the fashion of a

woman, nor even more prosaically after the likeness of a man." The Eastern artist's inspiration seeks no human symbol, "unnatural though it
seems to us." His Muse is "not kin to mankind"; she is too impersonal
for any personification, because she is nature. What impresses Lowell
most is that the Far Eastern artist "makes fun of man and makes love to
Nature." From this he concludes that the fundamental distinction between Western and Far Eastern art lies in this attitude toward humanity.[33]

In contrasting man with nature, Lowell is not atypical of Western
attitude; but once he sets out to elaborate this, his argument hardly
clarifies the real issue. "In dealing with man," he writes, "the Oriental
artist is emphatically a realist; it is when he turns to nature that he
becomes ideal." That is, nature is his *"beau ideal."* The fact is that the
Oriental mind, as Hearn puts it more aptly, is thoroughly realistic, for
its approach toward nature is not that of passional love, being free of
any sort of sentimentalism. Lowell makes no allowance for the existence of some ways of looking at nature other than his own. To follow
the line of his argument, love as the prime cause of everything runs in
two opposing directions, toward man and toward nature. In accepting
a basic antagonism between man and nature Lowell stands by the
traditional Western point of view, whereas the Oriental mind sees no
such schism between the two, in the belief that man is part of nature,
and that his ultimate goal is to become one with the way of nature.
Nature here, it must be said, is not the landscape of the human soul, if
we use the Lamartinean phrase; it is basically identical with what is
generally meant by the universe. Lowell fails to grasp the metaphysical
meaning of nature in Far Eastern art, and Far Eastern culture generally.

Both Lowell and Hearn agree that to the Far Eastern mind art and
nature are hardly separable; yet, Lowell fails to perceive the aesthetic
principle underlying Far Eastern art. According to this principle, art,
whenever at its highest, is infinitely near to nature, the inference being
obvious in view of the basic identity of man and nature. This is not to
condone such formlessness in art as may be found in physical nature,
but more positively to insist that art loses its artifice, whenever its form
perfects itself. Only in perfecting itself can art approximate nature as
metaphysical reality. Without this basis, art would mean little to the
Far Eastern mind. What interests Hearn is that to the Oriental mind
nature holds no suggestion of sex character, that is, nature is neither
masculine nor feminine, but neuter or nameless. In other words, nature,
metaphysically at least, is at once masculine and feminine. In this sense

alone we can say that nature, identical with reality, manifests itself in an eternal interaction between two principles, female and male, or the *yin* and the *yang,* and their consequential multiplication. It becomes the supreme goal of an artist to glimpse this reality in the changing particular, and thereby to express the principle of oneness in the many.[34]

Here some may like to return to Hearn's thesis of the Eternal Feminine and ask him about the other half of the Western ideal, the Eternal Masculine, if we can call it such. Along with the Eternal Feminine there has been always the Eternal Masculine in the Western world; and this male principle, which is best embodied in God the Father and in Christ, is in Hearn's scheme completely overshadowed by the opposing principle. But it must be remembered that Hearn is concerned here with art par excellence, or with that which has through centuries been manifest in Western art. Considered in this light, his theory seems to contain something that is fundamentally valid. Lin Yutang writes:

> . . . this worship of the human body, especially of the female body, seems to me to be the most singular characteristic of Western art. The most singular contrast between Chinese and Western art is the difference in the source of inspiration, which is nature itself for the East and the female form for the West. . . . Whereas the Chinese painter symbolizes spring by a fat and well-shaped partridge, the Western painter symbolizes it by a dancing nymph with a faun chasing after her. And whereas the Chinese painter can delight in the fine lines of a cicada's wings and in the full limbs of the cricket, the grasshopper and the frog, and the Chinese scholar can daily contemplate such pictures on his wall with continual delight, the Western painter cannot be satisfied with anything less than Henner's *Liseuse* or *Madeleine*.[35]

The meeting of two voices, one Eastern and the other Western, indicates that Hearn's conclusions are more than the vagaries of his fancy or the expression of his personal sexualism.

Curiously enough, a thesis similar to Hearn's is developed by Denis de Rougemont in his controversial study, *Love in the Western World.* In this book the author concerns himself with what he calls the Western heresy of passional love, the religion of love which has so far dominated the Western world in its preference of love to marriage, in its opposition of love to life, and in its pursuit of passion to death. Its foremost expression he finds in the Tristan myth, the most eloquent embodiment of Medieval Catharism, a heretic cult of Eros, "boundless desire," which came to eclipse the spirit of orthodox Christianity, the cult of Agape, "Christian love." He believes that Western literature, whether in the works of the Provençal poets, in the courtly love tradition, in the masterpieces of Renaissance literature, or those of subsequent literature, reflects the progressive secularization of this heresy, and that it is still alive in the modern West, in secular form, endangering the foundation of Western social structure. Only when marriage based on Christian love is accepted as a stronger tradition than this heresy of passional love, the author insists, will Western civilization be able to solve its age-old conflict for survival.[36]

Despite the differences between Hearn and Rougemont—in speculation about the origins of the cult of passion, and in basic philosophy, their similarity is noteworthy, especially when Rougemont illustrates the manner in which the Tristan myth has manifested itself through various stages of Western literature. He points out not only the druidical cult which "turned Woman into a prophetic being, 'the eternal feminine' and 'man's goal,'" but also the "yearning for what lies beyond embodied forms," such as may be found in Goethe's "The Eternal feminine leads us away" and Novalis' "Woman is man's goal." He considers "the woman we yearn after, of our nostalgia" as "the best definition of Iseult." Finally he distinguishes two kinds of love; "Passionate love wants 'the *faraway* princess,' whereas Christian love wants '*our neighbour.*'"[37]

In more than one respect, it is significant that Lowell, Hearn and Rougemont meet and part. They agree on the significance of this ideal of the Eternal Feminine permeating the Western world. In Lowell's opinion this phenomenon is the natural manifestation of what he calls personality, a characteristic of Western mentality; and for the same reason Far Eastern mentality, which tends otherwise, seems to him unnatural. Both Hearn and Rougemont, however, are alarmed at the fact that the West has cultivated this passionalism in one direction only, to an abnormal degree,—at the cost of what is far more valuable.

Aside from the main issue, there is one more point of agreement between Hearn and Rougemont. Both are seeking some possible means of rearranging the scale of values, that is, restoring to its rightful place what their own West has consciously and unconsciously neglected, whether it be Hearn's "Nature" or Rougemont's "Christian love."[38] This is the point where Lowell parts company with them. True, both Lowell and Hearn are agreed that the Western approach toward nature is fundamentally anthropomorphic. On this basis Lowell theorized his personality-impersonality; in like manner Hearn contrasted personification with its absence. When Lowell said, "Christianity is a personal religion; Buddhism an impersonal one,"[39] he was undoubtedly right,

right because he pointed to the difference between these two religions over apotheosis. Because of his thesis, however, Lowell sees this significant contrast on a scale of superiority-inferiority. Hearn, starting from the same point, notes the contrast as it is and thereby seeks to determine the benefit it may possibly have for his "intellectual health." In spite of their common effort to explore the symbolic contrast between the East and the West, they part gradually from each other as their investigations progress.

This difference of attitude becomes pronounced when we examine Hearn's aesthetic speculation. Dwelling on the Japanese aesthetic response to a common stone, we remember, Hearn said to those readers wondering what could be beautiful in such an object: "Many things; but I will mention only one—irregularity." Hearn merely intimates this regularity-irregularity theme in connection with the East-West contrast; yet, its possible direction is sufficiently clear when he relates it to anthropomorphism as the Western approach toward nature:

> We have learned something of the beauty of Nature through our ancient worship of the beauty of woman. Even from the beginning it is probable that the perception of human beauty has been the main source of all our aesthetic sensibility. Possibly we owe to it likewise our idea of proportion; our exaggerated appreciation of regularity; our fondness for parallels, curves, and all geometrical symmetries.[40]

Aside from the question, whether this principle of regularity, as Hearn believes, owed its main inspiration to the perception of human beauty, there is little doubt that, taken largely as intellectualization or abstraction, it has guided the direction of modern Western art. On the contrary, this principle of regularity is to a striking degree, if not entirely, absent from Eastern art, at least from traditional Eastern art.[41] Hearn's observations are worth remembering in view of the possible introduction of the irregularity idea into the West and its subsequent impact on Western art and life.

Dealing with Hearn's travel writings as a whole, we observed that they ultimately center on an ever-recurring theme, the basic relationship between man and nature, or man's true position in nature. What Hearn attempts in his essay, "Of the Eternal Feminine," should be valued in this light. His primary concern is neither to determine which of these two modes of approach is superior or inferior, nor to display his speculative power for its own sake. His intent is to re-examine the peculiar aspect of the Western aesthetic sensibility side by side with that of the Eastern aesthetic sensibility, so that the former may be rearranged, enlarged, and enriched. Hearn does not think this is by any means impossible, recognizing that the process of learning is always painful and slow because it involves transformation. He admits that "the deeper spirit" of Eastern art "seldom reveals itself at first sight to unaccustomed eyes, since it appeals to so little in Western aesthetic experience"; yet, he is confident that

> . . . by gentle degrees it will so enter into an appreciative and un-prejudiced mind as to modify profoundly therein almost every preëxist-ing sentiment in relation to the beautiful. All of its meaning will indeed require many years to master, but something of its reshaping power will be felt in a much shorter time when the sight of an American illustrated magazine or of any illustrated European periodical has become almost unbearable.[42]

Whether or not we are in the process of seeing something of Hearn's prediction come true, it indicates at least how far he has traveled in his philosophical voyage since his arrival in Japan, and also how well he has sublimated his early personal and literary sexualism to the realm of thought.

XII

"The Coming Race"

Beyond Western Individualism

Elaborating on his metaphorical statement: "The East has opened my eyes," Hearn wrote,

> He who would study impartially the life and thought of the Orient must also study those of the Occident from the Oriental point of view. And the results of such a comparative study he will find to be in no small degree retroactive. According to his character and his faculty of perception, he will be more or less affected by those Oriental influences to which he submits himself. The conditions of Western life will gradually begin to assume for him new, undreamed-of meanings, and to lose not a few of their old familiar aspects. Much that he once deemed right and true he may begin to find abnormal and false. He may begin to doubt whether the moral ideals of the West are really the highest. He may feel more than inclined to dispute the estimate placed by Western custom upon Western civilization. Whether his doubts be final is another matter: they will be at least rational enough and powerful enough to modify permanently some of his prior convictions.[1]

By recording his own process of transformation Hearn really clarifies the meaning of the philosophical voyage, an allegorical search for self-knowledge. Self-knowledge comes only to those who are willing to re-examine even their cherished values in fresh perspective. How his essay on the Western aesthetic ideal of the Eternal Feminine was born in the process of self-questioning we have considered in the foregoing chapter. But Western passionalism is also paired with another theme, Western individualism. Indeed, upon these two themes Hearn based his speculation regarding the symbolic boundary between the West and the East, and thereby attempted their final integration.

This time, too, Lowell's theory of personality-impersonality served him as a springboard. Lowell was always there whenever Hearn touched on the central issue—especially in his correspondence with Chamberlain. In August 1891, despite his renewed admiration for *The Soul of the Far East*, Hearn was "so much horrified" by some of Lowell's conclusions that he would "try very hard to find a flaw therein." One of these was Lowell's uncompromising stand that "the degree of the development of individuality in a people necessarily marks its place in the great march of mind." This, said Hearn, is "not true necessarily." "At least," he continued, "it may be argued about." Since our modern world tends toward class specialization and interdependent subdivision of all branches of knowledge and all practical application of that knowledge, the development of the individuality of every integer of a community would seem to him to unfit the unit to form a close part of any specialized class. In a word, Hearn doubted that the cultivation of individuality is really "a lofty or desirable tendency," for the simple reason that much of so-called personality and individuality is "intensely repellent," and is even the cause of "the principal misery of Occidental life." To him the word seemed to connote much that is connected with pure aggressive selfishness. In Hearn's opinion, the extraordinary development of individualism, such as one may find in America and England, confirms Viscount Torio's observation that "Western civilization has the defect of cultivating the individual at the expense only of the mass, and giving unbounded opportunities to human selfishness, unrestrained by religious sentiment, law, or emotional feeling." [2]

Lowell's contention, Hearn conceded, points to something that is ineluctable in view of the evolutionary law, as expressed by Spencer's seemingly contradictory and yet indisputably true utterance, that the "highest individuation must coincide with the greatest mutual dependence," and that evolutional progress is "at once toward the greatest separateness and the greatest union." But from this fact alone, that the West has cultivated "mental and physical force to the highest pitch so far known," Hearn pointed out, it does not follow either that our methods of cultivation are natural and right, or that "we may not have ultimately to abandon all our present notions about the highest progress and the highest morality." "Personally," he declared, "I think we are dead wrong." [3] The more thought he gave to the question, the more desirous he became of writing a chapter on "Morbid Individuality," so as to take issue with Lowell.[4] As the word "morbid" should suggest, Hearn's objection is not raised against individualism as such. As with his examination of the Western ideal of the Eternal Feminine, he is questioning whether this Western ideal of individualism is absolutely necessary to intellectual health.

Hearn came to tackle this question, really the second in his quest for self-knowledge, only after having lived in the East for several years. It was by no means a romantic escapist's irresponsible curse on his own hostile world, but a thinking mind's self-examination; and the answer came as a result of his reconsidering what Lowell termed the Oriental lack of personality. While contrasting his own method "from the bottom" with Lowell's "from the top," Hearn said explicitly that "the most beautiful, the most significant, the most attractive point of Japanese character" is due rather to the very absence of personality which Lowell designated as an Oriental phenomenon. As he himself warned, Hearn weighs not "the fact *in itself*" but "that which it signifies." If he came to know better than Lowell what is behind the apparent want of personality, in the Japanese, it was through his study of the Chinese classics, the *Kojiki,* Buddhist texts, and above all through his contact with the life of the native people, "observing, watching, questioning, wondering." His own experience seemed to suggest much that is contrary to Lowell's argument. As Hearn came to understand, the impersonality of the Japanese is to a great extent voluntary, the consequence of a traditional life that has been, from prince to peasant, "religiously regulated by the spirit of self-suppression for the sake of the family, the community, the nation." Therefore, their impersonality should indicate their "ancient moral tendency to self-sacrifice for duty's sake," certainly not a lack of personality. Since the sacrifice of self for others is "the highest possible morality from any high religious standpoint,—Christian or pagan," Hearn argues, the traditional Japanese civilization is morally as far in advance of the Western, as it is materially behind it. It is true, Hearn admitted, that this advance was made only "at some considerable sacrifice to character and mental evolution," because of its excessive stress on mutual dependence. "But," he concluded, "the loss does not signify that the moral policy was wrong." [5]

Hearn's criticism of the West in his correspondence with Chamberlain echoes the conversation with a Japanese student later to be recorded in "Jiujutsu." When the conversation came to his notice, Chamberlain immediately labeled his friend's notion of the West as based wholly on America, and added that "Yankey-dom is not the sum total of Western achievement." [6] In response to Chamberlain's retort Hearn readily admitted that there is "a vast spiritual side to Western life" in the sense that "noble effort must ever rest upon a spiritual basis." At the same time he pointed out that there is "what must be termed a material side to life,—the *real* materialism." Modern Western civilization, whether it be "Yankeedom" or "Anglodom," is basically industrial and commercial, with all its aspirations. In this competition that has made a civilization possible, there is no morality "worth priding ourselves upon." All facts around him, he pointed out, seem to indicate that "my young student is altogether right." "Without having studied philosophy," Hearn continued, "he perceives that emotional morality must yield to legal morality; and I am trying to make him consider cosmic law *the* law to study, and he understands." As it is, our whole Western civilization is based on immorality, that is, "if we are to accept either the Buddhist or the Christian system of ethics." Yet, the cold fact is that only by industrialism can we exist, "unless, like Thoreau, we prefer to live in the woods." As a student of evolutional philosophy, Hearn was still hopeful about the coming of a larger morality, a morality based on the cosmic law. "A larger morality," he said, "will come—but only when competition ends." [7]

These are the words of a Victorian, a man of the second half of the nineteenth century. Hearn's was a dilemma which profoundly disturbed many thinkers in the Victorian world. Like them, he was examining the moral basis of modern industrial and commercial society. As he admitted in his letter to Chamberlain, there is something like "a *comparative* morality," to be sure. But this kind of easy compromise Hearn could not accept. His stand was at heart a religious one, a craving for something absolute. Hearn did not see Christianity as offering a satisfactory solution. To him, as an avowed evolutionist, it seemed now outgrown and stripped of its central dogma; historically, the Church had too long been associated with "its exclusiveness, its narrowness, and its memories of blood and fire." Now impotent, Christianity had betrayed its incapacity to cope with or halt the all-demanding industrial and commercial materialism in the West. Hearn queried: ". . . what is left of Christianity? Why, nothing whatever essentially of Christ." With its spiritual and moral foundation weakened by compromise, the West would be a mere aggregate of individuals, each striving to expand his own individuality at the expense of that of every one else. The future danger of the West, Hearn reasoned, would therefore be this unbridled expansion of the individual. At this stage the so-called struggle for existence would be no longer a struggle for survival, having lost its own justification.[8]

At this point another question arose, side by side with the moral issue above,—the survival of the West. How could the West encounter the East in the arena of the world struggle for survival? Hearn's speculative imagination seized on Charles Henry Pearson's *National Life and Character,* which appeared in 1893. The author's thesis, as Hearn explained, is that "the future is not to the white race,—not to the Anglo-Saxon." [9] "As I wrote to you long ago," he said in his letter to Chamberlain, "I have been inclined to the same conclusions as Pearson reaches, for some years; but I arrived at them by different methods." His life in the West Indies, he recalled, taught him "what tropical life means for white races, —after the trial of three hundred years"; and his experience in America showed him "something about the formidable character of the Chinese," as well as "the enormous cost of existing civilization to the Western individual." Hearn considered it highly probable that "the white races, after having bequeathed all their knowledge to the Orient, will ultimately disappear, just as the ichthyosaurus and other marvellous creatures have disappeared,—simply because of the cost of their structure." [10] Strangely enough, it was not Japan but China that came to the fore in his speculative panorama of the West-East struggle for survival. This fact may partly explain his stand on China when he discussed the question in the *Kobe Chronicle* in the midst of the Sino-Japanese War, especially when he said "China, stirred into self-help by this contest with Japan, might become the mightiest Power on earth." [11]

Outside of his correspondence, it was in the postscript to the essay "Jiujutsu" that Hearn for the first time openly ventured his speculation on the future of the world races.[12] When he asserted that *"Japan has won in her jiujutsu,"* the implication was that Japan's current victory over China might signify two points, that she had passed out of Western tutelage, and had gained world recognition neither by her arts nor by her virtues, but by the first display of her new scientific powers of aggression and destruction, which she had been compelled to learn from the West and had mastered in less than a generation. Calling attention to the fact that the art of jiujutsu was originally invented in China, Hearn then meditated: Who can be sure that under Japanese and Western pressure China also will not be forced to apply the spirit of jiujutsu, to master our arts of war in self-defense, and thereby "avenge all those aggressions, extortions, exterminations, of which the coloniz-ing West has been guilty in dealing with feebler races"?

He found much truth in Pearson's prediction that the long history of Western expansion and aggression is even now approaching its close. Western civilization has so far "girdled the earth only to force the study of our arts of destruction and our arts of industrial competition upon races much more inclined to use them against us than for us." The enormous social machinery created to maintain our Western supremacy may now threaten, "like the Demon of the old legend," to devour us, once it is out of our control. Our civilization has become "not less monstrous than wonderful." It is true, Hearn says, that the West, intel-lectually, has "grown beyond the altitude of the stars," but it is also true that the West has evolved the most detestable, as well as the most noble, forms of individuality. Now we are developing the individual more and more, "much as artificial heat and colored light and chemical nutrition might develop a plant under glass." Even social transformations, in-cluding the establishment of "an absolutely perfect communism," will produce no effect on the future course it may take. Our racial superi-ority seems incapable of solving one more important question: "Are we the fittest to survive?" This is no longer a matter of intellectual superiority; it is a matter of survival in the battleground of nature. Any possible answer seems pessimistic. Just as Western civilization has main-tained its costly complex machinery and boasted of its supremacy by *"overliving"* feeble races—"by monopolizing and absorbing, almost without conscious effort, everything necessary to their happiness," so may Eastern races be now capable of *"underliving"* the Western, "of monopolizing all our necessities," because they are "more patient, more self-denying, more fertile, and much less expensive for Nature to sup-port." All this, Hearn believes, seems to be assured by the inexorable law of history and nature itself.

Hearn's thesis is given fuller treatment in his article, "China and the Western World: a Retrospect and a Prospect," which appeared in the *Atlantic Monthly* for April 1896.[13] Drawing upon the works of Galton, Lombroso, Huxley, Spencer, and, more frequently, Pearson, Hearn speculates on the destiny of China, the West and the East, and human-ity in general. Citing several conflicting views as to the causes of the Sino-Japanese War (1894–95), he dismisses them as superficial. The truth, Hearn points out, is that "the vast tidal wave of Occidental civili-zation, rolling round the world, had lifted Japan and hurled her against

China, with the result that the Chinese Empire is now a hopeless wreck." But what is to come next? To those critics who believe that Japan may annex China, thereby becoming "the next world's ruler," Hearn suggests the counter-fear that Russian control of China could be quite as dangerous to the West as Japanese domination. The present situation, Hearn suspects, is such that no one can be sure about its outcome. One thing is certain, that while Japan has become a major factor in determining the international balance of power in the Pacific area, China must now yield to Western pressure only to be "industrially exploited to the uttermost," which may likely make her "a source of peril,—the possible cause of a tremendous conflict." All in all, the Chinese question is in Hearn's opinion neither political nor military; it is rather dependent on the operation of natural laws.

Hearn finds this view confirmed by Pearson's *National Life and Character,* which had recently rendered a rude shock to Western pride of race, shattering the belief that "all weaker peoples are destined to make way for the great colonizing white races." Rightly interpreted, he believes, it should also suggest that the West is now facing peril from within and from without. The peril from within is the ultimate result of "moral laxity"; the one from without is the industrial competition to come from the Far East. Referring to the fancied mental supremacy of the Western nations, Hearn attempts to show how unwarranted is their assumption of superiority. As history bears witness, he says, they are intellectually and commercially incapable not only of competing with the Jews but also of maintaining themselves outside the temperate zone.

From this standpoint, Hearn sees the future as favoring China rather than Japan. In industry as well as in commerce, the Chinese excel even the Jews. They are perfectly capable of multiplying their population wherever they may be, as statistics show. Compared with the "fluidity" of the Japanese, they are at heart conservative, but their "conservatism in beliefs, ethics, and customs" has little to do with business. Even the Japanese are willing to admit this characteristic of the Chinese. The real danger from the Far East, he reasons, should come not from the Japanese but from the Chinese, especially whenever they are compelled to "do what Japan has voluntarily done." All these factors, latent and otherwise, would create "a phenomenon without parallel in the past history of the world." In the face of this menace from the Far East, modern Western civilization seems to be powerless mainly because of its "monstrous egotism." In Western society, Hearn says, the struggle for existence is no longer "a struggle to live"; it has now become "a struggle to enjoy," a struggle "far more cruel than a contest for the right to exist." Too obvious would be the outcome of the struggle between the luxurious races, accustomed to regard pleasure as the object of existence, and those who are "quite content to strive to the uttermost in exchange for the simple privilege of life."

Having carried his speculation to its logical extremity, Hearn poses to himself a series of questions: The decay of faith, the substitution of conventionalism for true religion, the ever-growing hunger for pleasure, the constant aggravation of suffering, etc., such as we may find in modern Western society,—may they not be symptomatic of the coming death of a civilization? Has Western civilization not fulfilled its historical role on this human planet? Is the West then doomed to disappear? Does the future belong to the East? To follow Pearson's logic, the answer must be yes. The whole picture, thus outlined, is singularly anticipatory of the Western nightmare, which we all know was to climax in Spengler's natural history of cultural cycles. Is there any alternative but the twilight of the Western world? Hearn definitely believes that "a more optimistic view of the future is also possible."

Indeed, in his world prospect there is little of fatalistic cultural determinism. Hearn sees a ray of hope in only one direction, a sort of internationalization on a world-wide basis. With all the symptoms of the Western disintegration there are assuredly "signs also of new latent forces that will recreate society upon another and a more normal plan." As unmistakable facts he refers to the growing trends toward international union and "the most complete industrial and commercial federation." Furthermore, international necessities, artistic, scientific, and cultural, are rapidly breaking down old prejudices and conservative forces; in this process they are bringing forth a high degree of internationalism and cosmopolitanism. In Hearn's view, Victor Hugo's dream of the "United States of Europe" is not at all visionary; the ultimate fusion of Western races into one vast social organism is something we must strive for. And such fusion is "even now visibly beginning." Going further than Hugo, Hearn declares that the West will find its veritable place only through extending this fusion beyond its own world:

> . . . the promise of international coalescence in the West suggests the probability of far larger tendencies to unification in the remoter future, —to unification not of nations only, but of widely divergent races. The evolutional trend would seem to be toward universal brotherhood, with-

out distinctions of country, creed, or blood. It is neither unscientific nor unreasonable to suppose the world eventually peopled by a race different from any now existing, yet created by the blending of the best types of all races; uniting Western energy with Far-Eastern patience, northern vigor with southern sensibility, the highest ethical feelings developed by all great religions with the largest mental faculties evolved by all civilizations; speaking a single tongue composed from the richest and strongest elements of all preëxisting human speech; and forming a society unimaginably unlike, yet also unimaginably superior to, anything which now is or has ever been.

In saying this, Hearn is well aware that to many the mere thought of a fusion of races is repellent because of traditional and powerful prejudices "once essential to national self-preservation." To believers in racial purity Hearn points out that the record of human history disproves their view, and that none of the present higher races is "really a pure race." All our prejudices of nationality, race, and creed have had their usefulness, he admits, and some of them will continue to have usefulness for ages to come. In order, however, to survive and reach the highest progress, the human race must go along with the evolution of the feeling of universal brotherhood. As the only way to this brotherhood Hearn suggests the final extinction of all prejudice, "the annihilation of every form of selfishness, whether individual or national or racial." The picture Hearn presents here, needless to say, is the logical consequence of his evolutional doctrine of human progress. To us it may be at once too sanguine and too visionary; we are too imperfect in every way even to dream of it. Whether or not we accept the implication that evil is but man's imperfection as a result of his selfishness, Hearn's vision of this earthly paradise indicates his conviction about the unlimited possibility of human evolution.

Yet, in this utopian view we cannot fail to notice the nature of his concern, at once radical and conservative. As an evolutionist Hearn came to believe that at this stage of history socialism would eventually arrive; but as his evolutionism took the moralist point of view, he could not entertain the delusion that an ideal society would come into existence through merely social and political reforms. In other words, by accepting the evolutional doctrine of human progress Hearn actually sought to find the moral basis of the individual in society, nature, and the universe. In this sense his utopian world is still based on what the individual can and ought to be. Hearn's criticism is directed at what he regards as the Western cult of individualism, or more strictly speaking, the Western overemphasis on individualism, certainly not at individual-

ism as such. That is why Hearn considered individual freedom impera-
tive as long as it would ensure the healthy development of society as
organism. Hearn would have accepted the *raison d'être* of the state
as only "negative interference." As a matter of fact, Hearn and Spencer
were of the same mind in denouncing the tyranny of the state as the
"Coming Slavery." Socialism, Hearn believed, would overreach itself,
entailing dictatorship and consequently anarchy for the very simple
reason that human nature is not perfect.[14] This was the view he held
while in Japan.

It was by no means a new thought to him, judging from what he
had already said in some of his early American editorials. His conservatism was not always imported from Spencer, but was in all probability
his own. While in New Orleans he had much to say about new ideolo-
gies, especially socialism and communism. He scoffed at them, standing
by his belief in the imperfection of human nature. "To some extent,"
Hearn argued at one time, "it is a fallacy that men are born equal." [15]
At another time he reasoned the ultimate failure of social movements:
Communism ignores the reality of human nature, whereas the humanitarian movement refuses to face "hard facts," say, the commercial
foundation of modern society.[16] As for communism, his objection was
uncompromising: it is savage because of its natural primitivism, and
fanatic because of its blind religious zeal. Its basic doctrine of equaliza-
tion is "to do away with necessity," the mother of invention in industry,
sciences and arts, and thus it disregards individual ability, capacity,
desires, and so forth. And finally the dream of communism is much like
"that of the negro at the dawn of emancipation," the ownership of a
glorious plantation. From all these factors he came to the conclusion
that it is "impossible in any event, that civilization and Communism
should co-exist." [17] The implication is that with the establishment of
communism there will be no civilization, only a reign of terror. By
the time Hearn set out to tackle the question of "morbid" individualism, some of these points had been rejected; nevertheless, conservatism
seemed to have persisted as the core of his social thought. Take, for instance, the following passage he wrote in 1904, the year of his death:

> . . . I fear that I must shock you by my declaration of non-sympathy with
> much of the work of contemporary would-be reformers. They are toil-
> ing for socialism; and socialism will come. It will come very quietly and
> gently, and tighten about nations as lightly as a spider's web; and then
> there will be revolutions! Not sympathy and fraternity and justice—but a
> Terror in which no man will dare to lift his voice.[18]

In Hearn's opinion this is not the way to universal fraternity. Such social and political coercion, he feels, will result in stifling the human heart. Transformation must come, if it should come at all, from within, not from without. It should signify rather man's moral transformation, which alone is total.

Here is Hearn's increasing emphasis on the moral nature of man. Now he has come to realize that man, with all his present limitations, should be capable of perfecting himself through his evolution, though it may take him millions of years. In accepting both the reality and the potentiality of man, Hearn differs from those whose faith centers around the doctrine of original sin. He thinks that the world of universal sympathy, fraternity, and justice is possible whenever and wherever man begins to realize his moral perfection. We do not have to concern ourselves with creating new ethics, Hearn suggests, since "ethics" means the ultimate growth of man's moral nature. There will be only the enlargement of man's morality free of selfishness and prejudice; and this enlargement of self means purgation, a progress from self-interest to self-annihilation. Hearn's earthly paradise is also the realization of Spencer's dictum: ". . . the highest individuation must be joined with the greatest mutual dependence," or ". . . the law of progress is at once toward complete separateness and complete union." Its scheme is such as to reconcile freedom and duty, the individual and society, the law of man and the law of nature. We may be curious to know where to seek its pattern. In reply, Hearn repeats the Hebrew aphorism: "Go to the ant, thou sluggard, consider her way."[19]

In recognizing the allegorical significance of the ant, Hearn joins those philosophers and poets who have eulogized the way of social insects. What is really interesting, however, is that Hearn's parable is a joint creation of Hearn the evolutionist and Hearn the insect-lover. His partiality for small things, animals and insects, was such that Tinker and Kirkwood among others felt obliged to devote some portion of their studies to this eccentricity of his.[20] The tendency, which may demand many explanations, was no doubt augmented by his evolutional faith in the unity of life. But his recognition of the ant symbolism showed itself far back in 1878, when in his *Item* editorial, "Insect Politics," he mentioned the peculiar analogy between the human world and that of the insect.[21] In another editorial, while making no reference to the ant, Hearn noted curious bits of hearsay about cats and dogs seeming to have instincts or habits beyond human comprehension.[22] In this case, too, Michelet might have been, in part at least, Hearn's source of inspiration. With specific reference to Michelet's book, *L'In-secte,* Hearn wrote: "We read so wonderful a history of the republican ants and monarchical bees, one feels the great tenderness of the man to all living creatures entering into himself." [23] In a third editorial, "Insect Civilization," Hearn brought out three points of interest: first, he called attention to Darwin's opinion that "the brain of an ant is the most marvelous particle of matter in the universe"; second, he observed that we may be "able to find a future application of that intelligence to the benefit of man," thanks to our scientific discovery of insect intelligence; and third, he thought it would be interesting to question whether ants can survive the catastrophe of the human animal.[24] All these views Hearn put together once again in "News about Ants," his *Times-Democrat* editorial occasioned by Sir John Lubbock's recent observations on the harvesting ants. Referring to Solomon's phrase (Prov. xxx, 25), Hearn pondered on "the Republic of the Ants" in Michelet's *L'Insecte,* and also on those curious parallels between human and ant society. "Barbaric indeed," he wrote, "are Assyrian monarchies of wasps and the Roman empires of bees compared with the Greek republics of the ants." Following Lubbock's belief about the "intellectual progress" of the ants, he again speculated on the possibility that some ants may establish "a new and peculiar civilization of their own," perhaps when the human race has perished.[25]

How profoundly Hearn, while in Japan, continued to be fascinated by the world of the ant, is shown in the fact that the topic was not only presented in classroom lectures but further amplified in his book, *Kwaidan.* When he entitled his lecture on the ant "Beyond Man," his intention was overtly to attempt a serious parody of Nietzsche's book. As his introductory note suggests, Hearn based the subhuman society upon the same evolutionary philosophy that was, in his view, distorted by the German thinker in enunciating his doctrine of the superman.[26] Compared with this lecture, his essay, "Ants," is far more complete.

Hearn opens this essay with a Chinese tale about a devotee whose one-day knowledge of the ant language led to his discovery of hidden treasure.[27] In like manner Hearn pretends to get access, by the aid of modern science, to the moral symbolism of the ant society. Taking as his authorities Herbert Spencer and David Sharp, a contributor to the new *Cambridge Natural History,* he develops the central theme that "ants are, in a very real sense, *ethically* as well as economically in advance of humanity,—their lives being devoted to altruistic ends." Their advanced state "beyond man" is, to use Spencer's words, "a state in which egoism and altruism are so conciliated that the one merges into the other." In this society the value of the individual exists only in relation to the society. Therefore, the question, whether his sacrifice for the sake of that society is good or evil, should necessarily depend on what the society may gain or lose through a further individuation of its members.

His concern, as he explains, is with "the awful propriety, the terrible morality, of the ant," which our most exacting moral ideals seem to fall short of. (At this point Hearn calls our attention to the Chinese character for the ant, which signifies "The Propriety-Insect.") Yet, the ant under consideration is not the ant in general, but only the highest type of ant, the result of millions of years of evolutionary progress. This differentiation suggests that the ant possesses "a considerable power of independent thinking," and, therefore, individual character. When we say that the ant has no individuality, it means merely that the ant has "no individuality capable of being exercised in a purely selfish direction." Since its "superlatively practical mind" is incapable of moral errors, it may have no need of "spiritual guidance," though it would be difficult to prove that the ant has no religious ideas. No human mind, at least as now constituted, could attain "a mental habit so impeccably practical as that of the ant." Perhaps for this reason the ant society, Hearn says, deserves our serious study.

To follow Hearn's analysis: The labor force in this society is made entirely of females, which supervise all phases of daily work, from construction to the care of the children of the race. There is no private property allowed or even conceivable, "except as a res publica." Everything runs in an orderly fashion. On the other hand, males, which are inferior, are "equally incapable of fighting or working, and tolerated only as necessary evils." Their sole duty is to be accepted, at particular seasons, by a special class of females called "the Mothers-Elect." As a general rule the female laborers, while capable of parthenogenesis, have lost their sex, like "the Dragon-Maiden in the Buddhist legend." In addition there is a special military corps, all Amazons or "semi-females." More startling than this complete distribution of social function is the fact that the suppression of sex is possible in this ant society; and, to our surprise, *"this practical suppression or regulation, of sex-faculty appears to be voluntary!"* In other words, by "some particular mode of nutrition," the ant has succeeded in exercising "perfect control" over sex, admittedly "the most powerful and unmanageable of instincts." Every individual member of the society, as this single instance should indicate, "can exist, act, think, only for the communal good; and the commune triumphantly refuses, in so far as cosmic law permits, to let itself be ruled either by Love or Hunger."

This observation leads Hearn to questions pertaining to the possibility of human moral growth to the highest point, where egoism and altruism are in perfect harmony. His final question is: "Will humanity ever be able, on this planet, to reach an ethical condition beyond all its ideals, —a condition in which everything that we now call evil will have been atrophied out of existence, and everything that we call virtue have been transmuted into instinct;—a state of altruism in which ethical concepts and codes will have become as useless as they would be, even now, in the societies of the higher ants"? This question, Hearn is delighted to find, Spencer has answered partly in the affirmative. But in spite of his reverence for Spencer, Hearn speculates on the correlation between population pressure and sex suppression. Moral transformations such as have been predicted by Spencer could, in Hearn's opinion, come true only with the aid of physiological change, and at a terrible cost. Those ethical conditions in the ant society can have been reached "only through effort desperately sustained for millions of years against the most atrocious necessities." This may suggest that the human race may also have to meet and master its possible necessities, equally merciless. One of these necessities to come, Hearn agrees with Spencer, will be "concomitant with the period of the greatest possible pressure of population." As a result of that long stress there will be, no doubt, "a vast increase of human intelligence and sympathy"; yet, this increase of intelligence will be effected "at the cost of human fertility." The trouble is that the decline in reproductive power never will be "sufficient to assure the very highest social conditions"; it will "only relieve that pressure of population which has been the main cause of human suffering." In order to achieve the state of perfect social equilibrium, mankind must discover *"some means of solving economic problems, just as social insects have solved them, by the suppression of sex-life."* Should sex-life be transmuted to some higher purposes, there might be an eventual state of polymorphism. Should this come true, the "Coming Race" might then be represented "in its higher types,—through feminine rather than masculine evolution,—by a majority of beings of neither sex." "The higher types of a humanity superior to sex," Hearn continues, "might be able to realize the dream of life for a thousand years." Would this finally promise "a prodigious increase of longevity," the "Elixir of the Alchemists' hope," which science is not likely to discover? There is one more question of "largest significance": it concerns the "relation of ethics and cosmic law." If the highest possible strength is that of unselfishness, Hearn concludes, the parable of the ant should also suggest that the cosmic process seems to "affirm the worth of every human system of ethics fundamentally opposed to human egoism."

Any utopian scheme is bound to suffer from the criticism that it is impractical and fantastic to the point of absurdity. History also testifies that, no matter how nobly inspired, no matter how ingeniously contrived, utopian theory, once put into practice, often tends to be corrupted into some kind of collectivism. Viewed critically, Hearn's utopia seems to leave no room for individual choice or ability. Like any other, it seems completely devoid of moral value,—but only because we look at it from the world of actuality. No utopian thought can be grasped in terms of our existing human values; it is never meant to be. And no such criticism can deny the real potency inherent in its "hypothetical and conditional reasoning," as Rousseau called his own mode of thinking. Impossibility itself is of the very essence of utopianism. As Goethe said, "To live in the ideal world is to treat the impossible as if it were possible." Only in this way may we deal with a world of purely imaginary perfection.[28]

It must be pointed out that in this essay Hearn carried out his own early suggestion about insect civilization: "to find a future application of that intelligence to the benefit of man." Beyond this general significance of the parable there is one more point to be noted, that in this parable Hearn sought to solve at once sexualism and individualism, the two cults which, in his opinion, the West has developed to excess and now must reconsider for its own intellectual health. But these two questions are not to be confined to the West alone; they are universal, and must be treated as such. In viewing sex as "what is commonly supposed to be the most powerful and unmanageable of instincts," and then relating it to human egotism, Hearn would agree with the Buddha, who also designated the lure of sex and the pride of egotism as the two greatest hindrances and temptations on man's path to spiritual salvation. According to the Buddha, no matter how keen he may be mentally, no matter how he may be able to practice *dhyāna,* no matter to how high a degree of *samādhi* he may attain, unless he has wholly annihilated the lure of sex and the pride of egotism, man will eventually fall into the lower realms of existence.[29] In freeing himself from the bondage of sex and selfishness man enters Nirvana. Nirvana is reached when human morality expands as large as the universal law, an equivalent to what Hearn regards as the cosmic law in evolutional philosophy. Hearn's utopia comes into existence when egotism and altruism merge into one another, freedom and duty fuse with one another, and the individual wills the will of the whole universe. While this is an ideal, it is not a fantasy; for in the hearts of men Hearn saw the reality and the potentiality of utopia. It will never be created by either scientific advancement or socioeconomic reform or political revolution alone. On this point Hearn differs decidedly with many modern writers about utopia. A brave new world of his type can come only with the total spiritual rebirth of humanity.

On the human or historical level Hearn's two questions of sexualism and individualism may be still more suggestive. Hearn's solution to sexualism is as extreme as Plato's in his ideal republic. But they differ radically in point of emphasis; Hearn maximizes its importance, whereas Plato minimizes it. This difference seems to foreshadow our own age, far more so than we would like to admit, for twentieth-century man lives not in the antiquity which regarded love as "sickness," "frenzy," or "madness," [30] but in the world which has pursued the cult of passion, a world which has had to accommodate Freud. As for Hearn's critical observations about the cult of individualism, we must judge them by his intent, an intent to discover in his terms how to correct it. As has been pointed out, he does not deny individualism as such, for we recall his advice to modern Japan, that more personal freedom be allowed. His criticism is directed at Western overemphasis on the individual at the expense of the whole, a tendency which he believed has reached the point of morbidity. Accordingly, his criticism is extreme. Whatever our personal reaction to his stand, however, the issue still remains with us—in view of the fact that many of the recent intellectual movements in the West have centered around the re-examination of the meaning of the individual in relation to society, and also that, since Plato's classical analogy of microcosm-macrocosm, much of utopian literature in the West has attempted to redefine the individual primarily as part of a larger framework.[31] If Hearn saw the West of his time in such a way, it was because he was able to see stereoptically from the East which, due to its ultimately monistic position, has recognized "the other side of man, man the member of the family, of society, of the universe," thus defining him as "more than an individual." [32]

Here we are brought back once again to Japan, or rather Old Japan; to Hearn it is a symbol, just as is his parable of the ant. As the ant society is his insect pattern of utopia, so is Old Japan his human pattern. In criticizing the Western cult of individualism Hearn is really urging his own world to return to man's most important question. He has no intention of being a self-styled prophet of doom for the Western world. In him there is no trace of the prophet's self-righteousness. In his book, *Japan,* Hearn questions what constitutes that inscrutable charm of Old Japan: "Are we really charmed by the results of a social discipline that refused to recognize the individual?—enamored of a cult that exacted the suppression of personality?" To his own question Hearn responds:

> No: the charm is made by the fact that this vision of the past represents to us much more than past or present—that it foreshadows the possibilities of some higher future, in a world of perfect sympathy. After many a thousand years there may be developed a humanity able to achieve, with never a shadow of illusion, those ethical conditions prefigured by the ideals of Old Japan: instinctive unselfishness, a common desire to find the joy of life in making happiness for others, a universal sense of moral beauty. And whenever man shall have so far gained upon the present as to need no other code than the teaching of their own hearts, then indeed the ancient ideal of Shinto will find its supreme realization.[33]

Both Old Japan and the ant society are at best an intimation of a better world which could come if we desire and strive to that end. It is in this light that we must reconsider our common image of Hearn as a Japanophile, and even more, Hearn as a romantic escapist.[34]

XIII

"A
Perfect
Sphere"

*An
Integration
of the
World*

Some months after the publication of his essay, "Of the
Eternal Feminine," Hearn wrote to Henry Watkin, his "Dad" in Cincinnati:

> When one has lived alone five years in a Buddhist atmosphere, one
> naturally becomes penetrated by the thoughts that hover in it; my
> whole thinking, I must acknowledge, has been changed, in spite of my
> long studies of Spencer and of Schopenhauer. I do not mean that I am a
> Buddhist, but I mean that the inherited ancestral feelings about the uni-
> verse—the Occidental ideas every Englishman has—have been totally
> transformed.
> There is yet no fixity, however: the changes continue,—and I really
> do not know how I shall feel about the universe later on.[1]

Here the slow but far-reaching transformation Hearn had referred to
in the essay is described in a personal manner. This would come as no
surprise to those who remember his early conversion to evolutionism.
Eight years before, he had written to H. E. Krehbiel about his "very
positive change":

> Talking of change in opinions, I am really astonished at myself. You
> know what my fantastic metaphysics were. A friend disciplined me to
> read Herbert Spencer. I suddenly discovered what a waste of time all my

Oriental metaphysics had been. I also discovered, for the first time, how to apply the little general knowledge I possessed. I also learned what an absurd thing positive skepticism is. I also found unspeakable comfort in the sudden and, for me, eternal reopening of the Great Doubt, which renders pessimism ridiculous, and teaches a new reverence for all forms of faith. In short, from the day when I finished the *First Principles,*—a totally new intellectual life opened for me; and I hope during the next two years to devour the rest of this oceanic philosophy.[2]

Taken together with the fact that Hearn himself wished to be buried, and as a matter of fact, was buried by the Buddhist rite, these two statements seem to corroborate the assertion of his loyal defender, Yone Noguchi: "I like to vindicate Hearn from the criticism that his writing is about one third Japanese and two thirds Hearn. Fortunately his two thirds Hearn is also Japanese."[3] Noguchi actually does disservice to Hearn, however, and further fortifies the very slander that Hearn betrayed the West in order to imbibe the alien culture. We recall Dr. Gould's portrait of Hearn the hater of Occidentalism and lover of "the vapid, and even pitiful childishness of semi-barbaric Orientalism," as well as Matthew Josephson's charge against Hearn the enemy of the West.[4]

On the other hand, Nobushige Amenomori is cautious enough not to lift Hearn out of the total context. In a warm tribute to his old friend, Amenomori pointed out that those thoughtless charges would amount to confessing "to a dead failure to perceive the evolutionist ideas that pervade his works on Japan." "Unless," he continued, "a person has mastered the works of Herbert Spencer, whom Hearn almost adored, especially the *Principles of Biology, Psychology,* and *Ethics,*—he cannot read Hearn's books on Japan in the light in which the author meant that they should be read." That is, as a poet Hearn saw in Buddhism and Shinto "the emotional side of Evolutionism." Implying that his old friend was at heart an evolutionist, Amenomori said: "I am inclined to think that, had Hearn lived longer and taken to versifying, he would have been to Evolutionism what, in a sense, Pope was to the philosophy and theology of Bolingbroke."[5] This testimony deserves special attention, being from one like Amenomori, whom Hearn, in dedicating *Kokoro,* called "poet, scholar and patriot," and who proved to be his best informant on Buddhism and related subjects. No one need remind us of Hearn's whole-hearted acceptance of evolutionism, especially Spencerian philosophy. It is ever present in his thought and work, whether it be in his ambition to write "evolutional fiction," in his aesthetic theory, in his evolutional basis of literary study, in his interpretation of Japan, in his advice to modern Japan, or in his social thought.

Amenomori is undoubtedly right in warning against underestimation of the importance of evolutionism in Hearn's thought; however, Buddhism permeates his Japanese works as completely as evolutionism. This point, ironically enough, seems to support Noguchi's declaration, if it does not entirely confirm it. Before making any hasty conclusion we should listen to what Hearn himself has to say. In 1898 he wrote to a Yale student who had sought for an autograph: "I am not a Buddhist, but still a follower of Herbert Spencer." [6] Toward the end of his career he put it more explicitly—in his book, *Japan:* "I venture to call myself a student of Herbert Spencer; and it was because of my acquaintance with the Synthetic Philosophy that I came to find in Buddhist philosophy a more than romantic interest." [7]

What are the implications of Noguchi's assertion, and of Dr. Gould's and Josephson's accusations in the face of Hearn's own statement that he remained "a student of Herbert Spencer"? What does Hearn mean by "a more than romantic interest"? Does this refer to Hearn's seeing in Buddhism what Amenomori called "the emotional side of Evolutionism"? The issue is too important to be dismissed lightly, for it has been the focal point of the controversy over Hearn's intellectual consistency and integrity.

The critics cited err on at least one point; that is, they all fail to notice that evolutionism and Buddhism as an inseparable pair had been Hearn's life-long interest, as he made plain in the two statements of 1886 and 1894, quoted above. In Hearn's mind this pair had undergone a sort of dialectical development for two decades,—always, though sometimes vaguely, connected with the question of science and faith, and also that of the West and the East. As early as 1879, while reviewing Edwin Arnold's popular poetic account of the Buddha's life, *The Light of Asia,* Hearn wrote: "Today European thinkers are becoming deeply interested in the study of the ancient ethics of the East and those apparently wild doctrines of Indian metaphysics which, after all, appear to be founded upon scientific truths we are only now beginning to discover." [8] By 1884, when he wrote two articles, "The Buddhistic Bugaboo!" and "What Buddhism Is," Hearn had somehow sobered down his wild enthusiasm to the level of calm interest, but still with much of romantic vagueness.[9] From this point of view his statement expressing his conversion to evolutionism not only shows that his was one of those many voices testifying to the profound impact of Spencer on his generation but also indicates that Hearn was reacting strongly against his romantic zeal for Buddhism. When he regained his balance, the old dialectical pattern asserted itself again. In 1887, writing to Dr. Gould, Hearn suggested that modern science, namely evolutional science, would be able to provide for "an harmonious commentary" upon all the basic tenets of Buddhism, but not upon those of Christianity. Labeling Christianity as "the more barbarous faith of the Occident," he then pondered on "the possibility of the invasion of the Oriental philosophy into the Occident." [10]

As has already been said in the chapter on Hearn's travel writing, it is in the first group of his Japanese books that the pattern of evolutionism and Buddhism emerged as a central theme only to become one with his West-East theme, as he set out to investigate some of the most basic doctrines of Buddhism in terms of those of evolutionism. *Out of the East,* with its chapters, "The Stone Buddha" and "In Yokohama," marks his theoretical initiation, whereas *Kokoro*'s center of interest is its chapter, "The Idea of Preëxistence." The exploration culminates in "Nirvana," a chapter in *Gleanings in Buddha-Fields.* All that has been discussed is tied together in *Exotics and Retrospectives,* a study of comparative aesthetics. And finally "The Higher Buddhism," in his *Japan,* becomes the précis of his ten-year-long study of evolutionism and Buddhism.

"The Stone Buddha," a piece of interior monolog between the West and the East, and also between science and religion, concerns the mystery of the universe and the riddle of life and death.[11] Science suggests both that man's evolution is "a progression into perfection and beatitude," and that when it reaches its goal of equilibrium, integration must in turn yield to disintegration. Through science, Hearn thinks, the West has now discovered "mathematically" what the East has known since time immemorial; yet, science is capable of offering no answer to questions about the meaning of life,—"of this phantom-flash between darknesses," swinging between the past and the future, whose extremities are deeply steeped in the Unknowable. Science, while systematizing human experience, fails to enlighten us as to "the Whence, the Whither, or, worst of all!—the Why," man's innermost quest for certitude. Because of its rationalistic stand, he continues, science cannot explain the quintessence of the Eastern religion, that acts and thoughts are not merely the incidents of life, but really its creators,—the law of karma, which ultimately centers on the mystery of self. In search of the Unknowable beyond human prayer, Western faith loses its power of rendering service, thus leaving us to our own resources. We have no possible refuge but in ourselves. Our only comfort, Hearn says, is the Buddha's teaching: *"Be ye lamps unto yourselves; be ye a refuge unto yourselves. Betake yourselves to no other refuge. The Buddhas are only teachers. Hold ye fast to the truth as to a lamp. Hold fast as a refuge to the truth. Look not for refuge to any beside yourselves."*

This method of dialog Hearn carries over along with the theme in another chapter, "In Yokohama." [12] The conversation between a Western evolutionist and an Eastern priest once again centers on the awful three, "the Whence, the Whither, and the Why," the questions perpetually tormenting the Western mind. To these riddles, which Western science fails to solve, the priest suggests as a solution the Buddhist concept of the universe as "emanation of the infinite Entity," and of man as mixture of the original Self that is the universal mind and the primal illusion. Their discussion eventually leads to the notion of ego, where Buddhism and evolutionism meet, and the concept of salvation, Nirvana, where they part.

Hearn attempts to pursue the question of the awful three to its ultimate point, self, in the two essays, "The Idea of Preëxistence" and "Nirvana." Here he finds fundamental metaphysical explanations to fortify his criticism of the Western concept of individuality. The idea of preëxistence, Hearn writes, pervades the Eastern world and governs its mentality. [13] As Hearn explains, the Buddhist concept of preëxistence has little to do with Western ideas of metempsychosis, whether Pythagorean or Platonic; nor does it resemble the gnostic concept of soul as "a definitely numbered multiple." Buddhism denies the conventional soul, a soul which the West considers the basis of individuality or personality. In Buddhism soul signifies "an aggregate or composite of inconceivable complexity—the concentrated sum of the creative thinking of previous lives beyond all reckoning." According to its basic doctrine, "psychical personality," the so-called self, is "a temporary composite of illusions" as a result of the karmic law. What is reincarnated is therefore the karma, "the sum-total of the acts and thoughts of countless anterior existences." Although what constitutes the ultimate nature of this karmic force may be beyond human comprehension, its cause at least is known as *tanhā,* the craving for life, corresponding to Schopenhauer's "will" to live, or more so to Spencer's polarities of the physiological unit. This correspondence, Hearn believes, indicates that both Buddhism and evolutionism recognize the same phenomenon, even if under different terms.

Western theology, he continues, fails to account for those many familiar feelings which compose no small part of our psychological life, because it conceives of soul as something "specially created out of nothing to fit each new body." Christian theology, while accepting the doctrine of physical evolution, still clings to the hypothesis of special creation, contrary to the phenomena of heredity, and thereby asserts that all feeling and cognition belong to individual experience. Hence, it forces itself to reject the possibility that much of our personal impulse and emotion is superindividual. In order to cope with the advance of modern science, Hearn believes, Christian theology must accept this reality of psychological evolution, too, just as it has accepted the law of physical evolution. Otherwise, modern psychological science would relentlessly go on to break down all those "present petty metaphysical" notions of personality and individuality as realities *per se,"* notions so dear to the Western mind. Hearn ventures to question whether the disintegration of the ego is really so dreadful as we imagine, and whether the ego is really essential to our spiritual salvation. He points out that the Buddhist concept of soul as an infinite multiple not only accords with what modern science has revealed of our psychical reality but also offers a more reasonable basis for our spiritual hope. To the Buddhist, salvation means but his struggle to "disengage his better self or selves from his worse selves," thus attaining Nirvana, or the supreme bliss—"only through the survival of the best within him." Is it not, Hearn asks, "for this very disintegration" of the ego that Christians and Buddhists alike perpetually pray? From this viewpoint the dissolution of self is not something to be feared, but rather the ultimate goal toward which our religious efforts should turn; for it is through the surrender of self that we are able to participate in the supreme revelation of the Absolute Reality.[14] Should any philosophy deny us this hope it never would deserve the name.

Buddhism and science are at one, Hearn believes, in pointing out that the concept of the individual ego is "a fiction of selfishness." A reconsideration of the question of the ego, with which the Western mind is confronted, may exert a significant influence in every phase of our life— even in creative art, he says. It would provide modern art with larger inspirations, absolutely novel and exquisite sensations, hitherto unimaginable pathos, and marvelously deep emotions. Of what modern literature in particular would gain with our final recognition of the idea of preëxistence, Hearn then writes:

> Even in fiction we learn that we have been living in a hemisphere only; that we have been thinking but half-thoughts; that we need a new faith

to join past with future over the great parallel of the present, and so to round out our emotional world into a perfect sphere. The clear conviction that the self is multiple, however paradoxical the statement seem, is the absolutely necessary step to the vaster conviction that the many are One, that life is unity, that there is no finite, but only infinite.[15]

In order for this to come, Hearn believes that we must forsake our conventional notion about soul as a finite unit. In fact, to acknowledge the composite nature of self would help to enhance rather than annihilate our profound sense of mystery.

Here he speaks as an artist, to be sure. But soon he turns to the main issue and warns us against overlooking the vital distinction between Buddhism and evolutionism. As to the awful three, science still remains mute, whereas Buddhism is capable of answering in its own fashion. As Hearn emphasizes, it is not science but faith, faith alone which provides this universe, "a vast phantasmagoria"—with moral purpose. This question once again takes him back to the Buddhist doctrine of karma in relation to Nirvana. By definition, Hearn points out, karma, as the sum-total of the acts and thoughts of countless anterior existences, has nothing to do with the popular Buddhist notion of personal transmigration. What it really signifies is moral causation. Once this chain of karma, the operating principle of reincarnation, is broken, there is a promise of blissful Nirvana. The complete annihilation of the individual self is the way of return to the one all-self, or universal Self. This is the kernel of Hearn's chapter "Nirvana," which, as Amenomori tells us, took him a little more than three years to complete.[16]

Hearn declares that Buddhism denies neither the reality of phenomena, including soul, as phenomena nor the forces creating phenomena as such. As he points out, to negate karma as karma would amount to negating the entire Buddhist system. His subtitle, "A Study in Synthetic Buddhism," suggests plainly that he is not concerned with either popular Buddhist beliefs or those doctrines peculiar to any one sect. Rather, he sets out to attempt a synthesis of the essentials, so as to present a satisfactory outline of Buddhist ontology.

Indeed, the question of Nirvana, as Hearn sees it, is of prime importance both because it is the essence of Buddhism, without a genuine knowledge of which one's understanding of Buddhism comes to little, and because it is the point where Buddhism and evolutionism must diverge, despite their common position as to the impermanency of this phenomenal world. At the outset Hearn attempts to correct one most prevalent notion about Nirvana as "complete annihilation."

Nirvana signifies an extinction only in that it leads to an emancipation. Should this sound paradoxical, it is simply because of our Western notion of self. "Nirvana is no cessation, but an emancipation," writes Hearn. "It means only the passing of conditioned being into unconditioned being—the fading of all mental and physical phantoms into the light of Formless Omnipotence and Omniscience." [17] Accepting this undoubtedly Mahayana Buddhist concept of Nirvana, he presents an illustrated account of the Eight Stages of Deliverance leading to Nirvana, the course of spiritual progress from the world of men to the state of divine bliss. In his opinion the Buddhist teaching, that "only after the lapse of millions of future lives," the average man can hope to free himself from his worse nature, is "much more of a truth than of a theory."

Buddhism, Hearn continues, is in complete accord with modern science—not only in stressing the impermanency of all phenomena, the ethical signification of heredity, the lesson of mental evolution, the duty of moral progress, but also in repudiating the Western doctrine of materialism and even of spiritualism, the hypothesis of special creation, and the belief in the immortality of the human soul. Though it negates the foundation of Occidental religion, Buddhism has been able to offer "the revelation of larger religious possibilities—the suggestions of a universal scientific creed nobler than any which has ever existed." Hearn concludes:

> Precisely in that period of our own intellectual evolution when faith in a personal God is passing away—when the belief in an individual soul is becoming impossible—when the most religious minds shrink from everything that we have been calling religion—when the universal doubt is an ever-growing weight upon ethical aspiration—light is offered from the East. There we find ourselves in presence of an older and a vaster faith—holding no gross anthropomorphic conceptions of the immeasurable Reality, and denying the existence of soul, but nevertheless inculcating a system of morals superior to any other, and maintaining a hope which no possible future form of positive knowledge can destroy. Re-enforced by the teaching of science, the teaching of this ancient faith is that for thousands of years we have been thinking inside-out and upside-down. The only reality is One;—all that we have taken for Substance is only Shadow;—the physical is the unreal;—*and the outer-man is the ghost.*

Having pursued the question of self to its logical limits, Hearn seems now well convinced of the possibility of the invasion of the Oriental philosophy into the Occident, the dream he had a decade ago.

If *Japan: An Attempt at Interpretation* is a summation of Hearn's many thoughts about Japan, it is also a summation of his study of synthetic Buddhism. In a chapter entitled "The Higher Buddhism," Hearn examines Buddhist metaphysics—again in the light of evolutionism.[18] It is more than a mere summation of what has been said about the subject. At the start he explains that he has written this chapter for three reasons: First, Western ignorance of philosophical Buddhism is conducive to our charge of atheism among the intellectual classes of Japan; second, some people have been misled into believing that the Japanese masses are quite resigned to vanish from the face of the earth because of an incapacity for struggle, supposedly created by the doctrine of Nirvana; and third, the subject could be "one of extraordinary interest to the student of modern philosophy."

Many Western thinkers, Hearn admits, have been drawn to Buddhism for "the strangeness of the intellectual landscape" it affords, to use Henry Clarke Warren's phrase. Hearn prefers to point out the startling analogy between Buddhism and evolutionism. Philosophical Buddhism, due to its monistic basis, contains some doctrines which accord with the scientific theories of the German and the English monists. What is striking, he says, is that Buddhism has formulated those doctrines through mental processes unknown to Western thinking, and unaided by any knowledge of science. Hearn lists some of the doctrines which he believes to be the most important of this higher Buddhism: the doctrine of Nirvana; the doctrine of monism, that there is but one Reality; the doctrine of self, that the consciousness is not the real self; and the doctrine of karma, that both mind and matter, as a result of the karmic law, represent "a strictly moral order."

Hearn examines these doctrines one by one in comparison with evolutionism, especially with Spencer's own statements. This comparative study continues until he comes to the point where Buddhism and evolutionism part company as regards the ultimate. In admitting their intellectual incapacity for grasping the Unknowable Reality, Spencer and his school are agnostic, whereas Buddhism is definitely gnostic in professing to know this. He notes here a resemblance between Buddhism and the German evolutionist school. For instance, Haeckel and his fellow-monists are gnostic, certainly not agnostic, when they admit "a universal sentiency," or more specifically, "a universal potential-sentiency." This hypothesis seems to Hearn to resemble very closely the Buddhist belief that all matter is sentient, though it may vary according to condition. The similarity ceases here, for there is "one immense, all-important difference" between the Western and the Eastern monism. "The former," says Hearn, "would attribute the qualities of the atom merely to a sort of heredity—to the persistency of tendencies developed under chance influences operating throughout an incalculable past. The latter declares the history of the atom to be purely moral!" Buddhism "proclaims a purely moral order of the cosmos, and attaches almost infinite consequence to the least of human acts." Thus describing Buddhism as a kind of monism based on the moral principle, Hearn reminds us that there is no good justification for declaring a man, especially an Oriental, irreligious because of his disbelief in a personal God, in an immortal soul, and in any continuation of personality after death, those doctrines characteristic of Christianity. Western accusation of his "atheism," in spite of his profound belief in the moral order of the universe, the ethical responsibility of the present to all the future, the ultimate disappearance of evil, and the possibility of salvation, simply betrays bigotry and ignorance.

Hearn has indeed come a long way since his Jesuit education drove him—"at the tender age of fifteen"—to what his religious tutor termed "the folly and the wickedness of pantheism." [19] This is as far as he has come for his personal need, the need to satisfy his whole being. Only in terms of such a personal necessity can we explain his conversion to evolutionism in 1886. What he saw in it and accepted is Spencer's synthetic philosophy, his systematic application of the evolutional theory, and his universal speculation on the basis of three grades of knowledge, everyday, scientific, and philosophical. That is why he said: "I also discovered, for the first time, how to apply the little general knowledge I possessed." It was his metaphysical awakening, so to speak, for in it he saw for the first time the possibility of an all-embracing view of the universe, a monistic view of life which he had been seeking unawares. Though he set out to devour Spencer's "oceanic philosophy," it would not gratify him entirely; it was too intellectual and too scientific. Neither science nor metaphysics alone could offer a sense of fullness. This forced Hearn back to his "Oriental metaphysics," —which at the moment of conversion to evolutionism he had called "a waste of time,"—or, more specifically, to Buddhism. What drove him on to this point was, as aforesaid, his existential need, not only metaphysical but also religious. Because of this Hearn sought in Buddhism something more than "the strangeness of the intellectual landscape," and found "a more than romantic interest." It would be far from the truth to dismiss Hearn's philosophy as merely an intellectual eclecticism.

The analogy between evolutionism and Buddhism, such as we have observed, leads us to consider Hearn's dream of unifying science and religion and thereby reconciling the West and the East. While in Matsue, Hearn reported local news for the *Japan Mail,* an English paper then appearing in Yokohama. In his despatch of June 23, 1891, he wrote about an interview with Enrio Inouye (1859–1919), Director of Tetsugakkwan, or the College of Philosophy, who was on a nation-wide lecture tour. With specific reference to Bunyiu Nanjo (1849–1927), an Oxford-educated Buddhist scholar, Hearn praised Inouye's effort to fuse the East and the West philosophically, that is, Eastern religion and Western science. As an envoy Hearn wrote a passage of special interest:

> What would be attempted as an ultimate end would be a synthesis of Oriental and Occidental philosophy,—an elucidation of cosmic philosophy through the study of the best thought of the human race, combined with the knowledge of the largest results of contemporary science.[20]

Once again, the occasion must have bestirred Hearn's old dream of meeting the world at large, and this time he felt more acutely its possibility and necessity. His subsequent study of Buddhism must have added more to his conviction, as can be found in his correspondence and Japanese books. In his letter to Chamberlain of June 4, 1894, Hearn touched on the subject. "Western Science and Eastern Faith," he wrote, "A comparison of results in the form of an address. Shall I, or shall I not try?"[21] As elsewhere, he was hopeful about the reciprocity of the East and the West. When in his first Japanese book Hearn expressed his satisfaction that Japan had "wisely" accepted Spencer's philosophy, it was not simply because of his personal interest in evolutionism, but also because of his belief that this would revitalize Japan.[22] In *Kokoro,* moreover, he pointed out that the higher forms of faith Japan needs most should be evolved from within, never from without. "A Buddhism strongly fortified by Western science will meet the future needs of the race," he added. At the same time he did not fail to remind his own world of the possible salutary influence from the East, especially its religion.[23] In *Gleanings in Buddha-Fields* he became more articulate while meditating on the future marriage of the East and the West: "I cannot but think," he wrote there, "that out of the certain future union of Western knowledge with Eastern thought there must eventually proceed a Neo-Buddhism inheriting all the strength of Science, yet spiritually able to recompense the seeker for truth."[24] Against this background we should be able to understand better Hearn's own studies, such as "The Stone Buddha," "In Yokohama," "The Idea of Preëxistence," "Nirvana," and "The Higher Buddhism."

In the process of these studies Hearn confided to Chamberlain his desire to teach philosophy rather than literature. What his lecture on philosophy would have been is not difficult to surmise from his special lectures on Victorian philosophy in relation to modern literature. After having systematically traced the development of evolutionism, Hearn once again ventured his hope:

> All of the old barriers set up by dogmatic faith have been broken down. The future is to be a new era of thought, a new era of philosophy. The ultimate question must, indeed, remain for us as far as ever—unless we should be able at some enormously remote time to develop new senses. The indications are that in the immediate future Western and Eastern thought will cease to be in opposition, and that a combination is very likely to occur between the fundamental truth of Oriental philosophy and of Occidental science. Should this come about, we might expect the inauguration of what might be called a new universal religion—a religion of humanity, not in the sense of Comte (which was an impossible dream), but in that ethical signification which would represent the unification of all that is best in human knowledge and experience.[25]

Here Hearn is convinced that science and faith, metaphysics and religion, and the West and the East should be symbolic of harmony, not discord.

This is Hearn's expression of the perennial philosophy, as we may call it. In presenting a view of the world as one, Hearn's intention is honorable, and even hopeful. Admitting this, some may still feel justified in suspecting that it is a poet's wishful but irresponsible dream. The central question, how to seek in science and faith the basis of world integration, philosophical as well as religious, is a difficult one. On the theoretical level it demands a certain set of generalizations; yet, at every turn it surprises us with frequent exceptions. What is more, the search leads through an area long and thickly entangled with prejudices, disagreements, and controversies. Yet, the question cannot be avoided; it must be pursued.

Through his study of evolutionism and Buddhism Hearn came to regard evolutional science as a manifestation of the Western genius, and philosophical religion as a manifestation of the Eastern genius. This kind of contrast necessarily involves the risk of oversimplification. We obviously must object that the West cannot be summed up in terms of science, especially Spencer's nineteenth-century conception of science, which is at best quasi-philosophical; and, furthermore, Hearn ignores a long Western religious tradition. Likewise, the East cannot be adequately described in terms of Buddhism, which is but one of its religions. Hearn's foundation itself, then, is inadequate. In broad outline, however, there is a measure of truth in Hearn's stand that is hardly touched by this categorical repudiation. One important aspect of Western philosophy, after all, has been its close affinity with rational science; and Spencer's philosophy of science is a characteristic example. Moreover, Buddhism best fulfills the role of representing the East, not only because it is one of the major religions but also because they all are at one over the nature of the Ultimate.[26] Now, when Hearn says that the union of science and religion is at once possible and logical, it is not merely because they are complementary, but rather because they have common ground. He believes their union to be possible only because of their common monistic basis, without which the union of science and religion would be merely verbal. Metaphysically, it seems almost indisputable that the East has been as much monistic as the West has been dualistic. Eastern religion, with some exceptions, has been consistently monistic in holding that the many are always and ultimately subordinate to the One. On the other hand, Western religion, whether Christian or non-Christian, has been dualistic and monotheistic.[27] This may account for the historical antagonism between science and religion experienced by the West. The schism between science and faith, which Hearn as a religious-minded Victorian sought to reconcile in his own way, is unquestionably Western. In the East, however, there is no such tension, not because science is a recent import from the West (even this point some may question), but because its traditional monism finds no serious objection in science itself. This is quite true of Buddhism, a religion professing to be continuous in exploring man's problems across all possible existential strata. Since Buddhism demands no theistic premise, its approach to science can be positive. Buddhism here, needless to say, is what Hearn calls philosophical Buddhism, Buddhism in its purest form, without its historical impedimenta.[28] In Buddhist phenomenology there is no fixity; it is a philosophy of change, as Hearn notes in the basic analogy between evolutionism and Buddhism. Thus Hearn's thesis, the union of evolutionism and Buddhism and, in a larger sense, science and faith, is philosophically tenable.

In Hearn's opinion the East has been ready to accept and master Western science, its theories, and their technical application, along with Christianity as social action; whereas the spiritual authorities of the West have for centuries attempted to impede the advance of science, and have also become alarmed at the possible impact of Eastern religion. As the most practical means of solving this discord Hearn then suggests that the East accept Western science while the West also become aware of the fructifying influence from the East, and more responsive to its spiritual challenge: "The soft serenity, the passionless tenderness, of these Buddha faces might yet give peace of soul to a West weary of creeds transformed into conventions, eager for the coming of another teacher to proclaim." [29] In this suggestion Hearn is not alone, of course, but singularly anticipatory of the way some thinkers, Western and Eastern, have in the recent years begun to attempt what they term world philosophical synthesis. With all their individual variances, they have come to the realization that such a philosophical integration should and could come, if at all, most likely through the complementary union between Western knowledge and Eastern wisdom, between the Western scientific spirit and the Eastern religious insight.[30] In view of this, too, Hearn's proposal for an integration of the West and the East in terms of science and religion deserves fresh appraisal.

At the end of his voyage into the Far East Hearn came to discover that science and religion are one at root, their difference being primarily in approach to the Ultimate. Buddhism seemed to him to assume a further significance as he turned to his own West. Throughout, Hearn repeated the question: Is it absolutely necessary for Christianity to insist on its own uniqueness based on its dogmas? As he saw it, Christian dogmas, like the hypothesis of special creation, faith in a personal God, belief in the continuation of personality after death,—whatever service they have done in the past—seem no longer tenable in the face of modern science. To him philosophical Buddhism appeared as evidence that faith is still possible without resorting to rigid dogmas, and that faith can embrace science and humanize it with its own profound spirituality. This led Hearn to suggest that the West cease to adhere to these dogmas as "the absolutely necessary step to the vaster conviction that the many are One, that life is unity, that there is no finite, but only infinite." As the most logical means to this he proposed a synthesis of Western science and Eastern philosophy. Therefore, "a new universal religion" or "a religion of humanity," the kind of religion Hearn called for, would come only when all religions are willing to go beyond the dogmas and rites which have clustered in their historical evolution, and return to the divine ground, that inexhaustible fountainhead of the spirit of religion, where all religions meet. Whatever his emotional bias against his early Jesuit education, whatever his personal reaction to the missionary cause, and whatever his violent objection to Christian dogma, Hearn never rejected what he took to be Christianity in the primal sense.[31]

Hearn's perennial philosophy, rightly understood, is his call for a recovery of faith in the reality of the divine ground which alone can reconcile religion and science, and also the West and the East. In distinguishing Christianity from historical Christianity, and Buddhism from historical Buddhism Hearn does not equate religion with morality, which is after all human, a fallacy committed by those who would make an easy compromise with science. Hearn's is rather an attempt to call attention to the primary function of religion, a function of assuring man's direct participation in the spiritual ground of the world and enriching his unitive knowledge of the Godhead. Many will complain that such suggestions carried into practice would destroy religion itself. In a sense it would, since in emphasizing its mystic core Hearn minimizes the importance of its dogmatic and ritual structure. But it must be pointed out that actually all religious doctrines, dogmas, and rites have at one time or another been subject to the mutation of time. Hearn is not unaware of their usefulness as principles of discipline and guidance in the temporal world. His point is that they are but symbols of truth, not truth itself, and that they should not be allowed to eclipse the goal of our spiritual pilgrimage and our ultimate salvation. This kind of approach and attitude, it must be admitted, involves a serious risk, but Hearn thinks one must take the risk to remain spiritually alive. He would agree to the Buddha's warning:

> Subhuti, do not think that the Tathagata ever considers in his own mind: I ought to ennunciate a system of teaching for the elucidation of the Dharma. You should never cherish such a thought. And why? Because if any disciple harboured such a thought he would not only be misunderstanding the Tathagata's teaching, but he would be slandering him as well. Moreover, the expression "a system of teaching" has no meaning; for Truth (in the sense of Reality) cannot be cut up into pieces and arranged into a system. The words can only be used as a figure of speech.[32]

In the same spirit Jesus opposed the legal-minded high priests and Pharisees who were crowding the temple of God. If it be agreed that religious doctrines, dogmas, and rites never can be a substitute for truth, though important as its symbols, it is then not impossible to recognize the essential value in Hearn's call for a recovery of faith.[33]

XIV

"The
Tree
of
Life"

An
Integration
of
Man

In Exotics and Retrospectives there is a prose poem called "Of Moon-Desire." In speaking of his little son's wish for the moon, Hearn mentions those wishes, innocent and yet natural, which we all nourish as "children of a larger growth," and thereon come to "the highest wisdom" that "commends us to wish for very much more than the Moon—even for more than the Sun and the Morning-Star and all the Host of Heaven." Against this background he sets his life course:

I remember when a boy lying on my back in the grass, gazing into the summer blue above me, and wishing that I could melt into it—become a part of it. For these fancies I believe that a religious tutor was innocently responsible: he had tried to explain to me, because of certain dreamy questions, what he termed "the folly and the wickedness of pantheism"—with the result that I immediately became a pantheist, at the tender age of fifteen. And my imaginings presently led me not only to want the sky for a playground, but also to become the sky!

Now I think that in those days I was really close to a great truth,— touching it, in fact, without the faintest suspicion of its existence. I mean the truth that the wish *to become* is reasonable in direct ratio to its largeness—or, in other words, that the more you wish to be, the wiser you are;

while the wish *to have* is apt to be foolish in proportion to its largeness. Cosmic law permits us very few of the countless things that we wish to have, but will help us to become all that we can possibly wish to be. Finite, and in so much feeble, is the wish to have: but infinite in puissance is the wish to become; and every mortal wish to become must eventually find satisfaction. By wanting to be, the monad makes itself the elephant, the eagle, or the man. By wanting to be, the man should become a god. Perhaps on this tiny globe, lighted only by a tenth-rate yellow sun, he will not have time to become a god; but who dare assert that his wish cannot project itself to mightier systems illuminated by vaster suns, and there reshape and invest him with the forms and powers of divinity? Who dare say that his wish may not expand him beyond the Limits of Form, and make him one with Omnipotence? And Omnipotence, without asking, can have much brighter and bigger playthings than the Moon.

Probably everything is a mere question of wishing—providing that we wish, not to have, but to be. Most of the sorrow of life certainly exists because of the wrong kind of wishing and because of the contemptible pettiness of the wishes. Even to wish for the absolute lordship and possession of the entire earth were a pitifully small and vulgar wish. We must learn to nourish very much bigger wishes than that! My faith is that we must wish to become the total universe with its thousands of millions of worlds—and more than the universe, or a myriad universe— and more even than Space and Time.[1]

Reading this, one recalls Wordsworth's phrase: "The Child is father of the Man." If Hearn's life is a record of his attempt to answer some of "the cruel enigmas of the Sphinx of Life," nothing, perhaps, could better depict his mode of approach. Hearn always stressed the prime importance of a faculty he called soul sympathy, a faculty he himself eminently possessed, as all his writings bear witness. He was supreme whenever he turned to media which demanded his exercise of that faculty,—as evident in his translations, his twice-told tales, his interpretative lectures, and his Japanese travel books. His approach was intuitive and fundamentally aesthetic, in that it aimed at obliterating the distance between the object and the subject, resolving the tension between "thou" and "I," and asserting the oneness of the many. Dr. Gould was undoubtedly correct in noting Hearn's "unique expertness of entering into the spirit of his models, refeeling their emotions, reimagining their thought and art," and in calling him "a true thaumaturgist." [2] To Dr. Gould and many others, this characteristic of Hearn's signified his spiritual emptiness. The irony is that Dr. Gould, despite his unkind intention, depicted the essence of Hearn's mode of existence and his aesthetic approach,—its logical manifestation. There is good reason that the last chapter of the present study should be concerned with the fundamental nature of Hearn's vision, the vision of a translator.

There is nothing novel about an artist's partiality to certain colors. It is a phenomenon as old as literature. As a recent case in literature there is Rimbaud's color symbolism; before him there was Gautier, whose obsession with the color white, triumphant in his poem, "Symphonie en blanc majeur," may be contrasted with that of Melville in *Moby Dick*. Like Gautier's and Melville's, an artist's color symbolism deserves special mention only when its manifestation is persistent, not incidental, and when its significance is both personal and more than personal. Color symbolism of this kind Hearn discovered in his master, Poe. "Poe's strange passion for the hue of crimson," he wrote in 1878, "indicate[s] a peculiar and abnormal condition of the imagination." With specific reference to Poe's later works he pointed out that this penchant grew as Poe's art proceeded.[3]

Whatever the pertinency of his observation about Poe, it almost predicts the future direction of Hearn's own color symbolism. As for his color consciousness in general, we have seen it in connection with his Gautierite technique of coloring; and, like Dr. Gould, we may explain it away as compensating for myopia coupled with a monocular defect.[4] Yet, this theory can hardly account for Hearn's singular passion for the color blue, which is treated not merely as one of many colors, but with special emphasis, favorite care, and deepening implication.[5] In short, blue or azure, as we shall see presently, is to Hearn symbolic in the way that crimson is to Poe.

It seems more than a coincidence that in the revealing passage from "Of Moon-Desire," Hearn wrote: "I remember when a boy lying on my back in the grass, gazing into the summer blue above me, and wishing that I could melt into it—become a part of it." Toward the close of another prose poem, "Noctilucae," Hearn noted: ". . . and I saw that the light which was mine shifted tint with each changing of thought."[6] As he gazes at the vast night sky, his light changes from ruby to sapphire, from topaz to emerald. Though there is no way of knowing fully the meaning of these changes, it seems to him that thoughts of the earthly life make the light burn red, while "thoughts of supernal being—of ghostly beauty and of ghostly bliss" kindle "ineffable rhythms of azure and of violet." To him, marveling at the fact that there are no white lights in all the visible, a Voice whispers:

> The White are of the Altitudes. By the blending of the billions they are
> made. Thy part is to help to their kindling. Even as the color of thy
> burning, so is the worth of thee. For a moment only is thy quickening;
> yet the light of thy pulsing lives on: by thy thought, in that shining mo-
> ment, thou becomest a Maker of Gods.

Might we not say that the color blue merging into the white is really
the color of his "burning"? That is because blue is symbolic of his
existential mode. To trace the process of his color symbolism is, in fact,
to follow his total evolution from its depth to its altitude. This seems
the best way of understanding the spirit of Hearn.

Precisely when and where Hearn's color symbolism crystallized it
may be impossible to determine. His delight with the color blue, however, seems to have a history much longer than Dr. Gould suggests in
his assertion that Hearn's southward itinerary down the Mississippi
concurred with his growing interest in colors.[7] It is nevertheless true
that his "Ozias Midwinter" series, the first of which Dr. Gould cites
for illustration, bears out Hearn's rich response to the colors abundant
in nature. Indeed, it forms a sort of color symphony. Already on the
orchestral stage of nature, the color blue tends to monopolize all the
parts of the violin, first and second, and is accompanied by the sky, as in
"the blue of the sky," "the sky-blue," "the Northern sky blue," and the
like. In the first despatch he wrote:

> Then the day broke quietly and slowly,—a day too vast for a rapid dawn,
> —a day that seemed deep as Space. I thought our Northern sky narrow
> and cramped as a vaulted church-roof beside that sky,—a sky so softly
> beautiful, so purely clear in its immensity, that it made one dream of the
> tenderness of a woman's eyes made infinite.[8]

Hearn's contrast between a vaulted church-roof and the sky, together
with that between the Northern and the Southern sky, accentuates his
obviously pantheistic tendency. His reference to femininity, too, already suggests his course. Although no color is specified, all these factors
tempt us to imagine the keynote of his blue symphony.

From this time on the color blue recurs in his writings, pantheistic
or aesthetic, until it becomes an overall symbol for everything natural
and spiritual, always associated with heaven, eternity, and the infinite,
as in "It is as though one might wish to wander through blue deeps of
eternity to reach a rosy paradise in some far-sparkling world," in his
editorial, "Spring Fever Fancies." [9] At last there comes a distinct turn
in his color symbolism. In 1884, while vacationing in Grande Isle,
Hearn wrote to Page Baker:

I'd like to melt into the water, and move with it lazily,—tumbling sleepily on the lukewarm sand under big lazy moons;—or become a half-conscious fish to be assimilated by the irresistible stomach of a man-of-war bird. To become a part of the infinite laziness of a man-of-war bird would delight me. Still better to become a cloud floating in the Eternal Blue Ghost and only draw my breath at long, long intervals, so enormously lazy have I been.[10]

The sea is an inseparable half of the sky-sea pair; it is a mobile symbol of the sky. In this poetic exclamation Hearn's pantheistic aspiration becomes immediate; beneath his jovial tone there is a momentary sense of exhilaration. Through union with the "Eternal Blue Ghost," self-annihilation becomes identical with self-emancipation and self-expansion.

But what is the Blue Ghost? How should we account for the sudden apparition looming mysteriously and luminously before his vision? An *Item* editorial of 1879, "The Secrets of the Infinite," seems convenient to begin with, in our attempt to answer these questions. In it Hearn first compares the modern scientific efforts to probe into the mystery of the universe to those of Egyptian neophytes who lifted the last veil of Isis. As Hearn sees it, "the last folds of the Veil" are symbolic of "the deeper-lying laws," or, "the Holy of Holies." Although Hearn regards "the Veil" as an emblem of the infinite or its inscrutability, there is no use of color, say blue, the color which we might expect to see.[11] Another article of 1881, "The Sexual Idea in French Literature," is a little more helpful on two counts: first, the Eternal Feminine is related to "a feminine Brahma"; and second, the term "Soul of the World" is then introduced in connection with Michelet.[12] This term suggests the Hindu concept of the Universal Soul, as suggested in "a feminine Brahma." Its possible correlation, however, is pointed out more positively in a third article, Hearn's obituary on Emerson. Undoubtedly Hearn had in mind Emerson's "Over-Soul," when he mentioned the thinker's belief in "the kindred of all souls with the Universal Soul." Emerson's philosophy, Hearn pointed out, represents an equally pantheistic tendency, "leading us to believe in the union of our own being with the All-being, and to regard death only as a Nirvana for the individual mind."[13]

All this should indicate that the term "the Blue Ghost" is the intensification of Hearn's early pantheism, augmented by his interest in Hindu philosophy. Why the word "Ghost" instead of "Soul," then? In all likelihood, Hearn here intends to attempt his own version of the Holy Ghost, without sacrificing his associations with the color blue. With this in mind we may read Hearn's article, "Tinted Art," written shortly before his first Grande Isle vacation, a defense of the tinted art of the Greeks as contrasted with the modern white art. A "perfect white statue," he argued, would have seemed to the Greeks something ludicrous or "an unfinished model, a sketch half-made." While dreaming of luminosity, the Greeks were too human to imagine or robe their Olympian gods and goddesses in white, the color which would have seemed only "spectral, weird—perhaps even shocking." Modern art has emphasized colorlessness, namely white, symbolizing "the infinite and the formless." Hence our traditional notion of "beauty in perfect whiteness," which is in Hearn's view the reverse of the Greek practice. This transformation, Hearn believes, is due mainly to the spirit of Christianity. Once connected with our spiritual ideas and holy tradition, the color white has become "sacred as a tomb, awful as a ghost." "Sanctified by the speech of the prophets and their visions," he continues, "it has been applied to the raiment of angels, the robes of the blessed dead, even to that great Throne from the face of whose occupant 'the heavens and the earth fled away, and there was found no place for them.' " [14]

Hearn is quite right in relating the color white to Christianity; but he seems to miss one point, that in liturgical color symbolism white usually represents purity, rather than the infinite or "formless." We may wonder, too, what he would have made of the fact that blue is Mary's color, even though he was to come later to the same point by a tortuous route. Be that as it may, we do find that the link between the two words, "white" and "ghost," had been anticipated since his childhood. In "My Guardian Angel," the first of his autobiographical fragments, Hearn, looking back at his ghost-haunted early years, tells us that as a child he had the impression, possibly from the folklore associations with the word "ghost," that the Holy Ghost or Holy Spirit is "a *white* ghost" and would not make "faces at small people after dusk." [15]

Thus Hearn's coinage, "the Blue Ghost," is a curious mixture of various factors, personal and suprapersonal, Christian and pagan. In spite of his attempt to contrast the Blue Ghost with "a white ghost," and in spite of his attempt to parallel the Blue Ghost with the World Soul, Hearn is not free from an unmistakably Christian tone: "My dreams now," so he wrote to W. D. O'Connor in 1887, "are full of fantastic light—a Biblical light: and the World-Ghost, all blue, promises inspiration. Could we not celebrate the Blue Ghost's pentecost together?"[16] God, as he defined elsewhere, is "only the World Soul, the mighty and sweetest life of Nature, the great Blue Ghost, the Holy Ghost which fills planets and hearts with beauty."[17] There is little doubt that his pantheism is permeated with the Christian symbolism of the Holy Ghost. As he grew aware of the ultimate oneness of the multiple components of his Blue Ghost, its shadow appeared over and again, coloring all his writings.

Hearn's conversion to evolutionism, of which he wrote so enthusiastically in 1886, only fortified this aesthetic symbolism of blue. As in other cases, evolutional science enabled him to theorize about what he had perceived intuitively. As he admitted, it showed him "how to apply the little knowledge" he possessed. The result was his sublimation of the Blue Ghost, as is plain in his *Times-Democrat* editorial of 1887, "Colors and Emotions." The piece was occasioned by "The Human Color-Sense as the Organic Response to Natural Stimuli," a pamphlet by G. M. Gould and L. Webster Fox, in Hearn's view "a remarkable amplification" of the theories advanced in Grant Allen's *Physiological Aesthetics*. As for some correlation between the primary colors and the emotional states of man, Hearn observed that emotionally those primary colors come in the order of red, yellow, green, and blue. As he explained, red, the color of blood, is the most emotional color, being symbolic of violence and passion; yellow, the color of the sun, is the color of life; green, the color of labor; and finally blue, the color of "the faraway sky," is also the color "most mysterious and holy—always associated with those high phenomena of heaven which first inspired wonder and fear of the Unknown." Blue is therefore "still the least violent, the most agreeable to the artistic sense." Then he concluded:

> Blue has always been, since man commenced to think—associated with his spiritual sense—his idea of many gods or of One—his hopes of a second life—his faith, his good purposes, his perception of duty. Still, all who pray turn their faces toward the eternal azure. And with the modern expansion of the Idea of God, as with the modern expansion of the Idea of the Universe, the violet gulf of space ever seems more mystical— its pure color more and more divine, and appeals to us as the color of the Unknowable—the color of the Holy of Holies.[18]

Here blue stands for the mystery of the indestructible Absolute, the Unknowable, which Spencer designated as the basis of reconciliation between faith and science. As Hearn later realized, it is also Brahman in the Hindu, or Nirvana in the Buddhist concept of the Absolute. In this process of apotheosis, too, there seems to be little conflict. The

Blue Ghost being, as he said in *Chita,* "something into which you would wish to melt utterly away," the process does correspond with the evolutionary theory of dissolution.[19] But once spiritualized, the process of dissolution ceases to be the evolutional mechanism; rather, it comes to signify the emancipation from the laws of nature, those of dissolution and evolution. It is in this sense similar to an eternal return to Nirvana. This must be what Hearn meant in his *Glimpses* by the following passage: ". . . and the remembrance of the sky, a sky spiritual as holiness, a sky with clouds ghost-pure and white as the light itself,—seeming, indeed, not clouds but dreams, or souls of Bodhisattvas about to melt forever into some blue Nirvana." [20] Thus Hearn's acceptance of evolutionism along with Buddhism seems to have affirmed his apotheosis of blue as a unifying symbol of the intellectual and the emotional. And probably in this process his "Ghost" finally tended to lose its anthropomorphic shadow in the mystery of blue itself.

It is only natural that Hearn came to the fullest theorization of his color symbolism in *Exotics and Retrospectives,* his attempt to seek a reconciliation between the East and the West in the meeting of Buddhism and evolutionism, more specifically the Buddhist doctrine of karma and the evolutional doctrine of organic memory. As the former indicates man's liberation from this world of illusion into space ("Exotics"), so does the latter accept its reality in terms of time ("Retrospectives"). The second part of the volume consists of ten essays or fantasies dealing with Hearn's "experiences in two hemispheres." These *"metaphysical idyls,"* as Hearn called them, are offered "merely as intimations of a truth incomparably less difficult to recognize than to define." [21] They fall into three groups: the first group, "First Impressions," "Beauty is Memory," and "Sadness in Beauty," is concerned with his theory of beauty as memory; the second group, with its five essays, is his attempt to investigate the physio-psychological basis of aesthetic feelings; and the third group, of the last two essays, is his aesthetic study of the ghostly.

The first group, already treated in connection with Hearn's aesthetic theory, will be dismissed from the present consideration. As for the second, it may be well to note Hearn's apparently deliberate arrangement of the five pieces: "Parfum de Jeunesse," "Azure Psychology," "A Serenade," "A Red Sunset," and "Frisson," which seems to indicate his primary concern to elucidate evolutionally the aesthetic bases of the human senses.[22] Here his effort is to delve, by way of the doctrine of organic memory, into the nature of the ghostly sense, as implied in the last group of essays or fantasies in "Retrospectives."

In these fantasies Hearn once again stresses the aesthetic symbolism of the color blue, along with red, so as to establish the basic correlation between sight and other functions. "Parfum de Jeunesse," a "revery about the riddle of the odor of youth," is a rather terse theorization. The pleasure of savory odor, Hearn says, is a pleasure of remembrance, namely "the magical appeal of a sensation to countless memories of countless lives." [23] Compared with this brevity, Hearn's treatment of the color sense in "Azure Psychology" and "A Red Sunset" is far more substantial in examining the fundamental contrariety between blue and red on the scale of the primary colors. As for red, Hearn first cites a tropical sunset as an example, and designates our emotional response to it as "a sense of distress like that which precedes a nightmare." As he qualifies it, red in this instance signifies crimson or scarlet, not its lower variations such as pink and rose. The question common to both Japan and other civilized societies, he writes, is how to explain the fact that a color insufferable to an adult may be delightful to a child. Hearn explains this phenomenon by organic memory. Since red suggests fire, passion, blood, and above all, violence, it excites children and savages not only emotionally but also aesthetically. With adults in civilized societies, on the other hand, the emotional is more or less subdued by the aesthetic feeling, which in turn is much subject to the modern abhorrence of violence, and anything related with it.[24]

"Azure Psychology" is a further amplification of Hearn's early American editorial, "Colors and Emotions," and yet it is more fully developed along the theory of organic memory.[25] In this essay Hearn first introduces his own impression that the color blue seems to be "the latest pure color developed in the evolution of flower and scale and feather." Among the primary colors, Hearn points out, blue alone, as "the color of heaven," has remained "a color pleasurable in its purest intensity to the vision of highly civilized races." While rejecting "large and opaque *solidity*," blue has always associated itself with the "ghostly and semitransparent." To Hearn's delight, this color sense is the same in Japan, "the land of perfect good taste in chromatics." With all the individual emotional variations it creates, the color blue evokes "in the *general* mind one common quality of pleasurable feeling"—"a tone of emotional activity unmistakably related to the higher zones of sentiency and of imagination," as vast as cosmic emotion. In order to explain the symbolism of blue as "divine," "pantheistic," and "ethical," he suggests, we might possibly refer to the evolutional interpretation, that the emotion should owe its origin to the total accumulation of the "sensuous race-experience of blue skies," transmuted to each of us in organic memory, an experience "vastly older than the religious idea" itself. Hearn does not reject this speculation; but he goes further to venture his own: *"All moral pulsations in the wave of inherited feeling which responds to the impression of blue, belong only to the beautiful and tender aspects of faith."* Thus the vision of blue, he concludes, is "spiritual, in the fullest ethical meaning of the word." As symbolic of the "everlasting Peace," it suggests something of "all human longing for all the Paradises ever imagined," "of all preëxistent trust in the promise of reunion after death," and "of all expired dreams of unending youth and bliss." In a word, it suggests "something of all the aspirations of the ancient faiths" and "the power of the vanished gods," and "the passion and the beauty of all the prayer ever uttered by lips of man." Especially from *"the beautiful and tender aspects of faith,"* it is now clear that Hearn regards the color blue as representative of the non-theoretical or rather pre-theoretical basis of any faith, that is, its emotional, aesthetic, mystical, intuitive, and all-unifying core, the spirit of all great religions which alone makes man a religious being far beyond his multitudinous warring credos and churches.

Hearn's emphasis on the femininity underlying human psychical experiences may certainly tempt us to dismiss this as the symptom of his peculiar mentality. Although there is some truth in this reaction, we should not allow ourselves to overlook a more important fact, that with Hearn the personal experience always becomes the basis of the theoretical speculation sublimating it to the superpersonal. With this in mind let us examine the rest of his "Retrospectives." "A Serenade," a psychological study of hearing, is a revery about the sweetness of the tropical melody. As in his color study, Hearn attempts to explain the mystery of his sensation in terms of the general theory, and then disentangles the bundles of reviving memories of the dead. A sudden revelation, that the whole spell of the melody was "supremely and uniquely *feminine,*" convinces him that "the primal source of all human tenderness has been the Eternal Feminine." But how is it possible to explain the fact that man could compose the melody "uttering only the soul of woman"? To this Hearn offers his answer: *"Every mortal man has been many millions of times a woman."* "Undoubtedly," he further speculates, "in either sex survives the sum of the feelings and of the memories of both. But some rare experience may appeal at times to the feminine element of personality alone,—to one half only of the phantom-world of Self,—leaving the other hemisphere dormant and unillumined." [26]

Hearn's obsession with the feminine in organic memory dominates his next study. The title, "Frisson," comes from the unexplainable word which he fondly used all his life, with a meaning drawn from his own experience rather than from his poetic association with the Gautier-Baudelairean term, *"frisson nouveau."* Hearn rejects all purely categorical theories of the *frisson* such as the thrill of a human touch and the thrill of pleasure. Like Alexander Bain, he regards the phenomenon as "electric" or "magnetic," and as a most perplexing example he cites the phenomenon of love at first sight. An enigmatic attraction such as this, Hearn says, "depends upon an inherited individual susceptibility to special qualities of feminine influence, and subjectively represents a kind of superindividual recognition,—a sudden wakening of that inherited composite memory which is more commonly called 'passional affinity.'" This, according to Hearn, should suggest "something corresponding to an inherited ideal within himself, previously latent, but suddenly lighted and defined by result of that visual impression." [27]

The same emphasis on the feminine aspect of our psychical inheritance can be found in "Vespertina Cognitio," an account of the ghostly nightmare Hearn himself experienced in the West Indies. The cause itself, once uncovered, is but "the cracking of the floor" at a Creole house where he and his half-breed guide Louis happened to take shelter. The point of the story is that both Hearn and his servant simultaneously saw the apparition, though they visualized it differently. What the guide saw in his nightmare was "a familiar creation of West Indian superstition—probably of African origin," whereas the shape Hearn saw was a childhood phantom nourished by "a certain horrible Celtic story." Hearn describes the moment of the apparition: "Gradually then, and without sound, the locked door opened; and the Thing entered, bending as it came,—a thing robed,—feminine, reaching to the roof,—not to be looked at." Louis' account is: *"Fenm-là?* . . . That Woman? . . . Tall, tall—high like this room, that Zombi. When She came the floor cracked. I heard—I saw." Instead of going further, Hearn then turns to ruminate on what he believes is the evolutional origin of nightmare in general. The clue has already presented itself in the fact that the femininity of the apparition, which is indeed stranger than the coincidence, is common to the whole of humanity, or more strictly its masculine half, regardless of varying race experience.[28]

Now we are with the last piece, "The Eternal Haunter." [29] Among a set of Tokyo color prints, studies of all sorts of Far Eastern specters, one piece by Chikanobu bestirs Hearn's fancy. The lovely girl-figure in the picture is neither "some Psyche of the most Eastern East" nor "the personification of any season" nor a dream girl who haunts "the slumbers of Far-Eastern youth." The falling cherry-flowers are "passing *through* her form," and the folds of her robe, below, melt "into blue faint mist." Who is she? What is she? She is a tree spirit, the spirit of the cherry tree. "Only in the twilight of morning or of evening She appears, gliding about her tree;—and whoever sees her must love her. But, if approached, she vanishes back into the trunk, like a vapor absorbed." What is "the use of drawing the Impossible"? In reply to this question Hearn defends the vision of all the poets. "The Impossible," he writes, "may not be naked truth; but I think that it is usually truth,—masked and veiled, perhaps, but eternal." It is for this reason that every man is haunted by ghosts. We are asked whether we have seen this haunter in dreams or her presence when "boyhood begins to ripen into youth." This glimpse of the haunter, ever returning but never remaining, leads us to "wander over the world in search of somebody like her." "Ancient her beauty as the heart of man,—yet ever waxing fairer, forever remaining young." She has always been loved but untouchable, deceiving but adored, undescribable but only worshipped, always sought after but never clasped. Then follows Hearn's poetry:

But who is she?—What is she? . . . Ah! that is what I wanted you to ask. Well, she has never had a name; but I shall call her a tree spirit.

The Japanese say that you can exorcise a tree spirit,—if you are cruel enough to do it,—simply by cutting down her tree.

But you cannot exorcise the Spirit of whom I speak,—nor ever cut down her tree.

For her tree is the measureless, timeless, billion-branching Tree of Life,—even the World-Tree, Yggdrasil, whose roots are in Night and Death, whose head is above the Gods.

Seek to woo her—she is Echo. Seek to clasp her—she is Shadow. But her smile will haunt you into the hour of dissolution and beyond—through numberless lives to come.

And never will you return her smile—never, because of that which it awakens within you—the pain that you cannot understand.

And never, never shall you win to her—because she is the phantom light of long-expired suns—because she was shaped by the beating of infinite millions of hearts that are dust—because her witchery was made in the endless ebb and flow of the visions and hopes of youth, through countless forgotten cycles of your own incalculable past.

This search for the Impossible ensures man an eternal youth. It was Poe indeed who designated this human aspiration for the Impossible as "the desire of the moth for the star," and believed our sense of the "Supernal Beauty" to be an "immortal instinct, deep within the spirit of man." [30] Because of his evolutional doctrine of organic memory, Hearn was able to go beyond Poe and identify the haunter as a creation of "the beating of infinite millions of hearts that are dust."

At first glance the Eternal Haunter may appear identical with the Eternal Feminine. As we remember, Hearn's theory of the Eternal Feminine was that such a feminine personification of man's metaphysical rage for the Impossible is characteristic of the Western mentality. His repeated emphasis on the feminine in the psychical inheritance, such as we have observed all through his "Retrospectives," seems to affirm the point beyond doubt. "Of the Eternal Feminine," it is true, could have been written by another scholar, whereas "The Eternal Haunter" is something created out of a poet's vision. Indeed, there is a world of difference between the Eternal Feminine and the Eternal Haunter. As we know from his modest preface to *Exotics and Retrospectives,* Hearn offered these pieces as intimations of a truth incomparably less difficult to recognize than to define. As a poet of deep feeling he could best utilize his own experiences in two hemispheres as the basis of his metaphysical exploration. Having crossed many realms within man, physiological, psychological, aesthetic, and religious, his quest became also a quest of human psyche. In exploring the psychical world, Hearn could expand the implication of the Eternal Feminine to its limits and discover within its most profound meaning, the meaning of Goethe's words, "Das Ewig-Weibliche/ Zieht uns hinan." This is as far as he could come in pursuing his own symbolism of the color blue. It was here, surprisingly enough, that Hearn saw the meeting of the East and the West, too, as implied in his experiences in both hemispheres, and more specifically in his recognition of the common meaning that the tree spirit should have to these two worlds. In this sense the Eternal Haunter, Hearn came to see, is truly symbolic of man's, not merely the Western man's, way to the Ultimate, a way of man's unitive knowledge of the divine.

As it is, Hearn's feminine symbolism may still invite the Freudian interpretation. Some may like to explain Hearn's ruling passion as simply a mother fixation, and as good evidence may refer to a passage from Hearn's letter to his brother James, whom he never met after their childhood. He mentioned their father briefly: "I suspect I do not love him. . . . The soul in me is not of him." But of their mother, he wrote:

> Whatever there is of good in me—and, I believe, whatever there is of deeper good in yourself—came from that dark race soul of which we know so little. My love of right, my hate of wrong, my admiration for what is beautiful or true, my capacity for faith in man or woman, my sensitiveness to artistic things, which gives me what ever little *success I have*—even that language-power whose physical sign is in the large eyes of both of us—came from Her.[31]

Such was his love for the woman who left her children behind to return home to the Mediterranean, and was never heard from again.[32] True, many of his works suggest something of this mother fixation: the loss of mother, a theme common to all his romances, *Chita, Youma,* and "Karma"; and also the spectral love theme which virtually weaves the warp and woof of all his twice-told legends, to name just two examples. What Hearn's critics usually fail to note, however, is the fact that the manifestation extends beyond the personal realm. Compared with the above passage, another one from "My Guardian Angel," the first of Hearn's autobiographical fragments, suggests much more:

> To the wall of the room in which I slept there was suspended a Greek icon,—a miniature painting in oil of the Virgin and Child, warmly coloured, and protected by a casing of fine metal that left exposed only the olive-brown faces and hands and feet of the figures. But I fancied that the brown Virgin represented my mother—whom I had almost completely forgotten—and the large-eyed Child, myself.[33]

In this piece, intended to create the poetry and truth of his life, Hearn's search for a mother image becomes as symbolic as his reference to the Eternal Haunter as "the beautiful shape bending above your rest," the pattern which recurs through all his legends dealing with the spectral love theme. Here the Eternal Haunter, losing its sex connotation, comes to signify motherhood, a symbol of life creation.

Here, Hearn reached the ultimate expansion of the idea he glimpsed in his essay, "Of the Eternal Feminine." There he remarked that evolutionism has enormously enhanced our notion of character values, tending toward "the highest possible spiritualization of the ideal of woman."[34] It was then a mere suggestion, which was to serve as the springboard for his further speculation. In reply to Chamberlain's question regarding this evolutional idealization of woman, Hearn theorized on the essential goodness of woman's heart. Evolutionism alone, he pointed out, could account for the "mother-soul" inherent in a sweet young girl, by way of "the sacrifices, and the love, and the sense of goodness acquired by countless millions of mothers." Of the symbolic significance of this "mother-soul" in human evolution, Hearn wrote:

> Here is a woman, for example, who is good, sweet, beautiful. Since the being [beginning] of the world, all life, all humanity, all progress has been working against evil and death in one line. The end of the line only is visible. It is that girl. She represents the supreme effort. But she is a creator. Her place is to continue the infinite work of the dead. He who weds her has an awful responsibility both to the dead and to the unborn. To the dead, if he should mar their work. To the future, if he plant in that bosom a life incapable of continuing the progress of the past.[35]

As he carefully qualifies, Hearn speaks "from the masculine point of view" here. He suspects that even in the ideal man there is no such divinity as we can glimpse in the perfect woman. It is to her rather than to him that "soul-things," such as devotion, mercy, pity, infinite love, and tenderness, belong. Granted that the man is superior morally as well as physically, and that the woman never can be his equal for physiological reasons, says Hearn, ". . . *it is only the woman who really sees the man,*" and "it is only for her that he takes off his armour and mask." [36]

Singularly enough, the East is at one with the West here. Hearn was right in speaking of "feminine Brahma" or "blue Nirvana," "feminine" and "blue" being interchangeable. In this connection, we should remember that what is represented by Tao, Jen, Nirvana, and Brahman, is, according to F. S. C. Northrop, often referred to throughout all Oriental religions, as the female principle. In *The Meeting of East and West,* he quotes from Lao Tzu: "The Spirit of a Valley is to be undying./ It is what is called 'The Original Female,'/ And the Doorway of the Original Female is called/ 'the root from which heaven and earth sprang.'" [37] The "Original Female" here cannot be confounded with a man-to-woman sexualism; rather it signifies the original sex, or the originator of sex. This larger and deeper concept of love as the female principle, or as the divine motherhood, must be what Hearn finally reached in "The Eternal Haunter" by way of "Of the Eternal Feminine." The point will be made more clear if we note the coincidence between Hearn's emphasis on the "Tree of Life," and the "World-Tree," and the phrase from Lao Tzu, "the root from which heaven and earth sprang." And the West and the East are agreed as to what this tree signifies, the divine creativity of the love that is the source of life.[38]

In proportion to our concept of this female principle, love also enlarges itself far beyond the limits of sex. That Hearn regarded love as what motherhood symbolizes is plain enough in his definition of the perfect woman with such divine attributes as devotion, mercy, pity, infinite love, tenderness, etc. In his essay, "Revery," he wrote:

It has been said that men fear death much as the child cries at entering the world, being unable to know what loving hands are waiting to receive it. Certainly this comparison will not bear scientific examination. But as a happy fancy it is beautiful, even for those to whom it can make no religious appeal whatever—those who must believe that the individual mind dissolves with the body, and that an eternal continuance of personality could only prove an eternal misfortune. It is beautiful, I think, because it suggests, in so intimate a way, the hope that to larger knowledge the Absolute will reveal itself as mother-love made infinite. The imagining is Oriental rather than Occidental; yet it accords with a sentiment vaguely defined in most of our Western creeds. Through ancient grim conceptions of the Absolute as Father, there has gradually been infused some later and brighter dream of infinite tenderness—some all-transfiguring hope created by the memory of Woman as Mother; and the more that races evolve toward higher things, the more Feminine becomes their idea of a God.

Conversely, this suggestion must remind even the least believing that we know of nothing else, in all the range of human experience, so sacred as mother-love—nothing so well deserving the name of divine. Mother-love alone could have enabled the delicate life of thought to unfold and to endure upon the rind of this wretched little planet: only through that supreme unselfishness could the nobler emotions ever have found strength to blossom in the brain of man;—only by help of mother-love could the higher forms of trust in the Unseen ever have been called into existence.[39]

This distinction between motherhood and fatherhood, expressed, on a personal level, in the letter to his brother, James, has become an integral part of Hearn's thought. In his last book, *The Romance of the Milky Way,* two pieces, "The Romance of the Milky Way" and " 'Ultimate Questions,' " seem to mark the climax of this contrast between the maternal and the paternal. Retelling in the former the famous Far Eastern legend, Hearn depicts what every man dreams of as "a love unchanging, immortal,—forever yearning and forever young, and forever left unsatisfied by the paternal wisdom of the gods." [40] The paternal wisdom, Hearn implies, is not love but righteousness, not mercy but justice. To it "soul-things" never belong because the paternal wisdom is based on law, ultimately. It represents the realm where reason is supreme. In spite of his reverence for Spencer, and in spite of his acceptance of evolutionism, Hearn admits his dissatisfaction with the master's "purely scientific position," and asks: "But how do *you* feel in regard to the prospect of personal dissolution?" In Spencer's essay, "Ultimate Questions," Hearn attempts to search for his master's personal answers to the ultimate questions which profoundly disturb the minds of those unable to "accept the creed of Christendom." Spencer, Hearn points out, has plainly declared that "the human intellect, as at present constituted, can offer no solution." His mind "confessed itself, before the Riddle of Existence, scarcely less helpless than the mind of a child." [41] Hearn realizes that there is a world between him and his avowed master, for he can now go further than Spencer to seek the answers in religion. The implication is clear: As science is, to Hearn, symbolic of the paternal wisdom, so religion is symbolic of the maternal wisdom. When Hearn says in "Revery" that this mode of imagining is "Oriental rather than Occidental," that is simply because the East has always placed prime emphasis on the mystical rather than the doctrinal component of religion.

Yet, Hearn would not merely have us see the antithesis between the paternal wisdom and the maternal wisdom, the father love and the mother love; he simply points to the inadequacy of the former alone, in man's attempt to solve that riddle of existence. "I confess," Hearn writes in *Kokoro* "to being one of those who believe that the human heart, even in the history of a race, may be worth infinitely more than the human intellect, and that it will sooner or later prove itself infinitely better able to answer all the cruel enigmas of the Sphinx of Life." [42] In asserting the primacy of the human heart, the maternal wisdom, and the mother love, Hearn is really concerned with restoring the divine femininity to the Holy Ghost as unity of Father and Son, and thereby perfecting the meaning of the Trinity. Only in the mother love can man find the key of knowledge, a knowledge of God. Thus this mother love, so poetically rhapsodized in "The Eternal Haunter," seems to suggest man's dream of the Tree of Life by the river of the Water of Life —in the Garden of Eden. As the Tree of Knowledge marks his exile therefrom, so should the Tree of Life complete the pilgrimage of redemption and salvation that is the meaning of his existence.

Hearn's attempt here is more than a defense of the emotional, the aesthetic, and the human heart against the universal trend to overprize the rational, the theoretical, and human intellect. It is an attempt to restore human values to their proper places, a quest of the unity and wholeness of life in a world of disconcerting multiplicity. This knowledge of unity comes only through our wish *"to become,"* not through our wish *"to have,"* as Hearn said in his prose poem, "Of Moon-Desire." This aesthetic and fundamentally mystical approach to the Ultimate is summed up more symbolically in his favorite fable of Salmacis and Hermaphroditus. "The beauty," he once wrote, "is really in that psychic truth of the desire to melt into another being." [43] Indeed the fable reveals the nature of Hearn's mode of cognition and approach and, at the same time, suggests much more. First, it insists on restoring man's most basic way of knowledge to its original dignity against the menace of the overweening rationalism which alone may stifle his instinct to be a whole being. The desire to know is not sufficient in itself; it must be initiated and completed with the desire to be, because that desire alone can satiate man athirst for God. Second, the fable of Salmacis and Hermaphroditus suggests the goal of man, to be complete and whole. Androgyny, as implied in the fable, may indicate the real meaning of Hearn's emphasis on the originator of sex. From this standpoint he also defined the poet as "a man who is half a woman." [44] In his essay, "Suggestion," Hearn again expounded this completeness as man's ideal:

A man or a woman is scarcely more than half-a-being,—because in our present imperfect state either sex can be evolved only at the cost of the other. In the mental and the physical composition of every man, there is undeveloped woman; and in the composition of every woman there is undeveloped man. But a being complete would be both perfect man and perfect woman, possessing the highest faculties of both sexes, with the weakness of neither. Some humanity higher than our own,—in other worlds,—might be thus evolved.[45]

Here it may be well to remember the Far Eastern belief that man attains the highest state when *yin* and *yang,* namely the feminine and the masculine, are in harmony. It is no mechanical complement, but the fulfillment or completion of man's potentiality. Whatever difference we may make between Western personalism and Eastern impersonalism, the West and the East are at one over the spiritual goal of man.

Criticism cannot be more superficial than when it complains that Hearn betrayed himself and his own world only to imbibe that of others. His revolt was a serious warning against the divided man and world, not a betrayal by any means. It was his plea for healing the awful division characteristic of modern man and his world. When he envisioned "a perfect sphere" in the integration of the West and the East, Hearn was really concerned to see man in the harmony of the masculine and the feminine. Man, the microcosm, is divided as is the world, the macrocosm. The boundary between the East and the West is symbolic of the division, and because Hearn had faith in man he believed a fusion was possible. His attempt was a meaningful one, even a noble one, for to perfect the microcosm after the fashion of the macrocosm is the true meaning of self-discovery, an ideal common to the East and the West. In consecrating his existence to its realization Hearn proved in his own way that man is fundamentally an artist ever dreaming of completion of his only material—his life.

Conclusion

A quarter of a century after Hearn's death there appeared Matthew Josephson's provocative essay, "An Enemy of the West: Lafcadio Hearn." Whatever the writer's intention, he summed up logically the hostile accusations invariably echoing the oracular denouncement of Dr. Gould. In this verdict on Hearn the artist and the man, Josephson itemizes his charge: As a dreamer of romance in America's Gilded Age, Lafcadio Hearn is "a belated romanticist living for his natural emotions, pursuing always, in the face of everything, his scandalous, sensational existence." This, Josephson believes, is evidenced in Hearn's life, a record registering his "great pattern of flight—toward the blue Gulf, to the tropical islands, ultimately to the Far East":

> . . . we have no single masterpiece, no Complete Works, but their torso: fragments that compose a character—a character of the sinful, rebellious type met with in older literatures—who flourishes secretly and stubbornly for a time in the inhospitable atmosphere of America's Gilded Age, and offers himself always in the ornate over-colored and rhythmic prose of the romantics whom he adores and emulates.

All in all, Hearn was "a minor artist; he contributed no invention, no energizing principle of form, that could give his work a significant order and force."[1] This is one judgment: As an artist Hearn is a failure; and as a man he is worse because he is an "Enemy of the West." On the other hand, Paul Elmer More rejected Josephson's verdict, while admitting that there is "something almost romantic" in Hearn's life as in his books. Of Hearn's significance as the meeting of three traditions, the religious instinct of India, the aesthetic sense of Japan, and the interpreting spirit of Western science, More wrote:

> . . . these three traditions (Hindu, Japanese, and European) are fused by the peculair sympathies of his mind into one rich and novel compound,— a compound so rare as to have introduced into it a psychological sensa-

tion unknown before. More than any other recent author, he has added a new thrill to our intellectual experience.[2]

Undoubtedly Josephson bases his verdict on what he knows of Hearn's career, not the whole but only a fraction of it, the American period of his career, especially those days of his flamboyant, romantic revolt. More concerns himself primarily with Hearn's Japanese years, the period of his maturity. Yet, the disparity of opinion between the two is not due to this alone. Josephson's judgment, compared with More's, indicates the critical failure likely to occur when one sees an artist's work only in terms of the surface of his life. Josephson is unable to see Hearn in the light of his total growth, in the light of the intensity, consistency, and largeness of his growth. But every artist demands that he be judged in his own terms, and we must comply with this demand. Only then can we determine what he has added to our tradition, what we really owe to him. If an artist has contributed "a new thrill to our intellectual experience," he has a claim on us. Lafcadio Hearn, I believe, is such an artist.

With this guiding principle in mind I have undertaken my study of him and have subjected to scrutiny those aspects of his achievement which I believe to be of vital importance for understanding his art and thought. As my investigation reveals, there are places where Hearn erred and failed. He erred in his wild dream of "English in splendid Latin attire," and in his pathetic effort to create romance, his kind of fiction. But there are more places where he achieved distinction, a distinction far greater and more lasting than he himself intended and desired. These are his twice-told tales, his travel literature, his commitment to major issues of American literature during the eighties, his defense of idealism against naturalism, his double strategy in literary study, his aesthetics of organic memory, and his proposal for a world literature based on humanity. Also there are his attempts to present Japan with her two phases, his re-evaluation of Western passionalism, his criticism of Western individualism, his labor to reconcile science and faith in terms of evolutionism and Buddhism, and his final plea for integration of the West and the East on the basis of man as a whole being.

In art all his efforts, beginning with translations of many levels, are consummated in his travel books. In criticism his critical perception and his sense of literary values made possible his Japanese lectures; and his belief in idealism provided his theory of literature with its necessary foundation. In philosophy his enquiry into the cultural ideals of the

West, undertaken for his personal need, led him across some questions of great import to recognizing the urgency of reconstructing our divided world and selves into "a perfect sphere." His art confronts his criticism, and both merge with his philosophy. The intensity, consistency, and integrity with which this growth has come about is all the more remarkable if we remember Hearn's point of departure as worshipper of "the Odd, the Queer, the Strange, the Exotic, the Monstrous." In the mature Hearn there is little trace of his early romantic Bohemian pose. What we find in the mature Hearn are instead the classical qualities called balance and sanity.

Once Hearn is restored in his entirety and viewed in his own terms, there is little difficulty in perceiving that his career was one of maturation. The real difficulty arises, however, as soon as we try to accommodate him within the context of literary history and thereby determine his possible claims to a place in an already established literary pantheon. The reason for this is obvious. To be well received in this hierarchy, where "greats" and "majors" reign supreme, one must either prove some "connections" or "influences" or establish himself first of all in poetry and fiction. Otherwise, he is bound to be sealed away in the class of "miscellaneous writers." Such has been Hearn's lot. What further complicates the matter is his identity. By birth he is both Greek and Anglo-Irish; by literary inclination he is rather French; by adoption he is Japanese; and at no time did he consider himself American. In spite of all this he was offered a place in American literature, but not without uncertainty. In our standard literary history of America, Hearn, a "deracinated" Bohemian, is consequently lumped together with Ambrose Bierce, Edgar Saltus, and James Huneker. His life record begins: "Lafcadio Hearn is not less completely the Bohemian for having remained a foreigner, a transient contributor to American literature. On his devious pilgrimage from the Old World toward the Orient, he spent more than twenty years in this country, and nearly all of his work encountered its audience here." And it ends: "He never escaped from what he had never found: himself. 'Ironically,' as Katherine Anne Porter points out, 'he became the interpreter between two civilizations equally alien to him.'"[3]

This view of Hearn is sympathetic, certainly. But it is too limited to stand up to Josephson's forthright charge; it is too narrow in perspective to support More's testimonial. Before it can be taken as a standard estimate of Hearn, this view needs considerable revision, as my investigation should suggest. For one reason or another, many Hearn critics have failed to take a total view of his career and his achievement. They have failed to recognize the importance of this simple fact, that at the beginning of his career Hearn figured in the tradition of American literature and then gradually went beyond national boundaries.

First of all, Hearn is entitled to a place in American literature at least on three counts: his active participation in the national forum of major literary issues of the 1880's; his many-sided involvement in Franco-American literary relations; and his contribution to American literary exoticism. First, as an artist-journalist Hearn not only familiarized himself with the contemporary situation of literary journalism but also sought to explore ways of raising its general standard above the national mean. An an artist-critic he defended the artistic potentialities of the Southern movement and also the local color movement. At the same time he did not remain blind to their possible pitfalls but made these known. While upholding catholic principles of art and exercising his cosmopolitan taste, he made a colorful addition to American literature by his romances, *Chita* and *Youma*. In dealing with the then rising realism Hearn more than once challenged the Olympian authority of Howells and in fact crossed swords with him over the doctrine of *vraisemblance,* which was in Hearn's opinion tantamount to confusion of life and art. Nor did he welcome aestheticism without chiding its intellectual paucity. Although his activities were limited to the South, although his voice was largely unheeded, it is unfair for us today to deny his share in the formation of literary opinion during that decade. Looking back at that significant moment in the history of modern American letters, we can hardly afford to ignore his critical opinions which are far from dated, owing to his insight into the question of artistic creation and his uncompromising quest for literary excellence.

Second, as an artistic translator Hearn helped in many ways to create an atmosphere hospitable to French writers like Gautier, Flaubert, Baudelaire, Daudet, Coppée, France, Loti, Bourget, and L'Isle-Adam. He also helped to shape the American response to Zola, Maupassant, and their naturalist followers, both because as a translator he demanded artistic competency and integrity from fellow translators, and because as a critic he countered Zola's scientific determinism with his own idealism. Even his admitted failure to create "English in splendid Latin attire" is no common failure in this sense; it has its own significance, when taken as an ambition to exact stylistic excellence, and also as an attempt to unify three traditions—English, American, French—of poetical prose, the romantic prose traditions of Blake, Coleridge, and De Quincey, of Poe, and of Bertrand, Nerval, and Baudelaire.

Third, Hearn extended the tradition of American literary exoticism in two directions, first toward the primitive tropics by his *Two Years in the French West Indies,* second toward the Orient by his *Stray Leaves, Some Chinese Ghosts,* and also his Japanese books. In this he aligned himself with the primitive tradition of young Melville, with the mythopoeic tradition of Irving and Hawthorne, and with the Orientalism of Emerson, Thoreau, and Whitman. In furthering America's passage to the East, especially, Hearn went well beyond the circle of American literature proper. His involvement with these three important literary situations and traditions may not necessarily prove that he is a major figure, but there is little doubt that he belongs legitimately to American literature.

While Hearn's early work is clearly part of American literature proper, his mature work goes beyond national limitation, though he never forsakes his own American and Western heritage. The question, then, is how and where to accommodate him and his output during his last period: Japanese studies, lectures, and philosophical writings. Hearn refuses to belong to either Japanese or American literature alone. But this can hardly justify our looking at him as an anomaly.

Future Hearn criticism, I believe, needs to look at Hearn with more catholic appreciation. The trend has already set in, as evident in Malcolm Cowley's recent estimate of Hearn's achievement, even though it has not come as far as one might expect. Of Hearn's volumes of criticism Mr. Cowley writes: "The volumes do not prove that Hearn was a great critic or that he always preferred the best to the second-best. What they do prove is that he was a great interpreter who, belonging to English literature, could still explain it as if he formed part of a Japanese audience." And with special emphasis on Hearn's retold legends among others, Mr. Cowley concludes: "I think it will be apparent that his folk tales are the most valuable part of [his work] and that he is the writer in our language who can best be compared with Hans Christian Andersen and the brothers Grimm." [4] As for the first point, Mr Cowley's distinction between "critic" and "interpreter" is neither clear nor convincing. How can Hearn be one without being the other? Nor is it necessary to insist on greatness for Hearn. Not discarding but simply modifying Mr. Cowley's opinion, I should like to call Hearn an interpretative critic, and a good one. As for the second point, I suspect that Mr. Cowley is right in appraising the ultimate significance of Hearn's legends. But there are still Hearn's philosophical observations on the cultural issues of the West and the East, and of man and the world at large. Would Mr. Cowley dismiss these writings on cultural philosophy as merely irrelevant and amateurish? What is disappointing about his otherwise perceptive and generous estimate is his reticence about Hearn's philosophical writings and his failure to tie them all together as an integral part of Hearn's total achievement.

The question, whether Hearn has a place in world literature and world culture, therefore, depends on our willingness to redefine Hearn's so-called exoticism in broader perspective, to expand its meaning to its limits, and to consider it primarily as a philosophical voyage, that is, representative of man's voyage of self-discovery. Few would deny that Hearn, encompassing the West and the East, carried out his literary exoticism on a grand scale; but this alone, I am aware, does not preclude the possibility of labeling his career that of an impressionistic and rootless cultural dilettante. To avoid this possibility I should like to call attention to one point where Hearn stands far apart from fellow literary exotics. To most literary exotics, exoticism usually signifies surrender to the charm or fascination of the unfamiliar. This kind of exoticism is not only superficial but also dangerous, because it often deprives them of their anchor, namely, their existential center; hence their chameleon-like cultural relativism, their intellectual bankruptcy, and their spiritual impasse. Hearn's exoticism, on the other hand, is more than literary; it is basically philosophical. To him it signifies discovery of the sameness of multi-colored world cultures. In exploring the East, not only its surface but also its foundation, Hearn could ascertain the oneness of humanity at its primitive core. And if he could repossess this primitive core without sacrificing his own intellectual dignity and spiritual heritage, that is because evolutional science and philosophical Buddhism as a pair of vehicles served well his precarious voyage across the world. It was in this way that Hearn achieved his own view of the world at large. In this regard, Yone Noguchi was right when he wrote of Hearn:

> To call him primitive, as one might wish to say of him, does not mean that he was undeveloped, but on the contrary, his soul was a thousand years old. Primitiveness was strength in him; and the wonder about him was how he succeeded in remaining primitive under such an age's intrusion of knowledge.[5]

In his thought, as in his life, Hearn suggests clearly the possibility of reintegrating divided modern man into one whole being, the very question that has come to occupy the major Western writers and thinkers in our century, such as Gide, Mann, Joyce, Lawrence, Eliot, and Jung. Hearn does not belong to the past alone; in posing this important, and singularly modern question and exemplifying one of its means of solution he is still much alive to us, and will remain so for many years to come. Thus considered, Hearn is no longer a minor exotic; he is undoubtedly a major exotic. And perhaps even no longer an exotic in the light of world culture.

Hearn's exoticism, redefined in this way, becomes everyman's. Here is the essence of Hearn's art that never tarnishes with the passage of time. Here is also the "something permanent" which Edmund Gosse found in Hearn's fame. Mr. Cowley is no exception when he is surprised to find that so much of Hearn has remained new and genuine, and when as a matter of fact, after comparing Hearn with many of his contemporaries, say Howells and Norris, he confesses that "Lafcadio Hearn at his best was independent of fashion and was writing for our time as much as his own." [6] Hearn's permanency, to which Gosse and Cowley, among many others, bear witness, is remarkable especially in view of his meager academic education and his lack of formal discipline. Whatever he acquired was through self-education, with no other guidance than his insatiable curiosity, versatile mind, and honest heart. As he himself admitted, he was not a scholar in any sense—in any field. As we all know, he was not a literary historian, nor a Japanologist, nor a Buddhist scholar, nor a systematic philosopher; nor was he even an artist of inventive imagination. It would be a serious mistake not to admit this and to try to present him as something that is not Hearn. At the same time we need not be apologetic about this fact. What we must remember is that with Hearn these weaknesses did not remain necessarily mere weaknesses; they acquired instead a positive quality. This point is quite true, paradoxical as it may be. Owing to the very inadequacy of his formal discipline, Hearn had no fear of making mistakes and maintained the naïve boldness vital for speculation. More often than not, it is true, he made mistakes, and ran to extremes, being unable to stay safe within the boundary clearly prescribed by rules of rigid discipline. He might have been led to complete disaster had he not been genuinely motivated by his own existential necessity and preserved sufficiently intact by his artistic instinct. He sought knowledge for the sake of transformation, not merely for the sake of information. If this mode of approach to knowledge as a way of life is eminently Oriental, it is also that of the artist—as representative of the whole man.

The secret of Hearn's permanent appeal lies in the fact that he always remained an artist whether he was assuming the role of a critic, a teacher, a traveler, or a man. Whatever role he might play, he was at heart an artist intent on completing the circle of his own existence. Few of us today can imitate or even understand his genuflection to Spencer; but in this sort of excessive response Hearn is one of many artists of like mentality. What is important is that it was the best way Hearn, not as a philosopher but as an artist, could absorb Spencer's "oceanic philosophy." What Hearn really needed was "suggestion," and that was sufficient food for his thought. For this reason, whenever he maldigested Spencer he remained a disciple parroting his master; and consequently his voice was often unconvincing. On the other hand, whenever he assimilated Spencer's philosophy, his comprehensive view of the universe, Hearn remained an artist, and consequently his voice was authentically his own with a ring of truth. Here it is well to recall Coleridge's words: ". . . deep thinking is attainable only by a man of deep feeling." When considering Hearn's seemingly blind acceptance of Spencer one must not exaggerate his intellectual limitations and thereby refuse to note what significant result it has actually brought out. It is far more important to recognize how imaginatively Hearn, seizing on Spencer's unitive view of time and space, came up with an aesthetics of organic memory which sheds much light on the aesthetic tradition of Poe, Baudelaire, and others; came up, indeed, with an insight into the human psychic structure, anticipating Jung, though without the latter's clinical apparatus; and also how imaginatively, by way of evolutionism and Buddhism, he not only penetrated into the mental foundation of Japan but also made a serious attempt to resolve the cultural contrast between the West and the East in terms of world integration.[7]

Hearn's great gift was soul sympathy, the secret of the artist as a translator. His life was a long, tortuous process of testing those many intimations every artist can utilize if he listens carefully. In order to remain faithful to the singular presentiments that were the dictates of his existence, Hearn set out to search for his own medium of utterance. When he accepted his failure in fiction he probably knew it was but an episode, no matter how painful, in the long search for his own medium. He was right in choosing translation as this medium and enlarging it as far as he possibly could. Out of his life-long search grew his twice-told legends, his critical writings, and his travel books; for these were his translations in the best and largest sense of the word—as a result of his attempt to recreate the body and the spirit, the essence of his given subject. In spite of his initial determination, translation became something more than only the first step to his literary career. Hearn's achievement is neither that of a creator nor an inventor; he was a translator, a discoverer. Hearn not only launched into his career as a translator but ironically completed it as a translator.[8] More strictly speaking, he was a rediscoverer of those old mysteries that are man's. Here is the ultimate significance of Hearn the man and the artist. Breaking through his narrow artificial cult of art, he voyaged further, to the point where it was possible to reconcile life and art once again.

All great art has "its source in the rich soil of sorrow," Hearn observes, and quotes in one of his Japanese lectures: "Who ne'er his bread in sorrow ate,—/Who ne'er the lonely midnight hours,/Weeping upon his bed has sat,—/He knows ye not, ye Heavenly powers."[9] To this quatrain of Goethe, Hearn would fondly refer as an expression of the poet's awareness of the intimacy between life and art. Like Goethe, Hearn saw both life and art "under the same sun," while rejecting their confusion. Art, he believed, must be created out of life; and in this sense art never can be an escape from life. Life is tragic because it is imperfect. He held that the pain of life is due to one's ignorance of this fact. The primary function of art is to complete life by making this clear.

As he himself professed, Hearn was a Romantic in that he accepted his innermost urge to experience life itself. "It is," said he of the ideal artist, "the man who has had to fight with the world's rough weather that can feel life to several dimensions."[10] His exoticism is but the manifestation of this courageous acceptance of existence. Because of it, not in spite of it, Hearn could both live and think in terms of his time and his world, and go beyond. If he is "a civilized nomad" as he called himself, wholly isolated from the historical context, it is simply because he lived the world anew in the midst of the cross-currents of the modern world. He was no mere mirror which reflected diverse trends; he determinedly sought their integration at the foundation where alone it is possible.

Convinced of the intimacy between life and art, Hearn could see the possibility of re-evaluating the relationship between man and the universe. Hence his attempt to unify the disconcerting multiplicities peculiar to modern man, as is evident in his labored union of various cultural elements, from North, South, East, and West. Once he asked: "Why must there always remain the width of a world between us?"[11] Kipling could simply say: "Oh, East is East, and West is West,/And never the twain shall meet," but Hearn could hardly accept such a position. The marriage of the West and the East was symbolic of his dream of "a perfect sphere." Hearn needed the East because he was a man of the West. To him, the West was only a half-world, and a man of the West was only a half-man. On this point many of his admirers and critics have erred. Dr. Gould, for instance, spoke of Hearn as essentially "an Oriental mind and heart, an exotic weed. . . . dropped by some migrating bird upon the strange crabbed soil of the crudest of Occidentalism." [12]

The contrast between the West and the East is, in Hearn's opinion, an allegory suggesting the necessity of enlarging man's inner world and perfecting it into unity. There is a singular parallel between two spheres, global and human. As the world can be one only with the union of the West and the East, man can be a whole being only with the ideal harmony of the male and the female, the human intellect and the human heart. In the spiritual marriage of these opposing principles lies the meaning of his beloved fable of Salmacis and Hermaphroditus. His faith in man as a whole being is the core of his thought. His version of world literature, world society, and world religion has its original inspiration in the ultimate perfection of man. It is his reaffirmation of man as microcosm and his universe as macrocosm. This points to the characteristic failure of even such a sympathetic critic as F. L. Pattee: "He [Hearn] obliterated his very self: he was neither Occidental nor Oriental. He died the loneliest death in the whole history of romanticism." [13] But the truth is that Hearn became simply a man, a representative man, by living in his life the whole history of man anew. When Hearn, parodying Darwinism, defined man as "an ape of gods," his intention undoubtedly was to liken man's potentiality to the perfect image of God.[14] If this ideal completion is the basis of Western individualism, it is nowise foreign to the East. In the *Great Learning* Confucius emphasized the complete development of the individual as the very foundation of the universal harmony: "From the Son of Heaven down to the mass of the people, all must consider the cultivation of the person the root of everything besides." Indeed, to be a citizen of the universe was the one life dream of Hearn even in his boyhood, when like so many children he gave his whimsical address as: "P. L. Hearn, Esq., Ushaw College, near Durham, England, Europe, Eastern [sic] Hemisphere, The Earth, Universe, Space, God." [15] With Hearn this dream survived through his life, as it rarely does for the rest of us.

Hearn's destiny led him over the world: the Mediterranean, Ireland,

England, France, America, the West Indies, and Japan. In circling the world he was incessantly haunted by the peace of the Heights. On the summit of Mt. Fuji he noted in the summer of 1897: ". . . there is a silence that I remember from West Indian days: the peace of High Places."[16] Doubtless he had in mind Mt. Pelée, which is the structural and thematic center of his *Two Years*. While gazing at the peak of St. John, on his winter journey across Canadian prairies in 1890, Hearn wrote:

> But still, over them all, shines the eternal white peace of that supreme peak,—growing ever taller to look down upon us,—to mock our feverish hurrying with the perpetual solemnity of its snowy rest. And watching it, there returns to me, with a sudden new strange pleasure, as of fancied revelation in slumber, the words:—"He maketh peace in His high places."[17]

Hearn dealt with the same topic in a fragment describing a youth's pilgrimage to "the place of the Vision" under the guidance of the Bodhisattva.[18] The mountain symbolism which recurs throughout his writings seems to indicate Hearn's vision of spiritual paradise, whether it be Nirvana or New Jerusalem. Thus his wanderlust comes to assume an entirely different meaning: it is a search for something higher and ultimate, and a pilgrimage toward the Absolute.

His was a soul in many ways more than usually handicapped. His was a life frustrated continuously as a result of his quest of certitude and peace. He was not unaware of personal limitations and flaws. His life and work, it seems to me, is a record of how succesfully one can overcome them. He described his method as learning "to take all possible advantages of his myopia—to utilize his physical disability to a good purpose."[19] With the imperfections common to us all, he fought all his life to make a virtue of necessity. His life is thus exemplary of what Wordsworth meant by "glorious gain." Turning flight into search, exile into pilgrimage, Hearn lived out his life on his own terms, as all his writings attest. When he strove to perfect life as art, his life itself tended to become an allegory of man's destiny.

Appendix

A
Sketch

Hearn's
Life
and
Works

I. *An Autobiographical Letter* (*written by Hearn to one of his early admirers*) *
Dear Mr. ___,

I have done so little, and am so painfully conscious of the imperfections of what I have done in a literary way, that I feel unworthy of the kindly attention you propose to give me.

I am not an American by birth, but a Greek. My father was an army physician,—Charles Brush [Bush] Hearn, surgeon-major in the 76th British Infantry. My father passed most of his life in India; but married in the Ionian Islands,— his regiment being stationed there during the English protectorate. My mother was a native of Cherigo;—I was born in Santa Maura, in 1850. I was educated partly in Ireland, partly in England, partly in France, and soon forgot my mother's language. After my father's death in India and a business-failure at home which swept away the fortune of relatives on whom my future depended, I came to the United States alone, at nineteen years of age. A good old English printer, named Henry Watkin, of Cincinnati, taught me the rudiments of his craft, and my first practical lessons in earning a living. After holding various situations as proof-reader, as subordinate mailing-clerk in a printing office, as a writer for weekly newspapers, I began my apprenticeship in journalism on the *Enquirer,* then controlled by Mr. John A. Cockerille, afterwards editor of New York *World.* Subsequently Mr. Murat Halstead employed me for several years on the *Commercial,* as reporter, and occasionally as travelling correspondent. I went South for the first time on a vacation-journey; but I left sleet and gloom to sail into the warmth and perfume of a Louisiana autumn-day,—into a blaze of violet and gold. The sharp contrast affected me as it has many another; I re-

* Quoted in *Harper's Weekly,* LXVIII (October 15, 1904), p. 1593.

solved never to go back North, and I had no reason to regret the decision. In New Orleans I obtained not only editorial work of a more agreeable sort, but work as a specialist in certain directions that enabled me to cultivate literary tastes I could not gratify without the greatest difficulty elsewhere.

Still, I had found time to study a little even while employed upon Western journals. It was during intervals of night-work on the Cincinnati *Commercial* that I attempted a translation of Théophile Gautier's most powerful short stories. Part of the MS. found a publisher some years after; it was issued by Worthington, under the title *One of Cleopatra's Nights* ("Une Nuit de Cléopâtre" being the original French title of the opening story of the collection).

The observation uttered by Baudelaire,—*Quel est celui de nous qui n'a pas, dans ses jours d'ambition, rêvé le miracle d'une prose poétique, musicale sans rhythme et sans rime,*—haunted me, and inspired me to attempt something in another direction, after having made various translations which never found a publisher because they never deserved it. Oriental literature had always had a strong charm for me; gradually, in the course of years, I had built up a tolerably extensive library of exotic poetry and legend; and while studying the singular beauties which one finds in these writings, I began to rewrite such of the myths as most impressed me in a style which represented an attempt at poetic prose. In this way I formed a collection of oddities, *Stray Leaves from Strange Literature.* I had only begun, however, to learn that good work requires care and time; my production bore a few evidences of hasty execution. But I found I had the power to please—this encouraged me. My next effort resulted in the production of another little volume of exotic stories, entitled *Chinese Ghosts.* (One of the stories it contains first appeared in *Harper's Bazar,* and reappeared with special permission.) This little book represents, I think, a much better effort in the direction of poetic prose, and much more serious study than *Stray Leaves.* I do not wish to appear as one proud of what he has done,—only as one full of hope regarding what he *will* do. With best regards,

Lafcadio Hearn

II. *Curriculum Vitae (communicated by Hearn to Waseda University in 1904)** Koidzumi Yakumo (Lafcadio Hearn), originally British subject. Born at Leucadia (Santa Maura), Ionian Islands, 1850. Brought up in Ireland, England, and Wales,—also for some time in France. Went to America in 1869. Lived as printer and journalist. Became eventually literary editor of New Orleans Newspaper. At New Orleans met Ichizo Hattori, Esq.,—then Commissioner at the New Orleans Exhibition, afterwards Governor of Hyogo Ken. From 1887 to 1889 in Martinique, French West Indies. Sent to Japan in 1890, by the publishers Harper Brothers. Obtained, through the goodwill of Mr. Hattori, then Vice-Minister of Education, a position as teacher of English in the Ordinary Middle School of Matsue, Idzumo. In the autumn of 1891 went to Kumamoto, and taught in the Fifth Higher Middle School until 1894. In 1894 went to Kobe, and acted for some time as editor of the *Kobe Chronicle.* In 1895 became a Japanese citizen. Called to

**Some New Letters and Writings of Lafcadio Hearn,* ed. Sanki Ichikawa (Tokyo, 1925), pp. 429–30.

lecture at the Tokyo Imperial University in 1896 and held the chair of English Literature as lecturer until 1903,—6 years and 7 months. Author of eleven books about Japan.

III. *A Supplementary Chronology*

(Based on the Hearn studies by R. Tanabe, E. L. Tinker, and O. W. Frost.)

The European Period (1850–69)

1850	Patrick Lafcadio Hearn born June 27, on the Isle of Santa Maura (Leucadia), off the west coast of Greece, as second child of Charles Bush Hearn and Rosa Cassimati, a native Ionian.
1852–63	In Dublin, Ireland. Stays most of the time with his great-aunt, Mrs. Sarah Brenane. Mother returns to her native country in the summer of 1854. Later at the Petit Séminaire, a Roman Catholic school, at Yvetot, France.
1863–68	At St. Cuthbert's College, a Roman Catholic school, Ushaw, near Durham, England. His left eye seriously injured in a game of "Giant's Stride." Father dies on the S. S. *Mula,* buried at sea on his return voyage from India.
1868–69	For some time as a paying guest at the house of Catherine Delaney in London, Mrs. Brenane's ex-parlor-maid.

The American Period (1869–87)

1869	Arrives in Cincinnati, Ohio, via New York.
1872–75	On the Cincinnati *Enquirer.*
1875–77	On the Cincinnati *Commercial.*
1877	Arrives in New Orleans, La.
1878–81	Associate Editor of the *Item* (June 1878–December 1881). Contributor to the *Democrat.*
1881–87	Editorial Staff of the *Times-Democrat.*
1882	*One of Cleopatra's Nights.*
1884	*Stray Leaves from Strange Literature.* Vacations at Grande Isle, La.
1885	*Gombo Zhèbes,* and *La Cuisine Créole.* Takes a spring trip to Florida with Charlie Johnson of Cincinnati.
1886	Vacations again at Grande Isle, La.
1887	*Some Chinese Ghosts.*

The West Indian Period (1887–89)

1887	New York City (June–July). First West Indian trip (July–September). New York and Metuchen, N.J. (September–October).
1887–89	In Martinique, the French West Indies.
1889	*Chita.* Stays at Dr. George Gould's in Philadelphia (May–October).
1890	*The Crime of Sylvestre Bonnard,* translation of Anatole France. *Two Years in the French West Indies. Youma.* "Karma" (*Lippincott's Magazine,* May). Leaves New York for Montreal with Charles Weldon, a *Harper's* artist (March). After a trans-Canadian journey, arrives in Vancouver, sailing thence on the S. S. *Abyssinia.*

The Japanese Period (1890–1904)

1890   Arrives in Yokohama (April). In Matsue as teacher of English in the Ordinary Middle School (September).

1891   Marries Setsu Koizumi (age 22) probably in January.
Moves to Kumamoto and teaches at the Fifth Higher Middle School (November 1891–October 1894).

1892   A summer trip to Kobe and Kyoto, and also to the Oki Islands.

1893   Trips to Hakata and to Nagasaki. Eldest son, Kazuo, born November 17.

1894   Trips to Kompira, and to Yokohama and Tokyo.
The Sino-Japanese War (1894–95). Acts as editor of the *Kobe Chronicle*.
Glimpses of Unfamiliar Japan, 2 vols., first of his Japanese works.

1895   *Out of the East.* Naturalized and adopted into his wife's family, Koizumi. Approached by B. H. Chamberlain for professorship at the Imperial University of Tokyo.

1896   *Kokoro.* Moves to Tokyo and begins to lecture on English Literature at the University.

1897   *Gleanings in Buddha-Fields.* Climbs Mt. Fuji with his former student, Fujisaki, in late August.

1898   *Exotics and Retrospectives.*

1899   *In Ghostly Japan.*

1900   *Shadowings.*

1901   *A Japanese Miscellany.*

1902   *Kotto.*

1903   Resigns from the University in March.

1904   The Russo-Japanese War (February 1904–September 1905).
Begins to lecture at Waseda University in April.
Kwaidan. Dies September 26, and is buried according to the Buddhist rite, named: "Believing Man Similar to Undefiled Flower Blooming like Eight Rising Clouds, Who Dwells in Mansion of Right Enlightenment."
Japan: An Attempt at Interpretation.

1905   *The Romance of the Milky Way.*

Notes

AM, (I, II)	*An American Miscellany*, 2 vols.
AP	*Appreciations of Poetry*
BB	*Barbarous Barbers and Other Stories*
BCT	*Buying Christmas Toys and Other Essays*
BH	*Books and Habits*
CC	*Cincinnati Commercial*
CE	*Cincinnati Enquirer*
EAL	*Essays on American Literature*
EEOL	*Essays in European and Oriental Literature*
EKC	*Editorials from the Kobe Chronicle*
ER	*Exotics and Retrospectives*
FF	*Fantastics and Other Fancies*
GBF	*Gleanings in Buddha-Fields*
GJ	*In Ghostly Japan*
GUJ, (I, II)	*Glimpses of Unfamiliar Japan*, 2 vols.
HEL, (I, II)	*A History of English Literature*, 2 vols.
IL, (I, II)	*Interpretations of Literature*, 2 vols.
JAI	*Japan: An Attempt at Interpretation*
JL	*The Japanese Letters of Lafcadio Hearn*
JM	*A Japanese Miscellany*
KC	*Kobe Chronicle*
LDI	*Leaves from the Diary of an Impressionist*
LE	*Literary Essays*
LH, (I, II)	*The Life and Letters of Lafcadio Hearn*, 2 vols.
LL	*Life and Literature*
LR	*Letters from The Raven*
LS	*Lectures on Shakespeare*
LSK	*Letters from Shimane and Kyushu*
NR	*The New Radiance and Other Scientific Sketches*
OA	*Oriental Articles*
OE	*Out of the East*
OG, (I, II)	*Occidental Gleanings*, 2 vols.
PR	*Pre-Raphaelite and Other Poets*
RMW	*The Romance of the Milky Way*
SCG	*Some Chinese Ghosts*
SL	*Stray Leaves from Strange Literature*
SNL	*Some New Letters and Writings of Lafcadio Hearn*
TD	*New Orleans Times-Democrat*
TY	*Two Years in the French West Indies*
VP	*Victorian Philosophy*

Notes

Chapter 1

1. Letter to Wayland D. Ball, 1882. *LH*, I, 251.
2. Joseph S. Tunison's account, as quoted by Elizabeth Bisland:

   But it was impossible for even this slavery of journalism to crush out of him his determination to advance and excel. In the small hours of the morning, into broad daylight, after the rough work of the police rounds and the writing of columns in his inimitable style, he could be seen under merely a poor jet of gas, with his one useful eye close to book and manuscript, translating from Gautier (*LH*, I, 61).

   George M. Gould offers a similar account by Edwin Henderson, the city editor of the Cincinnati *Commercial* (*Concerning Lafcadio Hearn*, Philadelphia, 1908, p. 47).
3. Letter of 1882. *LH*, I, 237–38.
4. There is no separate complete list of Hearn's translations made for the three New Orleans newspapers. Gould lists only those made for the *Times-Democrat* (pp. 376–87). For a general list of Hearn's newspaper writings, including his translations, see P. D. and Ione Perkins, *Lafcadio Hearn: A Bibliography of His Writings* (Boston, 1934).
5. The five articles discussed here are collected in *LE* (pp. 39–41, 59–61, 62–65, 42–44, 45–47 resp.). Of Mary Neal Sherwood's translations of Zola, Albert J. Salvan writes:

   "Il faut dire, cependant, que le style un peu lâche et plein d'inexactitudes de Mary Neal Sherwood se lit très facilement. Ce que l'oeuvre perdait en force, en précision et en poésie, elle le regagnait en quelque mesure par son aisance" (*Zola aux États-Unis* [Providence, 1943], p. 36).
6. *TD*, September 24, 1882, as quoted in E. L. Tinker, *Lafcadio Hearn's American Days* (New York, 1924), pp. 158–60. For the episode, see also Tinker (pp. 163–64).
7. Henry James's two reviews, "Gautier's *Winter in Russia*" (*The Nation*, November 12, 1874) and "*Constantinople* by Gautier" (*The Nation*, July 15, 1875), are collected in *Literary Reviews and Essays by Henry James*, ed. Albert Mordell (New York, 1957), pp. 89–94.
8. *Dayton Journal* (Ohio), September 30, 1904. Quoted in Gould, p. 204.
9. See note 7 above.
10. Théophile Gautier, *One of Cleopatra's Nights and Other Fantastic Romances* (New York, 1882), p. 25. The French original reads:

    Maintenant que Cléopâtre dort, remontons sur le pont de la cange et jouissons de l'admirable spectacle du soleil couchant. Une large bande violette, fortement chauffée de tons roux vers l'occident, occupe toute la partie inférieure du ciel; en rencontrant les zones d'azur, la teinte violette se fond en lilas clair et se noie dans le bleu par une demi-teinte rose; du côté où le soleil, rouge comme un bouclier tombé des fournaises de Vulcain, jette ses ardents reflets, la nuance tourne au citron pâle, et produit des teintes pareilles à celles des turquoises. L'eau frisée par un rayon oblique a l'éclat mat d'une glace vue du côté du tain, ou d'une lame damasquinée; les sinuosités de la rive, les joncs, et tous les accidents du bord s'y découpent en traits fermes et noirs qui en font vivement ressortir la réverbération blanchâtre (Gautier, *Nouvelles* [Vienne, n.d.], pp. 382–83).

11. Letter to J. A. Hart, May 1882. *LH*, I, 244.
12. James, "Flaubert's *Temptation of St. Anthony*" (*The Nation*, June 4, 1874), *Literary Reviews* . . . , pp. 145–50. The French original reads:

Sa robe en brocart d'or, divisée régulièrement par des falbalas de perles, de jais et de saphirs, lui serre la taille dans un corsage étroit, rehaussé d'applications de couleur, qui représentent les douze signes du Zodiaque. Elle a des patins très-hauts, dont l'un est noir et semé d'étoiles d'argent, avec un croissant de lune,—et l'autre, qui est blanc, est couvert de gouttelettes d'or avec un soleil au milieu.

Ses larges manches, garnies d'émeraudes et de plumes d'oiseau, laissent voir à nu son petit bras rond, orné au poignet d'un bracelet d'ébène, et ses mains chargées de bagues se terminent par des ongles si pointus que le bout de ses doigts ressemble presque à des aiguilles.

Une chaîne d'or plate, lui passant sous le menton, monte le long de ses joues, s'enroule en spirale autour de sa coiffure, poudré de poudre bleue; puis, redescendant, lui effleure les épaules et vient s'attacher sur sa poitrine à un scorpion de diamant, qui allonge la langue entre ses seins. Deux grosses perles blondes tirent ses oreilles. Le bord de ses paupières est peint en noir. Elle a sur la pommette gauche une tache brune naturelle; et elle respire en ouvrant la bouche, comme si son corset la genait.

Elle secoue, tout en marchant, un parasol vert à manche d'ivoire, entoure de sonnettes vermeilles;—et douze négrillons crépus portent la longue queue de sa robe, dont un singe tient l'extrémité qu'il souleve de temps à autre.

Elle dit:

Ah! bel ermite! bel ermite! mon coeur défaille! (G. Flaubert, *La Tentation de Saint-Antoine* [Paris, n.d.], pp. 33–34.)

13. Gustave Flaubert, *The Temptation of St. Anthony* (New York, 1911), pp. 60–61.
14. So far as I know, Hearn's translation of this Baudelaire piece has never been reprinted. For another, impromptu version by Hearn, see *IL*, II, 84. "Spring Phantoms" (*Item*, April 21, 1881) is his free adaptation of the same piece (*FF*, pp. 147–51). The French original reads:

La Lune, qui est le caprice même, regarda par la fenêtre pendant que tu dormais dans ton berceau, et se dit: "Cette enfant me plaît."

Et elle descendit moelleusement son escalier de nuages et passa sans bruit à travers les vitres. Puis elle s'étendit sur toi avec la tendresse souple d'une mère, et elle déposa ses couleurs sur ta face. Tes prunelles en sont restées vertes, et tes joues extraordinairement pâles. C'est en contemplant cette visiteuse que tes yeux se sont si bizarrement agrandis; et elle t'a si tendrement serré à la gorge que tu en as gardé pour toujours l'envie de pleurer.

Cependant, dans l'expansion de sa joie, la Lune remplissait toute la chambre comme une atmosphère phosphorique, comme un poison lumineux; et toute cette lumière vivante pensait et disait: "Tu subiras éternellement l'influence de mon baiser. Tu seras belle à ma manière. Tu aimeras ce que j'aime et ce qui m'aime: l'eau, les nuages, le silence et la nuit; la mer immense et verte; l'eau informe et multiforme; le lieu où tu ne seras pas; l'amant que tu ne connaîtras pas; les fleurs monstreuses; les parfums qui font délirer; les chats qui se pâment sur les pianos et qui gémissent comme les femmes, d'une voix rauque et douce!

"Et tu seras aimée de mes amants, courtisée par mes courtisans. Tu seras la reine des hommes aux yeux verts dont j'ai serré aussi la gorge dans mes caresses nocturnes; de ceux-la qui aiment la mer, la mer immense, tumultueuse et verte, l'eau informe et multiforme, le lieu où ils ne sont pas, la femme qu'ils ne connaissent pas, les fleurs sinistres qui ressemblent aux encensoirs d'une religion inconnue, les parfums qui troublent la volonté, et les animaux sauvages et voluptueux qui sont les emblèmes de leur folie."

Et c'est pour cela, maudite chère enfant gâtée, que je suis maintenant couché à tes pieds, cherchant dans toute ta personne le reflet de la redoutable Divinité, de la fatidique marraine, de la nourrice empoisonneuse de tous les *lunatiques.* (Charles Baudelaire, *Petits Poëmes en Prose, Œuvres complètes,* IV, 133–34.)

15. See "The Favours of the Moon," *Baudelaire: Prose and Poetry,* trans. Arthur Symons (New York, 1926), pp. 65–66; and "The Moon's Favors," *Paris Spleen,* trans. Louise Varèse (New York, 1947), pp. 79–80.
16. Cf. the following passage from his essay, "The Literature of the Dead":

> In the rendering of Chinese sentences this duty presents itself under a peculiar aspect. Any attempt at literal translation would result in the production either of nonsense, or of a succession of ideas totally foreign to far-Eastern thought. The paramount necessity in treating such texts is to discover and to expound the thought conveyed to Oriental minds by the original ideographs,—which are very different things indeed from 'written words.' The translations given in this essay were made by Japanese scholars, and, in their present forms, have the approval of competent critics (*ER,* p. 152).

17. "Songs of Japanese Children," *JM,* p. 212.
18. "Dragon-flies," *ibid.,* p. 115.
19. "Bits of Poetry," *GJ,* pp. 157–58.
20. "Frogs," *ER,* p. 164.
21. These three versions are from R. H. Blyth, *Zen in English Literature* (Tokyo, 1948), pp. 217–18; Curtis H. Page, *Japanese Poetry* (Boston, 1923), p. 110; and D. Keene, *Japanese Literature* (New York, 1955), p. 39.
22. For treatment of this much-neglected subject, see Gould's chapter, "As a Poet" (pp. 133–44), and Kenneth Kirkwood, "Hearn as Poet and Craftsman," in *Unfamiliar Lafcadio Hearn* (Tokyo, 1936).
23. Letter to Masanobu Ōtani, December 1897. *LH,* II, 343–44.
24. "Note on the Study of Shakespeare," *IL,* II, 36–37.
25. "On Reading in Relation to Literature," *LL,* p. 16.
26. "Edward Fitzgerald and the *Rubaiyat,*" *IL,* I, 304.
27. Quoted in Caroline Ticknor, *Glimpses of Authors* (Boston, 1922), pp. 125–26.
28. Gould, pp. 69–70.

Chapter 2

1. Letter to Jerome A. Hart, January 1883. *LH,* I, 248.
2. Letter of 1882. *Ibid.,* I, 250–51.
3. Letter to W. D. O'Connor, August 1883. *Ibid.,* I, 270.
4. Letter to Elizabeth Bisland. *Ibid.,* I, 82.
5. Letter of 1882. *Ibid.,* I, 252–53.
6. Letter to W. D. Ball, 1883. *Ibid.,* I, 262–64.
7. Letter of June 29, 1884. *Ibid.,* I, 328.
8. Letter to W. D. O'Connor, 1883. *Ibid.,* I, 290–91.
9. "But I think a man must devote himself to one thing in order to succeed: so I have pledged me to the worship of the Odd, the Queer, the Strange, the Exotic, the Monstrous. It quite suits my temperament" (Hearn's letter to O'Connor, June 29, 1884. *Ibid.,* I, 328). Hearn's vow leads Mr. Malcolm Cowley to write: "It seems to us now that Hearn started by misestimating and underestimating his own gifts" (Introd., *Selected Writings of Lafcadio Hearn,* ed. Henry Goodman [New York, 1949], p. 10). But Hearn is merely restating his old stand, as evident in the following self-portrayal:

> Now, in those days there was a young man connected with the *Daily Enquirer* whose tastes were whimsically grotesque and arabesque. He was by nature a fervent admirer of extremes. He believed only in the Revoltingly Horrible or the Excruciatingly Beautiful. He worshipped the French school of sensation, and reveled in thrusting a reeking mixture of bones, blood and hair under people's noses at breakfast time. To produce qualms in the stomachs of other people affords him special delight. To borrow the picturesque phraseology of Jean Paul Richter, his life-path was ever running down into vaults and out over graves. He was only known to fame by the name of "The Ghoul" (*"Giglampz!"* CE, October 4, 1874. *AM,* I, 16).

10. Letter to W. D. Ball, July 1885. *LH*, I, 344.
11. Letter of April 1886. *Ibid.*, I, 364.
12. Letter to H. E. Krehbiel, 1886. *Ibid.*, I, 370–72.
13. Hearn's letter appeared in *Harper's Weekly*, October 15, 1904. See Appendix.
14. Gould, p. 167.
15. "In Algeria," *TD*, April 1, 1883. *Stories from Pierre Loti* (ed. Albert Mordell [Tokyo, 1933]), p. 73. For Hearn's interest in Loti, see Mordell's introduction.
16. "A New Romantic" (*TD*, September 23, 1883), *EEOL*, pp. 131–32; "The Most Original of Modern Novelists: Pierre Loti" (*TD*, September 7, 1884), *ibid.*, p. 136.
17. Letter to H. E. Krehbiel, October 1884. *LH*, I, 333–34. According to Hearn's plan, his Grande Isle piece, "Torn Letters" (*TD*, September 14, 1884. *AM*, II, 56–65), was to form the opening of this little book.
18. "To the Reader," *One of Cleopatra's Nights*, p. xxi.
19. Letter to W. D. O'Connor, February 1883. *LH*, I, 268.
20. Letter to O'Connor, August 1883. *Ibid.*, I, 275.
21. Letter to H. E. Krehbiel, May 1884. *Ibid.*, I, 324.
22. Letter to H. E. Krehbiel, October 1886. *Ibid.*, I, 379.
23. Letter to H. E. Krehbiel, 1886. *Ibid.*, I, 373–74.
24. See note 22 above.
25. Hearn's early prose poems are collected in *FF*. See Charles W. Hutson's introduction to this collection. In connection with Hearn's stylistic experiment it is interesting to compare "A Dead Love" (*Item*, October 21, 1880) with its later version, "L'Amour après la Mort" (*TD*, April 6, 1884), also "The Fountain of Gold" (October 15, 1880), with "A Tropical Intermezzo" (*LDI*).
26. *SCG*, p. 46. Of this particular passage, Edward Thomas writes:

> For example, in "the great citron-light of the sunset faded out," either the mind will think only of citrons, or it will painfully discover for itself a resemblance between one of the sunset colours and the colours of a citron, leaving the words of the writer a merely accurate statement incapable of producing a pure impression related to its context. This is far too often the reader's fortune (*Lafcadio Hearn* [Boston, 1912], pp. 46–47).

27. *Youma*, p. 152.
28. Letter of February 6, 1893. *JL*, pp. 58–59.
29. Letter of June 5, 1893. *Ibid.*, pp. 105–7.
30. Letter of June 14, 1893. *Ibid.*, pp. 112–16.
31. Letter of February 18, 1893. *Ibid.*, p. 62.
32. Letter of 1893. *Ibid.*, p. 201.
33. Letter of December 12, 1892. *Ibid.*, p. 27.
34. "Note on Some French Romantics," *LL*, pp. 261–65.
35. "Studies of Extraordinary Prose," *IL*, II, 85.
36. Roughly classified, Hearn's Japanese studies consist of 60 sketches, 58 essays, 50 legends, and 35 prose poems. To these we may add several fairy tales.
37. "The Prose of Small Things," *LL*, pp. 108–28.
38. *GUJ*, II, 582.
39. "A Mid-Summer Trip to the Tropics," *TY*, p. 4. The original form of this is found in Hearn's notebook:

> 2nd Day
> Ink-blue extraordinary the sea is. It is beautifully marbled beside the ship. It looks like marble,—a black-blue marble white-veined and exquisitely clouded.
> A sign of prodigious depth. There are no ships visible, we shall not see another for days. Mild wind, white clouds. A long ground swell. The sea is a great blue-black circle. Light cumuli and cirrhi [sic] are climbing up over its edge in every direction,—a few slightly shaded on the under side. The sky is still pale blue; but the blue of the water continually changes. It brightens with the sun's ascent,—wonderfully, deliciously" (quoted from Ichiro Nishizaki, "The Apprenticeship of Lafcadio Hearn," *The Bulletin of the Institute for Research in Language Teaching*, No. 231, January 31, 1956, p. 2).

Hearn's unpublished notebook, from which the above quotation originally comes, is in possession of Henry E. Huntington Library.

40. *JM*, pp. 225–30.
41. *Kwaidan*, pp. 45–49.
42. See "Note on Some French Romantics" (*LL*, pp. 246–65) and "Studies of Extraordinary Prose" (*IL*, II, 50–89).
43. *Kotto*, pp. 248–51. This piece is actually based on Hearn's early version found in "Three Dreams" (*TD*, April 11, 1885. *AM*, II, 69–71). The American version, though identical in substance with the Japanese, has no framework.
44. *Shadowings*, pp. 197–200. Compare this piece with Hearn's early prose poem, "A Dream of Kites" (*Item*, June 18, 1880. *FF*, pp. 57–59), which deals with a similar situation, but has no sense of sublime drama.
45. "Notes on American Literature," *HEL*, II, 885. For Hearn's part in the introduction of Baudelaire into America, see Jacob Canter, "The Literary Reputation of Baudelaire in England and America," unpublished doctoral thesis, Harvard University, 1940.
46. Letter to Mr. and Mrs. John Albee, February 1898. *LH*, II, 359.
47. "On Composition," *LL*, pp. 61–66.
48. Letter to B. H. Chamberlain, January 23, 1893. *JL*, p. 42.

Chapter 3

1. *SL*, p. 7.
2. *CE*, March 1, 1874. *AM*, I, 1–12.
3. See "The Restless Dead" (*CC*, August 29, 1875), "Some Strange Experience" (*CC*, September 26, 1875), and "Banjo Jim's Story" (*CC*, October 1, 1876), all collected in *AM*, I.
4. *Item*, August 4, 1878. *AM*, II, 25–27.
5. Letter to H. E. Krehbiel, March, 1884. *LH*, I, 314.
6. Letter to H. E. Krehbiel, 1886. *Ibid.*, I, 370–71.
7. In his letter to Mrs. Wetmore (formerly Elizabeth Bisland) of 1903, Hearn wrote:

   I have also something to say about your proposed *Juvenilia*. I think this would be possible:—To include in one volume under the title of *Juvenilia*—(1) the translations from Théophile Gautier, revised; (2) *Some Chinese Ghosts*; (3) miscellaneous essays and sketches upon Oriental subjects, formerly contributed to the *T.-D.*; (4) miscellaneous sketches on Southern subjects, two or three, and fantasies,—with a few verses thrown in (*ibid.*, II, 500).

8. *SCG*, p. vii.
9. *Ibid.*, pp. 97–114.
10. *Ibid.*, pp. 11–27. For a brief comparative study of Paul Claudel's "La Cloche," in *Connaissance de l'est*, and Hearn's "The Soul of the Great Bell," in *SCG*, see Gilbert Gadoffre, "Claudel et Lafcadio Hearn," *Studies in Modern French Literature*, ed. L. J. Austin, G. Rees, and E. Vinaver (Manchester University Press, 1961), 104–8.
11. *Ibid.*, pp. 71–96.
12. "Lest the reader should suppose, however, that I have drawn wholly upon my own imagination for the details of the apparition, the cure, the marriage ceremony, etc., I refer to No. XCVI of Giles's *Strange Stories from a Chinese Studio*, entitled, 'A Supernatural Wife,' in which he will find that my narrative is at least conformable to Chinese ideas" (*ibid.*, p. 179).
13. *Ibid.*, pp. 115–42.
14. See Chapter 1, p. 10.
15. *SCG*, pp. 143–74.
16. Hearn supplies an English version of Father d'Entrecolles' account, *ibid.*, pp. 181–82.
17. *Ibid.*, pp. 29–69.
18. "Some Fairy Literature," *LL*, pp. 324–39.
19. Introd., *Selected Writings of Lafcadio Hearn*, p. 15. Cf. also: "Long before coming to Japan he had shown an instinct for finding in legends the permanent archetypes of human experience—that is the secret of their power to move us—and he later proved

that he knew which tales to choose and which details to emphasize, in exactly the right English" (*ibid.*).

20. Such as "Chin Chin Kobakama," "The Goblin Spider," "The Old Woman Who Lost Dumplings," "The Boy Who Drew Cats," and "The Fountain of Youth."

21. The word "weird" is defined by Hearn:

> "Weird" is a later form of the Anglo-Saxon word meaning fate. The northern mythology, like the Greek, had its Fates, who devised the life histories of men. Later the word came also to be used in relation to the future of the man himself; the ancient writers spoke of "his weird," "her weird." Still later the term came to mean simply supernatural influence of a mysterious kind. Poe found it so used, and made it into a living adjective, after it had become almost forgotten, by using it very cleverly in his poems and stories. As he used it, it means ghostly, or ghostly looking, or suggesting the supernatural and the occult. Hundreds of writers imitated Poe in this respect; and now it is so much the rule, that the word must be used sparingly. It is the mark of a very young writer to use it often ("Poe's Verse," *IL*, II, 158).

Yet the word "weird" remained Hearn's great favorite.

22. "The Stone Buddha," *OE*, pp. 171–77. See also his letter to Chamberlain, of June 1, 1893 (*JL*, p. 104).

23. Originally published as part of *Japanese Fairy Tales* (Tokyo, 1898).

24. "Yes, after all, to devour one's own legs for hunger is not the worst that can happen to a being cursed with the gift of song. There are human crickets who must eat their own hearts in order to sing" ("Kusa-hibari," *Kotto*, p. 241).

25. "The Romance of the Milky Way," *RMW*, pp. 3–49.

26. Cf. Malcolm Cowley:

> The great weakness of his early sketches is that they aren't sufficiently odd or monstrous or differentiated from one another. The best of them—including many reprinted in this volume—are folk tales adapted from various foreign literatures. The others keep reverting to the same situation, that of a vaguely pictured hero in love with a dead woman or with her ghost (just as Hearn was in love with the memory of his mother, disappeared from his life when he was seven years old). They are obsessive rather than exotic; and they are written in a style that suggests the scrollwork on the ceiling of an old-fashioned theater" (Introd., *Selected Writings*, p. 11).

27. "The Eternal Haunter," *ER*, pp. 294–95. The general significance of this particular piece will be discussed in Chapter 14, pp. 268–69.

28. "The Value of the Supernatural in Fiction," *IL*, II, 101.

29. *Ibid.*, II, 103.

Chapter 4

1. Letter of 1883. *LH*, I, 276.
2. *Ibid.*, I, 350.
3. *Ibid.*, I, 352.
4. Tinker, p. 126.
5. *AM*, II, 56–65.
6. Letter to H. E. Krehbiel, 1886. *LH*, I, 371–72.
7. Tinker, p. 367. Though no date for this letter is given, the context indicates that it was written in the summer of 1886 during Hearn's second Grande Isle vacation.
8. "Alden is, of course, deliberating over the 'Legend of l'Ile Dernière'" (letter to Krehbiel, October 1886. *LH*, I, 378).
9. Letter to George M. Gould, June 1888. *Ibid.*, I, 426–27.
10. Letter of September 6, 1887. "Newly Discovered Letters from Lafcadio Hearn to Dr. Rudolph Matas," ed. Ichiro Nishizaki, *Ochanomizu University Studies in Arts and Culture*, VIII (Tokyo, 1956), 106.
11. *Chita*, pp. 14–19.
12. Letters to B. H. Chamberlain, January 23 and May 12, 1893. *JL*, pp. 41, 96 resp.
13. Letter to G. M. Gould, April 1887. *LH*, I, 393.

14. Letter to H. E. Krehbiel, 1887. *Ibid.*, I, 405.
15. *Chita*, p. 136.
16. *Ibid.*, p. 21.
17. Letter to Mitchell McDonald, January 1898. *LH*, II, 347. In this letter Hearn offers further explanation:

> It gave me no small pleasure to find that you liked *Youma:* you will not like it less knowing that the story is substantially true. You can see the ruins of the old house in the Quartier du Fort if you ever visit Saint-Pierre, and perhaps meet my old friend Arnoux, a survivor of the time. The girl really died under the heroic conditions described—refusing the help of the blacks, and the ladder. Of course I may have idealized *her*, but not her act. The incident of the serpent occurred also; but the heroine was a different person,—a plantation girl, celebrated by the historian Rufz de Lavison. I wrote the story under wretched circumstances in Martinique, near the scenes described, and under the cross with the black Christ.

18. *Ibid.*, I, 445. From the context of the letter it is evident that this was written shortly after Hearn's arrival in Philadelphia, some days later than May 8, 1889.
19. *Youma*, pp. 84–85.
20. Hugh Walker, *The English Essay and Essayists* (London, 1928), pp. 321–22.
21. "Editor's Note," *Karma*, ed. Albert Mordell, p. 5.
22. Letter of 1889. *LH*, I, 454–55.
23. *Karma*, pp. 55–56.
24. *The Dial* (December 14, 1918), LXV, 568.
25. Gould, pp. 98–99.
26. This quotation is from Hearn's letter of October 1888 (*LH*, I, 437–38).
27. R. L. Stevenson, "Victor Hugo's Romances," *Works* (New York, 1924), XIV, 42.
28. "By right of this single but profoundly remarkable book, Mr. Hearn may lay good claim to the title of the American Victor Hugo. . . . so living a book has scarcely been given to our generation"—from a review of *Chita*, *Boston Evening Transcript*, November 2, 1889, as quoted in Gould, p. 226.
29. See Tinker, pp. 290–93.
30. *Ibid.*, p. 311. In his letter of 1889 to Dr. Gould Hearn wrote: " 'Ruth' maketh progress; but I had to murder the 'Mother of God.' Anyhow the simile would have had a Catholic idolatrousness about it, so that I don't regret it" (*LH*, I, 468).
31. Letter of April 1895. *Ibid.*, II, 246.
32. Letter of July 1895. *Ibid.*, II, 267.
33. Letter of November 1897. *Ibid.*, II, 341–42. Even while working on *Chita*, Hearn wrote to H. E. Krehbiel: "Ticknor writes that if I should undertake a novelette, he is certain it would succeed. So I shall try. In trying I must study from real material; I must take models where I can find them. Still the work will be ideal to the verge of fantasy" (*ibid.*, I, 372). Cf. "I can only think that I have found superb material for a future story, in which the influence of New York on a Southern mind may be destroyed." (Letter to Henry Watkin of June 1887, *LR*, pp. 85–86).
34. Letter to Henry Alden, July 17, 1888. "Some Martinique Letters of Lafcadio Hearn," *Harper's Monthly Magazine*, March 1921, 520.
35. *Loc. cit.*
36. Letter of November 1897. *LH*, II, 342.
37. See note 34 above.

Chapter 5

1. *LH*, I, 97.
2. This undated letter is quoted in Tinker, p. 85.
3. "A Ghost," originally printed in *Harper's Magazine* for December 1889, is collected in *Karma*, pp. 59–69.
4. "Travel as an Educational Influence," *Item*, February 24, 1879. *BCT*, pp. 31–33.
5. All thirteen letters in the series appeared in the Cincinnati *Commercial* at irregular intervals from November 6, 1877, to March 31, 1878. Except for the last two dealing

with Louisiana politics, they are collected in *OG*, I, 144–275. They are also extensively quoted in *LR*, pp. 153–201.

6. *LR*, pp. 42–43; *OG*, I, 162.

7. Ferris Greenslet's introduction to *LDI*, which he edited in 1911, states that Hearn apparently intended to add to the "Floridian Reveries" a little collection of "Fantastics," with such titles as "Aïda," "The Devil's Carbuncle," "A Hemisphere in a Woman's Hair," "Tho Fool and Venus," etc. "A Tropical Intermezzo," the second piece in the "Reveries," however, is actually a revision of Hearn's early piece called "The Fountain of Gold" (*Item*, October 21, 1880, *FF*, pp. 110–19).

8. "Midsummer Trip to the Tropics" (July–Aug.–Sept. 1888), "Les Porteuses" (July 1889), "La Grande Anse" (November 1889), and "La Vérette" (October 1888), all in *Harper's Monthly*.

9. "Preface," *TY*. Cf. his letter to Chamberlain, August 1891 (*LH*, II, 58):

> I could not finish my book on the West Indies until I saw the magical island again through regret, as through a summer haze,—and under circumstances which left me perfectly free to think, which the soporific air of the tropics makes difficult. (Still the book is not what it ought to be, for I was refused all reasonable help, and wrote most of it upon a half-empty stomach, or with my blood full of fever).

10. "Creole Women in the French West Indies" (originally in *Harper's Bazar*, February 1, 1890), *LDI*, p. 113.

11. *TY*, p. 24.

12. *Ibid.*, p. 34.

13. *Ibid.*, p. 302.

14. *Ibid.*, pp. 308–9.

15. *Ibid.*, p. 440.

16. *Ibid.*, p. 188.

17. *Ibid.*, p. 326.

18. "You will understand why the tropics settled by European races produce no sciences, arts, or literature,—why the habits and the thoughts of other centuries still prevail where Time itself moves slowly as though enfeebled by the heat" (*ibid.*, p. 416).

19. *Ibid.*, p. 423. For a personal aspect of this drama of temptation, see Hearn's letter to Dr. Matas, written from Barbados in July (?) 1887: "I tried to read, to study, to indulge intellectual pursuits. Herbert Spencer has become totally uninteresting, or rather incomprehensible; the poets are dullards; the novelists are stupid beyond endurance. Heaven and Sea make so mighty a poem here, that mind refuses to consider any other (*Ochanomizu University Studies*, VIII, 92). See also his letter of September 6, 1887 (*ibid.*, 106–7).

20. *TY*, p. 449.

21. See Tinker, pp. 290–93. The episode of Lys, as we have it now, is far removed from the original plan, in which the heroine was to die of "consumption," a malady of civilization. This plan was later abandoned for something "much more artistic." See also his letter to Dr. Matas, of August 28, 1887 (*Ochanomizu University Studies*, VIII, 102).

22. Letter of November 28, 1889, as quoted in Tinker, pp. 328–30. To list the proposed subjects: "City life to the foreigner"; "Art in everyday life: effect of foreign influences on art products"; "The new civilization"; "Amusements"; "The Guéchas (dancing girls) and their profession"; "The new Educational system,—child life—child games, etc."; "Home life and popular domestic religion"; "Public cults—Temple ceremonies and the duties of worshippers"; "Curiosities of Legends and superstitions"; "Woman's life in Japan"; "Old popular melodies and songs"; "The Old Masters of Japan—in the arts: their influence as a survival or a memory; their powers or value as reflectors of the life and the nature of the country"; "Curiosities of popular speech,—singularities of verbal usage in everyday life"; "The social organism,—political and military conditions"; and "Japan as a place to settle in; the situation of the foreign elements, etc."

23. "Yokohama," *OE*, p. 325.

24. *ER*, p. 11. In August 1897, Hearn climbed Mt. Fuji, accompanied by his former student Fujisaki. He also requested Ōtani, his student assistant, to collect materials on

the subject, "Relations of Mt. Fuji and Shinto" (Ryuji Tanabe, *Koizumi Yakumo* [Tokyo, 1914], p. 385).

25. *ER*, p. 14.

26. "A Winter Journey to Japan" (originally printed in *Harper's Magazine* for November 1890). *AM*, II, 262–63.

27. *GJ*, p. 7. In this connection it may be well to note Chita's terrifying experience when she saw a skull through a chink in the roof of a ruined tomb (*Chita*, pt. III, ch. 1).

28. See Hearn's letter to Ernest Fenollosa, May 1898:

> As for the Mountain of Skulls—yes: I have written it,—about seven or eight times over; but it still refuses to give the impression I feel, and can't define,—the impression that floated into my brain with the soft-flowing voice of the teller. I shall try again later; but, although I feel tolerably sure about the result, nothing but very hard work will develop the thing. Had I only eleven more stories of such quality, what a book could be made out of them! Still, it is quite impossible that a dozen such tales could exist. I read all the Jatakas to no purpose: one makes such a find only by the rarest and most unexpected chance" (*LH*, II, 383).

29. *ER*, p. 14.

30. *LL*, pp. 122–23.

31. "Frogs," *ER*, p. 172.

32. Letter to H. E. Krehbiel, December 1883. *LH*, I, 294–95.

33. "A Winter Journey to Japan," *AM*, II, 245.

34. Time-consciousness is hardly characteristic of the West only, as evident in the Eastern doctrine of karma, for instance. The real difference may be that the West is primarily interested in differentiated time, and the East in undifferentiated time. Considering the question in terms of a sense of history, Denis de Rougemont has recently written: ". . . a sense of history is characteristic of the West, and may even turn into an obsession (to judge by the present century), whereas it was completely wanting in Orientals till they came under Western influences" (*Man's Western Quest* [New York, 1957], p. 85). For an attack on the time obsession of modern literature, see Wyndham Lewis, *Time and Western Man* (New York, 1928). For a more helpful treatment of this time theme in literature, see Hans Meyerhoff, *Time in Literature* (Berkeley and Los Angeles, 1955).

Chapter 6

1. "Newspaper Book Critics," January 12, 1879. *EAL*, pp. 14–16.

2. Albert Mordell, Introd. *EAL*, pp. xxxii, vii, ix, resp. For a more detailed treatment of the subject, see Ray McKinley Lawless, "Lafcadio Hearn, Critic of American Life and Letters" (unpublished doctoral thesis, University of Chicago, 1940).

3. "Death of American Literature," *Item*, December 31, 1880. *EAL*, pp. 62–64. See also "Novelists and Novels" (*TD*, December 31, 1882), *ibid.*, pp. 104–7.

4. "Cheap Books," *TD*, December 20, 1883. *Ibid.*, pp. 143–45.

5. "Dime-Novel Wickedness," *TD*, April 12, 1884. *Ibid.*, pp. 146–48.

6. "Pictures vs. Texts," *TD*, September 19, 1886. *Ibid.*, p. 214.

7. "The Journalism of the Future," *Item*, June 24, 1879. *Ibid.*, pp. 27–29.

8. "Decline of the *Atlantic*," *Item*, November 4, 1878. *Ibid.*, pp. 4–6.

9. "The New Departure in Periodical Literature," *Item*, January 17, 1879. *Ibid.*, pp. 17–20.

10. "Novelists and Novels," *TD*, December 31, 1882. *Ibid.*, pp. 104–7.

11. "Latterday Reviews," *TD*, November 13, 1883. *Ibid.*, pp. 138–42.

12. For a list of Hearn's contributions to these American periodicals, see Perkins' *Bibliography*, pp. 223–33.

13. *TD*, March 16, 1884. *EEOL*, pp. 34–39.

14. "More Biography—*About Grant*," *Item*, March 4, 1880. *EAL*, pp. 49–53.

15. "Southern Novels," *Item*, November 26, 1879. *Ibid.*, pp. 43–44.

16. "A Southern Magazine," *Item*, March 24, 1881. *Ibid.*, pp. 65–69.

17. *TD*, April 15, 1883. *Ibid.*, pp. 112–17.

18. "Southern Literature and *Observer*," *TD*, May 6, 1883. *Ibid.*, pp. 118–21.
19. Jay B. Hubbell, *The South in American Literature* (Durham, N.C., 1954), pp. 723–24.
20. *"Marjorie Daw and Other People,"* *CE*, November 2, 1873. *LE*, pp. 134–38.
21. "Bret Harte and the Critics," *Item*, July 26, 1878. *EAL*, pp. 1–3.
22. "A Louisiana Idyl," *Item*, February 25, 1879. Tinker, pp. 145–46.
23. May 26, 1881. *EAL*, pp. 73–75.
24. "Mark Twain on the Mississippi," *TD*, May 20, 1883. *Ibid.*, pp. 127–33.
25. For Hearn's literary friendship with Cable, see Tinker, pp. 183–86.
26. *TD*, October 5, 1884. *EAL*, pp. 64–70.
27. "One of Mr. Howells' Realisms," *TD*, April 12, 1887. *Ibid.*, pp. 238–40.
28. "Howells on Critics," *TD*, May 29, 1887. *Ibid.*, pp. 248–50.
29. See note 17 above.
30. "Authors and Success," *TD*, May 18, 1884. *Ibid.*, pp. 153–56.
31. "The Apostle of Aestheticism," *TD*, April 16, 1882. *LE*, pp. 118–22. "Oscar Wilde as a Fashion Designer," *TD*, May 14, 1882. *Ibid.*, pp. 123–26.
32. The only serious study of Hearn's criticism of Zola, so far as I know, is Albert J. Salvan's article, "Lafcadio Hearn's Views on the Realism of Zola" (*PMLA*, LXVII [1952], 1163–67). No mention is made of Hearn in his earlier comprehensive investigation, *Zola aux États-Unis* (1943).
33. *"Helene—A Love Episode,"* *Item*, November 24, 1878. *LE*, pp. 50–51.
34. Quoted in William C. Frierson and H. Edwards, "Impact of French Naturalism on American Critical Opinion: 1877–1892," *PMLA*, LXIII (September 1948), 1007–16. Incidentally, this article makes no mention of Hearn.
35. "Translating and Mutilating," *Item*, January 30, 1880. *LE*, pp. 39–41. For Hearn's remarks on Stirling's art, see Chapter 1, pp. 4–5.
36. "The Value of Novels," *Item*, January 23, 1879. *EAL*, pp. 21–23.
37. *Item*, May 30, 1879. *LE*, pp. 52–55.
38. *Item*. *Ibid.*, pp. 19–20.
39. *"Au Bonheur des Dames,"* *TD*, May 13, 1883. *EEOL*, pp. 113–20.
40. *TD*, May 25, 1884. *Ibid.*, pp. 10–15.
41. Letter of Henry James (I, 104–5), as quoted in Frierson and Edwards (1012). Cf. the opinion of an anonymous critic: ". . . utterly contemptible, a disgrace to literature, to science, to civilization" (a review of *La Joie de Vivre*, *Literary World*, April 19, 1884, as quoted in Frierson and Edwards, 1013).
42. Frierson and Edwards, 1013–14.
43. *Harper's Magazine*, LXXIV (April 1887). Quoted in Frierson and Edwards, 1014.
44. *TD*, February 28, 1886. *EEOL*, pp. 16–18.
45. "Science and Literature," *TD*, August 15, 1886. *Ibid.*, pp. 23–27.
46. *"L'Œuvre,"* *TD*, June 20, 1886. *Ibid.*, pp. 121–24.
47. "A Great Prosateur," *TD*, April 20, 1884. *Ibid.*, pp. 80–86.
48. "Literary Pessimism," *TD*, July 5, 1885. *Ibid.*, pp. 87–92.
49. "A Lesson of Literary Evolution," *TD*, December 19, 1886. *Ibid.*, pp. 19–22.
50. *TD*, September 23, 1883. *Ibid.*, pp. 125–32.
51. "The Most Original of Modern Novelists: Pierre Loti" (*TD*, December 7, 1884), "Plot-Formation in Modern Novels" (*TD*, August 22, 1886), and *"The Nation* on Loti" (*TD*, March 13, 1887) are collected in *EEOL*. For Hearn's translations of Loti, see *Stories from Pierre Loti*.
52. *TD*, September 6, 1885. *EEOL*, pp. 183–88.
53. "A Terrible Novel," *TD*, November 22, 1885. *Ibid.*, pp. 189–94.
54. "Academical Triumphs," *TD*, December 20, 1885. *LE*, pp. 85–91.
55. *TD*, February 21, 1886. *EEOL*, pp. 153–57.
56. *TD*, February 7, 1886. *Ibid.*, pp. 3–9.
57. *TD*, May 1, 1887. *EAL*, pp. 245–47.
58. "Prejudices of Prudes," *Item*, August 9, 1880. *BCT*, pp. 151–53.
59. "Sins of Genius," *TD*, June 6, 1886. *EAL*, pp. 189–93. Cf. "He [Hearn] had courage and vision and was not scared by big names of the time, many since then no longer big" (Mordell, Introd. pp. vii–viii). For Hearn's unexpected encounter with Howells

at a dinner party given by J. Henry Harper in 1890, see Tinker, pp. 322–24.
60. "The Age of Dr. Johnson: Preliminary Survey," *HEL*, I, 341.
61. See Hearn's editorial, *"Leaves of Grass," TD*, July 30, 1882 (*EAL*, pp. 91–95). For his further remarks on Whitman, see his letter to W. D. O'Connor, one of the poet's loyal defenders (August 1883. *LH*, I, 270–74).

Chapter 7

1. For Hearn's teaching in Japan, see particularly Y. Noguchi, *Lafcadio Hearn in Japan* (New York, 1911); R. Tanabe, *Koizumi Yakumo* (Tokyo, 1914); M. Maruyama, *New Commentary on Lafcadio Hearn* (Tokyo, 1936); and B. Negishi, *Lafcadio Hearn in Izumo* (Matsue, 1936).
2. "You modestly depreciate your qualifications, for the post, but if as you say, English literature will be taught emotionally and historically on the principles of evolution I cannot see how it could be taught better" (Professor Masakazu Toyama's letter to Hearn, December 13, 1895, quoted in *More Letters from Basil Hall Chamberlain*, ed. Kazuo Koizumi [Tokyo, 1937] p. 185).
3. Letter of February, 1899. *LH*, II, 429–30.
4. Letter to Ellwood Hendrick, September 1902. *Ibid.*, II, 480–81.
5. John Erskine, Introd. *IL*, I, ix. Noting Hearn's basically French approach to literature, Erskine writes: "Lafcadio Hearn lectured upon English literature in Japan as we should like to see it taught in America and England,—as a total expression of racial experience, in which ideas, however abstract, often control emotions and conduct, and in which conduct and emotions often explain or modify ideas" (*ibid.*, p. xi).
6. For the same editor's reassertion, see Introd., *AP*, pp. ix–xiv.
7. A review of *IL, The Dial*, LX (February 3, 1916), 112–14.
8. S. P. B. Mais, "Lafcadio Hearn," *Books and Their Writers* (New York, 1920), p. 242. See also his conclusion (*ibid.*, p. 276).
9. *Times Literary Supplement*, August 18, 1927, p. 563.
10. Cf. Mordell, Preface, *EEOL*:

> But the literary criticism that Hearn wrote in the nineties of the last century was not his first effort in that direction. It was merely a continuation of his work on the New Orleans *Times-Democrat* in the eighties. His later views are very much the same as those there recorded, although in his editorials there is not as much stress laid on the moral and sociological aspect of art. His preference, however, for the French Romantics, to the Naturalistic School of writers, persisted throughout his life (pp. vi–vii).

11. All of Hearn's remarks on these American authors, unless otherwise indicated, are found in "Notes on American Literature" (*HEL*, II, 861–914).
12. "Ralph Waldo Emerson," *TD*, April 30, 1882. *EAL*, pp. 83–86.
13. "Walt Whitman," *On Poets*, pp. 817–41. For Whitman's influence on Japanese literature, see Saburo Ota, "Walt Whitman and Japanese Literature," *Asia and the Humanities* (ed. Horst Frenz [Bloomington, 1959]), pp. 62–69.
14. In his survey of Victorian fiction Hearn also said:

> Except Meredith, nobody has done anything in the shape of a purely psychological novel of really surprising kind. But psychological stories and novelettes have been introduced with excellent results; and the work of Mr. Henry James is a striking example. However, the short stories of Henry James deal with abnormal rather than with normal psychology—that is to say, his stories, although perfectly true to life, picture to us the strange and fantastic aspects of character rather than the natural ones (*HEL*, II, 808).

> Cf. a contemporary opinion: "Certain of Mr. James' later and more elaborate novels of English life . . . are as full of covert suggestions of foulness as the worst French novel of the last forty years" (*Atlantic Monthly*, XCI [1903], as quoted in Frierson and Edwards, p. 1016).

15. *LL*, pp. 246–65. For Hearn's other remarks on French literature, see "On Modern

English Criticism" (*ibid.*), "Some French Poems on Insects" (*ibid.*), "The Prose of Small Things" (*ibid.*), and "Studies of Extraordinary Prose" (*IL*, II).

16. For a general list of Hearn's university lectures, see Tanabe, *Koizumi Yakumo,* pp. 399–418.

17. Editors' Note, *HEL,* II. With this remark Hearn closed his first series of lectures on the history of English literature.

18. "Summary of 18th Century Literature," *HEL,* I, 478.

19. F. L. Pattee, *The New American Literature* (New York, 1937), p. 227.

20. See Hearn's remarks on literary "schools," *HEL,* II, 480.

21. "On Modern English Criticism," *LL,* pp. 80–107. For Hearn's comment on Matthew Arnold's criticism, especially in connection with Sainte-Beuve, see *HEL,* II, 841–42.

22. "On Composition," *LL,* pp. 43–68. For further discussion, see Chapter 8.

23. Cf. Mais, in *Books and Their Writers:*

> That is perhaps one of Hearn's greatest charms: although he is only attempting to give the simplest account of our great writers, he never approaches them along the lines of stereotyped criticism; consequently, even though we may imagine that we have heard the last word on a poet whom we have carefully studied, we shall do well to look up Hearn's comments before we conclude that there is no more to be said (pp. 249–50).

24. "On Reading in Relation to Literature," *LL,* pp. 1–20.

25. *CC,* January 9, 1876. *LE,* p. 201.

26. "Poe's Verse," *IL,* II, 150–66.

27. "Studies in Browning," *AP,* pp. 172–238.

28. *"The Shaving of Shagpat,"* *IL,* I, 381–90.

29. "Tennyson and the Great Poetry," and "The Minor Singers," *HEL,* II, 637–704.

30. See "Studies in Tennyson" (*AP*), "Studies in Browning" (*ibid.*), "Studies in Rossetti" (*ibid.*), "Studies in Swinburne" (*ibid.*), "Matthew Arnold as Poet" (*ibid.*), and "The Poetry of George Meredith" (*LL*).

31. "Philosophical Poems of the Victorian Age," *IL,* I, 348–80.

32. "Matthew Arnold as Poet," *AP,* pp. 298–333; "Pessimists and their Kindred," *IL,* I, 321–47. For Hearn's early remarks on Arnold, see "The Two Arnolds" (*TD,* November 4, 1883), *EEOL,* pp. 200–3; letter to W. D. O'Connor, March, 1884, *LH,* I, 318–19; and letter to Chamberlain, January 12, 1894, *JL,* p. 218.

33. "Note upon Tolstoi's *Resurrection,*" *LL,* pp. 300–307.

34. "Tolstoi's Theory of Art," *ibid.*, p. 288.

35. "On a Proper Estimate of Longfellow," *IL,* II, 199.

36. "On the Lyrical Beauties of Keats," *ibid.*, I, 200.

37. "On Reading," *LL,* pp. 9–11.

38. "Pessimists and their Kindred," *IL,* I, 328–29.

39. E. Gosse, "Lafcadio Hearn," *Silhouettes* (London, 1925), p. 226. Pointing out that Hearn's lectures "represent, to a very unusual degree, the impact of masterpieces on a mind unimpaired by previous cultivation," Gosse writes:

> There is no metaphysical ingenuity and no great subtlety of thought in these lectures, which are marked by an almost naïve simplicity. We seem to be returning in them to the infancy of criticism, where everything is good or bad, beautiful or ugly. But this does not detract from their merit, which depends on their freshness, their artless enthusiasm and also on the vigour with which impressions independently made on the enthusiasm of the lecturer are passed on to his audience. Moreover, when we examine these judgments carefully, we discover them to be more intelligently based, and more consistently guided by principle, than we at first thought them to be. We see poetry frankly described as Hearn saw it, and we are struck by the vigour of his analysis and the delicacy of his taste (loc. cit.).

Chapter 8

1. See Chapter 7, note 2.

2. Letter of September 1902. *LH,* II, 480–81.

3. "The Question of the Highest Art," *IL*, I, 7–10.
4. *HEL*, I, 285.
5. "Byron," *IL*, I, 117.
6. "The Victorian Spasmodics," *LL*, p. 207.
7. "On the Relation of Life and Character to Literature," *ibid.*, p. 40.
8. *Ibid.*, pp. 43–68.
9. Cf. Baudelaire, in *L'Art romantique:*

> L'enfant voit tout en *nouveauté;* il est toujours *ivre.* Rien ne ressemble plus à ce qu'on appelle l'inspiration, que la joie avec laquelle l'enfant absorbe la forme et la couleur. J'oserai pousser plus loin; j'affirme que l'inspiration a quelque rapport avec la *congestion,* et que toute pensée sublime est accompagnée d'une secousse nerveuse, plus ou moins forte, qui retentit jusque dans le cervelet. L'homme de génie a les nerfs solides; l'enfant les a faibles. Chez l'un, la raison a pris une place considérable; chez l'autre, la sensibilité occupe presque tout l'être. Mais le génie n'est que *l'enfance retrouvée* à volonté, l'enfance douée maintenant, pour s'exprimer, d'organes virils et de l'esprit analytique qui lui permet d'ordonner la somme de matériaux involontairement amassée (*Œuvres complètes*, III, 59–60).

10. *ER*, pp. 187–96.
11. *Ibid.*, pp. 199–207.
12. *Ibid.*, pp. 211–17.
13. Edgar Allan Poe, "The Philosophy of Composition" and "The Poetic Principle," *Complete Works*, ed. James A. Harrison (New York, 1902), XIV, 193–208, 266–92 resp.
14. In his essay on Gautier, Baudelaire writes: "C'est cet admirable, cet immortel instinct du Beau qui nous fait considére la Terre et ses spectacles comme un aperçu, comme une *correspondance* du Ciel. La soif insatiable de tout ce qui est au delà, et que révèle la vie, est la preuve la plus vivante de notre immortalité. C'est à la fois par la poésie et *à travers* la poésie, par et *à travers* la musique, que l'âme entrevoit les splendeurs situées derrière le tombeau; et quand un poëme exquis amène les larmes au bord des yeux, ces larmes ne sont pas la preuve d'un excès de jouissance, elles sont bien plutôt le témoignage d'une mélancolie irritée, d'une postulation des nerfs, d'une nature exilée dans l'imparfait et qui voudrait s'emparer immédiatement, sur cette terre même, d'un paradis révélé" (*L'Art romantique, Œuvres complètes*, III, 159).

    Quoting this passage, Jacques Maritain remarks: "Knowledge, not rational and conceptual, but affective and nostalgic, the knowledge through connaturality which the artist has of beauty in his creative experience, is *in itself* (I do not say for him or for his consciousness) an advance toward God, a spiritual inclination in the direction of God, an obscure and ill-assured beginning of the knowledge of God—vulnerable, indeed, on all sides because it is not disengaged in the light of intelligence and because it remains without rational support" (*Approaches to God,* trans. Peter O'Reilly [New York, 1954], p. 86).
15. Carl G. Jung, "The Psychology of the Unconscious," *Two Essays on Analytical Psychology, Collected Works*, VII, 64–65. Philip Wheelwright calls this mode of imagination "archetypal." See his chapter, "Four Ways of Imagination," *The Burning Fountain* (Bloomington, 1954), pp. 76–100. Hearn's interest in mythology, as well as his theory of idealism, could better be understood in this light.
16. Ernst Cassirer, *An Essay on Man* (New Haven, 1944), pp. 76–77, 153–54. For the author's theory of art, see especially his two chapters, "Myth and Religion" and "Art."
17. "On Composition," *LL*, pp. 52–61. See also his letter to B. H. Chamberlain, January 23, 1893 (*JL*, pp. 41–43) and another quoted in N. Amenomori, "Lafcadio Hearn, The Man," *Atlantic Monthly*, XCVI (October 1905), 513.
18. Letter to B. H. Chamberlain, February 18, 1894. *JL*, pp. 256–57. Cf. Poe's essay "The Poetic Principle": "The struggle to apprehend the supernal Loveliness—this struggle, on the part of souls fittingly constituted—has given to the world all *that* which it (the world) has ever been enabled at once to understand and *to feel* as poetic" (*Complete Works*, XIV, 274).

19. "First Impressions," *ER*, pp. 193–94. Cf. Jung, on the collective unconscious:

> In so far as through our unconscious we have a share in the historical collective psyche, we live naturally and unconsciously in a world of werewolves, demons, magicians, etc., for these are things which all previous ages have invested with tremendous affectivity. Equally we have a share in gods and devils, saviours and criminals; but it would be absurd to attribute these potentialities of the unconscious to ourselves personally. It is therefore absolutely essential to make the sharpest demarcation between the personal and the impersonal attributes of the psyche. This is not to deny the sometimes very formidable existence of the contents of the collective unconscious, but only to stress that, as contents of the collective psyche, they are opposed to and different from the individual psyche (*Two Essays on Analytical Psychology, Collected Works*, VII, 92).

20. *LL*, pp. 77–79.
21. "On the Relation of Life and Character to Literature," *ibid.*, p. 25.
22. "Shakespeare" and "Note on the Study of Shakespeare" are collected in *IL*, II, 1–38. See also *LS*.
23. "The Prose of the Classic Age," *HEL*, I, 302–3.
24. *LL*, pp. 37–38.
25. "Note upon Rossetti's Prose," *ibid.*, p. 191.
26. "Some Musical Literature," *TD*, May 31, 1886. *LE*, p. 193.
27. *LL*, p. 25. Here we find the consummation of Hearn's artist-lover theme (Chapter 3) and his concept of idealism (Chapter 6). Of the modern poet's nostalgic complaint that the "golden age" of poetry is "a lost paradise," Cassirer writes:

> But this complaint of the modern poet appears to be unfounded. For it is one of the greatest privileges of art that it can never lose this "divine age." Here the source of imaginative creation never dries up, for it is indestructible and inexhaustible. In every age and in every great artist the operation of imagination reappears in new forms and in new force. In the lyrical poets, first and foremost, we feel this continuous rebirth and regeneration. They cannot touch a thing without imbuing it with their own inner life (*An Essay on Man*, pp. 153–54).

Chapter 9

1. Gould, pp. 103–4.
2. Noguchi, p. 128.
3. T. Saito, "English Literature in Japan: A Sketch," Inazo Nitobe and others (eds.), *Western Influences in Modern Japan* (Chicago, 1931), p. 191.
4. For a comprehensive treatment of the subject, see Hisao Homma, *Meiji Bungakushi (A History of Meiji Literature)* (Tokyo, 1935), I. In his introduction the author designates the period as the Renaissance of modern Japan. See also Yoshie Okazaki, *Japanese Literature in the Meiji Era*, trans. V. H. Viglielmo (Tokyo, 1955), especially its first part, "A General Survey of Meiji Literature" (pp. 1–110).
5. Tanabe, pp. 202–4.
6. Saito, in *Western Influences in Modern Japan*, p. 197.
7. "Literature and Political Opinion," *IL*, I, 391–99.
8. "Notes on American Literature," *HEL*, II, 863–66.
9. For a list of Hearn's special lectures, see Tanabe, pp. 399–418. Cf. "It is greatly to be regretted that we have not in English a system of arrangement enabling the student to discover quickly all that has been written upon a particular subject—such as roses, for example, or pine trees, or doves, or the beauties of the autumn season" ("Some Poems about Insects," *IL*, II, 239).
10. Letter to Masanobu Ōtani, January 1900. *LH*, II, 461–64. See also "Note upon the Abuse and the Use of Literary Societies," *LL*, pp. 69–76. Cf. "The Japanese of our day have taken kindly to societies and associations of all sorts" (B. H. Chamberlain, *Things Japanese* [London, 1905], p. 434).
11. "Farewell Address," *IL*, II, 369–74.
12. Homma, I, 485.

13. For an extensive discussion of the question, see Okazaki's chapter, "The Universalization of Meiji Literature," in his *Japanese Literature in the Meiji Era*, pp. 93–110.
14. For a further discussion of the question, see Okazaki's chapter, "The Changes in Literary Style," *ibid.*, pp. 38–49.
15. "Studies of Extraordinary Prose," *IL*, II, 72–76. Years before, Emerson wrote: "I do not hesitate to read all the books I have named, and all good books, in translations. What is really best in any book is translatable; any real insight or broad human sentiment— . . . I rarely read any Greek, Latin, German, Italian—sometimes not a French book—in the original which I can procure in a good version" (as quoted in Richard G. Moulton, *World Literature* [New York, 1921], p. 5). For Goethe's view of translation as the most important instrument of world literature, see Fritz Strich, *Goethe and World Literature*, trans. C. A. M. Sym (London, 1949), pp. 6–9.
16. "On Modern English Criticism," *LL*, pp. 80–107. See also "Note on Some French Romantics," *ibid.*, pp. 246–65.
17. "Notes on American Literature," *HEL*, II, 865.
18. Goethe, *Werke*, 38: 137. Quoted in René Wellek, *A History of Modern Criticism:* I (New Haven, 1955), 221.
19. For a discussion of *West-Eastern Divan* as Goethe's attempt in this direction, see Strich's chapter, "New Light from the Far East," in *Goethe and World Literature*, pp. 136–51.
20. Designating modern Japanese literature as the result of the universalization of Meiji literature, Okazaki writes: ". . . Meiji literature indicated the possibility of a complete fusion of the literary currents of East and West. . . . This assertion leads us to the conclusion that from our present vantage-point this Meiji literature of ours was the most remarkable microcosm of universal literature conceivable" (Okazaki, p. 110).
21. "On Modern English Criticism," *LL*, p. 100. For the Far East in French literature, see William L. Schwartz, *The Imaginative Interpretation of the Far East in Modern French Literature, 1800–1925* (Paris, 1927).
22. "Some Poems on Death," *LL*, p. 323. The oft-quoted verse from "Locksley Hall"—"Better fifty years of Europe than a cycle of Cathay"—may explain Hearn's refusal to accept Tennyson as a world poet.
23. "Realistic Fiction," *TD*, September 10, 1882. *EAL*, pp. 100–3.
24. *"The Epic of Kings," TD*, April 22, 1883. *EEOL*, p. 318. For Emerson, Thoreau, and other contemporaries in relation to the Orient, see F. I. Carpenter, *Emerson and Asia* (Cambridge, Mass., 1930) and Arthur Christy, *The Orient in American Transcendentalism* (New York, 1932).
25. "The Renaissance: I—The Palette," *Poetry*, V, No. 5 (February 1915), 233. Quoted in S. K. Coffman, Jr., *imagism* (Norman, Okla., 1951), p. 42.
26. "Note upon the Shortest Forms of English Poetry," *IL*, II, 363. For Japanese influence on Anglo-American literature, see Earl Miner, *The Japanese Tradition in British and American Literature* (Princeton, 1958).
27. John Gould Fletcher, "The Orient and Contemporary Poetry," *Asian Legacy and American Life*, ed. Arthur Christy (New York, 1945), pp. 148–49.
28. For a rather negative view of this question, see James Baird, "Critical Problems in the Orientalism of Western Poetry," in *Asia and the Humanities*.
29. Letter to Ellwood Hendrick, September 1895. *LH*, II, 271.
30. Strich's book discusses in detail Goethe's concept of world literature. For further discussion of the term "world literature" (Goethe's *Weltliteratur*), see Strich, pp. 4–5; Moulton, pp. 1–9; and René Wellek and Austin Warren, "General, Comparative, and National Literature," *Theory of Literature* (New York, 1949), pp. 38–45.
31. "A Language Question," *TD*, May 16, 1885. *OG*, II, pp. 20–23. In the same article Hearn writes: "Humanity, emotionally considered, is the same the world over;—love, whether in India or among the Esquimaux, expresses itself in words of beauty;—faith whether in the sea of sand, or in the heart of strange Chinese cities, is the utterance of a universal truth;—and the incense of prayer is not less sweet whether it rises from the banks of the Volga or of the Mississippi."
32. "A Peep at Japanese Poetry," *TD*, May 27, 1883. *EEOL*, pp. 330–39.
33. "Some French Poems on Insects," *LL*, p. 266.

34. Letter to B. H. Chamberlain, May 10, 1894. *JL*, pp. 307–8. The correspondents are concerned with Mallarmé's poem, "L'Après-midi d'un faune," as shown in the following passage from the same letter: "The only really fine line in it,— '—*meurtries/ De la langueur goutée à ce mal d'être deux*—' (you will acknowledge a sensual but weird beauty in that!) is not original. I have read it before, though I can't tell where. I think it was better in the other form—to my taste the word *goutée* spoils the charm. The beauty is really in that pyschic truth of the desire to melt into another being—the fable of Salmacis and Hermaphroditus."

35. This judgment may also be due to Hearn's emphasis on what Goethe called "world poetry" in connection with "world literature." For Goethe's concept of world poetry as the essence of world literature, see Strich, pp. 307–18.

36. "Tolstoi's Theory of Art," *LL*, p. 293.

37. "The Prose of Small Things," *ibid.*, p. 128.

38. Letter to B. H. Chamberlain, November 1893(?). *JL*, pp. 197–98.

39. Cf. "We repeat, the idea is not that the nations should think alike, but that they shall learn how to understand one another, and, if they do not care to love another, at least they will learn to tolerate one another" (Goethe, *Werke*, 38: 170. Quoted in Wellek, *A History of Modern Criticism*, I, 221).

40. Letter to Wayland D. Ball, 1882. *LH*, I, 251.

Chapter 10

1. In his letter to Chamberlain of August 21, 1894, Hearn recalls his childhood: "—Carnarvon Castle was a favorite visit. I used to climb the Eagle-tower, and look down upon the crawling of the ships. I remember a *white* peacock there.—In Carnarvon also I had my first knowledge of the farther East. One year I lived there all alone with my nurse in the cottage of a seaman of some sort,—he was on the Chinese run; and every time he came back he used to bring all sorts of curious things from China,—porcelains, grotesques, gods. . . ." (*JL*, p. 370).

2. See, for instance, "Porcelain Painting," *CC*, August 29, 1875, *BB;* letter to Henry Watkin, June 27, 18—, *LR*, p. 69; "Tropical Literature," *TD*, December 12, 1886, *LE;* etc.

3. See, for instance, "Butterfly Fantasies," *CC*, May 9, 1876, *AM*, I, 190–93; "The New Orleans Exposition: The Japanese Exhibit," *Harper's Weekly*, January 31, 1885, *OG*, II, 209–14; "The East at New Orleans," *Harper's Weekly*, March 7, 1885, *ibid.*, II, 215–19; *TY*, p. 269.

4. Hearn's contributions to the *Japan Mail* consist, so far as is known, of 19 pieces, covering the period from November 3, 1890, to February 4, 1893. His editorials for the *Kobe Chronicle*, numbering 48, cover the period from October 11, 1894, to December 14, 1894.

5. Letter of August 4, 1891. *Letters from Basil Hall Chamberlain to Lafcadio Hearn*, ed. Kazuo Koizumi (Tokyo, 1936), pp. 57–58.

6. Letter of February 2, 1894. *JL*, pp. 243–44.

7. Letter of May 16, 1894. *Ibid.*, p. 309.

8. Letter of July 15, 1894. *Ibid.*, p. 341.

9. Letter to S. Nishida, October 23, 1894. *SNL*, p. 133.

10. Letter to Chamberlain, April 19, 1893. *JL*, pp. 85–89. See also that of March 4, 1894. *Ibid.*, pp. 261–62.

11. Letter of May 10, 1894. *Letters from Chamberlain*, p. 140.

12. Letter of July 17, 1894. *More Letters from Basil Hall Chamberlain to Lafcadio Hearn*, ed. Kazuo Koizumi (Tokyo, 1937), p. 142.

13. Letter of 1893. *SNL*, p. 81.

14. Letter of January 17, 1893. *JL*, p. 38.

15. Letter to Chamberlain, September 11, 1894. *Ibid.*, p. 382.

16. Letter to E. Hendrick, September 1894. *LH*, II, 186.

17. Letter of October 16, 1894. *JL*, p. 388.

18. Editorial of October 16, 1894. *EKC*, p. 10.

19. Letter of 1895. *LH*, II, 223.

20. Letter to S. Nishida, December 18, 1896. *SNL*, p. 174
21. Letter to E. Hendrick, 1902. *LH*, II, 485.
22. "At Mionoseki," *GUJ*, I, 243.
23. "From Hōki to Oki," *ibid.*, II, 585.
24. "The Japanese Smile," *ibid.*, II, 664.
25. See "From the Diary of an English Teacher," *ibid.*, II, 430–90. The Yokogi episode related in the chapter was provided by Hearn's Matsue pupil, Azukizawa (later Fujisaki). Cf. "Official Education," *JAI*, pp. 457–82.
26. "Sayōnara!" *GUJ*, II, 687.
27. "Jiujutsu," *OE*, pp. 230–34. The conversation actually took place between Hearn and his student Asakichi Yasukochi (later Vice-Minister of Home Affairs). The episode is in a similar manner related in his letter to Chamberlain of June 4, 1894 (*JL*, pp. 315–18) and also his letter to E. Hendrick of June 1894 (*LH*, II, 177–80).
28. Letter of June 17, 1894. *More Letters*, p. 135.
29. Letter of June 15, 1893. *JL*, p. 121.
30. "Jiujutsu," *OE*, pp. 230–31.
31. *Ibid.*, p. 229.
32. April 15, 1891. *LSK*, pp. 24–25. See also his letter to Chamberlain, of February 25, 1894 (*JL*, pp. 257–58).
33. "A Conservative," *Kokoro*, pp. 170–209.
34. R. L. Stevenson, "Yoshida-Torajiro," *Works* (New York, 1924), XIV, 152.
35. B. H. Chamberlain, *Things Japanese*, p. 65.
36. The editorials discussed here are "The Policy of Interference," October 12; "Barbarism and Civilization," December 11; and "As to the 'Golden Rule,'" December 14, 1894, all collected in *EKC*.
37. The editorials discussed here are "Some Possible Results of the War," October 15; "The Need of Generosity," October 17; "Sympathy with China," November 1; "The Future of China," November 12; "The Need of Generosity," December 10; "A Triple Alliance in the Farther East," December 12; and "The Korean Riddle," December 13, 1894, all collected in *EKC*. Cf. his letter to Hendrick, December 1895:

> And I hope to see a United Orient yet bound into one strong alliance against our cruel Western civilization. If I have been able to do nothing else in my life, I have been able at least to help a little—as a teacher and as a writer, and as an editor—in opposing the growth of what is called society and what is called civilization. It is very little, of course,—but the gods ought to love me for it (*LH*, II, 281).

38. See William W. Clary's study, *Japan: The Warnings and Prophecies of Lafcadio Hearn* (Claremont, Calif., 1943).
39. Letter to Chamberlain, January 17, 1893. *JL*, p. 35.
40. Letter to Mrs. Wetmore, November 1902. *LH*, II, 486. Cf. Chamberlain, in his letter to Hearn, August 5, 1893: "The longer I live among the Japanese the more strongly does the conviction strike into me that I know nothing of them but the outside" (*Letters from Chamberlain*, p. 32).
41. "Strangeness and Charm," *JAI*, p. 10.
42. William E. Griffis, a review of *Japan*, in *The Critic* XLVI (February 1905), 185, as quoted in Gould, pp. 322–23.
43. Letter of 1903. *LH*, II, 504–5. Cf. his letter to Mrs. Wetmore, in 1903:
> For the sake of the lectures, it is better that I should wait a little longer in Japan. Most of them have been written twice; but I must write them all once more—to polish them. They will form a book, explaining Japan from the standpoint of ancestor-worship. They are suited only to a cultivated audience. If never delivered, they will make a good book. The whole study is based upon the ancient religion (*ibid.*, II, 499).

44. See Chaps. XII, "The Triad of Principles"; XIII, "The Quality of Impersonality"; XIV, "The Patriarchal System"; and XV, "The Position of Woman," *Chosön, The Land of the Morning Calm* (Boston, 1886).
45. *Occult Japan* (Boston, 1894), p. 21.
46. *The Soul of the Far East* (New York, 1888), p. 15.

47. *Ibid.*, p. 26.
48. "Imagination," *ibid.*, pp. 194–226.
49. Letter to Chamberlain, August 1891. *LH*, II, 39–40.
50. *JAI*, p. 13.
51. Letter to Chamberlain, May 1891. *LH*, II, 28.
52. "The Japanese Smile," *GUJ*, II, 682.
53. "Jiujutsu," *OE*, pp. 182–202.
54. Letter to Chamberlain, January 14, 1893. *JL*, pp. 31–33. For the same question see Hearn's chapter, "The Japanese Smile" (*GUJ*, II, 656–83).
55. Letter to Chamberlain, June 10, 1894. *JL*, pp. 322–23.
56. Irving Babbitt, "Romanticism and the Orient," *On Being Creative and Other Essays* (Boston, 1932), pp. 235–61.
57. "Nature and Art," *The Soul of the Far East*, pp. 122–23. In his letter to Hearn of August 5, 1893, Chamberlain quotes Lowell: " 'Oh! art, you know, beautiful as it is, belongs to a lower stage of culture before science is evolved' " (*Letters from Chamberlain*, p. 33).
58. Letter to Chamberlain, May 1891. *LH*, II, 30.
59. Letter to S. Nishida, November 1893. *Ibid.*, II, 160.
60. Letter to Chamberlain, January 1895. *Ibid.*, II, 200.
61. Letter to Chamberlain, February 1895. *Ibid.*, II, 208.
62. Letter to Chamberlain, January 14, 1893. *JL*, pp. 30–31.
63. *The Soul of the Far East*, p. 226.
64. E. Miner, *op. cit.*, p. 65.
65. For an extensive study of Japan as viewed by Americans and other Westerners, see John Ashmead, Jr., "The Idea of Japan 1853–1895," unpublished doctoral thesis, Harvard University, 1951.
66. B. H. Chamberlain, *Things Japanese*, p. 65. The Japanese are not always the best judges in this matter. Read for instance the following: "Koizumi Yakumo (Lafcadio Hearn), who came to Japan in 1890 and became a Japanese citizen five years later, wrote tens of books praising the beauty of Japan, and introduced Japanese culture to the Western world. It was unavoidable that he should have been unable to have a true understanding of Japan and have seen it as a dreamlike world of mystery, in spite of his love for and aspirations with regard to Japan" (Okazaki, *Japanese Literature in the Meiji Era*, p. 572).

Chapter 11

1. Letter of October 1891. *LH*, II, 64.
2. Albert Mordell, Introd., *AM*, I, lxxvi. Cf. "Without his Japanese work Hearn would have died as a litterateur in the year he died as a physical body" (Gould, p. 183).
3. Gould, pp. 175–76.
4. Tinker, p. 71.
5. Albert Mordell, "The Ideas of Lafcadio Hearn," *The Erotic Motive in Literature* (New York, 1919), p. 237.
6. Letter of 1887. *LH*, I, 401.
7. See Tinker, pp. 229–36.
8. *JAI*, p. 393.
9. "We discover in his [the Far Oriental's] peculiar point of view a new importance,— the possibility of using it stereoptically" (*The Soul of the Far East*, p. 4).
10. "The Insuperable Difficulty," *IL*, I, 5.
11. See his American editorial, "A Mad Romantic," *TD*, February 24, 1884, *EEOL*, p. 47. The *Catalogue* of the Hearn Library indicates that the Nerval version, purchased in America, is *Le Faust, suivi du second Faust* (Paris, M. Lévy, 1868).
12. See the *Catalogue*, p. 92, No. 1721. Gautier's *Histoire du romantisme*, which customarily includes his Baudelaire essay, is the one purchased in America. The edition is a Charpentier of 1874.
13. *Editorials*, pp. 142–46. The article is also quoted in Tinker, pp. 71–75.
14. Letter of November 1882. *LH*, I, 256. See the *Catalogue*, pp. 86, 98–100. In addi-

tion to *Le Femme, L'Oiseau, La Sorcière,* and *Légendes démocratiques du nord,* all purchased in America, Hearn owned a complete set of Michelet's *Works.* It is indeed Michelet who said: "Woman is a religion" (*Woman,* trans. J. W. Palmer [New York, 1860], p. 79).

15. Letter of March 1884. *LH,* I, 315–17.
16. Letter of May 1884. *Ibid.,* I, 326–27. *Stray Leaves* appeared in June 1884.
17. Letter to Chamberlain, 1891. *LH,* II, 35–36. Cf. "Japanese women are most womanly,—kind, gentle, faithful, pretty" (Chamberlain, *Things Japanese,* p. 500). Disagreeing with the majority of foreigners in Japan, Henry Adams wrote to Elizabeth Cameron, August 13, 1886, from Nikko: "The Japanese women seem to me impossible. After careful inquiry I can hear of no specimen of your sex, in any class of society, whom I ought to look upon as other than a *curio.* They are all badly made, awkward in movement, and suggestive of monkey" (*Selected Letters,* ed. Newton Arvin [New York, 1951], p. 95).
18. Letter to E. Hendrick, November 1892. *LH,* II, 98–99.
19. Letter of April 1893. *Ibid.,* II, 110–14.
20. *Ibid.,* II, 120. Here again Henry Adams disagrees with Hearn. For Adams' distinction between Europe and America in the matter of sex, see Chapter XXV, "The Dynamo and the Virgin," *The Education of Henry Adams* (Modern Library ed.), pp. 383–85.
21. Letter of June 19, 1893. *JL,* p. 122.
22. Letter of April 17, 1893. *Ibid.,* p. 81.
23. Letter to Hearn, April 25, 1893. *More Letters,* p. 61.
24. Letter to Chamberlain, June 25, 1893. *JL,* p. 125.
25. Letter to Chamberlain, September 9, 1893. *Ibid.,* pp. 162–63.
26. Letter to Hearn, April 20, 1895. *More Letters,* p. 163.
27. "Of the Eternal Feminine," *OE,* pp. 85–125.
28. Cf. Lin Yutang:

> To a Chinese, nothing is more striking than that the statue of a woman should be placed high up in the harbor of New York, to be looked at by all people coming into the country. The idea of feminine exposure is indecorous to the extreme. And when he learns that the woman there does not represent the feminine but the idea of liberty, he is still more shocked. Why should Liberty be represented by a woman? And why should Victory and Justice be represented by women? The Greek ideal to him is new. For in the West man's imagination has somehow deified woman and conferred on her a spiritual, ethereal quality, representing all that is pure, noble, beautiful and unearthly. To a Chinese, a woman is a woman, who does not know how to enjoy herself. (*My Country and My People* [New York, 1935], p. 149).

29. "The Insuperable Difficulty," *IL,* I, 5. See also *OE,* pp. 111–12.
30. *The Soul of the Far East,* p. 51.
31. *Chosön,* p. 130. Cf. Henry Adams' letter to John Hay, August 22, 1886: "In spite of [Clarence] King, I affirm that sex does not exist in Japan, except as a scientific classification. I would not affirm that there are no exceptions to my law; but the law itself I would affirm as the foundation of archaic society. Sex begins with the Aryan race" (*Selected Letters,* p. 101).
32. *The Soul of the Far East,* p. 31.
33. "Nature and Art" and "Art," *ibid.,* pp. 110–41, 142–61 resp.
34. For general treatment of the Eastern art principle, see Laurence Binyon, *The Flight of the Dragon* (London, 1911); Ananda K. Coomaraswamy, *The Transformation of Nature in Art* (Cambridge, Mass., 1935); and Mai-Mai Sze, *The Tao of Painting* ("Bollingen Series" XLIX, New York, 1956).
35. Lin Yutang, pp. 310–11.
36. Denis de Rougemont, *Love in the Western World,* trans. Montgomery Belgion, rev. ed. (New York, 1956). A recent criticism is voiced by Alan W. Watts in *Nature, Man, and Woman* (New York: Pantheon Books, 1958).
37. Rougemont, pp. 74, 64, 283 resp.
38. T. S. Eliot speaks of the "harmony with nature" which "must be re-established if

the truly Christian imagination is to be recovered by Christians" (*A Choice of Kipling's Verse* [New York, 1943], p. 33).

39. "Religion," *The Soul of the Far East*, p. 185.

40. *OE*, pp. 112–13. L. Binyon expresses the same view in *The Flight of the Dragon* (pp. 75–76).

41. For further discussion of this contrast, see Northrop's provocative work, *The Meeting of East and West* (New York, 1947), pp. 407–9. As for some exceptions, such as we find in Buddhist art, Northrop follows René Grousset's theory that they are due to Greek influence.

42. *OE*, p. 120. For Hearn's other observations on the aesthetic aspect of Japanese life, see "In a Japanese Garden" (*GUJ*, II), "About Faces in Japanese Art" (*GBF*), "Frogs" (*ER*), "Bits of Poetry" (*GJ*), "Old Japanese Songs" (*Shadowings*), "The Story of Kwashin Koji" (*JM*), "The Story of Kōgi the Priest" (*JM*), "Dragon-flies" (*JM*), "Songs of Japanese Children" (*JM*), "Fireflies" (*Kotto*), etc. Relative to Hearn's prediction, see *House Beautiful*'s two issues (August and September 1960) dealing exclusively with Japanese art and its possible impact on American life.

Chapter 12

1. "The Eternal Feminine," *OE*, pp. 103–4.

2. Letter of August 1891. *LH*, II, 39–40. Lowell's original statement is as follows: ". . . *the degree of individualization of a people is the self-recorded measure of its place in the great march of mind* (*The Soul of the Far East*, p. 195). Cf. W. E. Hocking:

More practically, individualism has in practice tended to destroy the capacity of our democracies to achieve unity of action and feeling: the claim of rights has eaten up the awareness of common duty. And the totalitarian reaction expresses a distrust of the moral bases of democracy. We cannot meet the totalitarian case by simply reasserting our confidence in democracy. We have to reconsider the philosophical basis of democracy and the meaning of such individualism as we shall continue to hold. In this respect, the Orient is likely to be very instructive to us ("Value of the Comparative Study of Philosophy," *Philosophy—East and West*, ed. Charles A. Moore [Princeton, 1946], p. 8).

3. Letter to Chamberlain, January 14, 1893. *JL*, pp. 30–33.

4. Letter to E. Hendrick, November 1893. *LH*, II, 150.

5. See note 3 above.

6. Letter to Hearn, June 17, 1894. *More Letters*, p. 135. Hearn's dialog with his student became part of the essay "Jiujutsu." It is quoted and discussed Chapter 10, pp. 190–92.

7. N.d., *JL*, pp. 325–27.

8. Letter to Chamberlain, January 19, 1893. *Ibid.*, pp. 38–40.

9. Letter to E. Hendrick, August 1893. *LH*, II, 137–38. In spite of Hearn's testimony, the similarity between his position and Pearson's is not as significant as their difference, as is evident in Pearson's estimate of non-Western cultures:

Even during historical times, so-called, the world has mostly been peopled by races, either like the negro very little raised above the level of brutes, or at best like the lower-caste Hindoo and the Chinaman, of such secondary intelligence as to have added nothing permanent to our stock of ideas (*National Life and Character: A Forecast* [London, 1893], p. 341).

10. Letter of September 16, 1893. *JL*, pp. 166–67.

11. "The Future of China," November 12, 1894, *EKC*, p. 50. See also his letter to Chamberlain, April 28, 1893. *JL*, pp. 89–90.

12. "Jiujutsu," *OE*, pp. 234–42. See also "The Future of the Far East" (*SNL*, pp. 383–402). Hearn's view of the pattern in the struggle between the Western and the non-Western world is strikingly similar to that of Arnold Toynbee in *The World and the West* (London, 1953).

13. Collected in *Karma*, pp. 110–63.

14. Letter to E. Hendrick, September 1894. *LH*, II, 184–85.
15. "American Aristocracy," *Item*, April 30, 1881. *BCT*, p. 150.
16. "Will the Time Come When All Men Will Be Wise?" *Item*, October 5, 1881. *Ibid.*, pp. 137–39.
17. "Communism," *Item*, August 17, 1878. *Ibid.*, pp. 128–30.
18. Letter to Ernest Crosby, 1904. *LH*, II, 511.
19. Quoted by Hearn in his lecture, "Beyond Man," *IL*, II, 227. Under the chapter title, "Go to the Ant," Philo M. Buck, Jr., makes a study of Jules Romains' Unanimism—in the same spirit (*Directions in Contemporary Literature* [New York, 1942], pp. 193–217). In this manner we may profitably approach Michelet's *L'Insecte*, which was Hearn's favorite, and also Maeterlinck's interest in the intelligence and will to live of flowers, bees, termites, and ants.
20. See Kenneth Kirkwood, Chap. II, "Hearn the Animal Lover," in his *Unfamiliar Lafcadio Hearn*, and Tinker, Chap. IX, "Mrs. Courtney Mothers Hearn." Tinker Hearn as saying:

> Why, no, Mrs. Courtney, I'm only watching those ants. They seem so superior to us. They never fight among themselves, or backbite, or loaf. They're always working, working for the common good of their community. At a second's notice they are willing to sacrifice their lives—everything—to the general welfare. People are not like this. The propriety and morality of the ant is far higher than that of the human. If people could only learn to cooperate and all work for the public weal, to forget themselves and their egotism—how much better the world would be (p. 200).

21. Editorial of July 11, 1878. *Editorials*, pp. 17–18.
22. "Cat and Dog Stories," *Item*, April 1, 1881. *NR*, pp. 53–55.
23. "The Sexual Idea in French Literature," *Item*, June 17, 1881. *Editorials*, p. 146. Cf. Jules Michelet:

> The ant is frankly and strongly republican, having no need of a living and visible symbol of the community, lightly esteeming and governing with sufficient rudeness the soft and feeble females who perpetuate the race. The bee, on the other hand, more tender apparently, or less reasoning and more imaginative, finds a moral support in the worship of the common mother. For her community of virgins it is, so to speak, a religion of love. Among both the ants and bees maternity is the social principle; but fraternity also takes root, flourishes, and springs to a glorious stature (*The Insect*, trans. W. H. Davenport Adams [London, 1875], p. 333).

24. *Item*, October 4, 1881. *NR*, pp. 56–58. Cf. C. G. Jung:

> Modern investigation of animal instinct, as for example in insects, has brought together a rich fund of empirical findings which show that if man acted as certain insects do he would possess a higher intelligence than at present. It cannot, of course, be proved that insects possess conscious knowledge, but commonsense cannot doubt that their unconscious action-patterns are psychic functions (*Modern Man in Search of a Soul*, trans. Cary F. Baynes and W. S. Dell [New York, 1936], p. 214).

25. Editorial of August 27, 1882. *OG*, II, 48–52.
26. "Beyond Man," *IL*, II, 220–27.
27. "Ants," *Kwaidan*, pp. 215–40. Cf. R. L. Stevenson:

> We look at our feet where the ground is blackened with the swarming ant; a creature so small, so far from us in the hierarchy of brutes, that we can scarce trace and scarce comprehend his doings; and here also, in his ordered politics and rigorous justice, we see confessed the law of duty and the fact of individual sin ("*Pulvis et Umbra*," *Works*, XV, 296–97).

Cf. also S. Radhakrishnan:

> The holiness of life in all things, the equality of origin in the flower, the insect, the animal and the man were the fundamental ideas of the Upaniṣads, which betrayed them into an acceptance of this position. It has also great practical value. The tenderness shown to animals in the āśranas of the forests favoured the doctrine. Proud man was required to get rid of his snobbery and exclusiveness, and admit with the

humility of a St. Francis that the black beetle was his brother. This is not strange when we think of the modern theories of evolution and their emphasis on the close affinity between men and animals (*Indian Philosophy*, I [New York, 1923], 252–53).

28. These two statements by Rousseau and Goethe are quoted in E. Cassirer, *An Essay on Man*, pp. 61–62. In the same place Cassirer writes: "The great mission of the Utopia is to make room for the possible as opposed to a passive acquiescence in the present actual state of affairs. It is symbolic thought which overcomes the natural inertia of man and endows him with a new ability, the ability constantly to reshape his human universe."

29. From *The Surangama Sutra* (trans. Wei-Tao and Dwight Goddard), as quoted in Lin Yutang, *The Wisdom of China and India* (Modern Library ed., 1942), pp. 542–44. Cf. Confucius, *The Analects*, Bk. IX, xvi. Indian philosophy includes the art of love as one of its legitimate subjects. For discussion of the Kāma literature, see Heinrich Zimmer, "The Philosophy of Pleasure," *Philosophies of India* (New York, 1951). With specific reference to the "frankly sexual symbolism" found in the Tantaric Hinduism, F. S. C. Northrop also writes: "A culture born of such a religion would hardly need a Freud. Even so, Hinduism is more subtle and restrained than Freudian psychology" (*The Meeting of East and West*, pp. 372–73).

30. Denis de Rougemont observes:

Antiquity has left no record of an experience akin to the love of Tristan and Iseult. It is well known that the Greeks and Romans looked on love as a sickness—the expression is Menander's—whenever it went, no matter how little, beyond the sensual pleasure which was considered to be its natural expression. Plutarch calls love "a frenzy." "Some have believed it was a madness. . . . Thus those who are in love must be forgiven as though ill" (*Love in the Western World*, p. 60).

31. For a view of individualism as the product of the post-Renaissance West, see René Guénon, *The Crisis of the Modern World*, trans. Arthur Osborne (London, 1942).

32. Charles A. Moore, "Comparative Philosophies of Life," *Philosophy—East and West*, p. 307. Cf. W. E. Hocking: "In my judgment, we shall have no just estimate of our own social order until we have understood the philosophical bases of this Oriental outlook, in which the lot of the individual is not immersed in, but entwined with, the fortunes of a corporate group or groups, whether the family, the occupational group, or the nation" ("Value of the Comparative Study of Philosophy," *ibid.*, p. 10). Cf. *The Doctrine of the Mean*, xxx:

All things are nourished together without their injuring one another. The courses of the seasons, and the sun and moon, are pursued without any collision among them. The smaller energies are like river currents; the greater energies are seen in mighty transformations. It is this which makes heaven and earth so great.

For a comparative discussion of the question, see E. R. Hughes (ed.), *The Individual in East and West* (Oxford, 1937).

33. "Reflections," *JAI*, pp. 504–5.

34. Fumio Hozumi, *Lafcadio Hearn's Views of Society* (Tokyo, 1949), a Japanese text, is, so far as I know, the only serious study of Hearn's social thought.

Chapter 13

1. *LR*, pp. 99–100.

2. Letter of 1886. *LH*, I, 374–75. Of Hearn's interest in Spencer, Dr. Rudolph Matas remarked:

When he became acquainted with the work of Herbert Spencer,—through the enthusiasm of his friend Ernest Crosby for that philosopher and for the Darwinian theory of evolution, which we were all discussing with deep interest at that time—he used that thinker's philosophy as a foundation upon which to base his marvelous speculations as to the ultimate development of the race and the infinite truths of the universe (quoted in Charles W. Hutson, Introd., *FF*, p. 21).

Compare Hearn's enthusiasm to O. W. Holmes's tribute to Spencer, in which he expressed his doubt that "any writer of English except Darwin has done so much to affect our whole way of thinking about the universe" (quoted in Richard Hofstadter, *Social Darwinism in American Thought* [Philadelphia, 1945], p. 19).

3. Quoted in *LR*, p. 17.
4. See Gould, p. 192, and also Matthew Josephson, "An Enemy of the West: Lafcadio Hearn," *Portrait of the Artist as American* (New York, 1930), pp. 199–231.
5. "Lafcadio Hearn, The Man," *Atlantic Monthly*, XCVI (October 1905), 521.
6. Mentioned in his letter to Mitchell McDonald, December 1898. *LH*, II, 409.
7. *JAI*, p. 232.
8. "*The Light of Asia,*" *Item*, October 24, 1879. *OA*, p. 77.
9. "The Buddhistic Bugaboo!" *TD*, January 10, 1884, *OA;* "What Buddhism Is," *TD*, January 13, 1884, *EEOL*. See also Hearn's article, "Recent Buddhist Literature," *TD*, March 1, 1885, *EEOL*.
10. *LH*, I, 400–1.
11. "The Stone Buddha," *OE*, pp. 157–82.
12. "In Yokohama," *ibid.*, pp. 304–30. " 'In Yokohama' is a Buddhist paper,—a conversation with an old priest. Amenomori helped me magnificently with it—answering questions in the most beautiful way. His MS. is a wonder in itself. Any man who can write such English as Amenomori, and think so profoundly, ought to be able to render the *Tao-te-king* into perfect French" (letter to Chamberlain, September 22, 1894. *JL*, p. 384).
13. "The Idea of Preëxistence," *Kokoro*, pp. 222–56.
14. Cf. Eckhart: "Thou must love God as not-God, not-Spirit, not-person, not-image, but as He is, a sheer, pure absolute One, sundered from all two-ness, and in whom we must eternally sink from nothingness to nothingness" (Quoted in Aldous Huxley, *The Perennial Philosophy* [New York, 1945], p. 32).
15. *Kokoro*, pp. 248–49. Cf. Hearn's own ambition in "evolutional fiction."
16. "Nirvana," *GBF*, pp. 211–66. See also Amenomori, "Lafcadio Hearn, the Man," *Atlantic Monthly*, XCVI (October 1905), 513.
17. In his American editorial, "What Buddhism Is," Hearn attempted to define "Nirvana": "We have said annihilation; but it is still a vexed question whether Gotama regarded Nirvana as an utter extinction of being, or as a reabsorption of the soul into God, like a drop of water returning to the ocean whence it came. We do not know whether Nirvana always signified annihilation of the *Ego*,—as it seems to do today. A whole library of the treatises have been written on this one point alone" (*TD*, January 13, 1884. *EEOL*, p. 208). Evidently Hearn was aware of the conflicting definitions of the term, and yet his noncommital attitude indicates his merely intellectual grasp.
18. "The Higher Buddhism," *JAI*, pp. 229–50.
19. "Of Moon-Desire," *ER*, p. 177. Quoted more fully in Chapter 14, pp. 257–58.
20. *LSK*, p. 38.
21. *JL*, p. 320.
22. "The Japanese Smile," *GUJ*, II, 682–83. See also Michio Nagai, "Herbert Spencer in Early Meiji Japan," *Far Eastern Quarterly*, XIV (1954–55), 55–64.
23. "A Conservative," *Kokoro*, p. 193. Cf. "A few—a very few—men trained in European methods fight for the Buddhist cause. They do so, not as orthodox believers in any existing sect, but because they are convinced that the philosophical contents of Buddhism in general are supported by the doctrine of evolution, and that this religion needs therefore only to be regenerated on modern lines in order to find universal acceptance" (B. H. Chamberlain, "Buddhism," *Things Japanese*, p. 79).
24. "Buddhist Allusions in Japanese Folksong," *GBF*, pp. 209–10.
25. *VP*, p. 46.
26. For a discussion of the relationship between Western philosophy and rational science, see Heinrich Zimmer, "The Claims of Science," *Philosophies of India*, pp. 27–34. For further discussion of the whole question here, see Radhakrishnan, *Eastern Religions and Western Thought* (Oxford, 1939) and Northrop, *The Meeting of East and West*.
27. For a discussion of this question, see George P. Conger, "Eastern and Western Metaphysics," *Philosophy—East and West*, ed. Charles A. Moore, pp. 235–47.

28. Cf. Matao Noda:

> It is quite common for Orientals to think that the way of "nothingness," in the sense of being free from egocentricity, is much higher in value than the way of "being," in the sense of valuing finite beings and egos. One may find a similar estimate of "nothingness," of course, even in the Christian idea of "poverty." But in contrast to the Christian idea of God as absolute "being," in Buddhism and Taoism "nothing" is raised to the status of the ultimate ontological principle itself. The Absolute is conceived here as nothing rather than as being. And, according to Nishida and some other modern interpreters of Buddhism, this principle of nothingness has the advantage of being more compatible with modern science and humanism than does the Christian idea of God. They contend that the Oriental ontology of nothingness can accept human freedom and scientific cosmology more consistently than the theistic idea can ("East-West Synthesis in Kitarō Nishida," *Philosophy—East and West*, IV, No. 4 [January 1955], 350).

29. "In the Twilight of the Gods," *Kokoro*, p. 211. For a violent rejection of such a proposal as Hearn's, see Henri Massis, *Defense of the West*, trans. F. S. Flint (New York, 1928), and Arthur Koestler, *The Lotus and the Robot* (New York, 1961). From the same Catholic viewpoint, however, René Guénon argues very differently. See especially *East and West*, trans. William Massey (London, 1941).

30. See *Philosophy—East and West* (Princeton, 1946), *Essays in East-West Philosophy* (Honolulu, 1951), and *Philosophy and Culture—East and West* (Honolulu, 1962). These volumes are the results of the East-West Philosophers' Conferences held at the University of Hawaii in the summers of 1939, 1949, and 1959. According to Charles A. Moore, the editor of all these volumes, the conferences are "dedicated to the search for greater mutual understanding between the Eastern and Western philosophical traditions and to the effort to discover avenues of progress toward a significant synthesis of the ideas and ideals of the Orient and the Occident" (*Essays in East-West Philosophy*, p. vii). For more systematic expositions of this theme, see Radhakrishnan, *Eastern Religions and Western Thought*, and Northrop, *The Meeting of East and West*.

31. "Profound as may be the difference between his religion [Buddhism] and our own [Christianity], in respect of symbols and modes of thought, the moral conclusions reached in either case are very much the same" (*JAI*, p. 250). "Buddha, Confucius, Christ—all were of their time and place, and though different, were the same in spirit" (Hearn as quoted in Kazuo Koizumi, *Father and I* [Boston, 1935], p. 160).

32. From *Diamond Sutra*, quoted in A. Huxley, *The Perennial Philosophy*, p. 263. Here the Buddha merely points out the ultimate insufficiency of a doctrinal approach to spiritual salvation.

33. In this respect Hearn's is but one among many voices we hear the more we strive toward integrating our divided world. Cf. W. E. Hocking: "We have to recognise that a *world religion exists*. We give religious systems separate names, but they are not separate; they are not closed globules. They merge in the universal human faith in the divine being" (quoted in Radhakrishnan, *Eastern Religions and Western Thought*, pp. 347–48). Cf. also Radhakrishnan, in *Recovery of Faith*:

> Though our age has largely ceased to understand the meaning of religion, it is still in desperate need of that which religion alone can give. The recognition of a Transcendent Supreme, the freedom of the human individual as a manifestation of the Supreme and the unity of mankind as the goal of history are the foundations of the major religions. The religion of spirit reasserts these fundamental truths. It does not regard dogmas and rites as anything more than a necessarily inadequate symbolism. It calls upon the leaders of religions to set faiths from hardening into moulds of orthodoxy, religious and social. The religion outlined in these pages may be called the sanātana dharma, the eternal religion. It is not to be identical with any particular religion, for it is the religion which transcends race and creed and yet informs all races and creeds. We can so transform the religion to which we belong as to make it approximate to the religion of spirit. I am persuaded that every religion has possibilities of such a transformation. We must look upon Hinduism or Christianity

as part of an evolving revelation that might in time be taken over into the larger religion of the spirit" ([New York, 1955], pp. 204–5).

Chapter 14

1. *ER*, pp. 177–79.
2. See Gould, pp. 69, 191 resp.
3. "Crimson Madness," *Item*, November 20, 1878. *Editorials*, pp. 39–42. For the symbolic significance of Gautier's and Melville's obsession with the color white, see James Baird's chapter, "Whiteness," *Ishmael* (Baltimore, 1956), pp. 256–77.
4. See Gould, "Lafcadio Hearn," *Biographic Clinics*, IV (Philadelphia, 1906), pp. 200–37.
5. Albert Mordell, in " 'Letters to a Pagan' Not by Hearn," *Today's Japan*, V, No. 1 (1955–60, 5th anniversary issue), 89–98, questions the authenticity of Hearn's letters to Annetta Halliday (*Letters to a Pagan* [Detroit, 1933]). If it be forgery, the following passage, supposedly written from Martinique, indicates the pseudo-Hearn's awareness of a color sense to which Hearn's own writings attest:

> I am wondering where the esthetic difference between one color and another lies. And I am trying to classify the innumerable, unspeakable blues, like a crucible-glow, about me here in St. Pierre. Azure, indigo, sapphire, cerulean, ultra-marine, aquamarine, sky-blue, navy-blue, midnight blue, cadet blue, robin's egg-blue, baby blue, steel blue, electric blue—have I left any unnamed? A monstrous gamut of blue fire in ocean sky, hollow, mountains, distance, atmosphere, blossom, costume, foulard, fruit, shadow (Letter to Annetta Halliday, August 1887, *Letters to a Pagan*, p. 55).

6. *Shadowings*, pp. 197–200. Quoted in full, Chapter 2, above, pp. 42–43.
7. Gould, *Concerning Lafcadio Hearn*, p. 60.
8. "Memphis to New Orleans," *CC*, November 23, 1877. *OG*, I, 160–61; also quoted in Gould, pp. 61–62.
9. "Spring Fever Fancies," *Item*, March 16, 1879, *Editorials*, p. 44.
10. Quoted in Tinker, p. 255.
11. Editorial of August 15, 1879. *Editorials*, pp. 50–53.
12. *Item*, June 17, 1881. *Ibid.*, pp. 142–46.
13. "Ralph Waldo Emerson," *TD*, April 30, 1882. *EAL*, pp. 83–86.
14. *TD*, June 8, 1884, *Editorials*, pp. 238–42.
15. Quoted in *LH*, I, 16–25.
16. Letter of February 1887. *Ibid.*, I, 381–82.
17. Letter to Henry Watkin, June 1887. *LR*, p. 86.
18. *TD*, May 8, 1887, *Editorials*, pp. 349–53.
19. *Chita*, p. 21.
20. "A Pilgrimage to Enoshima," *GUJ*, I, 95.
21. See Hearn's Preface. In his letter to John Albee, May 1898, Hearn wrote: "My next volume will have a series of what I might call *metaphysical idyls*, perhaps, at its latter end. I fear you will think them too sombre,—now that I have felt something of the sunshine of your soul. However, each of us can only give his own tone to the thread which he contributes to the infinite warp and woof of human thought and emotion" (*LH*, II, 361).
22. Cf. S. Radhakrishnan, in *Recovery of Faith*:

> Spiritual apprehension insists on a participation of the knowing subject in the spiritual reality, a touching (haptus) and tasting (gustus) of the object of knowledge. We see, feel and taste the truth. This is the immediate awareness of Being itself. It is experience by participation, by a renewal of the self. We apprehend it with all sides of our being, sarvabhavena. Jesus defines the first Commandment thus: "Hear, O Israel: The Lord our God, the Lord is One; and you shall love the Lord your God with all your heart, and with all your soul, and with all your mind and with all your strength." Truth is the vision of reality which satisfies one's whole being. It is grasped by the complete man (p. 105).

23. "Parfum de Jeunesse," *ER*, pp. 221–26.
24. "A Red Sunset," *ibid.*, pp. 251–62.
25. "Azure Psychology," *ibid.*, pp. 227–40. This piece was first printed in *The Teikoku Bungaku* for January 1895.
26. "A Serenade," *ER*, pp. 241–50.
27. "Frisson," *ibid.*, pp. 263–74.
28. "Vespertina Cognitio," *ibid.*, pp. 275–92.
29. "The Eternal Haunter," *ibid.*, pp. 293–99. See "The Story of Aoyagi," a story about a young man in love with the spirit of a willow-tree (*Kwaidan*), and also Hearn's special lecture, "On Tree Spirits in Western Poetry," *IL*, II, 228–37.
30. "The Poetic Principle," *Complete Works*, XIV, 273.
31. Quoted in Tinker, p. 325. For Hearn's earlier mention of his father, see "Among the Spirits," *CE*, January 25, 1874 (*OG*, I, 24–35).
32. For a detailed account of the complicated circumstances, see O. W. Frost, *Young Hearn* (Tokyo, 1958).
33. Quoted in *LH*, I, 17.
34. *OE*, p. 112.
35. Letter of January 12, 1894. *JL*, pp. 222–23.
36. Letter to Chamberlain, January 22, 1894. *Ibid.*, p. 231.
37. Northrop, pp. 371–72. For Lao Tzu's repeated emphasis on the feminine principle, see his other poems: 1, 25, 28, 52, 59, 61, etc.
38. Compare this tree with the great Aswattha, a fig tree mentioned in the *Bhagavad-Gita* (XV).
39. *Kotto*, pp. 209–10. See Blake's poem, "Infant Sorrow": "My mother groan'd! my father wept,/Into the dangerous world I leapt:/Helpless, naked, piping loud:/Like a fiend hid in a cloud. //Struggling in my father's hands,/Striving against my swadling bands,/Bound and weary I thought best/To sulk upon my mother's breast." See also Michelet: "And so she has no fear of God; but advances peacefully towards Him, wishing only what He wishes, but sure of the life to come, and saying: 'Lord, I still love thee.' Such is the faith of the heart" (*Woman*, p. 263).
40. *RMW*, p. 49. Cf. "La force de l'homme est d'abstraire, de diviser, mais la force de la femme est de ne pas savoir abstraire, de conserver toute chose, toute idée entière et vivante, et par là de pouvoir la faire plus vivante et la féconder" (Michelet, *L'Amour* [Paris, 1861], pp. 181–82).
41. *RMW*, p. 112.
42. "The Genius of Japanese Civilization," *Kokoro*, p. 38.
43. Letter to Chamberlain, May 10, 1894. *JL*, p. 308.
44. "On the Relation of Life and Character to Literature," *LL*, pp. 24–25.
45. *GJ*, p. 200. Cf. "Sex complexes completely controlled his life,—in fact he was a strange combination of an illassible, masculine, physical passion married to a mentality that, in refinement and sensitiveness, was almost feminine, and so this particular subject had such an especial appeal that he treated it 'con amore'" (Tinker, p. 71). In his *Times-Democrat* editorial, "Memoirs of Michelet" (May 4, 1884), Hearn noted: "In such books especially as *L'Amour* and *La Femme*, this singular though beautiful androgynism of sentiment at once startles and charms; but the same characteristic makes itself felt in all his best works, whether in those wonderful essays upon natural history whose titles are too familiar to cite, or in the magnificent pages of his matchless history of France" (*LE*, pp. 101–2).

For discussion of androgynism, see C. G. Jung and C. Kerényi, *Essays on a Science of Mythology*, trans. R. F. C. Hull (New York, 1949). In his chapter, "The Hermaphroditism of the Child," Jung writes:

As civilization develops, the bisexual "primary being" turns into a symbol of the unity of personality, a symbol of the *self* where the war of opposites finds peace. In this way the primary being becomes the distant *goal* of man's self-development, having been from the very beginning a projection of unconscious wholeness. Man's wholeness consists in the union of the conscious and the unconscious personality.

Just as every individual derives from masculine and feminine genes, and the sex is determined by the predominance of the corresponding genes, so in the psyche it is only the conscious mind, in a man, that has the masculine sign, while the unconscious is by nature feminine. The reverse is true in the case of a woman. All I have done in my anima-theory is to rediscover and reformulate this fact. It has long been known (pp. 130–31).

Jung's interest in the Far Eastern theory of *yin-yang* is well known. When Fung Yu-Lan defines the Chinese ideal of man as "sageliness within and kingliness without," there is little doubt that he is simply restating this classical notion. See *A Short History of Chinese Philosophy* (ed. Derk Bodde [New York, 1948]).

Conclusion

1. Matthew Josephson, *Portrait of the Artist as American*, pp. 199–31.
2. Paul Elmer More, "Lafcadio Hearn," *Shelburne Essays*, 2nd ser. (New York, 1906), p. 48.
3. Harry T. Levin, "The Discovery of Bohemia," *Literary History of the United States*, ed. Robert E. Spiller and others (New York, 1957), pp. 1070–72.
4. Malcolm Cowley, Introd., *Selected Writings of Lafcadio Hearn*, pp. 14–15.
5. *Lafcadio Hearn in Japan*, p. 12. For a discussion of Hearn's position in the history of modern primitivism, see James Baird's *Ishmael*, especially pp. 156–61.
6. Introd., *Selected Writings . . .*, pp. 1–2.
7. For a recent assertion that any future dialog between the East and the West be based on our understanding of their underlying philosophies, see Charles A. Moore, "East-West Philosophy and World Understanding" and "East-West Philosophy and the Search for Truth," *Asia and the Humanities*. W. E. Hocking also writes:

There are three historic attitudes in dealing with what is beyond our own circle of ideas. First, "This is strange and alien—avoid it." Second, "This is strange and alien —investigate it." Third, "This appears strange and alien—but it is human; it is therefore kindred to me and potentially my own—learn from it." Until two centuries ago, we were for the most part acting upon the first maxim. For another two centuries, the eighteenth to the twentieth, we have acted on the second: we have been concerned with an objective study of the East. The two centuries ahead of us must be devoted to the third, an attempt to pass beyond scholarly objectivity to a working human association and the common pursuit of universal truth ("Value of the Comparative Study of Philosophy," *Philosophy—East and West*, ed. C. A. Moore, p. 11).

8. Cf. Baudelaire, in his essay on Victor Hugo: "Or, qu'est-ce qu'un poëte (je prends le mot dans son acception la plus large), si ce n'est un traducteur, un déchiffreur?" (*L'Art romantique, Œuvres complètes*, III, 305). Marcel Proust wrote: "Je m'apercevais que pour exprimer ces impressions pour écrire ce livre essentiel, le seul livre vrai, un grand écrivain n'a pas dans le sense courant à l'inventer puisqu'il existe déjà en chacun de nous, mais à le traduire. Le devoir et la tâche d'un écrivain sont ceux d'un traducteur" (*Le Temps retrouvé*, II, 41).
9. This quatrain from *Wilhelm Meister* is quoted in "On the Relation of Life and Character to Literature," *LL*, p. 39.
10. Letter to Chamberlain, January 30, 1894. *JL*, p. 238.
11. *JAI*, p. 473.
12. Gould, *Concerning Lafcadio Hearn*, p. 49.
13. F. L. Pattee, p. 227. Cf. "The symbolism of the Orient completed the disintegration of his baffling personality" (James Huneker, "The Cult of the Nuance: Lafcadio Hearn," *Ivory, Apes and Peacocks* [New York, 1915], p. 248).
14. "Of Moon-Desire," *ER*, p. 184.
15. Quoted in Nina H. Kennard, *Lafcadio Hearn* (London, 1911), p. 48.
16. "Fuji-no-Yama," *ER*, p. 17. For Hearn's mountain symbolism, see Chapter 5.
17. "A Winter Journey to Japan," *AM*, II, 254.
18. "Fragment," *GJ*, pp. 3–7.

19. "Artisitc Value of Myopia," *TD*, February 7, 1887. *Editorials*, p. 347. Hearn wrote to W. D. O'Connor in March 1887:

> Out of the misfortune, good came to me; and I notice that Nature is really very kind when we obey her;—she gives back more than she takes away, she lessens energies to increase mental powers of assimilation; she compels recognition, like the God of Job "who maketh silence in the high places," and after having taught us what we *cannot* do, then returns to us a hundredfold that which she first took away (*LH*, I, 383).

A
Selected
Bibliography

*The
Writings
of
Lafcadio
Hearn*

A. *Separate works published during his lifetime:*

Chita: A Memory of Lost Island. New York: Harper & Bros., 1889.

The Crime of Sylvestre Bonnard. By Anatole France. New York: Harper & Bros., 1890.

La Cuisine Créole, A Collection of Culinary Recipes. New York: Will H. Coleman, 1885.

Exotics and Retrospectives. Boston: Little, Brown & Co., 1898.

Gleanings in Buddha-Fields. Boston and New York: Houghton, Mifflin & Co., 1897.

Glimpses of Unfamiliar Japan. 2 vols. Boston and New York: Houghton, Mifflin & Co., 1894.

Gombo Zhèbes, Little Dictionary of Creole Proverbs. New York: Will H. Coleman, 1885.

In Ghostly Japan. Boston: Little, Brown & Co., 1899.

Japan: An Attempt at Interpretation. New York: Macmillan Co., 1904.

Japanese Fairy Tales. 5 vols. Tokyo: Hasegawa, 1898–1922.

A Japanese Miscellany. Boston: Little, Brown & Co., 1901.

Kokoro. Boston and New York: Houghton, Mifflin & Co., 1896.

Kotto. New York: Macmillan Co., 1902.

Kwaidan. Boston and New York: Houghton, Mifflin & Co., 1904.

One of Cleopatra's Nights and Other Fantastic Romances. By Théophile Gautier. New York: R. Worthington, 1882.

Out of the East. Boston and New York: Houghton, Mifflin & Co., 1895.

Shadowings. Boston: Little, Brown & Co., 1900.

Some Chinese Ghosts. Boston: Roberts Bros., 1887.

Stray Leaves from Strange Literature. Boston: James R. Osgood & Co., 1884.

Two Years in the French West Indies. New York: Harper & Bros., 1890.

Youma. New York: Harper & Bros., 1890.

B. *Posthumous collections:*

The Adventures of Walter Schnaffs. By Guy de Maupassant. Ed. Albert Mordell. Tokyo: Hokuseido Press, 1931.

An American Miscellany. 2 vols. Ed. Albert Mordell. New York: Dodd, Mead & Co., 1924.

Appreciations of Poetry. Ed. John Erskine. New York: Dodd, Mead & Co., 1916.

Barbarous Barbers and Other Stories. Ed. Ichiro Nishizaki. Tokyo: Hokuseido Press, 1939.

Books and Habits. Ed. John Erskine. New York: Dodd, Mead & Co., 1921.

Buying Christmas Toys and Other Essays. Ed. Ichiro Nishizaki. Tokyo: Hokuseido Press, 1939.

Children of the Levee. Ed. O. W. Frost. With an Introduction by John Ball. Lexington, Ky.: University of Kentucky Press, 1957.

Creole Sketches. Ed. Charles W. Hutson. With illustrations by the author. Boston and New York: Houghton Mifflin Co., 1924.

Editorials. Ed. Charles W. Hutson. Boston and New York: Houghton Mifflin Co., 1926.

Editorials from the Kobe Chronicle. New York: Privately printed, 1913.

Essays in European and Oriental Literature. Ed. Albert Mordell. New York: Dodd, Mead & Co., 1923.

Essays on American Literature. Ed. Sanki Ichikawa. With an Introduction by Albert Mordell. Tokyo: Hokuseido Press, 1929.

Fantastics and Other Fancies. Ed. Charles W. Hutson. Boston and New York: Houghton Mifflin Co., 1914.

A History of English Literature. 2 vols. Tokyo: Hokuseido Press, 1927.

The Idyl: My Personal Reminiscences of Lafcadio Hearn. By Leona Queyrouze Barel. Tokyo: Hokuseido Press, 1933.

Interpretations of Literature. 2 vols. Ed. John Erskine. New York: Dodd, Mead & Co., 1915.

The Japanese Letters of Lafcadio Hearn. Ed. Elizabeth Bisland. Boston and New York: Houghton Mifflin Co., 1910.

Japanese Lyrics. Boston and New York: Houghton Mifflin Co., 1915.

Karma. Ed. Albert Mordell. New York: Boni & Liveright, 1918.

Leaves from the Diary of an Impressionist. Early writings, with an Introduction by Ferris Greenslet. Boston and New York: Houghton Mifflin Co., 1911.

Letters from The Raven. Being the Correspondence of Lafcadio Hearn with Henry Watkin. Ed. Milton Bronner. New York: Brentano's, 1907.

Letters from Shimane and Kyushu. Privately printed for Sanki Ichikawa. Kyoto: Sunward Press, 1934.

Letters to a Pagan. Detroit: Robert Bruna Powers, 1933.*

The Life and Letters of Lafcadio Hearn. 2 vols. Ed. Elizabeth Bisland. Boston and New York: Houghton Mifflin Co., 1906.

Life and Literature. Ed. John Erskine. New York: Dodd, Mead & Co., 1917.

Literary Essays. Ed. Ichiro Nishizaki. Tokyo: Hokuseido Press, 1939.

* See Chapter 14, Note 5, p. 321.

"Newly Discovered Letters from Lafcadio Hearn to Dr. Rudolph Matas," ed. Ichiro Nishizaki. *Ochanomizu University Studies in Arts and Culture,* VIII (Tokyo, 1956), 85–118.

The New Radiance and Other Scientific Sketches. Ed. Ichiro Nishizaki. Tokyo: Hokuseido Press, 1939.

Occidental Gleanings. 2 vols. Ed. Albert Mordell. New York: Dodd, Mead & Co., 1925.

On Poets. Ed. Ryuji Tanabe, Teizaburo Ochiai, and Ichiro Nishizaki. Tokyo: Hokuseido Press, 1934.

Oriental Articles. Ed. Ichiro Nishizaki. Tokyo: Hokuseido Press, 1939.

Pre-Raphaelite and Other Poets. Ed. John Erskine. New York: Dodd, Mead & Co., 1922.

The Romance of the Milky Way and Other Studies and Stories. With an Introduction by Ferris Greenslet. Boston and New York: Houghton Mifflin Co., 1905.

Saint Anthony, and Other Stories. By Guy de Maupassant. Ed. Albert Mordell. New York: Albert and Charles Boni, 1924.

Sketches and Tales from the French. Ed. Albert Mordell. Tokyo: Hokuseido Press, 1935.

"Some Martinique Letters of Lafcadio Hearn." With an Introduction by Elizabeth Bisland. *Harper's Monthly,* CXLII (March 1921), 516–25.

Some New Letters and Writings of Lafcadio Hearn. Ed. Sanki Ichikawa. Tokyo: Kenkyusha, 1925.

Stories from Emile Zola. Ed. Albert Mordell. Tokyo: Hokuseido Press, 1935.

Stories from Pierre Loti. Ed. Albert Mordell. Tokyo: Hokuseido Press, 1933.

The Temptation of St. Anthony. By Gustave Flaubert. New York: Alice Harriman Co., 1911.

Victorian Philosophy. Ed. Ryuji Tanabe. Tokyo: Hokuseido Press, 1930.

References

A. *Biography, criticism, etc.:*

Amenomori, Nobushige. "Lafcadio Hearn, The Man," *Atlantic Monthly,* XCVI (October 1905), 510–25.

Ashmead, John, Jr. "The Idea of Japan 1853–1895." Unpublished doctoral thesis, Harvard University, 1951.

Barel, Leona Queyrouze. See *The Idyl,* under Posthumous Collections.

Bisland, Elizabeth. See *Life and Letters,* under Posthumous Collections.

Canter, Jacob. "The Literary Reputation of Baudelaire in England and America, 1857–1934." Unpublished doctoral thesis, Harvard University, 1940.

Catalogue of the Lafcadio Hearn Library in the Toyama High School. Toyama: 1927.

Christy, Arthur E. (ed.). *The Asian Legacy and American Life.* New York: John Day Co., 1945.

Clary, William W. *Japan: The Warnings and Prophecies of Lafcadio Hearn.* ("Claremont Oriental Studies," No. 5.) Claremont, Calif., 1943.

Cowley, Malcolm. "Lafcadio Hearn," Introduction to *Selected Writings of Lafcadio Hearn,* ed. Henry Goodman. New York: Citadel Press, 1949.

Crofts, Alfred. "A Study of Change in the Writings of Lafcadio Hearn." Unpublished Master's thesis, University of Chicago, 1930.

De Smet, Joseph. *Lafcadio Hearn, l'homme et l'œuvre.* Paris: Mercure de France, 1911.

Flanagan, Virginia. "Lafcadio Hearn." Unpublished Master's thesis, Ohio State University, 1927.

Foerster, Norman. *Interpretations of Literature* (review), *The Dial,* LX (February 3, 1916), 112–14.

Frost, Orcutt W. *Young Hearn.* Tokyo: Hokuseido Press, 1958.

Garig, Aminie Ruth. "Lafcadio Hearn: The Man and His Works." Unpublished Master's thesis, Louisiana State University, 1929.

Gosse, Sir Edmund. *Silhouettes.* London: William Heinemann Ltd., 1925.

Gould, George M. *Biographic Clinics,* IV. Philadelphia: P. Blakiston's Son & Co., 1906.

———. *Concerning Lafcadio Hearn.* With a bibliographical list by Laura Stedman. Philadelphia: George W. Jacobs & Co., 1908.

"A History of English Literature" (review), *Times Literary Supplement* (London), August 18, 1927, p. 563.

Hozumi, Fumio. *Lafcadio Hearn's Views of Society*. Tokyo: Yuhi-Kaku, 1949. (Japanese text.)

Hubbell, Jay B. *The South in American Literature 1607–1900*. Durham, N.C.: Duke University Press, 1954.

Huneker, James. *Ivory, Apes and Peacocks*. New York: Charles Scribner's Sons, 1915.

Johnson, Katherine. "Primitive Japanese Literature in the Writings of Lafcadio Hearn." Unpublished Master's thesis, University of Chicago, 1929.

Josephson, Matthew. *Portrait of the Artist as American*. New York: Harcourt, Brace & Co., 1930.

Kennard, Nina H. *Lafcadio Hearn*. New York: D. Appleton & Co., 1912.

Kirkwood, Kenneth P. *Unfamiliar Lafcadio Hearn*. Tokyo: Hokuseido Press, 1936.

Koizumi, Kazuo. *Father and I*. Boston and New York: Houghton Mifflin Co., 1935.

———— (ed.). *Letters from Basil Hall Chamberlain to Lafcadio Hearn*. Tokyo: Hokuseido Press, 1936.

———— (ed.). *More Letters from Basil Hall Chamberlain to Lafcadio Hearn*. Tokyo: Hokuseido Press, 1937.

———— (ed.). *Re-Echo*. Caldwell, Idaho: Caxton Press, 1957.

Koizumi, Setsuko. *Reminiscences of Lafcadio Hearn*. Boston and New York: Houghton Mifflin Co., 1918.

Lafcadio Hearn in New Orleans. Ed. the Lafcadio Hearn Society (New Orleans). New York: Japan Institute Inc., 1941.

Lawless, Ray McKinley. "Lafcadio Hearn, Critic of American Life and Letters." Unpublished doctoral thesis, University of Chicago, 1940.

Lewis, Oscar. *Hearn and His Biographers*. San Francisco: Westgate Press, 1930.

McWilliams, Vera. *Lafcadio Hearn*. Boston: Houghton Mifflin Co., 1946.

Mais, S. P. B. *Books and Their Writers*. New York: Dodd, Mead & Co., 1920.

Maruyama, Manabu. *New Commentary on Lafcadio Hearn*. Tokyo: Hokuseido Press, 1936. (Japanese text.)

Miner, Earl. *The Japanese Tradition in British and American Literature*. Princeton: Princeton University Press, 1958.

Mordell, Albert. *The Erotic Motive in Literature*. New York: Boni & Liveright, 1919.

————. " 'Letters to a Pagan' Not by Hearn," *Today's Japan*, V, No. 1 (1955–60, 5th anniversary issue), 89–98.

More, Paul Elmer. *Shelburne Essays, Second Series*. New York: G. P. Putnam's Sons, 1906.

Morrison, Robert Felix. "The Growth of the Mind and Art of Lafcadio Hearn." Unpublished doctoral thesis, University of Wisconsin, 1941.

Negishi, Bansei. *Lafcadio Hearn in Izumo*. Matsue: Matsue Hearn Society, 1936. (Japanese text.)

Nishizaki, Ichiro. "The Apprenticeship of Lafcadio Hearn," *Bulletin of the Institute for Research in Language Teaching*, No. 231 (January 31, 1956), 1–6.

Nitobe, Inazo, *et al. Western Influence in Modern Japan.* Chicago: University of Chicago Press, 1931.

Noguchi, Yone. *Lafcadio Hearn in Japan.* Yokohama: Kelly and Walsh, 1910.

Pattee, Fred Lewis. *The New American Literature 1890–1930.* New York: D. Appleton-Century Co., 1937.

Perkins, P. D. and Ione. *Lafcadio Hearn: A Bibliography of His Writings.* With an Introduction by Sanki Ichikawa. Boston: Houghton Mifflin Co., 1934.

Robert, Marcel. *Lafcadio Hearn.* 2 vols. Tokyo: Hokuseido Press, 1950–51.

Salvan, Albert J. "Lafcadio Hearn's Views on the Realism of Zola," *PMLA,* LXVII (December 1952), 1163–67.

Stevenson, Elizabeth. *Lafcadio Hearn.* New York: Macmillan Co., 1961.

Takada, Chikara. *The Profile of Lafcadio Hearn.* Tokyo: Hokuseido Press, 1933. (Japanese text.)

Tanabe, Ryuji. *Koizumi Yakumo.* Tokyo: Waseda University Press, 1914. (Japanese text.)

Temple, Jean. *Blue Ghost: A Study of Lafcadio Hearn.* New York: Jonathan Cape and Harrison Smith, 1931.

Thomas, Edward. *Lafcadio Hearn.* Boston and New York: Houghton Mifflin Co., 1912.

Ticknor, Caroline. *Glimpses of Authors.* Boston and New York: Houghton Mifflin Co., 1922.

Tinker, Edward Larocque. *Lafcadio Hearn's American Days.* New York: Dodd, Mead & Co., 1924.

Walker, Hugh. *The English Essays and Essayists.* London: J. M. Dent & Sons Ltd., 1928.

B. *Background material:*

Adams, Henry. *The Education of Henry Adams* (Modern Library ed.). New York: Random House, 1931.

———. *Selected Letters.* Ed. Newton Arvin. New York: Farrar, Straus & Young, Inc., 1951.

Babbitt, Irving. *On Being Creative and Other Essays.* Boston: Houghton Mifflin Co., 1932.

Baird, James. *Ishmael.* Baltimore: Johns Hopkins Press, 1956.

———. "Critical Problems in the Orientalism of Western Poetry," *Asia and the Humanities,* ed. Horst Frenz. Bloomington: Indiana University Press, 1959.

Baudelaire, Charles. *Œuvres complètes.* Ed. Jacques Crépet. Vols. III and IV. Paris: Louis Conard, 1925–26.

———. *Paris Spleen.* Translated by Louise Varèse. New York: New Directions, 1947.

———. *Prose and Poetry.* Translated by Arthur Symons. New York: Albert and Charles Boni, 1926.

Binyon, Laurence. *The Flight of the Dragon.* London: John Murray, 1911.

Blyth, R. H. *Zen in English Literature.* Tokyo: Hokuseido Press, 1930.

Buck, Philo M., Jr. *Directions in Contemporary Literature.* New York: Oxford University Press, 1942.

Carpenter, Frederic Ives. *Emerson and Asia*. Cambridge, Mass.: Harvard University Press, 1930.

Cassirer, Ernst. *An Essay on Man*. New Haven: Yale University Press, 1944.

Chamberlain, Basil Hall. *Things Japanese*. London: John Murray, Kelly and Walsh, Ltd., 1905.

Christy, Arthur E. *The Orient in American Transcendentalism*. New York: Columbia University Press, 1932.

Coffman, Stanley K., Jr. *imagism*. Norman: University of Oklahoma Press, 1951.

Coomaraswamy, Ananda K. *The Transformation of Nature in Art*. Cambridge, Mass.: Harvard University Press, 1934.

Eliot, T. S. *A Choice of Kipling's Verse*. New York: Charles Scribner's Sons, 1943.

Flaubert, Gustave. *La Tentation de Saint-Antoine*. With an Introduction by Émile Faguet. ("Collection Gallia.") Paris: J. M. Dent et Fils, n.d.

Frierson, William C., and Edwards, Herbert. "Impact of French Naturalism on American Critical Opinion," *PMLA,* LXIII (September 1948), 1107–16.

Fung, Yu-Lan. *A Short History of Chinese Philosophy*. Ed. Derk Bodde. New York: Macmillan Co., 1948.

Gautier, Théophile. *Nouvelles*. Vienne: Manz, n.d.

Guénon, René. *East and West*. Translated by William Massey. London: Luzac & Co., 1941.

———. *The Crisis of the Modern World*. Translated by Arthur Osborne. London: Luzac & Co., 1942.

Hofstadter, Richard. *Social Darwinism in American Thought*. Philadelphia: University of Pennsylvania Press, 1945.

Homma, Hisao. *A History of Meiji Literature*. 3 vols. Tokyo: Tokyodo, 1935–43. (Japanese text.)

Hughes, E. R. (ed.). *The Individual in East and West*. London: Oxford University Press, 1937.

Huxley, Aldous. *The Perennial Philosophy*. New York: Harper & Bros., 1945.

James, Henry. *Literary Reviews and Essays*. Ed. Albert Mordell. New York: Twayne Publishers, 1957.

Jung, Carl G. *Two Essays on Analytical Psychology*. Translated by R. F. C. Hull. (*Collected Works,* Vol. VII.) London: Routledge and Kegan Paul, 1953.

———. *Modern Man in Search of a Soul*. Translated by Cary F. Baynes and W. S. Dell. New York: Harcourt, Brace & Co., 1936.

——— and Kerényi, C. *Essays on a Science of Mythology*. Translated by R. F. C. Hull. New York: Pantheon Books, 1949.

Keene, Donald. *Japanese Literature*. New York: Grove Press, 1955.

Kim, Ha Tai. "Nishida and Royce," *Philosophy—East and West,* I, No. 4 (January 1952), 18–29.

Koestler, Arthur. *The Lotus and the Robot*. New York: Macmillan Co., 1961.

Lewis, Wyndham. *Time and Western Man*. London: Chatto and Windus, 1927.

Lin Yutang. *My Country and My People*. New York: John Day Co., 1935.

———. *The Wisdom of China and India* (Modern Library ed.). New York: Random House, 1942.

Lowell, Percival. *Chosön, the Land of the Morning Calm.* Boston: Ticknor & Co., 1886.

———. *Noto: An Unexplored Corner of Japan.* Boston and New York: Houghton Mifflin Co., 1891.

———. *The Soul of the Far East.* New York: Macmillan, 1888.

———. *Occult Japan, or the Way of the Gods.* Boston and New York: Houghton Mifflin Co., 1894.

Maritain, Jacques. *Approaches to God.* Translated by Peter O'Reilly. ("World Perspectives Series," Vol. I.) New York: Harper & Bros., 1954.

Massis, Henri. *Defense of the West.* Translated by F. S. Flint. With a Preface by G. K. Chesterton. New York: Harcourt, Brace & Co., 1928.

Meyerhoff, Hans. *Time in Literature.* Berkeley and Los Angeles: University of California Press, 1955.

Michelet, Jules. *L'Amour.* Paris: Librairie de L. Hachette et Cie., 1861.

———. *The Insect.* Translated by W. H. Davenport Adams. London: Nelson and Sons, 1875.

———. *Woman.* Translated by J. W. Palmer. New York: Rudd and Carleton, 1860.

Moore, Charles A. (ed.). *Philosophy and Culture—East and West.* Honolulu: University of Hawaii Press, 1962.

——— (ed.). *Philosophy—East and West.* Princeton: Princeton University Press, 1946.

——— (ed.). *Essays in East-West Philosophy.* Honolulu: University of Hawaii Press, 1951.

Moulton, Richard G. *World Literature.* New York: Macmillan Co., 1921.

Nagai, Michio. "Herbert Spencer in Early Meiji Japan," *Far Eastern Quarterly,* XIV (1954–55), 55–64.

Noda, Matao. "East-West Synthesis in Kitarō Nishida," *Philosophy—East and West,* IV, No. 4 (January 1955), 345–59.

Northrop, F. S. C. *The Meeting of East and West.* New York: Macmillan Co., 1946.

Okazaki, Yoshie. *Japanese Literature in the Meiji Era.* Translated by V. H. Viglielmo. Tokyo: Ōbunsha, 1955.

Page, Curtis H. *Japanese Poetry.* Boston and New York: Houghton Mifflin Co., 1923.

Pearson, Charles H. *National Life and Character: A Forecast.* London: Macmillan, 1893.

Poe, Edgar Allan. *Complete Works.* Ed. James A. Harrison. Vol. XIV. New York: Society of English and French Literature, 1902.

Radhakrishnan, S. *Indian Philosophy.* 2 vols. ("Library of Philosophy Series.") New York: Macmillan, 1923–27.

———. *Eastern Religions and Western Thought.* Oxford: Oxford University Press, 1939.

———. *Recovery of Faith.* ("World Perspectives Series," Vol. IV.) New York: Harper & Bros., 1955.

Rougemont, Denis de. *Love in the Western World.* Translated by Montgomery Belgion. New York: Pantheon Books, 1956.

Rougemont, Denis de. *Man's Western Quest.* Translated by Montgomery Belgion. ("World Perspectives Series," Vol. XIII.) New York: Harper & Bros., 1957.

Salvan, Albert J. *Zola aux États-Unis.* ("Brown University Studies," Vol. VIII.) Providence, R.I.: Brown University Press, 1943.

Schwartz, William L. *The Imaginative Interpretation of the Far East in Modern French Literature, 1800–1925.* Paris: H. Champion, 1927.

Spencer, Herbert. *A System of Synthetic Philosophy,* Vols. I, IV, V, IX, X. New York: D. Appleton & Co., 1887–93.

Stevenson, Robert Louis. *Works,* Vols. XIV, XV. New York: Charles Scribner's Sons, 1924.

Strich, Fritz. *Goethe and World Literature.* Translated by C. A. M. Sym. London: Routledge and Paul, 1949.

Sze, Mai-mai. *The Tao of Painting.* New York: Pantheon Books, 1956.

Watts, Alan W. *Nature, Man, and Woman.* New York: Pantheon Books, 1958.

Wellek, René. *A History of Modern Criticism: 1750–1950.* Vol. I. New Haven: Yale University Press, 1955.

—— and Warren, Austin. *Theory of Literature.* New York: Harcourt, Brace & Co., 1949.

Wheelwright, Philip Ellis. *The Burning Fountain.* Bloomington: Indiana University Press, 1954.

Zimmer, Heinrich. *Philosophies of India.* New York: Pantheon Books, 1951.

Index

Index

Works other than Hearn's are generally entered under their authors' names. For the abbreviations in parentheses, see the list on p. 296.

The manuscript was edited by Barbara Woodward and the book was designed by Richard Kinney. The text type face is Granjon, redesigned by George W. Jones from a face cut by Claude Garamond. The display type face is Mistral designed by Roger Excoffon, 1953.

The book is printed on S. D. Warren's Olde Style Antique, white wove paper and bound in Bancroft's Arrestox C, from the A. D. Smith & Co. Inc. Manufactured in the United States.